DEPARDIEU

Depardieu

A BIOGRAPHY

Paul Chutkow

HarperCollins*Publishers*

HarperCollins*Publishers*
77–85 Fulham Palace Road,
Hammersmith, London W6 8JB

Published by HarperCollins*Publishers* 1994
1 3 5 7 9 8 6 4 2

First published in the USA by
Alfred A. Knopf 1994

A catalogue record for this book is
available from the British Library

ISBN 0 00 255008 3

Set in Granjon

Printed in Great Britain by
HarperCollinsManufacturing Glasgow

For

ETHAN *and* JUSTIN

The genius resembles everyone and no one resembles him.

—Honoré de Balzac

Contents

Prologue
"Le Hold-Up"

3

PART 1
On the Road

19

PART 2
Châteauroux

45

PART 3
Paris

119

PART 4
Wings

207

PART 5
To America
239

Epilogue
315

Appendix
The Works of Gérard Depardieu
323

Acknowledgments
339

Index
341

DEPARDIEU

Prologue

"Le Hold-Up"

One day in the late summer of 1989, I had lunch in Telluride, Colorado, with the celebrated French director Bertrand Blier. Over steaks and salad, Blier told me funny stories about growing up in a theatrical family in Paris and about making movies with many of the finest actors in France. After coffee, we strolled back to Blier's guest chalet and settled ourselves out on a veranda surrounded by the snowcapped peaks of the Rocky Mountains. The sun was warm, the air smelled of pine, and now I pulled out my notebook and edged Blier toward the heart of what I wanted to know.

"So," I said. "Depardieu."

"Ahhhh, Gérard," Blier said with a bemused air. "Now there's a story." Blier pulled a pouch of Gauloise tobacco from his pocket and carefully refilled his pipe. I could see he was not quite sure where to begin. Finally, he struck a match and drew the flame down into the bowl. "Did you ever meet Gérard in Paris?"

"No," I said. "Strangely enough."

"Pity," Blier said. "He's extraordinary. A true phenomenon. Probably unique in the world."

"Yes, I can imagine."

"Oh, no, you cannot," Blier laughed. "No one can imagine it. With Gérard, you have to see it to believe it."

Of all of France's great *auteur* directors, Blier is probably the most comic and caustic, and over the years Depardieu has often been his most effective creative partner. Their first film together, *Les Valseuses,* shown in America as *Going Places,* created a sensation in France and catapulted them both to international acclaim. Their next, *Get Out Your Handkerchiefs,* won an Academy Award as best foreign film. Blier's scripts have helped Depardieu establish himself as one of the most gifted actors in the world, and from Blier's imagination have come many of Depardieu's most memorable moments on the screen: Depardieu wheeling down the street in a shopping cart; Depardieu in a café trying to recruit a lover for his melancholy wife; Depardieu breaking into a sumptuous chateau, lifting his nose into the air and declaring, "I smell tax fraud!"

"We are exact opposites," Blier explained, puffing on his pipe. "I'm a bourgeois from Paris, and Gérard is a peasant from the countryside. But what happens between us is pure magic. I write roles expressly for him, and since Gérard can do anything in front of a camera, I can write with total confidence and freedom."

Depardieu always leaves the writing to Blier, but he loves to play the role of muse. He is so intuitive, and his antennae are so acute, that when Blier is having trouble with a script, Depardieu will sense it, even when he is several countries away. Then, like a bolt from the blue, Depardieu will come crashing in and try to give his friend a fresh creative charge. Depardieu usually arrives without warning, and he always appears with such flair and theatricality that Blier has come to describe these visitations of his muse with a single vivid term: *"le hold-up."* Blier used this bit of franglais with such élan that I wrote it in my notebook in capital letters.

"If I'm down, or I'm having trouble writing, Gérard always knows," Blier went on. "I have no idea how he knows, but by some sixth sense he always does. He will be halfway around the world, making a movie, and suddenly he'll call me on the phone, to see how I am, to cheer me up. Or I'll be home in Paris and suddenly Gérard will be at the door, storming in: 'Where's the script? Is there a role for me? Let me read something! Let me read something!' This is *le hold-up*. Gérard is totally uninhibited, and being with him is very energizing and liberating. For me, he's pure tonic."

Blier and I were in Colorado for the annual Telluride Film Festival, which just the night before had featured the American premiere of his latest comedy, *Too Beautiful for You,* again starring Depardieu. The crowd and most of the American critics had loved it, subtitles and all. Depardieu works like no other actor in the world, Blier now told me, and he was just starting to recount a revealing anecdote about Gérard on the set when the telephone rang: Depardieu on the line from France, as though his ears had been burning half a world away.

"Ah, Gérard! Salut," Blier said. *"Merci, merci."*

As I eavesdropped, Depardieu congratulated Blier on the success of the premiere and demanded to know more about the reaction of the crowd. The two friends then discussed the weather in France, the price of cowboy boots in Telluride, and the splendor of the Rockies at sunrise. Then Blier politely excused himself.

"Listen, Gérard, I'll have to call you back. I'm right in the middle of an interview for the *New York Times*."

This did not stop Depardieu. As Blier later recounted to me, Depardieu then demanded: "Who's the journalist?"

"A freelance writer named Paul Chutkow."

"Passe-le moi! Passe-le moi!" Put him on! Put him on!

Blier waved me to the phone: "Here, he wants to talk to you."

Me? As I had never met Depardieu, this took me aback. And I was even more startled when I put the receiver to my ear: *"Paul! Gérard! Comment vas-tu?"* As if we had been pals since childhood.

Depardieu and I chatted awhile, his voice booming with the same energy and mischief he so often radiates on the screen, especially in Blier's comedies. Right away he addressed me with the familiar *tu* form and this surprised me; most Frenchmen I know use the formal *vous* on first encounter. But as I was to learn, Gérard uses *tu* with almost everyone, be they ministers of state, captains of finance, or stuffy aristocrats from the highest reaches of Parisian society. During our conversation, I mentioned that after twelve years of living in Paris and writing about France, I had just moved with my wife and two sons to northern California, near the Napa Valley. This led us straight into one of Depardieu's greatest passions: wine. We talked about California versus French wines and about the chateau he had just purchased in the Loire valley, so that he could make his own wine. Then Depardieu's tone suddenly turned intimate, conspiratorial.

"Paul, listen! If you want to know the truth about this *bastard* Bertrand Blier, give me your personal telephone number. I'll call you at home with the real story."

Bastard? The word hit me like a sock in the jaw. As I was to learn, Depardieu uses words as though they were grenades, the way an expressionist painter might use a flaming red: to shock, emphasize, and infuse with feeling. I took his request to be nothing more than high comedy, but I gave him my home phone number, said good-bye, and tried to pick up the thread of my conversation with Blier.

"What an amazing coincidence," I said. "Just as we're talking about him, up pops Depardieu."

Blier finished relighting his pipe and gave me a sly, knowing smile: "Listen, with Gérard, *nothing* is coincidence."

Indeed, Depardieu's call was not as spontaneous as it first appeared. Alain Vannier, a French film exporter who was traveling with Blier and handling the U.S. distribution rights for *Too Beautiful for You,* had called Depardieu in France to tell him the good news from Telluride. And when Depardieu heard that Blier was in the middle of an interview for the *New York Times,* he insisted on barging right in, somehow managing to arrive on cue. When Vannier recounted this to Blier and me, we both had a good laugh, and I figured that was that.

The next morning, I left Telluride for a long day's travel back to northern California. On the plane I went through my notes and transcribed parts of my tape, but I could see this profile was not going to be easy to write. By 10 p.m. I was back home, exhausted, and writing on a killer deadline: I had to file the story to New York by noon the next day, and I still had no lead. Then the phone rang: Depardieu on the line from France, at 7 a.m. his time. I was shocked.

"Paul! Gérard! How's it going, your article? Have you nailed that bastard?"

"Uh, sure," I lied, but there was no slowing Depardieu.

"We are like brothers. Did he tell you that?"

"Yes, Gérard. He said you shared a 'fraternal complicity.' "

"Yes! Fraternal complicity! But you must understand: in age, he is older, but I am the older brother. Bertrand needs protecting, and I protect him. And do you see why we work so well together?"

"Well . . ."

"It is because we are exact opposites. Like the sun and the moon. I am a peasant, he is a bourgeois. I grow grapes, he is an intellectual, a Parisian intellectual. But watch out: Bertrand can fool you. Being an intellectual, he can appear cold, dry, cerebral. But this I promise you: *il sait péter!"* He knows how to fart!

There it was, another grenade. In French, the verb *péter* is far less crude than its English translation, and it means far more. If a glass shatters or a lightbulb bursts, a Frenchman thinks *péter*. When Depardieu used the word, what came rushing to my mind were my two sons and some of the expressions they had learned growing up in Paris. In my ear, the word burst with schoolyard humor and . . . fraternal complicity. Then, in one sharp, clarifying jolt, I understood: Depardieu the impish peasant breaks open Blier's chilly intellectualism, frees him from his inhibitions, and puts him back in touch with what is primal and spontaneous. Exactly what you see in so many of Blier's movies.

"Paul! T'as compris?" Do you understand?

"I think so . . ."

"Listen, it's simple: Bertrand gives me his words and his vision, and I give him my emotions and power. If you can find the energy of the other, together you can sing. Understand?"

"Yes," I said, scribbling. "Got it, Gérard."

We talked for nearly an hour, and with quotes and insights like these, my story flowed easily onto the page. This was *le hold-up* first-hand; I was feeling the raw energy Depardieu routinely conveys to Blier and the other directors who write roles expressly for him. And as I was writing, who kept elbowing his way into Blier's story, and right into the Sunday Arts & Leisure section of the *New York Times*? Depardieu, of course. Oh, he had plenty of method wrapped in his mischief, and I wondered if *le hold-up* was always a ruse for stealing a scene. One day, I vowed, I'll have to meet this character and watch him work.

Five months later, in early 1990, I got my chance. I was going back to Europe for the Berlin Film Festival, the first cultural happening along the German divide since the collapse of communism and the tearing down of the Berlin Wall. At this juncture, Depardieu was on a fabulous roll. His *Cyrano de Bergerac* was about to open, and he was preparing to leave for New York, to make his first major film in English, a romantic comedy for Disney called *Green Card*. This seemed an ideal hook on which to hang a profile of Depardieu for the *Times*. The *Times* and he agreed, and so the morning after the Berlin festival I flew to Paris to meet Depardieu.

I had no idea what to expect. By now, Depardieu was dominating French cinema as no actor had since the legendary Jean Gabin. He had made his share of duds, but his performances in such distinguished films as François Truffaut's *Last Metro, The Return of Martin Guerre, Jean de Florette,* and *Camille Claudel* had earned him a huge following in Europe and America, and many film critics were ranking him among the greatest actors in the world. His energy was legend. He was not yet forty-five, but he had already made nearly eighty films—more than most actors make in a lifetime. He was making movies at the rate of three, four, or even five a year, and when he was not on a film set he was whirling around the globe promoting his newest release.

In France, Depardieu had become a true social and cultural phenomenon. With his distinctive look and talent, and by making so many movies, he had managed to weave himself right into France's collective consciousness and imagination. *Paris-Match* treated him as a superstar and cultural icon, and the European editions of *Newsweek* and *Time* had featured him in cover stories glowing with approval. Rarely had I seen any actor, in France or anywhere else, so lionized, romanticized, and mythologized in the press. In a nation where cinema is considered an art form, *le septième art,* and in a culture that expects great artists to be tempestuous, larger than life, and to burst the bonds of social and moral convention, Depardieu was being treated as a national treasure, as a living, breathing part of the patrimony.

"By his force, his charisma, his intelligence and sensibility, Gérard is more than an actor: he is the raw material, the stone with which we build our church," wrote Daniel Toscan du Plantier, a prominent producer, critic, and promoter of French cinema. "To our tired, intellectual, commonplace cinema he brings his freshness, his power, his irony, his fragility."

In the early years of his career, I used to read some of the interviews and profiles that inevitably accompanied the launch of a new Depardieu film, but I soon stopped. In the French press, and also in the American celebrity press, fact, fiction, and gossip all seemed to meld into a familiar legend. There were always the basic elements of his life story, painting him as a juvenile delinquent who was saved by acting, and there were always stock references to his wife Elisabeth and their two children, Guillaume and Julie. After a while, all the profiles and interviews seemed to have a similar ring, with one inevitable twist: if he was playing a thug in the movie he was promoting, Depardieu would play the thug for the profile. To promote a new comedy, he would play the comic.

Obviously, behind these deceptive public masks of humor and bravado there was a very serious, very complex artist, one of the premier artists of our time. Yet, for all my reading and talks with people like Blier, I still had no real clue what made Depardieu tick. What drove the man? What was the real nature of his gift? How could he be so compelling in Blier's light, thoroughly modern farces, and then glide so seamlessly into, say, playing a hunchback in the dark classical epic *Jean de Florette*? For me there was only one solution: I had to see this phenomenon for myself.

Depardieu lives in Bougival, a village just west of Paris, out along the Seine. I arrived in town on a crisp February afternoon and found my way up to a quiet residential neighborhood well above the river. Depardieu lives on a narrow lane that looks and feels more like Provence than Paris, and his house is hidden from the street by a simple wooden fence. The front gate opens into a private enclave, with a lovely garden, tree-shaded walkways, and a spacious country house that looks as though it has cheerfully sheltered families for several centuries and has every intention of doing so for several generations more.

Hélène Bordier, Gérard's sister, neighbor, and aide-de-camp, greeted me at the door, guided me to the family study, and promptly disappeared, leaving me to look around. Like Depardieu himself, the house has a labyrinthine eccentricity: narrow hallways twist through an odd assortment of rooms, some dark, but most of them bright and inviting, especially those facing the garden out back. The study was in a state of amiable chaos. Books filled the shelves and several more were strewn across an antique escritoire. Every surface seemed to hold knick-knacks and family memorabilia. Relegated to a corner, and laden with dust, was a César, France's Oscar, the one Depardieu had been awarded for his performance in Truffaut's *Last Metro*. I was busy admiring the César when all at once the whole house started to shake—earthquake!—and thundering down the staircase came the master of the house:

"Viens!" Not hello, *enchanté,* nice to meet you. Come!

Depardieu stormed past, waving me to follow, and only when we arrived in the music room did he stop to shake hands and inspect, nose to nose, like a big puppy might check your scent. I apparently passed muster, and Depardieu waved me to a couch beside the piano. He took over an adjacent couch, and even before I could take out my notebook and tape recorder, he was unleashing a torrent, a raging stream of consciousness, delivered in a rattling machine-gun French such as I had rarely heard. Rat-atat, rat-atat, RaTaTaTaTaT. His garb surprised me. He wore a suit of somber gray, with a black knit shirt buttoned right up to the neck. Without a pause in his stream, he fired up an unfiltered Gitane, put a battered cowboy boot across his lap, and sailed into a bizarre discourse on Molière, Rostand, Balzac, Musset, on and on, in a rush of words and thoughts spun forth in long, looping, seemingly endless sentences. His mood seemed dark, even tormented, and for a long moment I wondered if he might be hung over, stoned, or both.

Depardieu went on like a man possessed, and once his initial fury had subsided, his stream of consciousness began flowing into a single estuary: America. Gérard comes from a very poor family in one of the most backward regions of France. His father could barely read or write. Gérard told me he grew up feeling he was a misfit, in his family and in his town, and he spent much of his boyhood dreaming of America, of sailing to America, of seducing and conquering America. In the 1950s in his hometown of Châteauroux, there had been a U.S. air base, and that was where he hung out, where he had come of age, in a corner of France dominated by G.I.'s and James Dean, hamburgers and milkshakes, Budweiser and Brando. His group of friends was like an all-American rainbow: Marines and flyboys, whites, blacks, even an American Indian named Red Cloud, whom he called "Nuage Rouge."

"I soaked up everything," he said wistfully. "It was like being on an aircraft carrier adrift on an uncharted sea."

From those boyhood days on, America had been the lightning rod for his wildest hopes and fantasies, and now, at last, he was on his way. The day after next he was leaving for Manhattan, to make *Green Card,* his first major film in English. The chemistry felt good to him; he was going to be working with Disney Studios and Peter Weir, the director of *Dead Poets Society,* which right then was creating a sensation in France. What the movie had to say about schools, conformity, and creativity had prompted a national debate about the strengths and weaknesses of French education. There had even been a soul-searching article on page one of *Le Monde*. "Peter is a poet," Depardieu declared, and as I was soon to learn, in his pantheon there is no being more supreme.

Then something strange happened. As he talked about America, Depardieu's demeanor changed: the darkness worked its way out of his face, and when his stream of chatter had worn down to a trickle, he abruptly ripped open his collar, flung off his jacket, and jumped up into the sunlight pouring into an alcove he used as a bar. "Time to try my wine!" At once, all trace of the somber intellectual vanished and Depardieu seemed to transform into a different man; now he was an exuberant peasant eager to share the fruits of his vines and his soil and his sunshine. He poured two glasses of wine, a *cabernet franc* from his own Château de Tigné. He held one up to the light for inspection, then he put his nose down into the glass. "When I smell a wine," he said, "I want to smell nature and the genius of the winemaker."

As soon as the somber intellectual vanished, so did those long, looping sentences; what came out of Depardieu now were terse, pithy descriptions, a canny peasant's capsule portraits. Of his wife Elisabeth: "She's perfect for me; she goes very, very fast." Of Truffaut: "A punk-diplomat." Of Catherine Deneuve: "What a woman! And what a man!"

What also emerged from Depardieu now was a hint of panic. Just beneath his excitement about going to America was a web of fears and worries. He was worried about his English, worried that in working in a language he barely knew, he would lose the freedom and ease he needs to feel spontaneous, to connect and fly. He was worried that American audiences, so conditioned to leading men with trim physiques and handsome faces, would find him ugly and brutish. Never mind what he had accomplished in France and Europe; America was a whole new turf, and while it could bring him triumph, it could also bring him a disastrous, very public fall. "Look," he said, "there is France, there is Europe, and then again there is America. Face it: I am beginning either a great adventure or a tragic mistake."

I found Depardieu's swings of mood and character bewildering, and as our planned hour-long talk spun into the evening, I became even more bewildered. It was as though I had passed through a looking glass and entered a strange new world, with its own landscape, its own values, its own icons, even its own language. Most Frenchmen I know pride themselves on the power of their intellect; Depardieu prides himself on the power of his nose. Most Frenchmen I know admire reason, Cartesian logic, and rigor of analysis—hard facts hammered into thesis and argument, the whole set cogently down into talking points one, two, and three. With Depardieu, reason holds little sway; what he trusts are instincts, suspicions, impressions, feelings, whatever he senses in the look of an eye or the face of a stranger.

Language to Depardieu is mask and cape, and he talks in a kind of ongoing lyrical metaphor, using words with connotations which seem to dance to some private music. It took me aback. Usually when a Frenchman says, *"Il est fou!"*—He's mad!—he means it as a negative judgment, a criticism, a condemnation. Not Depardieu. When he says of Isabelle Adjani, for instance, *"Elle est folle!,"* he means it as a supreme compliment. On his side of the looking glass, madness is next to godliness; for without a touch of madness, an artist has no avenue into whimsy, poetry, or divine inspiration.

As the evening wore on, Depardieu took me through his wine cellars, opening bottle after bottle, and we talked about our wives and our children, about our mutual liking for Calcutta, and about his admiration for the Bengali director Satyajit Ray. But what Depardieu kept circling back to was America, always America. Robert De Niro, Al Pacino, Tom Cruise, Dustin Hoffman—he admires all of them, but he feels little rapport with the he-man style of acting found in most American action pictures. "I feel myself completely feminine in this craft. I don't believe in the Stallone image of the invincible hero, and much of the public doesn't either. The biggest success goes to actors like Cruise and Hoffman, who prefer to show their faults and weaknesses, rather than project an image of invulnerability."

Shortly after 11 p.m., and after we had consumed far too much wine, another curious thing happened. Big, bluff Depardieu, with hands like meat cleavers and a boxer's jaw that he waves right in your face, caught a look at his watch—and he started to get very, very nervous, almost timid. His wife, Elisabeth, was doing a play in Paris and soon she would be arriving home.

"Listen," he said, "it's been great, but you've got to go. I'm exhausted, and I have to be up early to get ready to leave for New York. Besides, Elisabeth will be home soon and I don't want her to see me like this." I left amazed. Blier had been right: with Gérard, you have to see it to believe it.

Now I wanted to see Depardieu at work. Six months later, this time on assignment for *Vogue,* I spent a week in the south of France, watching him on the set of a new Blier comedy, *Merci la Vie* (Thanks, Life). In two decades of reporting, I had been on many film sets, but never one like this; Hollywood would have been aghast. With Blier directing, and Depardieu acting and co-producing, everything was done low-budget and family-style, with a group of artists and technicians who worked and played more like a band of itinerant gypsies than any Hollywood cast or crew I had ever seen.

Nor did their values resemble Hollywood's. *Merci la Vie* was anything but a commercial picture: Blier was trying to weave the AIDS crisis into a larger reflection about the human condition and its periodic cataclysms, in this case Nazism. *Too Beautiful for You* had been a critical and financial success, and it had bought Blier the freedom to take this gamble; if the public and the critics ended up not liking *Merci la Vie,* well, too bad. What Blier felt he had to do now was experiment, expand his range as an artist, and he wanted to grapple in some meaningful way with the tragedy of AIDS. In Blier's case, small was not just beautiful, it was pure artistic freedom. Though his budget was $10 million, Blier usually made movies at half that cost, and by working on that scale, no investor would lose his shirt. If one of his movies failed, it would fail proudly, for reasons Blier deemed honorable: by aiming artistically high, not by pandering to mass audience tastes, or by using car chases and special effects to guarantee thrills, chills, and adolescent box-office appeal.

As for Depardieu, he was working for peanuts. His screen role was minor, the kind most Hollywood stars would never take—and the kind their agents would surely forbid them to take. But to Depardieu, Blier was family, and if Blier was making a new movie, he wanted to be a part of it, to lend him his power at the box office, no matter how small the role. Working on the set, Depardieu proved to be the exact opposite of the traditional Hollywood star. With him, there were no ego trips, no tantrums, no demands for limousines or personal trainers. Gérard organized the lunch canteen, with his handpicked chef, Richard, and on the set he worked like a master of ceremonies, joking, easing tension, smoothing rivalries, and creating the kind of intimate family atmosphere which would help Blier get what he wanted from his cast and crew.

Watching Depardieu act, even in a small role, is like watching a Bastille Day fireworks display. On camera he bursts, he explodes, he erupts with unexpected colors. Seeing his ease, his pure physical joy in creation, I immediately thought of Henri-Georges Clouzot's *Mystère Picasso,* a documentary done in 1956. On screen and up close, you see Picasso painting, improvising, experimenting on a sheet of glass, fixed in front of a camera. And what a wondrous sight it is, the artist in full, exuberant creation. What you see is not mental work; it is as though Picasso's mind shuts down and his eye and arm and hand alone channel his creative energy into color, movement, and sensual expression. So it is with Depardieu acting.

"On camera you must never think," Depardieu told me. "If you think, you stop. You block yourself. You just have to do it."

What struck me profoundly, watching him work and play, was that beneath his raucous bonhomie there seemed to be a terrible war going on inside Depardieu. He is a man of cascading moods and humors, with an emotional palette that ranges from timidity to flamboyance, from innocence to cunning, from an almost feminine delicacy to a blind, animal-like brutality. And his moods can turn in an instant. On one of his days off, a team from *Vogue* came to the set for a photo shoot. Depardieu, so at ease when facing a camera in character, despises sitting for a still portrait, and the morning of the shoot he went into a complete tizzy. To gird for the ordeal, he gorged himself on foie gras and white wine, and after the shoot he consoled himself with a steak big enough for three, a huge slab of Roquefort, and two bottles of young red wine from his chateau. After lunch, the *Vogue* team left, the cast and crew went back to work, and by the time we got to the plum brandy, Depardieu and I were alone in the lunch tent. He was going on about his wife, his children, the disruptions and loneliness of life on the road, and suddenly he stopped, right in mid-sentence, tears streaming down his cheeks.

This volatility and vulnerability, emerging straight from the warring extremes of his emotional palette, help fuel Depardieu's mesmerizing power on the screen. I think they also help explain the remarkable bond he has managed to forge with his viewing public. In the vast spectrum of emotions he so freely expresses, everyone can find some means of identifying with Gérard. At the start of his career, his rough appearance and the violent roles he often played put many people off. By the late 1980s, though, he had become an endearing part of the French national family. Depardieu is not some celluloid idol to be regarded from afar; he's down-home Gérard, as real and as human as a crazy uncle, or a cousin from the provinces, or the brother-in-law who comes to Sunday lunch or Christmas dinner and always plays the clown. At his core, he is an everyman and an openhearted peasant, and audiences feel it. Depardieu's appeal with the French public has reached the point where even when he is in a stinker of a film, his family of fans will go to see him anyway, if only to commiserate with his plight or the current state of his girth.

Depardieu seems to crave this close, family-style rapport, both with his fellow actors and with total strangers. Watching him in the south of France, I often had the impression that he wanted to charm every man, woman, child, dog, and cat who crossed his path, and that making movies was just an extension of his overwhelming desire to be welcomed into every household, not as a guest in the dining room, but as a member of the family at the kitchen table. One afternoon during the making of *Merci la Vie,* Depardieu took a break from the camera and went for a walk with his friend Jean Carmet. They were strolling leisurely down a quiet backstreet of Millau, headquarters for the shoot, when suddenly Gérard stopped and raised his nose into the air.

"Snnff! Snnff! Smell that, Jeannot? *Remarquable!"* Following his nose, Gérard tracked the scent to the kitchen of a tiny hotel, and without hesitation he rapped on the door. Soon a little old lady in an apron appeared, and her eyes lit up at the sight of two of the most famous actors in France.

"Madame!" Depardieu implored. "You are cooking something that smells magnificent, and I am willing to bet it is a *boeuf en daube!"*

"Ça alors! Oui, Monsieur!" It is a beef and carrot stew! In a moment, Depardieu and Carmet were happily ensconced in Madame's kitchen, tasting her stew and sampling her hearty red wine. In the process, of course, they charmed Madame and gave her a thrill she would cherish to the end of her days. And Madame, in turn, gave Depardieu a bit of the warmth and approval he so desperately craves.

Such spontaneous escapades are classic Depardieu. Like a merry troubadour of old, he spends most of his life on the road, and after a long day on the set, be it in France, New York, or Costa Rica, he loves to cut loose by following his nose and charming his way into some stranger's kitchen, refrigerator, or wine cellar. Barriers of language and culture do not deter him; they only stimulate his senses and imagination. On one of his many trips to India, Depardieu was traveling with his friend

Toscan du Plantier. One afternoon in New Delhi they took a drive into the country with a group of friends and stopped at a primitive village where no one had ever seen or heard of Depardieu. Gérard stepped from the car and promptly disappeared into a warren of huts and shanties. Two hours later, after searching the entire village, his friends found Gérard in a hut, sitting on the ground with a local family, and sharing with them a communal bowl of rice and dal. To the utter astonishment of his French friends, Gérard was regaling the family with stories, acting them out with pantomime and uproarious imitations of the local dialect. Toscan du Plantier would recount this episode for years to come, but to Gérard it was only normal; he was singing for his supper.

As I watched them in the south of France, Depardieu and Blier's film family seemed to me to embody a certain sensibility, a certain spirit, what many people equate with Paris when they read Hemingway or Gertrude Stein or Henry Miller, or when they see a Degas, or a Renoir, or a Toulouse-Lautrec. For anyone in search of that soaring artistic spirit, Paris today can be very disappointing; the city often seems too modern, too industrial, too expensive, too American. The warm, understanding embrace Paris used to reserve for painters and writers often seems to have disappeared under the relentless march of a new Europe where business is king, where Camembert is homogenized and pasteurized, where the cancan is ancient history, and where no one remembers the real La Coupole. No wonder the French press so lionized and romanticized Depardieu: he was not only France's greatest actor, he was a reminder of a more glorious time, when Montmartre and Montparnasse teemed with painters, poets, actors, and musicians, and when painters and writers the world over looked first to Paris for creative stimulus and inspiration.

During my stay in the south of France, the idea of writing a book about Depardieu became irresistible—provided he would agree to cooperate. So one night before dinner, while we were in the hotel bar sampling a wine, I broached the subject very tentatively. I knew he had written a lovely little memoir, *Lettres Volées* (Stolen Letters), but now I asked him, "Why have you never agreed to cooperate in a full-scale portrait, a biography?"

"Several writers have been after me for years," he said.

"But?"

"But I've never found the right chemistry," Depardieu said. "Why do you ask?"

"Oh, I don't know," I said. "I don't suppose . . ."

Now Depardieu inched in, locking me eyeball to eyeball, as if to look straight into the depths of my soul. Then he stuck out his massive hand: *"Avec toi, oui."*

"But, Gérard, I would need your complete cooperation."

"Si, si."

I put up my hand. "I would need your help, Gérard. But the ultimate vision would have to be mine. No interference." I also told him this would have to be entirely my book; he would not receive a centime from it.

"D'accord. Absolument."

We shook hands and clinked glasses to seal the accord. Depardieu surely had no idea what he was getting himself into, and neither did I. But over the next three years I tracked his life story back into the inner reaches of France, and I trailed Depardieu around France, America, Spain, and Costa Rica, interviewing him about his life and studying his unique approach to the art of acting. Being under such scrutiny might have driven anyone nuts, but with enormous patience and generosity, Depardieu brought me into the heart of his creative process, and into the heart of his extended film family.

As I found throughout my travels and interviewing, most of his friends are fascinated by Depardieu, and the images they conjure up to describe him are always vivid and surprising. Catherine Deneuve sees him as a caged lion, with a lion's nose and instincts. Fanny Ardant, the French actress, sees him as an oak tree. Australia's Peter Weir sees him as an aborigine with magical powers. The French director and cartoonist Gérard Lauzier thinks of him as a medieval sorcerer. Blier and other directors who write roles for Depardieu often portray him as a prankster, which is a cousin of the Trickster, a familiar figure in primitive folklore and in the psychological archetypes first discerned by Carl Jung. Toscan du Plantier thinks that Depardieu is simply the greatest actor of the century, and the producer Jean-Louis Livi hesitates to use the word but feels that in Depardieu's case it truly applies: genius.

To my mind, there is truth in all these characterizations, but they do not suggest the full richness of Depardieu's amazing life story. He was born in a village torn by war and Nazi occupation, and he was born into a family torn by poverty, alcohol, and emotional trauma. Gérard learned to speak only a strange patois at home, and he grew up with an array of humiliating speech problems. His mother often feared he was a dunce. School for Gérard was misery; at eleven he flunked the entire year, and at thirteen he dropped out and went to work as a printer's apprentice. By fifteen, he was sinking into a life of joy rides, aimless drifting, and petty crime. Many of his boyhood friends wound up in jail, or as alcoholics, or dead.

How did Depardieu escape a similar fate? With his background, how did he manage to become one of the greatest actors in the world? And how did a boy with severe speech handicaps wind up as Cyrano de Bergerac, the poet-warrior who could duel and woo with alexandrine couplets flowing from his lips like honey from a spoon? The answers reside in Depardieu's own hard work and amazing gifts, but also in his encounters with three brilliant individuals uniquely qualified to give him the help he so desperately needed: a professor of drama, a doctor specializing in speech disorders, and Elisabeth Guignot, an actress and psychologist who became Gérard's wife, the mother of their two children, and the unfailing anchor at the center of his stormy existence. With extraordinary patience and wisdom, these three mentors took a tongue-tied youth from the provinces and unlocked his hidden powers of language and expression. Then they guided Gérard into a stunning artistic and creative awakening, for all the world to see.

"Why did I become an actor?" Depardieu said during one of our many conversations. "Because I have always felt a need, a terrible need to communicate. As a child I never knew how to talk. I had to study theater in order to learn language. Acting for me is perhaps the adolescence I never had, what gives me the wings I need to fly up into the light."

PART I

On the Road

Cooking with Jean Bardet, one of the leading chefs of Châteauroux, 1979

1

The Appetite

This morning Depardieu is out searching for a chicken. His hand is on the wheel of his rented Citroën, and his eyes are on the road leading north out of France, but Depardieu's mind is on that chicken.

"Most of the chickens around here have no taste," he says. "It's as bad as New York. Worse. But I have found this one butcher in Belgium. You'll see."

For many people, shopping for a chicken is a dreary errand to be quickly dispatched; for Depardieu, it is very serious business, a challenge to be met and conquered with wit and gusto, and he has been planning this expedition to Belgium since breakfast yesterday morning. And since then he has been savoring in his mind the precise chicken he wants to prepare for everyone's lunch today: a plump, fresh chicken raised on a farm, preferably a small family farm where chemicals are never used in the feed and the birds are not kept in coops but are allowed to run free.

Depardieu eased the car through an unmanned border post, and in a few minutes he rolled into a pleasant little Belgian village with stone houses, freshly swept sidewalks, and a main square lined with flower shops, bakeries, and cheerful cafés. On market day, twice a week, the square fills with farmers from across the region who come to sell fruits and vegetables and their homemade sausages, cheeses, and peasant breads. But today was not market day, and on this cold, damp December morning the square was a bit glum. Depardieu drove on by the square and wound his way to the back of town. Near a church with an old stone face, he turned onto a quiet side street and nosed the car into a parking slot.

"Le voilà."

Across the road was a butcher shop. Not a fancy *boucherie* like you find in Paris, with rabbits and pheasants and maybe a partridge elegantly displayed in the window; this was a country shop with a modest front and very clean windows. Inside, alone behind the counter, was a wisp of a woman bent over her chopping block.

"Bonjour, Madame la Bouchère!"

Madame the Butcher, a matronly widow, looked a bit somber this morning, but the sound of that familiar booming voice made her face light up. "Ah, Monsieur Depardieu! What a pleasure to see you again!"

"Vous allez bien, Madame?" Government ministers he often addresses with *tu,* but Madame the Butcher merited a very respectful *vous*.

"Yes, I am well, Monsieur Depardieu. I have to be. And you?"

"A bit tired, to tell you the truth. But one of your farm chickens will fix me right up."

"Whatever you want, Monsieur Depardieu. You know the way."

Six plump farm chickens were neatly arrayed in Madame's window, and Depardieu did not inspect them just with his eye; one by one he placed his hand across their backs and inspected the meat with his fingers. Touch is very important to Depardieu. With his family, with close friends, or when he is admiring the small Rodin sculptures he bought after portraying the sculptor in *Camille Claudel,* Depardieu is always touching, always seeking physical contact—even with a chicken. Now, with a hand as massive as a butcher's, and just as knowledgeable, he inspected the birds for freshness, quality, and weight. None would do.

"Madame, these are not from that farmer to the north."

"Ah, non, Monsieur! Those arrived only this morning. Come."

In a moment, Madame the Butcher and Depardieu were squatting knee to knee inside her meat locker, expertly picking through two wooden crates heaped with freshly slaughtered chickens. It was an arresting sight: Madame the Butcher and one of the world's greatest actors squatting there, under huge slabs of red meat, both elbow-deep in chickens, both deeply and passionately committed to finding the very finest chicken to be had in the whole of northern France and southern Belgium. In a few moments, both of them were positively elated when Depardieu emerged from the locker gently clasping their mutual choice by the throat.

"Do you want it prepared in your usual way, Monsieur Depardieu? With the liver and gizzards wrapped separately?"

"Oui, Madame. And put in a few sprigs of thyme as well."

"Oui, Monsieur."

While Madame the Butcher prepared his chicken, Depardieu moved into the next phase of his culinary expedition: endive. In a shop across the street he was again greeted not as a star or an important client, but as a cheerful neighbor. This was December of 1992, and Depardieu had been living in the area for the past three months, during the filming of Claude Berri's *Germinal,* and he not only knew where to find the best chickens and the best meat and produce, he had settled in and become a local, part of the village landscape. Belgians are proud of their endive, as they are of their *moules frites* (mussels and French fries), and in the window was a lovely looking mound of endive. Depardieu emerged from a rigorous examination with an air of evident disappointment.

"Try below, Monsieur Depardieu," the shopkeeper suggested.

Below the counter were huge wooden bins, and Depardieu's head now disappeared into one of them. He rooted about and came out with a handful of the freshest, plumpest endive he could find. Fennel was his next quarry, and again his head plunged deep into a bin. Now, as anyone who has ever shopped in Paris knows, vegetable vendors usually have fits when a customer so much as puts a pinky on a tomato or a green pepper; only the vendor handles his produce. And yet here was Depardieu with the full run of the house. Now that inquisitive nose of his was emerging from a bin filled with heads of fresh garlic.

"A bit of cheese, Monsieur Depardieu?"

"Some Gruyère, please. The French. The Swiss is too salty."

Of course one reason he can do as he pleases, and usually get away with it, is that he is Gérard Depardieu, *artiste extraordinaire* and France's most prominent cultural icon and export. But that is a bit abstract to Madame the Butcher and Madame the Vegetable Vendor; what they can see and feel is a man with his hand on their chickens and his head in their bins—real, tactile. Yes, he is famous, but the true reason they respond to him and give him the run of their shops is not because Depardieu is a star, but because he is *not* a star. As they can see right in their shops, he is a man with no airs and no pretensions. As wealthy as he is, Depardieu could hire chefs to do his cooking and sous-chefs to do his marketing. Yet here he is, on a day off, doing the shopping and the cooking himself, and having the kind of taste and expertise these women admire. Food is Depardieu's way of remaining anchored to the soil, to his peasant roots, and when he greets these villagers, food and cooking are their common currency, their common language, even their common values.

"Will that be all, Monsieur Depardieu?"

"For today, Madame."

Depardieu carted off his endive and fennel and then picked up his chicken. But he was not satisfied with the butcher's thyme. So he went to a third shop, which had a supply of thyme as fragrant as he wanted. Depardieu next went to a café with a newspaper kiosk and picked up an armful of the day's papers from Paris. Then, missions accomplished, he headed back into France and to the chateau where he and his film family were camped during the long shoot of *Germinal*.

The chateau was set in seclusion and protected by an iron gate and a dense forest. The castle itself was a seventeenth-century monstrosity that may once have been a jewel of the French nobility but was now inhabited only by a caretaker, and it looked so sinister it appeared to be haunted. Depardieu and his friends would never stay there; instead, they were settled in the shadow of the chateau, in a carriage house beside the deserted stables. The carriage house was warm and cozy, ideal for the family-style intimacy Depardieu likes to maintain when he is away from home.

With Depardieu living there with five friends from the cast and crew of *Germinal,* the carriage house was a male bastion, a kind of fraternity house, and the center of its life was the kitchen. In a few moments, Depardieu, paring knife in hand, was at the kitchen table, crushing a head of garlic, cleaning the cloves, and slipping them artfully into the meat of the chicken. Zip, zip, and the chicken was in the oven, sprigs of thyme on its breast, and on the table were salads of endive and fennel. And open beside them was a bottle of young white wine, direct from Depardieu's chateau in the Loire.

Depardieu is even more passionate and exacting about wine than he is about chicken. In California's Napa Valley and Sonoma County, there are many rich and famous people who have bought wineries, for the prestige or the enduring legacy of having their name on the label. When Depardieu purchased his winery in 1988, he had two main motivations: to expand his knowledge of wine making and to create a large supply of the kind of wines he likes to drink and share with friends. The wines he makes are light and pure; in the process he uses, after the grapes are crushed, the juice is left to soak with the skins and pulp for an unusually long period of time, to gain added richness and flavor. Depardieu never uses chemicals, and he never chaptalizes, the process of adding sugar during fermentation to raise the alcohol content above the juice's natural level.

By 1 p.m., Depardieu and a small group of friends were sitting around his kitchen table, joking and enjoying his chicken and his wine.

And the more his friends ate and drank, the happier Depardieu became. For with Depardieu, a chicken is not just a chicken, and a bottle of wine is not just a bottle of wine; to him, good chicken and good wine are essential joys of the table, of his family, and of his life. To Depardieu, a good, pure chicken, properly cooked, and a good, pure wine, properly made, are highly personal means of expression; they are mediums of communication and sharing—just like acting. "What is an actor?" Depardieu says. "Someone who presents his friends with a big platter filled with the finest produce from his garden, so they can share the fruits of his labor and whatever talent and inspiration he brings to his craft."

To understand Depardieu's unique approach to acting, the place to begin is right here at his kitchen table. Here, the separate crafts of cooking, wine making, and acting all flow naturally together, and so do their guiding values, methodologies, and spirit. The way Gérard sees it, cooking, wine making, and acting are sister crafts; and all three can naturally elevate themselves into art forms and sensory celebrations—provided the artisan brings to them enough passion, expertise, "nose," and generosity of spirit. And in all three endeavors, Gérard insists on enjoying the process of creation as much as the final product. When he cooks a chicken, he turns it into an adventure; when he makes wine, he turns it into a consuming passion; and when he makes movies, he wants every day on the set to be like the big, bountiful Sunday lunches the French hold so dear.

"Oh, how I suffered in New York," Depardieu often complains. During the time he made *Green Card* in Manhattan, he lived in a hotel on the Upper East Side, and for his meals he went from restaurant to restaurant. But he never could find a chicken with the fresh farm taste he craved. "I would say to the chefs, show me just one farmer who raises free-range chickens, and I'll go kill one myself." He spent whole days looking for *fromage de tête*—headcheese—one of his favorite French specialties. He finally found an acceptable version at a small French restaurant. But what disturbed him most in making *Green Card* was that the American cast and crew did not sit down together for a proper lunch. The Americans ate sandwiches or salads or yogurt, and they ate quickly and often alone; there was little of the family-style closeness and camaraderie Depardieu yearns for on a movie set.

"To me, acting is intimately linked to the idea of sharing," he says, "and there is no better place to share than around a table filled with good food."

Film critics frequently call Depardieu a born actor, a "force of nature" who works on instinct alone. In fact, he went through a very rigorous apprenticeship under one of the leading professors of drama in Paris. His training was primarily in classical French theater. But from there, Depardieu evolved his own unique approach. While many actors today torture their soul or dredge up emotional strife from their past to channel to the camera, Depardieu prefers to emphasize joy and pleasure. And he encapsules his entire philosophy of acting in a word drawn directly from the joys of the table: *bien-être.* Well-being.

"What is *bien-être*?" he says. "A certain feeling of fullness. *Bien-être* is the happiness and *joie de vivre* I get from acting and being with other actors and creators. And I try to generate in the audience these same feelings of fullness and well-being."

Depardieu's methodology as an actor is in many ways akin to the way he works as a cook and a wine maker. Just as he grows his own grapes to make his own wine, he likes to "grow" his own scripts and projects, by working with a family of writers, directors, agents, and producers who develop movie projects especially for him. "Good scripts do not just pop up out of the ground," he says. "You have to cultivate them." When Depardieu pulls *le hold-up* and plays the muse with a writer, he is really gardening, tilling the soil, trying to give the writer and his script oxygen, nourishment, and sunshine.

In acting, as in food and wine, Depardieu's appetites are monstrous, even bulimic. Today's lunch of chicken and salad and wine was to Depardieu a light meal, fine for a day off. But to fortify himself for a day's work in front of the camera, Depardieu usually sits down to a lunch of steak—very rare and big enough for two—plus a salad, cheese, and plenty of red wine. If the weather is cold, as it was this week, he might sneak in a bowl of ice cream or a homemade tart. By dinner, he is again famished. Depardieu works with the same gusto with which he eats: he is perfectly happy to work fourteen, sixteen, or eighteen hours a day, and he is not content unless he makes three, four, or even five films a year, and has just as many in various stages of development.

Depardieu has maintained this frenetic pace since 1970, and his output of more than eighty movies suggests a creative energy as rich and relentless as Picasso's. And just as anarchic. Gérard is so consumed by his work that most of his adult life has been spent on the road, living in hotel rooms, eating restaurant food, and sharing his days and nights with itinerant film families. The pace is punishing for his wife, Elisabeth, and for their two children, and, as sturdy as he is, the pace also puts a terrible strain on Depardieu. During the making of *Germinal,* his weight ballooned to 260 pounds and his heart was racing at 110 beats a minute, a dangerous level. Today, after the chicken and wine, Depardieu simply collapsed in exhaustion and took a two-hour nap. Still, despite the strain, Depardieu seems unwilling, or unable, to slow down, or even to pause for breath. "Slow down?" he says. "That would be too depressing. Take time off for reflection? Why? For me the best way to reflect is to work."

Watch him run from film to film, from role to role, from country to country, and what soon becomes clear is that for Depardieu, acting is not a job or a career or a profession; it is food, nourishment, an almost daily need and craving. What drives this need? Money? Fame? Awards? No. For Depardieu these are welcome rewards, but they are not primary motivations. What drives him is far more complex and far more difficult to sate, as his choice of roles often suggests.

"I don't choose my projects according to their potential box-office appeal or the size of the paycheck," he explains. "I choose them for the size of the risk. And because I feel a rapport with the director. I would much rather make a high-risk film that fails in an interesting way than two safe films with obvious commercial appeal."

Depardieu finds little risk or intrigue in playing traditional heroes. Playing a hellion in *Les Valseuses* set the tone for his early acclaim, and from there his forte became incarnating trouble. With joyous abandon he played punks, thugs, con men, and a plethora of sexual provocateurs and misfits, including a husband who emasculates himself on screen and a transvestite working the hot zones of Paris in miniskirt and wig. This was his "mad dog" period, and part of the kick was that Depardieu belonged to a new generation of actors determined to thumb their noses at the French establishment and its values.

Whether Depardieu cared or not, his bad-boy roles played havoc with his public image. With his long hair and a face no one would mistake for Cary Grant's, Depardieu struck France in much the same way that Elvis Presley struck America and the Beatles struck Britain: young people lionized him, while older people found him downright contemptible. To traditional, bourgeois France, Depardieu was nothing but an eyesore from the provinces, and what he conveyed on screen was the mirror opposite of the image these Frenchmen preferred to project to themselves and to the world: the chic, Parisian image of culture so ideally embodied by Catherine Deneuve. And he was anything but the suave French lover so winningly portrayed to international audiences by Yves Montand, Charles Boyer, Louis Jourdan, and Maurice Chevalier in his youth. Caught in this generational split, Depardieu for years was either adored or detested; there seemed to be no middle ground. Either way, he stirred the passions and seemed to tap deep into viewers' psyches. *"Il dérange,"* people often said of him. He disturbs, he upsets.

During the 1980s Depardieu matured, and so did his work and reputation. Period costumes and scripts suited him especially well, no matter what the century. He seemed as genuine playing a medieval peasant in *The Return of Martin Guerre* as he did playing Danton. He was evocative as Rodin in *Camille Claudel,* and he was even more compelling as a naive hunchback in Claude Berri's tribute to Marcel Pagnol, *Jean de Florette*. But if anyone doubted Depardieu's talent, two films of the 1980s put those doubts to rest: Truffaut's *The Last Metro* and Jean-Paul Rappeneau's version of the nineteenth-century classic, *Cyrano de Bergerac*. Both *Cyrano* and *Last Metro* brought Depardieu Césars and world acclaim, and *Cyrano* earned him an Academy Award nomination as best actor. At the end of the 1980s, Depardieu was awarded a "Super César" as France's actor of the decade, and this was a confirmation of his artistry and popular appeal.

But all the prizes and popularity have done little to sate his monstrous appetites. Having conquered France, Depardieu began the 1990s with his sights set on the vast English-language audience, first with *Green Card* and then starring as Christopher Columbus in *1492*. At the same time, he kept extending his range in France. He made his first movie with Jean-Luc Godard, one of the creators of France's New Wave in the late 1950s and sixties, and still France's most idiosyncratic *auteur*. He also made a light romantic comedy called *Mon Père, Ce Héros,* and he lent a hand in *Tous les Matins du Monde,* a French tribute to baroque music that featured the acting debut of his son, Guillaume. At the end of 1993, Depardieu had almost every day of his life booked up for the next three years to come.

Feeding his monstrous appetites is more than a full-time job. Developing scripts, learning roles, shooting movies, and then promoting them around the world, plus growing grapes, running his winery, and trying to fulfill his multiple responsibilities as husband, father, and patriarch of his film family—all this demands enormous work. To call Depardieu a workaholic does not even begin to capture the frenzy of his days or the fury with which his metabolism burns. In order to keep up his energy, Depardieu eats and drinks enough for three, and that puts more stress and strain on himself and his family. Then, to relieve that additional stress, he eats more and drinks more, until he is imprisoned in a cycle of excess.

His pace, and the way he submerges himself in the skin and spirit of his fictional characters, can also wreak havoc on his sense of personal identity. His real life and his fictional lives are now so thoroughly entwined in his psyche that there is little boundary left between what is real and what is made up. Where do the roles leave off and the man begin? Depardieu sometimes has no clue. His worst time is between films. With no script to follow, no fictional skin to inhabit, he loses his way. Depardieu has turned to psychoanalysis more than once, and he returned to it intensively in 1990. Between films he often winds up spending every single morning on his psychiatrist's couch.

"There is always a lag period coming out of a role," he says. "I still respond to the name Danton, and I am sure that years from now I will still respond when someone calls out the name Columbus."

Working on *Germinal,* though, was for Depardieu relatively uncomplicated. He was working with a director he felt comfortable with, Claude Berri; he had a group of close friends around him, Jean Carmet in particular; and he was embodying a fictional character with a background similar to his own: a miner from a working-class family in a backward region of France. Though this was a very long shoot, and Berri had some very annoying directorial habits, for Gérard the making of *Germinal* was not a terrible strain. He could go home to Bougival on weekends, and on location he could eat well, drink well, and lead the life of a merry troubadour. Under such optimal conditions, Depardieu could work in front of the camera with the same fervor and joy with which he searches for a good farm chicken and prepares it for his friends.

To understand his unusual approach to acting, it is essential to spend time with him on a set. And it is essential to remember this: when Depardieu makes a movie, he feels he is preparing a great feast, a bountiful Sunday lunch to be shared with his immediate film family and with the viewing public. It is also essential to remember that for all his training in classical theater, Depardieu feels his most enduring values as an actor—and as a man—come from what he learned as a child tending the beets and leeks and radishes and scallions in the garden of his Grandma Denise. As he succinctly puts it:

"In life or art, in chicken or people, I always look for the same simple things: authenticity and purity of flavor."

As a rebellious miner in Claude Berri's *Germinal,* 1993

2

The Feast

Depardieu suffers from a severe case of telephonitis. Rotary, pushbutton, or cordless, car phones, cellular phones, and airplane phones, they all festoon his daily existence, often from dawn to well after midnight. Be it for business or for tending his network of friends and extended family around the world, this is a man who craves contact, who constantly needs to keep in touch.

This morning, a Monday, was typical. Depardieu had been home for the weekend, during a respite from the shooting of *Germinal,* and before dawn he was back in harness. Gérard usually sleeps only a few hours a night, and he always rises early. This morning he got up at 6:30 a.m., had coffee with Elisabeth, and, as usual, they started the day by reading several of Paris's daily papers. Depardieu has his own production company, D.D. Productions (named in honor of his father), and his office is comprised solely of his mind, his telephones, and his sister Hélène, who fields incoming calls and manages his agenda. Today, as usual, Gérard was on the phone by 8 a.m. To properly plan and route his telephone traffic, Depardieu seems to have a map of the world's time zones engraved in his brain; if he wants to call Peter Weir in Sydney or the French director Francis Veber in Hollywood, almost without thinking he knows the time difference from Paris or wherever else he happens to be. By 9:30 a.m., when he dashed out the door, he had already made a half-dozen calls.

Gérard had a 10 a.m. appointment in Paris, and he rode into town with a driver from Berri's production team. All the way in, he made calls on the car phone. Later today Depardieu would head back to the north of France, to shoot a major nighttime scene for *Germinal.* But first he had an important meeting with Jean-Louis Livi, his friend, adviser, and business partner for more than twenty years. Livi, the nephew of Yves Montand, was for a long time one of the chief agents and directors of Artmédia, a powerful talent agency that is to French cinema what Creative Artists Agency is to Hollywood. Livi left Artmédia in the late 1980s and became an independent producer specializing in small, high-quality films, many of which he develops as vehicles for Gérard.

At 10 a.m., Depardieu walked into No. 10, avenue Georges V, one of the most prestigious and influential addresses in French cinema. For Depardieu, as for Catherine Deneuve and many of France's leading stars, this is business central. The building houses a warren of offices, and behind its discreet façade and brass nameplates are the headquarters of Artmédia, Livi, Berri, and many other prime movers in the creation, production, and distribution of French movies. In Hollywood, the collection of film families housed here would be the makings of a studio with industrial-scale clout and reach; the residents here prefer to remain small, independent, and craftsmanlike in spirit, making movies not to feed any industrial demand but out of artistic compulsion or creative whim.

Livi's group is named Film Par Film, and by Hollywood standards his offices would be a closet, or perhaps an executive bathroom. And that is just the way Livi likes it. At the top of George V, on the Champs-Elysées, are the dazzling corporate headquarters of Ciby 2000, and across the Seine is Studio Canal Plus, two powerhouse production companies that entered French cinema loaded with cash from French television. They are now making movies on a Hollywood scale, and they are bankrolling top international directors like Bernardo Bertolucci, David Lynch, and Oliver Stone. But Livi prefers to make movies which are uniquely French in culture and spirit, a guiding philosophy he has turned into major commercial success. At this moment, his *Tous les Matins du Monde* was creating a sensation in Paris and New York.

Livi is a precise, fastidious, soft-spoken man, Italian by birth and Parisian by culture, and today he was dressed in an elegant blue blazer and tie. Depardieu arrived this morning in a rumpled black shirt and a pair of light cotton jeans the color of red wine spilled on a white tablecloth. His hair was unruly, there was stubble on his chin, and against the December cold he wore a jacket made from rough, oddly cut layers of canvas. The cumulative effect gave him the look of a caveman draped in bearskins.

Though they come from opposite poles of French life, Livi and

Depardieu are like brothers, and now they sat down to map the progress of three movie projects they had in development. One was a deal with Disney to make an American version of *Mon Père, Ce Héros,* a delightful comedy starring Depardieu as the absentee father of a teenage daughter. When he takes her on an island vacation in order to become reacquainted, Gérard becomes confused, angry, and ultimately enchanted as he watches his daughter come of age and approach the moment of sexual initiation. Livi and Depardieu then discussed their second project, a movie of Honoré de Balzac's *Colonel Chabert,* and then the third, a movie with a golden role for Depardieu: playing a larger-than-life writer with appetites and talents resembling those of Ernest Hemingway.

Two hours later, Livi and Depardieu had been through scripts, directors, crews, and shooting schedules, and Depardieu was famished. He embraced Livi and then headed out to his neighborhood canteen, Marius et Janette, a favorite hangout for the movie people who work in the *quartier*. As usual, Depardieu marched right into the kitchen and examined the day's fare firsthand, nose in the pots. He ordered a plate of fried baby squid, to be eaten standing up in the back by the kitchen. As with most of his hangouts, Marius et Janette stocks a large supply of wines from Depardieu's chateau, and this little snack merited a bottle of his own light white wine. Then, naturally, another plate of squid, just to carry him through to the end of the bottle and to set him up for the long ride north.

Depardieu's driver was parked outside Marius et Janette, and once they were on the road heading north, Depardieu was back on his car phone, calling his agent at Artmédia, Bertrand de Labbey, to keep him apprised of his talks with Livi. He then called Alain Goldman, the young French producer who put together the $46-million financing for *1492*. The movie had flopped in North America, but it did well in France and very well in Latin America, and though Depardieu was disappointed by the final outcome, he was relieved that most of the producers were at least going to get back their initial investment. Besides, his mind was already on his new projects; having so many movies in the works is always for him a cushion against a flop or two. Now, in the car, he went over a draft script that Veber had done for the remake of *Mon Père, Ce Héros*. Veber was like family. The two men had already made three successful comedies together: *La Chèvre, Les Compères,* and *Les Fugitifs,* which had been remade in English as *Three Fugitives,* with Nick Nolte playing Depardieu's role. Veber was working on the script in Los Angeles, and Depardieu planned to call him later that afternoon, just to pull a little *hold-up*.

As his monthly telephone bill would attest, Depardieu has now become the central switchboard of French cinema. In this small world of big egos, feuding clans, and a shrinking market share for French movies, there are deep-seated rivalries among directors, producers, and distributors; back-stabbing is not the exception, it is the rule. Depardieu talks to everyone. He has worked with most of the leading directors in France, and, with only a few exceptions, they all have become part of his extended film family. Besides, most directors and producers would love to have Depardieu in their next film; his presence is a guarantee of initial financing and box-office draw. Depardieu is also French cinema's principal bridge to Hollywood; not even Catherine Deneuve can rival his appeal in the American market. Over the past decade, French bankers have become deeply involved in financing ventures in Hollywood, but when Disney's Jeffrey Katzenberg, for example, comes to the Cannes Film Festival, the chief executive he wants to have dinner with is Depardieu.

On his way north, Depardieu put in a call to Claude Davy, his press agent for the past decade. Davy too is like family; his nephew Nicolas was serving today as Gérard's driver. Then Depardieu called the set of *Germinal* and talked to Patrick Bordier, probably his closest friend and aide. Patrick *is* family: he is married to Gérard's sister Hélène. Gérard introduced Patrick to Hélène, and, like her, Patrick serves Gérard in many different capacities. He helps Gérard run the wine business at the Château de Tigné, and he can be a settling influence when Gérard overworks or overdrinks. But Patrick is also an accomplished production manager, and he was now working for Claude Berri as one of the administrative anchors of *Germinal*. He was also running the carriage house where Gérard's film family was camped. On the car phone, Gérard asked Patrick what time he had to be on the set and if the house needed any supplies. With both Patrick and Gérard, the guiding spirit is always do-it-yourself, from buying soap and paper towels to planning the meals and doing the cooking. The following day, Patrick would come back from the set and cook everyone a proper lunch of steak with shallots, potatoes, and salad.

As the car wound its way into the north of France, into the gray, flat landscape surrounding Valenciennes, Depardieu looked out at all the old factories and shells of heavy industry, and he began talking about French coal miners. Berri's *Germinal* was inspired by Emile Zola's novel of the same name, and it recounted the story of a bloody miners' rebellion at the end of the nineteenth century. There was a crisis then, and there was a crisis now. Today most of the mines in northern France have shut down, and about the only work the miners and their wives can find is to be extras in Berri's movie, at 300 francs a night—about $60. For the miners of the last century, the owner of the mining company and his foremen ruled over their daily lives with almost absolute authority, the way kings had ruled all of France for centuries. Now, in Zola's story, the miners were sick of breaking their backs for slave wages. Depardieu was playing a miner and the father of a poor mining family, and now, passing through depressed villages and deserted mining company towns, a gnawing anger welled up inside him.

"This is the France I grew up in," he said. "Everything was patriarchal and caste-ridden. It was not easy for my family. In our town we were outcasts, almost untouchables, and it stayed that way right up through de Gaulle. I hated that France. It castrated us."

Nicolas pulled the Citroën off the main highway and wound around the back roads to the chateau where Depardieu and his family were staying, near the Belgian border. Depardieu and Nicolas dropped off their bags at the carriage house, and then Nicolas drove him another half hour to the location of the shoot. *Germinal* was a $32-million production, one of the largest ever undertaken in France, and Berri had spent $1 million transforming a huge, gutted factory into an entire underground coal mine. This week, though, Berri and his crew were doing outdoor scenes of the miners' rebellion, and for the daily operations the cast and crew were camped in a makeshift settlement of trailers, tents, and prefab offices, all set on an open slab of countryside. It had been pouring rain for days, some of the big tents had blown down, and now the *Germinal* encampment had an air as dismal as a nineteenth-century mining camp in the dead of winter.

Depardieu's car rolled into the encampment around 3 p.m. Gil Noir, his personal wardrobe woman for the past decade, was there to greet him, costume in hand. He spent twenty minutes in wardrobe and makeup and came out a very different man. Now Depardieu was clad in coarse wool pants, a wool vest, and a tattered old wool jacket. A rough moustache bristled across his upper lip, and his hands and face and neck were deeply ingrained with soot and ash. On his head was an old workman's cap, the bill pulled down in a way that made him look angry and menacing. The cut of the clothes made Depardieu look even more massive across the shoulders and trunk; at a glance, you knew that here was a man who spent his life heaving an axe and hauling coal.

Depardieu's demeanor changed subtly as well. Greeting Patrick and his friends in the crew, he became more ebullient, more forceful—not in a demanding way, just to energize the troops who had spent the entire day out in the cold. Once he was in costume, Depardieu's appetite came rushing back, and he rounded up Jean Carmet, who was playing his father in the film, and went to Chez Jannick, a nearby restaurant that had become his canteen on the set. It was a simple country place, run family-style and specializing in the kind of hearty cooking miners like. Of course, Depardieu headed right back into the kitchen and was greeted with hugs and kisses; here he was not a star but the prodigal son returning to his adopted family. The place was run by the family matriarch, La Mère Michèle, a short, stout, jovial peasant woman, with glasses steamed up from working her pots and an apron splattered with gravy and blood. Just behind her kitchen was a bank of dilapidated wooden cages, where Michèle raised chickens, rabbits, and even a turkey or two. The journey from the cage to the chopping block and into her pots was no more than fifteen meters.

Naturally, Chez Jannick was stocked with Depardieu's wines, and as this was sundown, it was time for a glass or two of young gamay. While Carmet and everyone else warmed up with wine, Depardieu slipped back into the kitchen for a private chat with La Mère Michèle. And Depardieu had very serious business on his mind: turkey. The Thursday before, the last week in November, Michèle had given Depardieu a fifteen-pound turkey, and he had used it to make his film family a huge American-style Thanksgiving dinner, with dressing and all the trimmings, including homemade cranberry sauce. Now, the two of them alone in her kitchen, the prodigal son was telling La Mère Michèle that he had followed her advice on the timing of the cooking and on the temperature of the oven, but he had made the dressing according to his own recipe. Clearly, that turkey was now a strong bond between them, for as Depardieu stood there with La Mère Michèle, both in rapt discussion of dressing and gravy, their peasant hands met and fused in a long, silent communion.

As a little pick-me-up, and to please La Mère Michèle, Depardieu ate a huge plate of lamb stew, and then he and Carmet went back to the encampment. Berri was running behind schedule, so they went to the dinner trailer to await their calls to come onto the set. They settled in at a table, and, surrounded by the pleasant odor of steak sizzling on the grill, Gérard began talking of his own parents, Dédé and Lilette. In Châteauroux, a small town in the agricultural heartland of central France, Dédé had worked as a skilled craftsman, specializing in sheet metal. Gérard now spoke of how his father would come home from work, eat alone, and often spend the entire evening saying nothing and doing nothing beyond sitting in his chair, lost in some distant reverie.

Dédé's great passion in life—beyond wine, fishing, and hunting mushrooms—was working sheet metal. To join France's fraternity of elite craftsmen, Les Compagnons du Tour de France, he spent an entire year crafting one piece of metal into the form of a fireman's boot, just like the boots he wore in his part-time job as a volunteer fireman. When he finished, the boot was exquisite, a masterpiece; under his skilled hands, the metal had become as smooth and supple as leather, with folds and wrinkles draping down around the ankle. In admiration, the boot was kept for many years in a privileged place in the Depardieu household; to his family, it seemed as though Dédé had wrenched that boot from his very soul. *"Une an à heures perdus,"* Dédé used to say, in his fractured French. One year of lost time.

Dédé was a dreamer, a poet of the spirit, and when he drank, as he did increasingly as he got older, he seemed to move into distant realms. For years, Gérard now recalled, Dédé imagined he was living in Spain. When his health disintegrated and he lapsed into serious illness, Gérard put him into a hospital outside Paris, an institution which cared for many elderly Moslems. One day, when Gérard came to visit, he asked his father if there was anything he needed. Dédé did have one request: He wanted a pair of *babouches,* those curl-toed slippers the Moslems wore. "I think by now he had moved south and was living in Morocco," Depardieu said, his own mind a long way away. When Gérard put Dédé into that hospital, he knew his father would never come out. "He was dying then," Gérard recalled, "but I could not bring myself to tell him. I had told Lilette she was dying. But when Dédé asked me how he was doing, I said, 'Fine, fine. Soon we'll go fishing together.' "

When Dédé died, Gérard found his body on a gurney in a corridor of the hospital, his mouth open in an expression of shock and surprise. "It was as if he had seen something at the very end," Gérard said, "something that made him gape in wonder."

Reminiscing about his father, stirring those very deep emotions, communing with La Mère Michèle, slipping into his miner's woolens, feeling the misery of the miners and their families in patriarchal France—through all this Depardieu had moved quietly and naturally, almost unconsciously, back into the skin and spirit of the coal miner he was embodying inside the world of *Germinal.* Through his own process of alchemy, like Dédé working sheet metal, Gérard had melded into the body and soul of the miner he was portraying. With his film father, Carmet, at his side, looking frail and covered with soot and ash, Depardieu was now ready to march into tonight's critical meeting of the miners. It was a strike meeting, tantamount to rebellion, and Gérard was ready to lend his full weight and anger to the miners' cause: he wanted to lash out at the heartless bosses, to spit on the oppressive caste system that had castrated his family.

"Putain," Depardieu cursed, standing up and buttoning his thick wool jacket. "Let's get going."

When Depardieu and Carmet arrived on the set, the strike meeting was already in full cry, on a cold hillside whipped by the wind. Some two hundred angry miners and their wives and children were pressed in between a roaring fire and a giant crucifix, the body of Jesus shimmering red and yellow and orange from the leaping flames. On a makeshift podium below the crucifix was the leader of the revolt, played by Renaud, a popular French singer in his first starring role. From the podium, his fists clenched, he was haranguing the miners, urging them to get off their knees and act like men; the time had come to strike! Soon Carmet and Depardieu were right by his side, Gérard swearing there would be no pity for scabs or traitors to the cause. He was angry now, bellowing and radiating an energy and fire that made the miners and their wives wave their fists and shout support for the strike.

"Cut!" Berri barked. "Not bad, not bad."

When the cameras stopped, it was clear that morale on the set was running very low, and there was a current of anger circulating against Berri. Directors like Ridley Scott, who did *1492* and *Thelma & Louise,* and Jean-Paul Rappeneau, who did *Cyrano de Bergerac,* have strong visual imaginations, and before their assistant director shouts Action!—*Moteur!* in French—they know exactly how they want a shot to look and unfold. Berri has a literary intelligence, and he puts his preparatory efforts into the words of his script, not into how a shot will appear on the screen. The visuals he then improvises on the set, by trial and error. His cameramen shoot a take, then Berri examines it on two video monitors he has rigged up in a small van he uses as his command center on the set. To get the visuals right, he ends up doing the same shot over and over and over again. This long and cumbersome procedure would drive most money-conscious producers berserk; Berri solves that problem by producing his own films and being accountable to no one but himself. Still, the process puts a terrible strain on the cast and crew and extras, especially when they are shooting out in the freezing cold.

Depardieu sensed the mood, and during breaks in the shooting, while Berri stared into his video monitors, Gérard joked with pals in the crew and mingled with the miners and their wives and children, signing autographs and posing for photos. On a set, Depardieu never goes into a corner or retreats to his star trailer to "stay in character." This is unnecessary. By the time he walks onto a set, Depardieu *is* the character; he is so totally fused into the being and essence of the character that he does not have to give it a single moment's more thought.

Many leading American actors spend months researching a role. Dustin Hoffman immersed himself in the world of autistic children to prepare for his award-winning role in *Rain Man*. In making *GoodFellas,* Robert De Niro called one New York mobster seven or eight times a day, to soak up detail and grit to strengthen his performance. Oliver Stone put Tom Cruise through weeks of simulated U.S. Marine boot camp, to force his recruit into the proper mind-set for making *Born on the Fourth of July*.

Depardieu does not like to do outside research. He starts from the conviction that already inside his being are all the emotions that animate and rule human behavior: love and hate, jealousy and rage, tenderness and compassion, strength and weakness, everything that is male and everything that is female. He also believes that buried somewhere inside his psyche, or deep within what he calls his "genetic memory," are shadows of all the characters and archetypes he might ever be called upon to embody, be they good or evil, king or beggar, murderer or saint, poet or prankster. So to prepare a new role, Depardieu does not look outward; he looks inward. He enters a period of reflection and introspection; he begins a deep interior search for the hidden shadow of the relevant archetype. With truly challenging roles, the search becomes a voyage into the emotional and spiritual unknown.

"The best research always begins in darkness and incoherence," he says. "To me, creating is trying to explore all those interior spaces that belong to me, but which I do not yet know or understand. Only in living them can I discover them."

To explore those interior spaces, Depardieu needs to have a map and directions. For this he looks to the director or the writer to reveal his guiding vision. But what is essential to Depardieu is a strong script. For *Germinal,* he looked to Berri and his script, but he also looked back to Zola and his novel. Every actor wants to work from a strong story line, but what Depardieu looks for in a script is not plot, action, or characterization. He looks for language and conflict, which for him are guideposts to his ultimate quarry: "emotional truths." For it is in the realm of the emotions that Depardieu does his exploring, and for his search to succeed, he desperately needs the right words and the right personal chemistry with his protagonists. Language is his probe and sonar, and words and conflict are the grenades he needs to dislodge his buried emotions.

Because his own background was so like that of Zola's miner in *Germinal,* Depardieu's interior research for this role was not too difficult. Tonight, he simply *was* the miner, dressed in a miner's woolens, with his hands and face ingrained with soot, and with a miner's anger roiling in his chest. By ten o'clock, the wind and cold and all the frustrations of shooting take after take after take had thoroughly fouled everyone's mood. So as Berri stayed buried in his van, staring into his video monitors, Depardieu took it upon himself to generate a little warmth by cracking jokes and publicly teasing some members of the crew.

"François Truffaut used to call me *un entremetteur,* a person who serves as a connector, a go-between," Depardieu says. "That is very true. I like to bring people together and catalyze."

By midnight, everyone was exhausted—everyone except Gérard. He was cheerfully doing take after take of a difficult scene in which he spouts a long, angry monologue. He had already repeated it a dozen times, but he seemed just as fresh and energetic as he had been all day long. He had been going hard, very hard, since 6:30 this morning, but he was now sailing along in the highest of spirits, laughing, clowning, telling bawdy stories, and groaning loudly whenever Berri emerged from his van to cry *"Moteur!"* Acting energized Depardieu, gave him nourishment; clearly, he was having the time of his life.

"To me, this is not work, it is pure fun," he explained. "For me, the mental work, memorizing lines—that is fatiguing and thankless. On location I can finally breathe. When I step in front of a camera, it is pure joy, a form of liberation. What is an actor? Someone who listens, listens, listens, and learns how to smile. I am constantly impregnating myself with people, with words, with feelings. Then, in front of a camera, I let them all go. I just try to show people everything I have inside me. And if I communicate what's inside me deeply enough, and purely enough, I will make them laugh or cry."

Another hour passed in the cold, with the cameramen shooting and reshooting the speeches of the strike leaders. What made all this particularly disheartening to many people in the cast and crew was that Berri, as usual, was using only two cameras, in fixed positions. Tonight the cameras were focused on the strike leaders; tomorrow night he would reshoot the same scene over again, this time with his two cameras aimed the other way, at the angry crowd. For the cast and crew and extras, it would be almost an exact replay, take after take. Berri was operating on a Hollywood-sized budget, but his techniques seemed archaic. An Oliver Stone or a Francis Coppola would use six or eight cameras to shoot this scene, doing all the wide-angles and closeups in one day of shooting, maybe less. Still, multiple cameras and modern technology do not guarantee high-quality movies. Fine scripts more often do, and Berri, the creator of such distinguished films as *Jean de Florette, Manon des Sources,* and *The Two of Us,* was not about to change his Old World ways.

By 1 a.m., Berri was still in his van, ordering take after take, and the open anger of the miner characters was now fusing with the silent anger of the real-life miners and their wives and children working as extras. They had been at it all night long in the cold, and now they were sick of it. Around 11 p.m. an urn of soup had been wheeled up, but only some of the extras had been able to break away for a little warmth and nourishment. And at $60 a night for ten hours of work, they were feeling exploited—as exploited as the miners in Berri's script and in Zola's novel. Still, they did not dare complain; they needed the money to feed their families, and outside the set were scores of out-of-work miners eager to take their place, no matter what the pay. So, on the set as in real life, the miners were pinned into submission, totally at the mercy of a hard-driving boss.

At last, Berri moved on to what he insisted would be the final round of closeups of the strike leaders. His cameramen shot several takes, until finally one unfolded with seeming perfection. Everyone on the set sensed it was just right, and even before the cameras stopped, a sigh of collective relief started spreading through the cast and crew and extras, as though they could already feel their feet thawing out and their heads hitting the pillow.

"Cut! Print! Excellent!" Berri called from his van. "Now we will do just one more take. As a guarantee. Places! *Moteur!*"

One more? A groan reverberated through the cast and crew, and then one angry voice burst from the crowd: *"Non! Pas de moteur!"* It was Depardieu, and a hush fell across the set. *"Merde, Claude, ça suffit!"* Shit, that's enough!

Depardieu now flew across the set, fuming and spouting all the way. Berri, his eyes swollen from hour after hour of staring into his video monitors, came out of his van to confront him. This was a clear challenge to his authority, all the more striking because Depardieu almost never second-guesses the director; he feels that an actor is there to make a director's vision come alive, and not to question his methods. But now Depardieu was furious, and Berri just stood there, taking it, unsure of what to do; he was the director and producer, but Depardieu was his gold at the box office and the anchor of the cast. Finally, Depardieu finished his harangue, and Berri just nodded in silent agreement, not so much in retreat but seemingly in relief. He had become so lost, so blind, in his creative quest that his only realities had become his video monitor and his private compulsions; now he seemed relieved that someone else had a clearer eye and the strength to act.

Afterward, as they rode back to the encampment to change out of their woolens and wipe off their soot and ash, Carmet turned to Depardieu: "You did a good thing there, Gérard, intervening like that."

"Oouaff," Depardieu said. *"Faut pas enculer les mouches."* You shouldn't try to screw flies. Meaning Berri had gone overboard.

Depardieu and Carmet changed out of their woolens and then headed back home to the carriage house. By the time they arrived it was 3 a.m., and there was Patrick standing at the stove, whipping up an omelette perfumed by thin slices of fresh black truffle, straight from the ground. The omelette was a gourmet delight, and to fete it properly, Gérard opened a bottle of his special Cuvée Mozart, one of the true jewels of his Château de Tigné.

For the next two hours, the carriage house rocked with hilarity and high spirits, as Depardieu's film family gathered for what amounted to a ritual Sunday lunch. Carmet, at seventy, and Patrick and Gérard, all fathers with sons of their own, let loose and told stories, bringing their young apprentices into the fold of their gypsy life and their troubadour spirit. Let other actors work for fame or money; Depardieu works for the myriad pleasures of nights like this. " 'Riches don't make a man rich, they only make him busier,' " Depardieu says, quoting one of his favorite lines from Columbus. "I never think about making a living. I just think about living. Even when my family was very poor, I always felt rich. If I have only a morsel of bread, I eat it with pleasure. I am lucky: I am blessed with a joyous nature, and that joy flows right into what I do as an actor. What is the best school for an actor? Life!"

Soon the omelette was gone, so was the Cuvée Mozart, and at the end of this marathon day, Depardieu was totally exhausted. He was far from Elisabeth and his children, and he missed them all, and he did not like going to bed alone, as he now would. Still, he was surrounded by his film family, Patrick had put a bountiful platter onto their communal table, and everyone had been eating and drinking and laughing with healthy appetites, family warmth, and generosity of spirit. Yes, his pace was maniacal and punishing, and to people on the other side of the looking glass it might seem like madness and a flight from reality; sometimes it looked that way to Depardieu as well. But this was his life, lived to the hilt, and now his demon appetites were finally sated. He would go to bed with a feeling of well-being—a feeling he can get only from creative expression and being around other actors and creators. As Depardieu knows painfully well, acting is his relief, his liberation, his joy, his fix, and acting and working on a movie set give him two vital nourishments he simply cannot get in any other way: poetry for his heart and music for his soul.

"What is the whole idea of *bien-être*?" he says. "Artists coming together in the spirit of creation, and everyone tapping into the collective energy and joy. *Bien-être* is the primal, prelanguage feeling of *ahhhhhhh!*"

PART 2

Châteauroux

Dédé and Lilette Depardieu at the time of their marriage, 1944

3

The Law of Silence

The road to Châteauroux runs due south from Paris, through the Parisian suburbs and out into unspoiled greenery. For miles and miles the road runs straight and flat, through farmlands and past villages with a single steeple, and as the road continues south, past herds of grazing cows, past mustard fields of brilliant yellow, and past acre upon acre of cultivated fields, no traveler needs to be reminded why France is the second largest agricultural power in the world. And when the road starts winding into the Loire valley, with its undulating vistas of chateaus and manicured vineyards, no one need wonder why so many generations of painters and poets in search of inspiration have been drawn to the bosom of France.

South of the Loire valley, the road flattens out again and the landscape becomes coarser, and so do the villages and farmhouses. Wander off the main road, turn into one of the rural villages, and along a country lane you might well see a weathered French peasant heading home for lunch with a baguette tucked under his arm. He might be wearing blue coveralls and a beret, and stuck in his lips there might be a *maïs,* one of those thick yellow cigarettes so characteristic of France. Peasants like this one, immortalized in the photos of Henri Cartier-Bresson, seem to belong to a different era, and many young Frenchmen resent being saddled with that cliché. But in the back reaches of central France, such peasants remain as much a fixture of country life as the distinctive Citroën Deux-Chevaux and the noontime pastis at the local café.

Stop at one of those local cafés for a sandwich and a glass of red wine, and standing next to you at the bar there may well be a local farmer on his lunch break. His hands and face and the creases on his neck will be permanently darkened by the sun, and he will be speaking a local patois you can barely understand, no matter how good your Parisian French may be. For his lunch, his friend the barkeeper might set before him a huge wedge of round country bread, a bottle of red wine, a slice or two of mountain ham, and a huge slab of Cantal cheese, or maybe a fresh chevre, made from the goat milk of one of their neighbors. The farmer might start in on his meal by cutting his bread or cheese with an old knife with the wooden handle rubbed smooth, or even with his Laguiole, the hand-crafted jewel so many French peasants guard in their pocket, a talisman with bone handles and a trademark bee at the neck.

From Paris to Châteauroux is a distance of only 160 miles, a leisurely three-hour drive. But to go from the Eiffel Tower to that farmer's Laguiole is like journeying from Manhattan to the Ozarks: you have to pass through radical changes of landscape, culture, mentality, and even language. Indeed, journeying from Paris to Châteauroux is like moving from one civilization to another. In the morning you are in the world capital of taste, sophistication, and intellectual enlightenment, and by lunch you are entering what Parisians call "La France Profonde," the depths of France, the dark, ageless core of the nation, the raw bedrock upon which village life, folklore, and superstition have been anchored since France was Gaul.

Châteauroux is situated in a region known as Le Berry, and the road leading toward the town passes through forests, pastures, and vineyards that are rough in appearance but which are considered some of the very richest in the whole of France, so rich, the locals refer to their countryside as "Champagne." But the comparison ends with the richness of the soil. By any standard, the back reaches of Le Berry remain surprisingly primitive. In some enclaves, the peasants still work their land in ways very similar to those their grandfathers used in the nineteenth century. In many families, bread, wine, and cheese are still made by hand, and the women still cure hams, smoke turkeys, make sausage and pâtés, and put up preserves for the winter.

Settled amidst the natural richness of the Berry landscape is the town of Châteauroux. On its outskirts there is little by way of suburb or outlying industry, and the town itself does not look large enough to hold 60,000 people; it looks more like an overgrown village. Which is just what Châteauroux turns out to be. In many ways it is a pleasant town, but to a newcomer arriving today it can seem a bit surrealistic, even schizophrenic; the kids appear eager to rush into the Americanized nineties, while their parents and grandparents still cling to the small-town France of the fifties.

The train station is one of the town's principal nerve centers and arteries, and its architecture reflects the town's time warps. The station itself is laid out in timeless French country style, with public washrooms at one end and the *buffet de la gare,* the station restaurant, at the other. The façade of the station used to be Napoleon III; now it is a modern slab of concrete with a big SNCF sign glowing in electric blue. In the main hall are the same bright-orange automatic ticket-punchers you see in Paris, and there are sleek vending machines, a new kiosk, even a photocopy stand. But walk into the *buffet de la gare* and you will swear that nothing, including the menu, has changed for the past forty years.

Turn right coming out of the station and the road leads around to the principal industry in town, a government-owned SEITA tobacco factory that each year churns out millions of packets of Gitanes and Gauloises for the rest of the nation. Walk straight out of the station and you are on the rue de la Gare, one of the town's main streets. The buildings here are modest, and several have upper reaches adorned with wood carvings done by the elite craftsmen of the Compagnons du Tour de France. Many of the storefronts just below are occupied by American-style hamburger joints, where the kids inside listen to Michael Jackson and wear baseball caps and T-shirts emblazoned with such concocted American team names as "New York Twins."

In the town's central plaza there are two city halls. One is a stately old Hôtel de Ville, with an elegant town clock, lovely green shutters and awnings, and, over the entryway, the inscription *"Liberté, Egalité, Fraternité."* The new city hall sits on an adjacent side of the plaza and nothing about it is distinctively French; it looks like a small office building imported whole from a town in Iowa or Arkansas. It is a block of drab concrete and glass, and its exterior is covered with a curious form of venetian blinds, to keep out the afternoon sun at no matter what aesthetic cost.

Châteauroux is built low and flat, with one notable exception. The town used to count among its small share of cultural treasures (the Michelin guide notes one church and gives the town no stars) a municipal theater and opera house more than a century old. The opera house was one of the great prides of Le Berry, with five hundred seats, and though its acoustics were poor, artists from Paris liked to come down to play the hall; it was so intimate they could literally smell the public. Now the only way to see the old opera house is in picture postcards; it was torn down in 1957 by a local aristocrat with evident delusions of grandeur. In its place he built a block of apartments a dozen stories high, an eyesore that towers over the town the way the Tour Montparnasse towers over the Left Bank of Paris. A band of purists fought to preserve the opera house, but it was a losing battle. And even after the new tower went up—never mind that it looked as if it had been designed by a five-year-old and built with Lego blocks—most of the townspeople showered it with praise. For this was progress, the modernity of Paris come to their province, a touch of the Chicago skyline come to Châteauroux.

Châteauroux today is a town of small shops, clean streets, many open-air markets, one department store, and little night life. As in many French provincial towns, there is a wealth of corner cafés and sporting-goods stores catering to local hunters and fishermen. To an American eye, Châteauroux is reminiscent of a small town in Iowa, Nebraska, or South Dakota, a town surrounded by corn or wheat, and where everybody knows everybody else. The locals here are known as Castelroussins, after the town, or as Berrichons, after the region. Like farm people in the American Midwest, folks in Châteauroux come across as honest, direct, hard-working, and incapable of pretense. Unlike Parisians, they are naturally warm and cordial, the kind of people who clap visitors on the back and put drinks in their hand, and who will go out of their way to help friends, strangers, and cats in the rain. If you suffered a flat tire on the main road near town, no Parisian passing by would ever dream of stopping; most Castelroussins would never dream of not stopping.

Like their architecture, the conversation of the Castelroussins quickly sorts itself out into decades and epochs. Sentences here often begin, "When the Germans were here . . . " or "During the time of the Americans. . . . " The Germans occupied the town by force during World War II, and the Americans occupied the town by invitation during the early stages of the cold war. But as different as these occupations were, both left deep imprints on Châteauroux and its villagers, in ways that older Castelroussins can still feel today. And in equally profound ways, the two occupations helped shape the life and destiny of Gérard Depardieu.

Dédé Depardieu, Gérard's father, was pure Berrichon. He was born in 1923 in Montchevrier, a hamlet of Le Berry surrounded by cows, wheat fields, vineyards, streams for fishing, and forests that were filled with mushrooms in the fall. Almost everyone in his family had two names, a given name and a nickname, often colorful, for everyday usage. His mother's given name was Emilienne; everyone called her Denise. His father's given name was Louis, but for some reason he was known as Marcel. Marcel and Denise had only one child and they named him René, but somewhere along the way he picked up the more whimsical name Dédé (pronounced Day-Day).

Marcel Depardieu fought in the French Army during World War I, and after the war he stayed on in the service. He died in 1931, when Dédé was only seven, of some grave malady never specified in family files. Dédé barely knew his father, and throughout most of his boyhood he lived alone with his mother, the two of them forced to cope as best they could in the tiny village and surrounding countryside. Dédé was raised on fresh meat and farm milk, and he grew into a big, healthy, hearty youth. By the time he reached manhood he was built like a bull, with a massive chest and neck, a beefy face, and very expressive eyes. Like most of the country boys in Le Berry, Dédé had almost no formal schooling, and he grew up barely able to read and write. All his life he signed his name with the initials "D.D.," and even that was a struggle. Dédé was never much of a talker. Even with family and friends, if he said much more than *"Salut, ça va?"*—Hi, how are you?—it was considered a long conversation. When Dédé did speak, his words often came forth in short bursts of onomatopoetic patter: *"Ouaff! Bof. J'sais-paw."*

Dédé had no gift for language, but he had talent in his hands. He had an easy, even graceful way with tools and wood and metal, and he might have settled into the countryside as an able craftsman, had it not been for Adolf Hitler. Le Berry felt the effects of Hitler's ambitions very early on. In the late 1930s, when Nazi storm troopers were rounding up Jews, gypsies, and dissidents, refugees from Germany poured into central France, and many sought shelter in Châteauroux. In 1939, when the German Army marched into Poland, Czechoslovakia, and Austria, whole trainloads of refugees streamed into central France. On May 10, 1940, German tanks and troops blitzed into Holland and France, and in the first days of Hitler's campaign, a key French air base outside Châteauroux was repeatedly bombed. So was the town's railroad station, strategically situated on one of the main lines to Paris. On June 22, with the 800,000-man French Army in ruins, France surrendered and signed an armistice allowing Germany to impose its formal Line of Demarcation cutting France into an occupied northern zone and an unoccupied south. That line of formal disgrace ran just a few kilometers north of Châteauroux.

Dédé was not yet eighteen when France fell. As German troops and the Gestapo started taking control of hundreds of French towns and villages, and as thousands of young Frenchmen were being rounded up and sent to German labor camps or conscripted into the defeated French Army, Dédé fled to Switzerland. He spent the early part of the war there in a camp for refugee youths. With France's defeat and occupation, and with Hitler and the Third Reich controlling Paris, millions of other Frenchmen were also uprooted from their homes and villages, including the young woman who would become Gérard's mother, Alice Marillier.

Her family roots were in another corner of La France Profonde, the Jura, the verdant, untrammeled range of forests, pastures, and mountains running from eastern France into Switzerland, just north of the Alps. Like Dédé, Alice was born in 1923. She grew up in St. Claude, a pleasant country town renowned among pipe smokers in Europe for the superb briar pipes its artisans have handcrafted for several generations. Her grandfather owned a small pipe factory in town, and her parents, Suzanne and Xavier Marillier, were sturdy, hard-working people. While they were by no means well-to-do in the harsh aftermath of World War I, they did provide a warm, stable home life for Alice and her sister, Colette.

Alice was a winsome young girl. She had dark hair and beautiful dark eyes, and she was vivacious and outgoing. The name Alice did not really capture her spirit, so early on everyone began calling her by the playful diminutive "Lilette." In the schools of St. Claude, Lilette learned how to read and write, but as with many girls growing up in provincial France in the 1930s, her real education took place at home, in the expectation that she would marry, raise children, and tend a household. But Lilette grew up with a head full of other dreams. She wanted to see the world beyond St. Claude; she wanted to travel to the romantic places she saw in picture postcards and magazines. From her vantage point, even Paris seemed exotic; it was a city her family and neighbors often talked about, but only the most privileged ever got a chance to see it. When she was nearing eighteen, Lilette did get to travel, but not to where she dreamed of going. Her father was a pilot in the defeated French Army, and in the first stages of the Occupation he was transferred to La Martinerie, the French air base three kilometers outside Châteauroux. His wife and two daughters soon joined him there in the occupied town.

When Alice and her family arrived, daily life in Châteauroux had a veneer of normalcy, but the town was actually living in a state of siege. In normal times, Châteauroux counted some 35,000 Frenchmen as natives, but the war had rapidly changed the complexion and the character of the town. In the early stages of the Occupation, 15,000 refugees poured in from northern France and Eastern Europe, and most of them were crowded into makeshift camps spread throughout Châteauroux and its environs. In town affairs Frenchmen retained titular positions, but what they mostly did was carry out German orders. For their occupation headquarters the Nazi command had requisitioned the best hotel in town, the Hôtel de France, and the Gestapo operated out of a villa they had seized on the rue Mousseaux. When Lilette's father was stationed as a flight monitor at La Martinerie, Luftwaffe pilots were using the field to train for missions on the Russian front. During the course of the war, thousands of German soldiers would pour into town for rest and relaxation, arriving from battlefronts across Europe, Russia, and North Africa.

In this state of siege, living in Châteauroux was not easy for any Frenchman, and especially not for pretty young women like Lilette and Colette. German officers and soldiers were in the streets, in the cafés, even in the shops and markets, and most were hungry for female companionship. With some exceptions, the French kept to themselves, in silent and sullen resignation, and parents tried to keep their daughters far away from German soldiers. But that was an almost impossible task. Food and essential items such as coal were all rationed and scarce; in most families, everyone but small children had to go out and work. The Marilliers were better off than many, as Xavier was in the French Army, but Lilette was obliged to work for a time in a German canteen, a potentially traumatic experience for a young, attractive woman.

Indeed, daily life in occupied Châteauroux was often traumatic. The texture of daily existence is clearly portrayed in a scholarly monograph written by Pierre Bellier, *La Vie à Châteauroux, Juillet 1940–Août 1944* (Life in Châteauroux, July 1940–August 1944). In August 1940, just after the defeat of the French Army, rationing was imposed on the sale of coal, sugar, fat, pasta, and soap. Real coffee all but disappeared. Concerts and dance halls were closed down. Blackouts were ordered on all homes, and listening to the BBC was formally banned. By winter, potatoes and shoes were added to the ration list. A tax was imposed on bicycles, and this was just the beginning. In April 1941, there appeared in Châteauroux the first signs of resistance: the letter *V* was scrawled on public walls. This was code for "Victory," and a sign of solidarity with the Resistance, being orchestrated by General Charles de Gaulle. De Gaulle was then in London, organizing the Resistance and broadcasting hope to occupied France.

The scrawled *V*'s elicited harsh repression by the Nazi command. In June 1941, a census was taken of all Jews living in Le Berry, as preparation for deportation. Sales of wine and tobacco were cut back. Establishments with public telephones were ordered to record the names and addresses of all users. In the fall of 1941, restrictions were imposed on anyone even suspected of being a Jew or a communist. The movement of cars and trucks was placed under strict control. The Gestapo stepped up its hunt for members of the Resistance, and Gestapo officers were using torture in their interrogations. Officers of the SS, habitually garbed in long leather coats, were easily recognized; what really terrified the Castelroussins was the Milice, the invisible network of French informers the Gestapo used to spy on their neighbors in exchange for cash, provisions, or special favors. No Frenchman could be sure who belonged to the Milice, so everyone was suspect, whether he was the grocer, the baker, the mailman, or the bartender; even some members of your own family might come under suspicion. No one could be trusted, and no one could open his mouth in public or in private without wondering if his partner in conversation belonged to the Milice. Or the Maquis, the underground. So a steely curtain of silence clanked down on the town, and even inside many individual homes.

When the situation in Le Berry seemed to have stabilized, Dédé decided to leave Switzerland and return to Le Berry, to look for work to support himself and his mother. Jobs in his village were few, so Dédé ended up going to the nearest promising place to find work: Châteauroux. Precisely how he and his mother got through this period is not clear, but Dédé apparently found work as a craftsman. Whatever he did, he had to keep his mouth shut, as each month the Germans were rounding up any suspected troublemakers and sending them to the labor camps and factories in Germany that were fueling Hitler's war machine. In May 1942, when Dédé and Lilette were in Châteauroux, Marshal Pétain paid a visit to what he thought was a town adjusting well to the Occupation. To his shock, the head of the collaborationist Vichy regime was greeted by defiant tracts from the Resistance and copies of the underground paper *Combat,* one of whose leading writers was Albert Camus. That July, all Bastille Day celebrations were banned, but some courageous townspeople hung out the French *tricolore* anyway.

By early 1943, any remnants of the town's veneer of normalcy had been stripped away. Electricity was added to the ration list. Frenchmen were ordered to turn in all their firearms. Bakers were fined for selling bread without ration tickets. To spur milk production, farmers were forbidden to make butter. Daily life was now so strictly controlled that barbers were ordered to turn in to the authorities all the hair they cut. Movie houses were ordered closed on Tuesdays. Sunday newspapers were banned, and those papers allowed to publish put out only German and Vichy propaganda. All lines of communication in town, including the rumor mills, were either cut or suspect.

Sometime during this period, Lilette and Dédé met and began courting. The details of their romance are unclear, but soon their flirtation blossomed into a full-scale romance. Lilette loved the movies, and if she and Dédé went to one of the three local theaters, they might have seen a lot more than the weekly newsreel and the feature film. Throughout the period of Nazi repression, one of the few ways the French could legally get together was at the movies, and the town's cinemas sometimes became points of symbolic resistance. In twin incidents at the Apollo and Alhambra theaters, when newsreels showed Marshal Pétain shaking hands with German commanders, angry disturbances erupted and the police had to be called in to break them up. A similar incident occurred once when the weekly newsreel showed Pierre Laval, the Vichy premier, extolling the benefits of his policies of collaboration. In the darkness, shielded from the eyes of anyone belonging to the Milice, the audience erupted in coughing, until everyone was drowning out the hated Laval with a chorus of hacking and spitting.

In early 1943, the Resistance started to score some serious hits on the Occupation forces. In April, British planes dropped morale-boosting leaflets promising total disarmament of the Axis powers. The Maquis circulated tracts urging citizens to make May 1, 1943, a national day of protest against deportation. Many Frenchmen were now resisting orders to go to German labor camps, and loads of wheat being shipped to Germany were being routinely torched. On May 31, in a stunning coup, a Resistance unit code-named Samson blew up eleven German trucks at La Martinerie. Stung, the Gestapo launched a counteroffensive of manhunts, arrests, and interrogations. The interrogations were carried out at Gestapo headquarters on the rue Mousseaux, and word of them quickly leaked out and spread terror through the populace. "People were tortured in the cellar. We sometimes heard their cries," recalls Maurice Croze, a local journalist who lived through it all.

This was a time when men and women were often forced to search their conscience and make painful decisions, with no idea of what the consequences might be. For many of them, these decisions and life in town combined to form a strange, schizophrenic existence: publicly compliant by day, privately defiant at night. Though their lines of communication were cut, and the newspapers were censored, the people of Châteauroux had their own way of mapping the course of the war: they surreptitiously inspected the quality of the German soldiers filling their cafés and harassing their women. In the early stages of the war, the town was filled with cocky pilots in dashing uniforms. In the next phase, the villagers saw in their midst some elite troops who were tanned, exceptionally fit, and outfitted in distinctive shorts. These turned out to be crack units of the fabled Afrika Korps, who were fighting in North Africa under the command of Field Marshal Erwin Rommel, the "Desert Fox." But by early 1944, the town was seeing a different breed of German soldier: shabby, less disciplined reservists, many forty-five or fifty years old. The villagers sensed that the tide might be turning.

Perhaps it was the changing course of the war, or perhaps it was just the natural culmination of their wartime romance, but on February 19, 1944, Dédé and Lilette went to the town hall and a French magistrate performed a civil ceremony and pronounced them man and wife. The young lovers were both twenty years old, they were both dreamy romantics, and they were outsiders to the encrusted provincial society of Châteauroux. In many ways they were a young, unwitting couple flung together by the uprootings and traumas of war, and their marriage was not destined to be easy. Indeed, they had nothing that could be described as a proper honeymoon.

In the spring of 1944, acts of Resistance sabotage increased. With the Allies stepping up their attacks on the Germans holding the north of France, refugees now poured in from Paris, most of them children. Now it was American planes bombing La Martinerie, and on March 14, members of the Maquis blew up five Messerschmitts parked on the ground. The Gestapo responded with more arrests and more interrogations of the townspeople. Gas and electricity were cut to a trickle, and rail and telephone links were frequently severed by Resistance saboteurs.

Then, on June 6, 1944, with General Dwight D. Eisenhower in command, the Allies launched the famous D-Day landing on the beaches of Normandy. American, British, Canadian, and Australian troops, along with a Free French contingent, hit the shores in one of the boldest and most painstakingly organized operations in the history of warfare. From towns and villages across Normandy, Brittany, and the whole of northern France, men, women, and children fled south and poured into central France, looking for shelter and safe haven. Châteauroux was now in total chaos. With sabotage and aerial bombing intensifying, ordinary citizens like Dédé and Lilette were in constant danger, and many townspeople fled to outlying villages for greater safety.

Finally, on August 20, 1944, with the Allies pressing their offensive south, the Germans pulled out. Members of the Resistance, including many communist commandos loyal to a charismatic Maquis leader named Robert Monestier, took control of Châteauroux. On the radio and in the newsreels shown at local theaters, Castelroussins now followed the liberation of France, crowned by the image of a triumphant General de Gaulle marching down the Champs-Elysées with U.S. and Allied troops and tanks trailing behind. But the town's nightmare was not over. Now began the period of recriminations and reprisals, when many of the individual decisions the townspeople had made during the course of the war brought very stark consequences.

In the town of Oradour-sur-Glane, 150 kilometers away, 642 men, women, and children were found massacred in a local church in an episode which was later exposed at the Nuremberg trials. Nothing that happened in Châteauroux would bring the town such collective infamy, but individuals did pay. Members of the Milice and many town officials who had collaborated with the Germans fled, hoping to shed their past and take up new identities in other towns and villages. A few local women had their heads shaved as a public humiliation for having consorted with German soldiers.

After the liberation of Châteauroux, Dédé and Lilette moved into a place of their own on the outskirts of town, in a residential enclave known as Omelon, and they tried to regain some sense of a normal life. At that time, Omelon was still under construction, but its future promised to be ideal for young families, as the enclave was going to have its own schools and playgrounds. The neighborhood that Lilette and Dédé moved into had wide streets and carefully mapped-out lots. Some of the houses going up or already built were large and well appointed, but most were small and unpretentious, including the house the Depardieus moved into at 39, rue du Maréchal Joffre.

The house was located on the corner of Maréchal Joffre and the rue Pierre et Marie Curie, and its side windows looked out onto a park with sumptuous gardens and orchards. The house itself was a drab, two-story box with a plain plaster façade, boxy windows, and a small, fenced-in box of a lawn out front. In a corner of the yard, Dédé would build a wooden shed for his bicycle. The Depardieus rented the upper floor, and they shared a common entryway with their landlords, Gaston and Memmette Gauriat and their son. The Depardieus' quarters included two bedrooms, a small living room, an alcove they used for meals, and a spartan kitchen with no oven. It was not the Ritz, but it was quite suitable for a young couple struggling in the wartime and postwar penury of Châteauroux.

When they moved into Omelon, the Depardieus were considered bumpkins and outsiders, and from then on they would be the subject of frequent gossip, especially as Dédé was one of the most colorful characters in the neighborhood. Marcel Pagnol would have loved him. Like so many of the peasants in Pagnol's novels, Dédé had a whimsy and presence all his own. In the morning, he would often ride to the *épicerie,* the grocer, to stock his *musette,* the lunch sack French workers of the time carried over their shoulder or on the handlebars of their bicycle. He would buy a loaf of bread; some ham, salami, or cheese; and, of course, a bottle of good, strong red wine.

Like many craftsmen in the French countryside, Dédé wore work clothes of a distinctive royal blue, with a denim jacket equipped with all sorts of pockets for pencils, measures, and tools. Rain or shine, summer or winter, Dédé went everywhere by bicycle, and even when he rode to work in the freezing cold, he never wore socks under his sandals, an eccentricity his neighbors found both memorable and endearing. Like Lilette, Dédé at heart was a dreamer, a voyager who imagined himself sailing to distant lands, and every morning when he set sail on his bicycle, he crowned his attire with a jaunty blue captain's cap, a small recompense for the painful reality that in his entire life he had never once cast his eyes upon the sea.

As soon as they were installed in Omelon, Dédé and Lilette began their own private baby boom. They would eventually bring six children into the world. In September 1945, just after the war was over, Lilette gave birth to their first child, a son they named Alain. In September 1947, she delivered a daughter they named Hélène. Providing for the children was not easy. By the time Hélène was born, the war had been over for two years. But the town had been devastated economically by four years of Nazi occupation, and the Depardieus and everyone else in Châteauroux were still suffering the consequences. Unemployment reigned in town and in the surrounding countryside, and bread, milk, meat, and many other staples of daily life remained in short supply and under ration. Dédé was working as a craftsman in a metal factory, but his wages were low—so low that to feed their family, he and Lilette were dependent on government welfare checks. In America, the baby-boom generation was born into a period of victory, renewal, and optimism; in Châteauroux, the same generation was born into a period of defeat, deprivation, cynicism, and ongoing recriminations against Nazi collaborators, real or suspected.

With two kids to take care of, Lilette found her life radically changed, and it was turning out nothing like the way she had dreamed it as a girl growing up in the Jura. Day and night Lilette worked—cooking, cleaning, marketing, and nursing and bathing her babies. All this she did mostly by herself, as Dédé also worked long hours and often did not come home until late at night. Lilette was constantly exhausted and she became homebound, feeling almost imprisoned in her home. In what little free time she did have, she would knit or read *CinéMonde,* a glossy film magazine filled with celebrity photos and gossip about France's leading movie stars of the day: Jean Gabin, Arletty, Danielle Darrieux, Michèle Morgan, Louis Jouvet, Michel Simon, Raimu, Fernandel. Once a week she and Memmette, who had become her closest friend, would go to the movies to see their favorite stars. Movies soon became Lilette's only means of escape and diversion, and, swept up by the romances she saw on the screen, Lilette often talked of running away to exciting places, just as she had dreamed as a child. But such fantasies were brought to an abrupt halt in 1948, when she became pregnant with her third child.

For Lilette, this was not an easy or a happy pregnancy. More and more she turned to Memmette for a helping hand with the housework and with little Alain and Hélène. In many ways, her neighbor became like a surrogate mother to her children, and "Milou," as everyone called her husband, Gaston, became akin to family as well. By the winter of 1948, Lilette was heavy with child, and she was starting to complain bitterly. She had been dreaming of taking a trip at Christmas time, but now the unborn baby she was toting spoiled all that, and she felt it was surely going to spoil her Christmas as well. Finally, on December 27, Lilette went into labor and gave birth to her third child, a strong, willful boy they named Gérard Xavier.

Lilette gave birth at home, with the help of a midwife. She and Dédé had no money for doctors and hospitals, and in any case, delivering at home was a common practice among peasant families in many parts of provincial France. Lilette's mother and sister were on hand to help and to take care of Alain and Hélène. But as was his custom, Dédé fled the house at the first sign of contractions. These births, with all their attendant ceremony and blood, terrified Dédé, and he figured the best thing he could do was to stay out of the way of the women—and seek the solace of his favorite café and medicinal doses of red wine.

With three children now in the household, the Depardieus' quarters became extremely cramped. Early on, Gérard was put into a bedroom with Alain, the corner room looking out onto the park, and Hélène wound up sleeping in the alcove next to the kitchen. Money was still scarce, and often, when the welfare checks were late, the family was forced to live on credit from local merchants. Never a talker, Dédé became even more withdrawn. Those times when he did come home for a hot meal at noontime he almost never ate with Lilette and the children; he would eat alone in his corner, tinkering or dreaming. "The ambiance in our house was not that of a real family, with a mother and a father," Hélène recalls. "There was love, but there was not what you would call a true family life."

On his days off Dédé would go fishing or, in the fall, hunt mushrooms in the forest. Whatever his bounty, he would bring it home to the family. Dédé also liked to work in the small vegetable garden he kept some years behind the house. But he never gave Lilette a helping hand with the kids, and he only rarely assumed the various responsibilities generally associated with being a father and a head of a household. Indeed, his children never called him "Papa" or "Father"; they called him Dédé. "My mother did everything," Hélène recalls. "And I think my father never lifted a finger. Dédé lived in a world of his own, and I think it was significant that he never knew his own father. As my mother often said, he lived alone. Like a bachelor. Like a little boy who never grew up."

With three active little kids running around, there was plenty of screaming in the Depardieu household, and there was plenty of yelling between Dédé and Lilette. But beneath the noise there set in an ever-present current of tension and a sullen, angry silence. Dédé spent more and more time drinking at the café, and Lilette became increasingly irritable. Even as a toddler, Gérard absorbed the family tension and felt his mother's discontent. "There was never violence or hatred in our house," he recalls, "only misunderstandings and this incomprehensible silence. One time I would be with my mother and she would caress me; another time she might be in distress, and she would push me away."

For all its raised voices, the Depardieu household was almost devoid of real language and familial communication. With his habit of speaking in onomatopoetic bursts and grunts, Dédé often left his thoughts suspended, unformed and unfinished. With Lilette he spoke a splintered Berrichon dialect, and they rarely talked in whole sentences or fully expressed their thoughts and feelings. As a result, their three children received no proper linguistic training or nourishment; their family communication was generally a chaotic rumble of grunts, aborted thoughts, stifled feelings, and yelling. His parents' battles frequently upset Gérard, and he would seek refuge downstairs with Memmette and Milou. Eventually the yelling would subside, but the pervasive tension only deepened, and the lack of communication would harden into an even stonier silence. In maturity, Gérard would see his childhood home and family as ruled by what he called *la loi du silence,* the law of silence.

Lilette and Dédé had trouble expressing themselves within their family, and they had even more trouble communicating with the world outside. Lilette did learn how to read and write, but she was never at ease writing or handling the paperwork necessary for coping with neighborhood schools or the French bureaucracy. In her later years, when she wanted to drop a note to her mother or to someone else, Lilette would often have Hélène do it for her. At the same time, Dédé was clearly handicapped by his problems with reading. Alain Depardieu believes that his father did know how to read, and he has memories of Dédé at home with a copy of *l'Humanité,* the Communist Party newspaper and the preferred journal of most of the workers in postwar Châteauroux. But Gérard believes Dédé had almost no ability to read, though he put on a very good act to the contrary.

"In fact, Dédé did not read *l'Humanité,* he sold *l'Humanité,*" Gérard recalls. "When he read the papers, he went *spssss, spssss, spssss,* as though he knew how to read. But he didn't really know how to read or write."

While Dédé may have been able to decipher some of the newspaper, writing for him was an almost impossible ordeal. Gérard often saw his father's frustration just in trying to sign his initials, and he has kept a letter Dédé wrote to his mother, Gérard's Grandma Denise. "It was written almost completely by signs and with the words spelled out phonetically," he says. In wishing to begin the letter *"Ma Chère Mère,"* Dédé wrote, *"Ma Chair Mere."* To make the point that the weather was good, he drew a tiny, childlike sun emanating rays. To Gérard, the writing was a highly personal form of hieroglyphics, weak in spelling and grammar but rich in Dédé's own strange, almost impenetrable poesy.

For Parisians, or anyone else who tends to equate the grandeur of France with elegance of language and with writers such as Hugo, Voltaire, Molière, Balzac, Jules Verne, Stendhal, Sartre, Camus, and countless others, it may come as a shock that in the middle of the twentieth century, in one of the most sophisticated cultures in the world, illiteracy still existed. But the Depardieu household was by no means unique in Châteauroux or in the rest of La France Profonde. Nor in those postwar years was Gérard's the only family marred by a dramatic lack of communication. In fact, many families in Châteauroux and across France lived for years after World War II in a strict, self-imposed "law of silence." The reason was rooted in the traumas of the war and the Occupation, and what many Frenchmen did to survive it. After the war, in countless villages and towns across France, a curtain of silence seemed to descend across France, like the curtains of sheet metal French shopkeepers slam down at night when they lock up their storefronts. Consciously or not, many Frenchmen seemed determined to wall off the past, to seal away the traumas of those nightmare years. Even in the privacy of their homes, the war and the Occupation became events it was best to forget; what Papa did during the war was not a subject parents wanted to discuss with their children, or among themselves.

The phenomenon was by no means unique to France. In Germany, Austria, Hungary, Poland, in almost every country in Europe, there were versions of the law of silence. Many Jewish survivors of the Holocaust would never utter a word of what they endured. The case of Austria's Kurt Waldheim was just one of the more visible instances of European leaders, in politics, government, or business, winding up haunted and shamed by wartime pro-Nazi pasts they had tried to hide and shutter away. This collective shuttering may have helped people get on with their daily lives, but it also produced some pernicious consequences. For decades to come, millions of French children would be left with the glorified impression that every Frenchman had been a Resistance hero and that General de Gaulle and his Free French forces had liberated France with only token help from their allies. And across Europe, many people born in the baby-boom generation would grow up uncertain about what their parents had done during the war. Were they members of the Maquis? Or the Milice?

It would take the French nearly thirty years to begin to pry up the curtain of silence they had rung down over their wartime traumas. And just as local movie theaters had provided a locus for symbolic wartime resistance, French cinema provided important levers for lifting the curtain. In his 1951 classic *Jeux Interdits* (Forbidden Games) René Clément depicted the horrors of the war through the eyes of a five-year-old girl (played by Brigitte Fossey, still one of France's finest actresses). The girl was fleeing Paris with her parents and her dog when Nazi warplanes strafed their bedraggled convoy, and she wound up an orphan. The film won an Oscar and prizes at the film festivals in Cannes and Venice. Because of its humanism and uncompromising realism, *Jeux Interdits* is considered one of the masterpieces of French cinema.

In 1969, the daring exploits of the Resistance were set forth in *L'Armée des Ombres* (The Army of Shadows), starring Simone Signoret and Lino Ventura. But it would take five other films to shed light into the darker sides of the Nazi occupation. In *The Sorrow and the Pity* (1970), Marcel Ophuls probed the response to the Occupation of those ordinary Frenchmen who did not join the Maquis. The film was commissioned by French television, which at that time was under complete government control, and when the film's findings were considered too negative and provocative, it was banned from the airwaves. It was not shown on French TV until 1981. Louis Malle shed more light on the Occupation years in 1974 with *Lacombe, Lucien,* his devastating portrait of a young French collaborator.

By the end of the 1970s, the complex issues of collaboration were still so shrouded in silence that the airing of the American TV series *Holocaust* triggered a national debate and soul-searching in France, as it did in Germany. In 1985, France was presented with its most comprehensive account yet of the Occupation, in Claude Lanzmann's stunning documentary *Shoah*. Marcel Ophuls enriched this tableau in 1987 with *Hotel Terminus,* which examined the terror tactics of Klaus Barbie, the Nazi zealot known as the Butcher of Lyons.

These films all helped to reopen France's collective consciousness. Most provoked extensive media coverage, and many sparked prime-time television discussions that aired collective and individual wartime traumas. This public exposure and debate in turn catalyzed private debates that helped to lift curtains of silence that had been rung down in many French families. In the Depardieu household, though, the ways in which Dédé and Lilette endured the traumas of the Occupation never became a topic of family conversation. Nor did the later national soul-searching ever prompt them to speak of the war with their children.

Just what role the war played in forging the family's reigning law of silence is now impossible to know. Nor is it clear what role the war may have played in generating the underlying current of tension that often characterized relations between Dédé and Lilette. But the family's problems of speech and communication, and the psychological tension within the household, clearly had a strong impact on Gérard, as a Parisian speech and ear specialist would later discover, after Gérard mysteriously lost almost all his powers of speech. In diagnosing and treating Gérard, the specialist would find that some psychological mechanism had "slammed down a curtain" inside Gérard, a curtain which impaired his ability to hear and speak.

Significantly, Gérard has spent most of his life thinking that Châteauroux did not suffer much during the war, and as far as he can remember, his parents never talked to him about how they endured the traumas of the Occupation. Most of what he knows about this decisive period in his parents' lives Gérard summarizes in a single word: *"Mystère."*

With brother Alain (rear) and sister Hélène, circa 1951

4

Pétarou

It all may have started at one Sunday lunch. On a weekend in the early 1950s, when Gérard was no more than three, the Depardieu family gathered for a big Sunday meal with Grandma Denise, Dédé's mother. Denise was a warm, earthy peasant woman with a lively spirit and a generous maternal bosom. A widow for years, Denise was now living in a little cottage outside Paris, and one of her greatest joys was to take the train down to Châteauroux to spend some time with Dédé and Lilette and her three grandchildren, Alain, Hélène, and little Gérard.

On this particular Sunday, the lunch was an especially festive occasion, enlivened by hearty country cooking, plenty of wine, and good humor. For Grandma Denise this was a heartwarming display, and she ate well and was very pleased, especially when midway through the meal she received a surprise visit from Gérard. He was an adorable tyke, with blond hair and big blue eyes, and with infinite sweetness he climbed up into grandma's lap, put his arms around her neck as if for a kiss, and stuck a pea right in her ear. With one tiny finger, Gérard jammed that pea in so deep that to this day some of her grandchildren fear old Denise may have gone to the end of her days with a sliver of pea embedded somewhere near her brain.

Imagine the hush that fell around that table. No one moved. How would the old lady respond? Would she fly into a rage? Would she grab the culprit and smack his bottom? Would she whisk him into a bedroom, slam the door, and sit him down for a stern lecture on good manners and the proper way to treat his elders? Well, once her initial shock subsided, Grandma Denise just burst out laughing. Roaring. She laughed so hard her sides shook, her eyes went teary, and the heavy folds of flesh along her arms and under her chin began shimmering and swaying to the music of her glee. Denise adored Gérard, and she knew there was no malice in the prank. By instinct or design, she treated that pea not as an insult but as a pearl, as a unique token of affection from her high-spirited grandson.

If Denise had not reacted with good humor and grandmotherly forbearance, Lord only knows what the consequences might have been. But once she gave this bit of mischief the blessing of her laughter, everyone joined in and showered little Gérard with laughter and applause. In one stroke, that humble pea turned into a family jewel, and its story was told and retold, forever fixing Gérard in the family spotlight. Though such events are impossible to pinpoint, perhaps it was right here that a star was born, along with an incorrigible prankster.

And what a prankster little Gérard turned out to be. Hélène was one of his prime accomplices and targets. The two of them loved to make mud pies in their backyard, and part of the fun was seeing which of them could make a pie filled with the foulest manure to be found in the surrounding gardens. By nature, Hélène was a quiet and obedient child, helpful to her mother, but Gérard always found devilish ways to get her goat. "My main chore was to do the floors of the staircase," Hélène recalls. "I would have to polish the stairs, down to the entryway. It was hard work, and just when I finished, inevitably Gérard would come along and, just to annoy me, he would march up and down the stairs, stomping his dirty feet, and I would take my brush and throw it at his head. I think a couple of times I actually hit him."

Even as a toddler, Gérard was a complete original. His brother and sister were docile children who gave Lilette and Dédé few worries; Gérard had boundless energy and was constantly into mischief. By the age of three, he was already so high-spirited, obstreperous, exasperating, irrepressible, and irresistible that the family called him "Pétarou," Little Firecracker. The nickname stuck, and it neatly defined and encapsuled his role as the family prankster and clown. The role came easily to Gérard, but it also proved useful within the Depardieu family. With the lack of communication between parents and children, and the evident strains between Dédé and Lilette, Pétarou's clowning proved necessary relief and diversion; in his own way, he served as an *entremetteur* and an antidote to the law of silence.

Many of the girls in the neighborhood found Gérard captivating, even when he was a toddler. One day he was playing in a sand pile outside his house and then suddenly he started crying so loud that half the neighborhood could hear. There was no sign of Lilette or his sister or brother, and he just kept on bawling and bawling, until a little neighbor girl came running to help. Monique Dagaud was then six and a playmate of Alain and Hélène. Gérard eagerly snuffled out to her his woe: he had lost his toy penguin. It was a trinket no bigger than his little fist, and when Monique sifted through the sand and found it, Gérard broke into a huge grin of relief. From that moment on, Monique has always felt a special tie to him, and later on they would become frequent playmates in the neighborhood.

Gérard has no recollection of that penguin, but his attachment to such a trinket would be understandable enough; he had few other toys. In the early 1950s, the Depardieus were barely getting by. Dédé was working sheet metal in a local factory, but his wages were still low. Alain and Hélène were now going to nursery school, the Ecole St. Denis, and that meant they had to have proper clothes and shoes. Lilette did manage to stretch the family budget far enough to put a proper lunch on the table, but at night the kids often ate nothing more than crêpes and jam. And once Lilette paid for food and clothes, there was no money left for cheering up the house. The bedroom Alain and Gérard shared was spartan and plain, with two beds and little more. The family bathed in a basin in the kitchen, and there was a single w.c. at the back of their quarters. From those years, Gérard recalls only a single adornment in the entire house: a picture of a hunting dog with a bird in its jaws.

Almost everyone else in Châteauroux was also hurting. The town's economy remained in postwar shambles. From 1948 to 1951, through the Marshall Plan for the reconstruction of Europe, the United States poured $12 billion into Europe, but little of the money had made it down the administrative chain to the industries or families of Châteauroux. Food staples were still in scarce supply, and most of the town's energy and capital were going into rebuilding and basic subsistence. In its economic and political shakiness, Châteauroux was a microcosm of the nation, which was now operating under the tentative structures of the postwar period's Fourth Republic.

Poverty only worsened the strains within the Depardieu family. With Dédé rarely home, and never helping when he was, Lilette was constantly exhausted and often exasperated. Alain and Hélène, though obedient, were still a handful; Gérard was just too much. Beneath his pranks and exuberant clowning, he was a boy of mercurial nature and moods. He was hypersensitive, and he often seemed overwhelmed by floods of turbulent emotions. His moods and behavior could change in an instant, depending on how he felt about whomever he was with. With some people he was timid and shy; with others he was aggressive, with others he would play the clown. Any modern, educated family would have had trouble enough trying to understand such an emotional volcano; little Gérard left Lilette and Dédé totally confounded. To them he was an *enfant sauvage,* a wild child, beyond anything they had ever seen. They could not fathom, penetrate, or even ease his moods, his torments, or his volatility. The Little Firecracker was so explosive that his parents never knew why or when he would burst into tears or fits of temper, and he kept his feelings strictly to himself.

"Gérard and I were always together, but he rarely talked, even when we were alone in our room," his brother Alain recalls. "And when he was small, he was so timid that if anyone came to the house, he would hide in the closet."

Gérard was usually happiest outside the house. Even as a boy of three or four, he would wander off on his own for hours at a time, turning up at Memmette's or at home only when he tired of his meanderings. Out on his own, Gérard seemed to have a knack for making friends, with other kids, with grownups, and with neighborhood cats. His parents may have refused to socialize in Omelon, but not their unusual son. "In a way, I became the child of everyone," Gérard says. "Because I was joyous, and I had a frank look and smile. I was unaffected, strong, blond, blue-eyed, and self-reliant."

Early on, Gérard became the family emissary to the neighborhood. When, for instance, the vital welfare check did not come on time, it was Gérard who was dispatched to charm the butcher and ask for a pound of meat, on credit. By appearance, Gérard was an unlikely diplomat. His look was always untamed; his clothes and hair were scruffy. The only thing Pétarou kept in spotless order was the slingshot he had personally crafted and which he kept in his back pocket. Nor was this a child who went to the butcher with a proper attitude of *"Oui, Madame"* or *"Non, Madame, merci."* But scruffy or not, the kid had charm; he almost always came home with the pound of meat.

Even as a little boy, Gérard provoked strong responses in other people, either very positive or very negative. While he could charm the butcher and other children, there was no way he could charm some of the family's prim, proper, bourgeois neighbors. They did not find him free-spirited; they found him a wild and unruly urchin, an unwelcome pest. In many ways, Omelon was typical of the caste and class system endemic to provincial France, and Pétarou fell far short of the bourgeois ideal of being *bien élevé,* well brought-up and well behaved. He was not considered *mal élevé,* badly reared; he was considered not brought up at all. Gossipy neighbors considered him a child whose parents too often left him to his own devices, even when he was very small: "His father was never there; he seemed to have no interest in his children. And his mother paid him little attention," Monique Dagaud recalls.

Monique's mother, with some trepidation, allowed her to play with Hélène, but when it came to Alain and Gérard, Monique was allowed to play with them only out in the street, not inside their house. Nor would Monique's mother ever dream of inviting Alain and Gérard into her home for lunch or dinner; they did not come from a proper family. Dominique Meunier lived down the street, at 26, rue Pierre et Marie Curie, and her mother's attitude was even more severe: Dominique was allowed to play with Hélène, but she was strictly forbidden from playing with the Depardieu boys—and with most other boys. Her mother was a teacher who had come from Paris, and she would not have her daughter mixing with provincial riffraff. Among bourgeois families in the neighborhood, there was a firm conviction that boys were boys and girls were girls; allowing the two to mix was not just improper, it was a recipe for disaster.

Even as small children, Gérard and Hélène felt the disapproval of their bourgeois neighbors, and it confused and angered them. It was belittling and made them feel like misfits, even untouchables. "We felt it strongly: we just did not come from the same milieu," Hélène says. "In the provinces, this is something you feel right away."

Lilette and Dédé knew they were outcasts in the neighborhood caste system, and around their bourgeois neighbors they kept their heads down and their eyes averted, as if they could pass through town—and life—unnoticed, invisible. It was a modus vivendi they tried to pass on to their children, but Gérard refused to accept it: "I was always educated with the saying, 'Shame is upon us.' Don't do this. Don't do that. You mustn't disturb anyone. We were still in the Middle Ages. There were always fears and worries. None of them were ever explained; they were just there. As a result, we were all inhibited."

From the vantage point of the proper and well-to-do families of Omelon, Pétarou was not just troublesome, and the Depardieus were not just primitive and poor; all of them were constant wellsprings for neighborhood gossip. Dédé's drinking, Lilette's credit problems at the butcher and the *épicerie,* Lilette's many pregnancies—these were all common knowledge. The novels of Balzac and François Mauriac are filled with this kind of village gossip and posturing, and in many ways these qualities of Omelon are typical of La France Profonde.

In later years, Jean Carmet often came home with Gérard to see Lilette and Dédé. Carmet came to know them well, and he admired their simple, modest ways. In Omelon, he always sensed the same "village curiosity" he grew up with in his own provincial village, nearby in the Loire valley. "In these villages, you see the eye of an old lady peering out through the cracks of a window or a blind, so that she can see what's happening out in the street," Carmet recalls. "My father put a tiny hole in the front gate, so he could see out to the corner, where someone passed by maybe once a half-hour." In these villages, no detail of a neighbor's life went unnoticed, from the daily comings and goings to what Madame was cooking for dinner. "We were always attracted by odors. We attached enormous importance to what kind of food our neighbors put on the table," Carmet says. "Lilette and Dédé were modest people with enormous qualities. Dédé had an unusual sense of fantasy, an opening into dreams and spirits."

Gérard resented the disapproval of his bourgeois neighbors, and to this day he remains allergic to bourgeois pomp and stuffiness. But that same disapproval gave him a definite cachet among the other kids on the block. "He was the *enfant terrible* of the neighborhood," says Dominique Meunier, "because he was not afraid to talk back to adults, to provoke people." "Everyone was afraid of Gérard," agrees Monique Dagaud, "and he was afraid of nothing."

With his urchin manners and free-spirited ways, Gérard was a taste of forbidden fruit for bourgeois daughters, and playing with him was heady adventure. "At the end of our street was a chateau, with a big garden and orchards, and we often sneaked in there to play," recalls Monique Dagaud. "For our lunch, we would take pears and apples and plums right off the trees. A retired school principal lived in the chateau and we called him *La Taupe,* The Mole. If he caught us in his orchard, he would run after us. Nothing was more exciting than running like that, through the formal paths in the garden. Your heart pounded and you felt like a bird in flight."

When he was about four or five, Gérard began spending a month every summer on a farm in the southern part of Le Berry, near where George Sand had lived and entertained Parisian intellectuals and artists. The farm belonged to a distant relative of Dédé. The family arranged for Hélène to spend part of the summer months nearby, with cousins named Maxime and Clémence. Hélène often cried during these summers away, out of homesickness, but Gérard loved being out on his own, away from the suffocations he felt in Omelon, both in the neighborhood and in the cramped family quarters. "I was happy in the country, in nature, even though the work was very hard and tiring," he says. "Getting up at four in the morning to lead the cows to the farm, the milking, the odors, the rhythm of the seasons. In nature, everything is clean, even the soil; there is no such thing as dirt. And there, when you go out walking, you can be rich or poor, and when you come across someone, no one knows anything. You can say what you want to say."

But even nature could turn hostile, as little Gérard discovered one day when he was minding the cows. "I was a child filled with curiosity, and like all such children, I could be dangerous. One day I found a prod, and I was making a circle around the eye of one of the cows. I was fascinated, because the cow never moved. She stood as if she were hypnotized. It was the first time I had been able to tame such a big animal, and I was doing it just by caressing her eye. Three or four days later, the cow's eye was completely infected, with flies all over it and a big scab. It was only then that I realized the poor beast had been neither hypnotized nor tamed; there had been a needle at the end of the prod, which had scratched her eye. What I had done was not sadistic or deliberate; I just didn't know any better. The veterinarian came, and in a day or so the cow was fine."

As a small child, Gérard seemed to develop a dual strategy for facing the world. Out on his own, either in the country or roaming around Omelon, he was happy, carefree, and outgoing, as long as he kept far away from snooty neighbors. But at home with Lilette and Dédé, when he was not clowning he could also be aloof and moody. No one in his family, least of all Lilette and Dédé, seemed to understand him or could offer him any help. Whether he was around cows or neighbors who treated him like a pest, Gérard lived in a world which seemed full of menacing contradictions and confusions, and when he returned home he found no warm, secure shoulder on which to rest his head. Lilette was too busy; Dédé was rarely there, and when he was, he was too self-absorbed to notice his son's emotional needs. During his early boyhood years, Gérard began suffering terrible nightmares, and they scared Lilette.

"I was a sort of monster, too precocious and hypersensitive," he wrote to Lilette in *Stolen Letters*. "I always sensed you were a little afraid of me. Afraid of my young strength, afraid above all of my nocturnal visions. Often in the middle of the night I would wake up sweating, convinced that some big rat had his teeth sunk into my neck. If I said anything or made a single move, he would bite me. And I would die soaked in my own blood, without disturbing anyone."

When he was still very little, no more than four or five, Gérard picked up a problematic habit from his father: he, too, started talking in fits and starts, a kind of stutter that would leave his sentences and thoughts fractured and aborted. Within the family circle this posed few problems; most of his clowning was nonverbal anyway. But outside the house, and later at school, his speech problems would become a source of frustration and embarrassment, and sometimes it made him ill at ease with strangers. Like Dédé, Gérard frequently withdrew into silence. Sometimes, though, an inchoate anger would erupt in the most unexpected ways. In *Stolen Letters,* he recounts the memory of one Easter morning when he rode to the bakery on the back of Lilette's bicycle.

At the bakery Lilette bought him Easter eggs; beautiful Easter eggs, which she carefully placed in her basket. When they returned home, a man was in their kitchen, listening to the radio. His name was Philippe Daudon, and little Gérard took an instinctive dislike to him. While he sat in his chair, Daudon reached over, picked up Lilette's basket, and when he saw the Easter eggs, he began feeling them, one by one, with his hand. Then he started to eat them, one after the other. Lilette said nothing, and did nothing to stop him, and Gérard burned with rage. Years later, Gérard ran into Daudon on the street in Châteauroux. "I was barely thirteen, but I was already a man in size, with the hands of a strangler and a menacing nose. I pointed my finger at him and screamed, 'Philippe Daudon!,' " Gérard wrote. Daudon was scared and did not recognize the young Depardieu. Gérard lifted him off the ground, pushed him against a wall, and pressed his fist against his throat; he was determined, years later, to make him cough up those Easter eggs. "Happily, I was with friends who stopped me from doing something truly foolish," he wrote. "Those stupid Easter eggs nearly ruined my future career as an actor!"

As this anecdote suggests, what permeated the Depardieu family in Gérard's early years was a heavy sense of resignation. In their childhoods, Lilette and Dédé had been romantics and dreamers; then the war and their marriage reshaped, and in some ways destroyed, their youthful dreams. Even after the Liberation, and well into the 1950s, a flag of enduring defeat hung over Châteauroux, and it hung over the Depardieu family as well. Lilette wanted to run away to some exotic place; all Dédé wanted, apparently, was to be left alone, to be left in peace. For both of them, their children were sometimes a delight, but more often they were a burden. Gérard sensed their ambivalence and resignation, but, of course, he was far too young to comprehend their feelings. And when Lilette paid him no attention, or even physically pushed him away, that only confused him all the more. As a result, he often felt little sense of personal worth. "My mother never told me I had talent," Gérard says. "She only told me I had cheek."

But some other members of the family suspected that Gérard might harbor some hidden talent, perhaps even a form of genius. Suzanne Marillier, Lilette's mother, was considered something of a medium, and she dabbled in the gentler forms of witchcraft, such as reading tarot cards and communing with family ancestors. One Sunday afternoon, after a big family lunch, everyone gathered around Grandma Suzanne for a seance. She dimmed the lights and called on friendly spirits to help her divine the futures of her grandchildren.

"Alain," Grandma Suzanne foresaw, "you will see your name on huge posters. And with it you will see the name of Gérard. He will be a *petit Mozart.*"

Suzanne proved prophetic. Alain began his career as a draftsman, but he later became a film production chief, and his name did appear on huge movie posters, often along with Gérard's. Lilette and Dédé always thought Alain had real potential, but despite Suzanne's prediction, they could not imagine their youngest child had potential of any sort, and they surely never believed he had hidden gifts. In fact, throughout much of Gérard's childhood, and especially when he did poorly in school, Lilette feared he was a dunce.

Dédé was an especially confusing character to young Gérard. Dédé was a gentle soul and Gérard said he never hit any of the children. But Dédé was always withdrawn and passive, and he offered his young son little example, guidance, or parental comfort. Still, Gérard loved to tag along when Dédé went fishing down at the river, and Gérard knew his father was capable of enormous energy and passion. One night he awoke in the middle of the night and found his father hard at work on a piece of sheet metal, the project that became his masterpiece fireman's boot. This was a night with a full moon, and Dédé wanted to take advantage of the special light.

"He always felt the best time to work the metal was during a full moon," Gérard says. "Dédé was a true poet, but a mute poet."

To an outsider, Gérard's formative years appear to have been marked by physical, emotional, and linguistic neglect. But Gérard and Hélène did not feel it as neglect; they had no idea family life could be any different. "We never considered ourselves poor," Gérard says, "because we had no idea what it meant to be rich. In a way, I was very lucky; I have never had any problems with money. If I have none, I can be happy with a piece of bread. I never feel the lack." Later in life, Gérard came to understand the lack of emotional sustenance and equilibrium he suffered as a child, but he also appreciated that at the root of it there was no malice on the part of Lilette and Dédé, only ignorance. He also came to see that being left on his own did have a positive side: freedom from parental expectations. "Lilette and Dédé never forced us to live up to their expectations. They had none."

Still, Gérard was often flooded with confusion and hurt. Sometimes, when his mother was feeling especially irritable, she would accuse Gérard of ruining her Christmas in 1948, and destroying her childhood dream of traveling. "Right from the beginning, I was the person who kept her from leaving. My mother swore she would have left and gone off somewhere, though who knows where," Gérard says now. "When your mother tells you something like that when she is in moments of distress and she looks at you and says, 'It's because of you. . . .' "

Dédé's absence and mental wanderings, Lilette's irritability, the inconsistency of her affection, the blame she put on Gérard for her own frustration and distress—all these plunged young Gérard into turmoil. His chief modes of response became acting out and turning inward. To the world he showed a smiling, clowning face; his interior confusions and roiling emotions he showed to no one. "I was too full," Gérard says now. "I could not understand all that I was absorbing, and I had no means of expressing myself."

Gérard endured other shocks as well. When he was just a little boy and Lilette was at her wits' end, she would tell him that she had tried to abort him. According to Gérard, she even described to him the method she had used: knitting needles.

"In poor families, no other form of abortion existed," Gérard says. "Rich French girls went to England or clinics in Switzerland. Doctors in France would not perform abortions, so everything had to be done clandestinely. Poor women had no other choice."

Whatever the rational explanation he understands now, hearing such words as a small child, right from the lips of his mother, was devastating for Gérard. In his nightmares, or in his waking imagination, he would look in the mirror and inspect his face and the top of his head, looking for scars from the needles. With this terrible shock and knowledge, Gérard became convinced he was an unwanted child. This conviction would deeply disturb him, and his relationships, for years to come.

Later, in adolescence, these childhood emotional traumas would feed into the mysterious breakdown in his ability to speak. According to the doctor who treated him, at the age of five or six, Gérard seems to have gone into an emotional shell. There, he was safe, protected from his parents and their primitive ways. There, inside his imagination, he was totally free to become whoever he wanted to be and to say whatever he wanted to say. In the face of similar traumas, the doctor explained, many children become emotionally crippled. But Gérard was blessed with a very strong constitution, and that shell served as a protective defense, helping him to tune out trauma and bounce back with more will and determination, the way a vine that has been pruned will grow back even fuller. It was as if some part of his being rose up and declared, "If I can survive those knitting needles, I can survive anything."

"I was afraid of nothing," Gérard says of his early boyhood years. "And I knew I had something special: my *joie de vivre.* That is an asset you are born with; it cannot be learned. It came along with the complexity of who I am, namely, 'The Preventer from Leaving,' someone who cut the legs off his mother and who somehow managed to live and grow in spite of it all."

At age six (second row, center)

5

Pennies from Heaven

In February 1951, when Gérard was two, an American general named Joseph Hicks paid a discreet visit to Châteauroux. With a team of three advisers, the brigadier general inspected first the airfield known as La Martinerie and then the adjoining airplane factory, which the Luftwaffe had bombed in the opening stages of World War II. Though the aim of his visit was kept secret, Hicks was on an urgent mission for NATO, the new Western alliance destined to transform the military, political, and economic landscapes of Europe and the world.

On March 19, 1951, *La Nouvelle République du Centre-Ouest,* the local paper in Châteauroux, announced the news: the U.S. Army was sending in four thousand troops to set up a military base at La Martinerie. The Castelroussins were shocked. Many of them had never heard of the new North Atlantic Treaty Organization, and they had no idea what this American influx would mean. Indeed, when the news broke, no one in the little town dreamed that Châteauroux was about to be radically transformed, in ways that would have a profound and lasting impact on the town and its people.

The background and the dimensions of the NATO operation soon became clear. In 1949, a dozen Western governments, including France and the United States, had decided to form a new military alliance, establishing a system of collective security and postwar peacekeeping designed to balance the power of the Soviet Union. To make NATO operational, in 1950 the NATO governments created a military high command for Western Europe headquartered in Rocquencourt, outside Paris. Its mission was to set up and command an invincible network of bases, supply depots, and communications centers across Western Europe. As a result of General Hicks's visit, Châteauroux was chosen to be a pivotal hub of the new network. Specifically, La Martinerie was to become the receiving end of a giant transatlantic supply line, with planes and materiel coming straight from a U.S. Army base in Dayton, Ohio.

NATO had sound reasons for selecting Châteauroux. According to a monograph on the American experience in Châteauroux, written by a local researcher named Valérie Besset, one reason was the town's strategic and geographic position in the heart of Western Europe; it was near Paris and Germany, and it was served by major rail and highway links. The town was also situated in a region that was hospitable to air traffic; it was flat and not prone to the heavy fog that often affected other parts of central France. La Martinerie had served as a training base in both world wars, and the adjacent aircraft plant, the Société Nationale des Constructions Aéronautiques du Sud-Ouest or SNCASO, would provide NATO with a pool of six hundred skilled aircraft technicians.

The French government was hoping that the NATO installation would bring new jobs and capital to a region with little industry and chronically high unemployment. The French government also hoped to jolt the town and the region out of their postwar economic malaise. Le Berry and Châteauroux clearly needed all the help they could get. Janine Gagné, the wife of an American who arrived in the first wave of NATO preparations, recalls that the town was in dire straits at the time: "When the Americans arrived, the town was dead. There were shortages of everything. There were no more vouchers for government-subsidized bread. There were no trains. There were few cars. Ice and beer were delivered by horse-drawn wagons. The French went everywhere by bicycle. The Castelroussins were barely able to cope."

After Hicks's initial visit, events moved rapidly. In April 1951, with America now in a full-scale war in Korea, Hicks returned to Châteauroux with an advance unit from the 7300th Material Control Group. Their mission had two urgent goals: to set up a base for NATO forces and support units, and to turn La Martinerie into an air base and supply depot able to provide supplies and maintenance to NATO aircraft and forces all across the European theater. This meant building hangars, workshops, and housing. To handle the big transport planes ferrying in supplies and the lighter craft relaying supplies across Europe, Hicks and his team had to construct mammoth airstrips three kilometers long.

To build the base and the rest of the network going into Europe, Eisenhower's commanders applied the same planning, organization, and mobilization they had used in preparing the massive D-Day landings.

And Châteauroux saw the results. Almost overnight, some two thousand troops poured into La Martinerie, and the process of transformation began. Bulldozers and earth movers began constructing the huge new runways. The buildup of troops and materiel was massive and rapid. Soon so many troops were bivouacked at the construction site that it became a makeshift village, complete with its own name: "Tent City."

The arrival of *"les boys"* and the Stars and Stripes both dazzled and divided the Castelroussins. The Nazis had been driven out of town just seven years before, and many people feared this was going to be a second foreign occupation, this time with American G.I.'s on French soil. "U.S. Go Home" became a standard theme of street rallies and editorials in the pro-communist newspaper, *La Marseillaise.* But the base, which the U.S. Air Force was leasing from the French government, did have many local supporters, if only because it was going to generate jobs for French workers, and at wages three times those anywhere else in town. Hundreds of jobs were to go to Frenchmen immediately, and by the late 1950s, five thousand Frenchmen would be working at the base. By contrast, the town's second largest employer, the government-run SEITA cigarette factory, employed seven hundred workers. At the same time, Le Berry's other main economic activities—textiles, metallurgy, and the aircraft plant—were all sunk in depression.

This influx of soldiers and activity brought Châteauroux powerful injections of energy and capital. Local companies began receiving contracts to help supply the base. For its officers' living quarters, the U.S. command rented rooms at the Hôtel de France and the Hôtel Sainte Catherine. The Air Force put its command headquarters at the Bourse de Commerce, a building that had served as a trading center. Local cafés and restaurants began to boom, catering to hungry G.I.'s. Alongside the French franc, the town instantly had a new currency: the U.S. dollar. The G.I.'s paid for everything in dollars and military certificates redeemable in dollars. With their high wages, French workers at the base could now find and afford goods that had been in short supply since the war: coffee, whiskey, chocolate, sugar, and electrical appliances. Inevitably a black market sprouted, with goods pouring through the American PX. Real estate boomed, with inflated prices and inflated profits for French families. In Omelon, French families eagerly moved out—sometimes into gardening shacks—and rented their homes to U.S. officers, who were now being joined by their wives and children. Even Dédé Depardieu profited. For a time, he worked at the airplane factory, making wooden mockups of plane components still in the design stage.

Janine Gagné and her husband, Joe, participated in the rapid transformation of Châteauroux. In a delightful wartime love story, they had met in Paris in March 1945, when Joe was on weekend leave from the U.S. Army. They met coming out of a Métro station at the Cité Universitaire, on the southern rim of the city. Joe was French Canadian by heritage and came from Maine; Janine was a *parisienne* and the daughter of a baker. It was love at first sight, and they married that May. After the war, Joe took his bride back to Maine, but in 1950 they returned to France to settle down. Joe went back to school on the G.I. Bill, studying cuisine at the famous Cordon Bleu cooking school, and he helped his father-in-law in the bakery. When he heard that NATO was going to open a base in Châteauroux, he went south to see if he could land a civilian job at La Martinerie. But when he saw Tent City and talked with the G.I.'s, Joe got another idea: "They had very little at all. And they certainly had nothing resembling a decent canteen."

Joe rushed back to Paris, fetched Janine, and returned to Châteauroux to set up "Joe from Maine," a family-style eatery that would bring to this little French provincial town all the wonders of gastronomic Middle America: hamburgers, hot dogs, milkshakes, and BLTs—served on sliced American bread straight from the PX. With American coffee, baseball pennants, and Budweiser on tap, Joe figured he could do a nice little business giving G.I.'s a home away from home. He underestimated: "The second day we opened, the line outside stretched around the block. It was outrageous. We could not keep up with the business. I was probably the first fast-food outlet in France."

Joe prospered, the base prospered, Châteauroux prospered, and before long, this pastoral little backwater of La France Profonde was being flooded with Americana. In the early 1950s, Frenchmen in their Renaults and Peugeots, small and painted a somber black or dark green, began yielding their narrow streets to Buicks, Chevrolets, and Fords, sumptuous machines with bumpers of gleaming chrome and paint jobs of pink, yellow, or robin's-egg blue. What also poured into town was standard U.S. Army nightlife with a French twist: G.I. bars and strip joints with names like Le Crazy Bar, the Rodeo Bar, Le Chat Qui Fume, and the Lido. With them came another novelty for the town: MPs in Jeeps making nightly patrols and breaking up brawls.

Those four thousand G.I.'s and pilots, with dollars in their pockets and carnal pleasure on their minds, attracted to Châteauroux whole trainloads of Parisian prostitutes. They would come down for a weekend of work, profit, and maybe some silk stockings from the PX. Soon wayward girls from nearby towns and villages started coming in and joining the pros. Joe brought in a real hamburger grill from America and stuck to burgers and milkshakes. But the bars and strip clubs turned into pickup joints and informal language schools: "You buy me ze drink, *cheri?*" "Wee, wee, *ma belle.*" The hotels by the railroad station began doing such a boom business that when all the rooms were rented, enterprising night clerks would add more dollars to the weekend haul by putting overflow couples into bathrooms and storage closets, at an hourly rate.

At the base, Tent City was soon replaced with proper barracks, mess halls, and offices. Many of the G.I.'s were reservists with wives and children, and soon the base added an officers' club, a school, a library, a bowling alley, baseball diamonds, a roller-skating rink, and even a golf course. By the mid-1950s, the base had turned into a small American suburb, offering American families all the comforts of home. "It was just like an American city," recalls Annette Gagné, Joe and Janine's daughter. "You had everything you could possibly hope for. I went to school on the base, in an American school bus, with an American driver. We even had pajama parties, just like at home."

This influx of Americana flooded the lives and the imaginations of French parents and children. Maurice Croze was now a reporter at *La Nouvelle République,* and he frequently covered events at the NATO base. To his astonishment, and in sharp contrast to the way the French Army had operated the base, Croze was allowed wide latitude to roam around and visit with the troops and officers. He mingled with army journalists who were putting out a sheet called *The CHAD News,* named after the Army acronym for the base, and he was invited to fly with U.S. pilots to get a firsthand taste of NATO exercises. Croze was stunned at how open and forthcoming everyone was with him. General Hicks, now commander of the base, wound up an interview by inviting Croze to lunch at the officers' mess. The meal was served in a way Croze had never seen before: cafeteria-style, now known in franglais as *"un self-service."* Croze was dazzled. "The choice, the speed, the efficiency, the trays dipped in disinfectant—for us Frenchmen, all this was extraordinary."

Soon many U.S. officers and their families moved into Omelon, arriving with their American cars, their refrigerators, their yellow school buses, and other shiny goods and appliances, all Made in U.S.A. In many of the American homes, French women came in to cook and French teenagers came to baby-sit. To the town's encrusted caste system there was now added a new French elite, one that had nothing to do with family background or levels of education or professional position. This elite had everything to do with money and with a person's proximity to the new powers in town. Nobility was now defined as a job at the NATO air base or with the Americans.

Still, the arrival of the Americans drew a mixed response. Because of their profound impact on the old order, the Americans were resented by many Castelroussins, including Dédé. "For my father, the arrival of the Americans was in no way a happy event; it was an invasion," Alain Depardieu says. Maurice Croze's wife, Josette, was among those who saw the NATO arrival in positive terms: "For many of us, this was not a second occupation; it was a panacea." And among the kids of Omelon, there was no ambivalence. "Our fathers didn't see them that way, but for us kids, the Americans were liberators," says Alain. "They came by in their trucks and threw us chewing gum and chocolate bars."

Dominique Meunier used to baby-sit for an American family which had moved in down the street, and for her, going to their house was an adventure. "It was like two different civilizations, and we envied theirs," she says. "They had those wondrous American loafers, with a penny tucked in the front. Our dream was to have a pair of those loafers. Sometimes they took us to the base to bowl. And we all had another dream: that they would give us peanut butter."

To win public support, and to help bridge the cultural, linguistic, and social barriers separating the French and American communities, U.S. commanders put on an open house for the French every Christmas, with American-style Christmas trees, colored lights, and presents for the kids. The fete was held in one of the giant hangars at the base, or out on the tarmac beside one of the monster C-47 transports that on working days were landing and taking off from the busy base every three minutes. It was a huge treat for the French, with champagne tours for the parents and games for the kids. Most children from proper bourgeois families were polite and restrained, but out on the tarmac there was usually one little hellion having the time of his life. He would stand in line for a present, then hide it and sneak back for a second. Yes, Pétarou.

For Gérard and Alain, their first American Christmas was like a new world opening before them. "The Americans brought us the grandeur of Christmas," Alain says. "They even passed out Christmas trees, complete with ribbons lettered 'Merry Christmas' and 'Joyeux Noel.' Until then, we had never had a Christmas tree at our house, but after that we always did, in the backyard."

From that moment on, the base and the Americans in town became focal points of the Depardieu boys' existence and their imagination. By the time he was six or seven, Gérard had learned pidgin English and had American friends whose parents would sneak him onto the base: "It was a different world at the base—the PX, the snack bar, life American-style. To get inside, to go to the roller rink, I would practically hide in the trunks of cars. I would be hiding and the American family would tell me, 'Gérard get down.' Once past the guard gate, I'd get up and go roller-skating. It was extraordinary."

In the mid-1950s, Gérard also discovered movies. French cinema was then in an unusually rich period, with directors like Max Ophuls, Robert Bresson, Jacques Tati, and Jean Cocteau. Most of his friends went to see French movies, but Gérard's interest was farther away, in America. "The first film I remember seeing was a Chaplin, in the youth club of the neighborhood church," he says. "After that I went regularly to the movies. In the church there was the most magnificent odor, and there were all those children huddled in the dark, facing the magical black curtain." From then on, movies became one of his favorite forms of fantasy and release. He saw Chaplin and Keaton, *Le Ballon Rouge* and *Around the World in 80 Days* and *20,000 Leagues under the Sea.* In 1954 there was Brando in *On the Waterfront,* and the next year came James Dean in *Rebel Without a Cause.* Dean, in jeans and T-shirts and with all that turmoil in his eyes, looked like the young G.I.'s Gérard and Alain were seeing around Châteauroux.

Alain idolized Dean, and Gérard was now thoroughly swept up by everything American: "All of us Berrichons after the war were completely fascinated by the Americans," Gérard says. "The Germans were terror; the Americans were liberty. The Americans had an odor which was completely different from ours—a freedom that was completely different from ours. Everything about them was different, even the pleat in their pants. They were these guys nineteen or twenty years old smelling of Palmolive and chlorophyll—that's America, chlorophyll—and they ate omelette sandwiches. We had never seen anyone put an omelette on bread before, and to us it seemed ingenious and wonderful."

By contrast, life inside the drab, cramped quarters of 39, rue du Maréchal Joffre was anything but wonderful. And as if Lilette did not have enough to do, in 1955 she became pregnant again. When she delivered her fourth baby, again at home with a midwife, Dédé fled the scene. But not Gérard, now six years old. As his mother went into labor and brought forth a baby girl, Catherine, he stayed and watched the drama from beginning to end, with an attentive and detached gaze. It was like his summers on the farm, watching cows give birth.

"My mother reminded me of one of those cows," he says. "She was flesh, milk, and blood. She was a mass of maternal instinct. This was not pejorative. Mine was an almost Hindu notion: I saw her as a sacred cow.

But at the same time, it was very real and natural, like a cow with her calf, when she literally gives life. All this I saw through my own eyes as a child."

During this period, Gérard saw other stark sights as well. By now Dédé's drinking had become a serious problem. One day, Gérard saw his father outside of his school, with his head in the gutter, and all the other kids could see him too. Gérard was not only ashamed; he was angry that the internal turmoils of his family had now been laid bare before all the neighborhood. But Dédé was having no easy time of it, either. By now he was trying to feed his wife and four children by working as both a craftsman and a volunteer fireman. He was often changing jobs, and he resented having all these Americans in town and around his job sites. Lilette, with four kids to take care of now, had little time for him. Over the next few years she would have two more babies, making for a family of eight and compounding all her stresses and strains.

With Lilette preoccupied with baby Catherine, Gérard was left entirely to his own devices, and he spent less and less time at home. He became a street child, hanging out with Alain and the kids on the block, sneaking into the park to smoke Gitanes, playing soccer or going fishing or swimming. In many ways he was running out of control, but even at his worst, what he seemed to elicit most from his parents was indifference. To a child like this, punishment might have come as a relief, as a boundary and a sign of caring. But there was little discipline and no boundaries or constraints. Sometimes he was verbally reprimanded, but Gérard says there was never corporal punishment. "Dédé was in no way violent," he says. "I was never hit. None of my brothers and sisters was ever hit. He was someone who would stand up and yell, '*Aaaarrgh, whaaaa, tchooo!*' And that was it. There was never violence, ever."

During this period, when Gérard was seven or eight, the kids of Omelon did have some wonderful times together, almost all of them out-of-doors. At night, after dinner, they would gather in the street or on someone's doorstep and play cards or hide-and-seek or *devinette,* a French version of twenty questions. In this period of the mid-1950s, one of their neighbors, a salesman specializing in Dijon mustard, bought the first television set in the neighborhood, and on summer nights he would leave his windows open so the kids on the block could watch the magical box. On hot days, the kids would group onto a few bicycles and pedal out of town to the swimming hole at Mousseaux. Next to the swimming hole was a café run by an old man named Monsieur Robinet. In his cellar he kept cold lemonade, in old-fashioned bottles with ceramic tops, and in those lean postwar years the kids considered buying a bottle of lemonade from Monsieur Robinet to be the height of luxury and high times. So was watching Pétarou play daredevil and ride a bike straight into the creek.

To bridge barriers between the American and French children in Châteauroux, there were exchanges between the schools. Dominique Meunier's class went to the American school on Thursday afternoons. She recalls being fascinated by details American kids would not even notice. "We attended their classes, we saw their rooms, and we saw something which struck us as fabulous: the freedom the students had. They wore no uniforms, as we did. There were water fountains in the hall. Most of us had never seen a water fountain, and that struck us as very advanced. In our classes we were always behind a table, at a desk and chair. They had classes with no tables or desk at all. We had the impression of a great, great freedom."

This sense of freedom made a strong impression on young Gérard as well. Growing up in an Americanized town, Gérard idolized the G.I.'s and emulated their behavior. At home, in the street, and at school he never became persistently naughty or malicious; he just became more active. Hanging around the American G.I.'s, he often felt a strong urge to cut loose, make noise, make waves, affirm his existence. It would be many years before he could fully comprehend and articulate his reactions, but as Gérard explains it now, he was rejecting his parents' resignation and passivity. In one way or another, he was determined to *act*—not in the theatrical sense, but in the sense of acting up and acting out, cutting through inhibition, cutting free.

Compared with the freedom he was feeling out on the streets, school for Gérard seemed rigid and stifling. For kindergarten, the three Depardieu children went to the local Ecole St. Denis; then they moved up to the neighborhood grammar school, the Ecole de l'Omelon. Here, even though the building was new and modern, with large classrooms and good facilities, old traditions prevailed. As is typical even now in the French provinces, and even in some schools in Paris, boys and girls attended separate, adjoining schools. And as is still true under the French system, students learned by rote and were rarely encouraged to question the teacher. Discipline was severe, and there was little communication between teachers and parents, or between the principal and the parents. And even when students did extremely well, teachers rarely gave them praise or encouragement.

For Gérard, one of the worst aspects of school was that it was steeped in the same caste system as the rest of Omelon—only here he could not flee the social strictures as they were too tightly woven into the life of the school. Just walking in the door made him feel like an outcast, a feeling he found suffocating: "When I was a child, I felt very strongly what class differences were. At school there were gypsy kids whose families lived in wagons, and, like me, they were not treated in the same way as kids from working-class or middle-class families." According to Gérard, his family was considered beneath working class, because Dédé did not have a regular job.

Alain and Hélène did well under this scholastic regime. They were both serious and studious, they earned good marks, and they rarely caused disciplinary problems. But Gérard was another matter. School bored him, and he paid little attention to his studies. This was a continual worry for Lilette, and she just did not know what to do about Gérard. With little schooling of her own, she never felt comfortable going to the school and talking with his teachers. Nonetheless, one day in autumn of 1956, when Gérard was seven, Lilette gathered her courage and paid a call on the principal, Roger Lucas. They met in his office, exchanged polite greetings, and then Lilette blurted out her fear:

"Monsieur, is my son a dunce?"

Lucas was taken aback. *"Mais non, Madame.* Your son is not a dunce. And he is not even a bad student." He went on to reassure Lilette that Gérard was average in math, good at drawing, and his handwriting was making progress. And he was good at reciting poems in front of the class—a claim Gérard still disputes. "He doesn't sing badly, either," the schoolmaster assured her. Lilette went home relieved but dubious.

Lucas, who was known to the children as Le Père Lucas, was to have a major impact on Gérard's life at school, as both the principal and later his homeroom teacher. Now retired, Lucas says he always liked Gérard's "peasant nature," as well as his simplicity and spontaneity. "He was the defender of the little ones," Lucas says. "If there was a little kid being shoved around by one of the big kids, Gérard would come up shouting, '*Haaaarrrrggg!* What are you doing? Leave him alone!' "

Lucas came away from Lilette's visit with a distinct sense that Gérard was having troubles at home. The principal occasionally ran into Dédé in the neighborhood, and, like everyone else in Omelon, he knew that Dédé spent far more time in cafés than he did with his family. But at school Gérard never complained, and Alain and Hélène were both good students who gave no indication of similar problems. So Lucas and his wife, who taught at the girls' school, did not worry about Gérard.

They figured that at home he was being as boisterous and exuberant as he was on the soccer field. "He played goalie and he loved to roll around in the mud," Madame Lucas recalls.

Grandma Suzanne may have sensed that hidden inside Gérard was a *petit Mozart,* but none of his teachers did. Like most public schools in France, which are under the central control of Paris, Omelon at that time had a regime of studies that was traditional and in no way geared to children possessing unusual forms of intelligence or creativity. With four hundred children crowding into the brand-new school, and classes running as large as thirty or thirty-five students, teachers rarely had time to give children personal attention. School opened at 9 a.m. with thirty minutes of *leçons de morale,* lessons in ethics and civics. Then came math, history, and geography, with only ten minutes of recreation lightening the morning routine. With a proper hot lunch being held sacred in France, the children went home for a two-hour lunch break. In the afternoon, they came back for grammar, composition, and *orthographe,* the spelling and writing of French. None of this excited Gérard, and his main interests at school were soccer and marbles.

After school, Gérard and Alain would go into town to gaze at the huge American cars and peek in the doorways of strip joints. On Saturdays they would try to find ways to go roller-skating at the NATO base or peer into Joe from Maine and watch the Americans eat hamburgers and drink milkshakes. Sometimes at night, while Dédé was home listening to Radio Moscow and riffling through *l'Humanité,* Gérard and Alain would go down around the railroad station to check out the hookers hanging out in the bars of the two hotels facing the station, the Faisan and the Berry. Even when they stayed in Omelon and played with friends, they would talk about the Americans. By now, a new phrase was entering their vocabulary and their consciousness: *le Rêve Américain,* the American Dream.

"I had a wild love for America," Gérard recalls. "Many of my friends went to America. To look. Because they were fascinated. Fascinated. These were the people who changed our dreams."

Gérard, about age ten, at Ecole de l'Omelon

6

The Four Hundred Blows

By 1957, when Gérard was eight, Châteauroux was no longer one town, it was two—with two languages, two cultures, two economies, two currencies, and two very different mentalities. What had begun as a contingent of four thousand U.S. servicemen had ballooned to twelve thousand men and some three thousand American wives and children. Now on the edge of town there were two new enclaves the Americans had built to house their troops and families. The first to be constructed was Touvent, a cluster of apartment blocks. The second was Brassioux, a genteel suburb that looked as if it had been airlifted in whole from Oklahoma or Arizona. Brassioux was mostly for officers and their families, and it had spacious, prefabricated ranch houses with a feel of the American Southwest. They even had tidy lawns and hedges out front and big American kitchens and bathrooms, all equipped with U.S. appliances, from refrigerators to faucets.

Many French parents remained upset about this cross-cultural cohabitation, but for the French kids the American homes were like candy shops. And some were nearly just that. American families introduced French children to popcorn, marshmallows, Baby Ruths, and sliced, packaged American bread, like Wonder Bread. In the summer, French kids playing with American friends sometimes got another treat: Popsicles. In the heart of gastronomic France, in a country town surrounded by goats and cows, any day of the week French kids could have raw-milk Camembert cheese, chevre, and fresh milk. But what they wanted was American milk, for it came not out of cows but out of something far more exotic: cartons. "Up until then, we had never seen milk in cartons," Monique Dagaud recalls.

For all their magic, Wonder Bread, Baby Ruths, and peanut butter were not enough to bridge the barriers separating the French and American communities. Language, mores, and pride prevented a deeper *entente cordiale.* The French resented the fact that the Americans shipped in not only their materiel but their food; was there something wrong with French milk or bread, or even with French tomatoes and lettuce? Nor did French mothers and fathers, with vivid memories of French girls having their heads shaved for consorting with Germans, look kindly upon their daughters flirting on the streets with young G.I.'s. For anxious middle-class parents, the only proper place for their daughters to meet *les boys* was at the Sunday-afternoon dances organized by officers' wives at the American Red Cross.

While dancing allowed proper French girls to straddle the line of demarcation that separated the two communities, Gérard jumped completely over to the other side. With no constraints at home, he and Alain did not just gaze at the Americans from a distance; they joined in G.I. life. They sneaked into bars and had milkshakes and cheeseburgers at Joe from Maine. Long before they hit adolescence, Alain and Gérard were emulating the G.I.'s and what they saw in American movies. They wore T-shirts and Levi's, listened to jazz, and picked up American slang. They carried dollars in their pockets and thumbed rides out to the base. "Châteauroux was one-hundred-percent Americanized, and so were we," Alain says. "We played softball at the base and we were completely clothed by the Americans."

During their amblings in town or at the base, among the G.I.'s and at Joe from Maine, the Depardieu boys enjoyed a special status as pals and mascots, as translators and go-betweens. Gérard was especially eager for this star-spangled embrace. At home he was lonely and felt estranged, and at school he was bored and felt like a misfit. Although still only a boy, he was already in search of ways to remake his family, his way. "I was a solitary child, and during my childhood, what I consider the first half of my life, I always sought to re-create my family," he says. "I always dreamed of having my own family with lots of children."

The Americans embraced Gérard as family, and the more time he spent with them, the further he drifted away from Lilette and Dédé. Alain and Gérard were now a study in contrasts. Alain was three years older, but it was Gérard who was the more restless, the more eager to create for himself a new life, a different reality. Alain kept up his studies and his appearance; he was so often in a blazer and tie that his brother and sister started referring to him as "The Snob." Alain was hoping to go to a *lycée,* French high school; Gérard at the age of eight and nine had no plans beyond dinner and the night's kicks. Though big for his age, he had not outgrown the nickname Pétarou, and in Omelon he was still the fearless *enfant terrible.* But now he found bolder ways to play daredevil and dazzle his friends. Along with his trips to the base for bowling or roller-skating, he would find ways to get into the American PX. "I went in with American adults, and I would buy their ration tickets," Gérard says. "They had ration tickets for everything. And I'd say, 'Look. You don't drink. You don't smoke. Let me buy your tickets.' It was my little deal." He would then resell the whiskey or cigarettes to the French, to help pay for his jeans and T-shirts, and his burgers and fries.

According to most everyone in Châteauroux, dealing in American cigarettes was, next to soccer, the most popular boys' sport in the local grade schools and high schools. It was not considered petty crime; it was deemed a mark of prestige, of street smarts, of access to the powers that be. To be a star among the kids, as among the adults, what you needed was visible proof of access to the base, to the Stars and Stripes. A carton of Camels was thus a coveted badge of youthful status and swagger. And such trafficking was child's play next to the adult action in town. "Châteauroux had become Europe's Havana," says Alain. "You found everything that was forbidden, and everything was trafficked. Guns. Cars. Trucks. Whole truckloads of goods from the PX. Once someone hijacked an entire airplane motor. Thank heaven, though, this was before the era of drugs. There were no drugs."

The journalist Maurice Croze watched Châteauroux's transformation into a wide-open town, and he saw the impact on the youngsters living near him in Omelon. "All the kids earned themselves a little pocket money by trafficking in American cigarettes," he says. "It was part of growing up, part of *les quatre cents coups."* When the French say a boy is "doing his four hundred blows," they mean he is raising hell, passing through the period of defiance and rebelliousness preliminary to manhood. Truffaut used the expression as the title for one of his first films, an autobiographical story of his own troubled youth. The movie is one of Depardieu's favorites, and it proved to be a strong bond between them when they later worked together. *The 400 Blows,* released in 1959, tells the story of a boy growing up in circumstances similar to Gérard's. In the film twelve-year-old Antoine Doinel is a sensitive but deeply confused boy upset by his parents' bickering, and he runs into problems at school. Inevitably, Antoine also runs into trouble with the law, not because he has any taste for crime, but because he is in turmoil and is unable to communicate with his parents or vent his confusions.

"He was totally alone," Gérard says. "No more parents. Just him, alone. Facing himself. A rebel. I like rebels, because they are people who, one day, confront themselves. Alone. Some of them become alcoholics or drug addicts. Today that is so easy. But back then, in simple families like mine, the only recourses for a rebel were writing, painting, passion, dreaming, or the movies."

While Gérard's rebellion led him into Americana and into dreaming that he belonged to an American family, nothing much changed with Lilette and Dédé; they just had more babies. After Catherine, Lilette gave birth to Franck, her fifth child, and then, barely stopping for breath, she became pregnant with a sixth child. As usual, she planned to deliver the baby at home, and also, as usual, Gérard was on hand to watch. But this time something went wrong. "With this sixth child—my brother Eric—my mother had terrible hemorrhaging. Dédé was at the fire station, and he was dead drunk. Someone sent word for him to come quickly, and thinking our house was on fire, he arrived with the big ladder and raised it up to the second-story window. All the while my mother was bleeding, and what we needed was an ambulance to take her to the hospital."

Confronted with such episodes, Gérard often responded with emotional detachment and black humor. He also drifted further away and created his own family of adopted friends, including many thoroughly colorful local characters. One of the most memorable was "Maurice au Bar," Maurice from the Bar, a rugged old salt who treated Gérard as his sidekick. Maurice had served in the French Foreign Legion and had fought in Indochina in the battle of Dien Bien Phu. Now he was a bit of a lost soul who spent his time painting murals in the local bars, murals filled with Oriental dragons from Vietnam. Like a miniature Pied Piper, Gérard would bring Maurice and his other waif friends home for a meal, often to the astonishment of the rest of the family. "Gérard knew everyone in town," says his sister Hélène. "We had no idea where he met them all. Alain and I were not like that."

Gérard's real family also included plenty of colorful characters. On Sundays the family would get a visit from Gérard's godfather, a hefty mason known as "the Fortress." Gérard awaited these visits with great anticipation. Inevitably, the Fortress would drink too much, and he would wind up passed out in Gérard's bed. It was an annoying habit, but as soon as the old fellow was zonked out, Gérard would come along and very carefully extract a few francs from the old boy's pocket, a small fee for use of his bed. "The joy of my existence, despite all the problems, was that I came from a family of true poets," Gérard says. "Put a hat on their heads and they would dream."

By nature, Gérard was clever and resourceful, what the French call *débrouillard.* He could fend for himself and make the best of a bad situation. His parents were poor, uncultured, nearly illiterate, and stuck in a mentality that in many ways seemed out of the Middle Ages, and yet now, in retrospect, Gérard feels they had a beautiful simplicity, almost an innocence. And for all his mental absences, Dédé had a strange and almost inexplicable force, which he in some ways shared with Gérard, especially when they went fishing together. "I love to fish, but I always hated hunting, because its only purpose was killing. Fishing is mysterious: the water, the fish below. Dédé would sit there for hours, never saying a word; he was off somewhere else and yet still there. He could have skipped work and spent his whole life fishing. I loved going with him. It was almost a communion."

By the late 1950s, though, when Gérard was about ten, he moved further away from the family circle. With six children now crowded into such cramped quarters, Gérard spent most of his days and many of his evenings away from home. He was now a regular at Joe from Maine. He would go right into the kitchen to watch Janine cooking omelettes or hamburgers or sit at the counter and talk with Joe as he made milkshakes or drew draft beers for the G.I.'s. By now Joe had become part of the folklore of Châteauroux. He had brought from America a hot new Ford Fairlane convertible, a red-and-white model with a black top, gleaming chrome fenders, and more interior space than many hotel rooms in Châteauroux. Being French Canadian by origin, Joe had no trouble talking with Gérard, and he was a big, strong, fatherly man who commanded Gérard's respect, and everyone else's. If G.I.'s wanted to get into brawls at the nightclubs or strip joints, that was their business, but Joe would not tolerate brawls at his eatery. He also had a very efficient way of breaking them up: he would spray any offender with his trusty fire extinguisher.

In this same period, another potent wave of Americana swept into Châteauroux and into Gérard's young fantasy life: rock and roll. Now, via record shops and popular radio shows like "Salut les Copains" (Hi, Kids), French youths discovered Elvis Presley, Chubby Checker, and Bill Haley and the Comets. Instantly, rock and roll became both a fad and a weapon of youthful rebellion. Elvis was an immediate star with the Depardieu children, and with their growing ability to wangle and barter, Gérard and Alain amassed a large collection of American records and one of the first record players in the neighborhood. On Saturday afternoons, the kids on the block would come over to listen to music. During one phase they listened to Chubby Checker and practiced the twist in the Depardieu kitchen. Rock and roll swept the clubs and the jukeboxes in town, and even Gérard's favorite swimming hole. This was a pond on the edge of town, near the slaughterhouses, and though the water was foul, Gérard loved to swim there because it had a loudspeaker that would blare out the latest hits.

When Elvis was drafted and sent to a U.S. Army base in West Germany, the kids of Châteauroux went wild, dreaming that the King would come play a concert at La Martinerie. Today there are those, including Gérard, who swear Elvis did come and sing. Others, like Annette Gagné, swear he did not. Alain remembers talk that the King was coming, but he does not remember it actually happening. Whatever the gauze now wrapping those childhood memories, America at that time totally colonized the imaginations of Gérard, Alain, and their friends in Châteauroux; reality often blended with wish. Elvis, rock and roll, Coca-Cola, and Levi's were their touchstones and cultural emblems. For them, growing up with Elvis and all those G.I.'s, the rite of passage of the four hundred blows came with southern drawls, Texas twangs, and dreamy visions of heartbreak hotels and blue suede shoes: "It's extraordinary what we experienced as kids," Alain says. "We saw so much. It was an opening toward the whole world. And our means of escape was always America."

For Alain and Gérard, America was a particularly important means of escape at Christmastime. For many French families, Christmas was a time to be shared together; even families who rarely went to church would attend Christmas Eve mass. Not the Depardieus. Though they were born Catholics, and the children were baptized, Lilette and Dédé were by no means churchgoers, at Christmas or any other time. Nor did Lilette and Dédé, with their limited means, make Christmas into a big celebration. Lilette's sister, Colette, usually had the entire family in for a big Christmas meal, but Alain and Gérard quickly drifted away from these events. To them, Christmas meant the annual American Christmas party out on the tarmac at La Martinerie and they spent time with American families or sometimes with lonely G.I.'s spending Christmas far away from home.

One Christmas, when Alain was about fifteen and Gérard twelve, they wangled their way into a private American club for a Christmas Eve bash. It was a makeshift club set up in someone's barn, and for the boys it was like entering their own fantasies. There was American food and drinks, a record player poured forth misty American love songs sung by Dean Martin and Tony Bennett, and the place was filled with maudlin G.I.'s aching to be home in Ohio or Texas or Oklahoma. All night long they danced cheek-to-cheek and necked with warm, fragrant French women, either their girlfriends or professionals who had come in from Paris for the holiday celebrations. The G.I.'s, as always, welcomed Alain and Gérard as family, and the two boys nestled right in, in utter contentment and fascination.

"We were far from our own family," Alain recalls. "We were in this universe smelling of cheeseburgers, gingerbread, and what's that gum that smells like fruit? Juicy Fruit. This was not France; this was some town in America. Somewhere in Arizona maybe. We spent both Christmas and New Year's there, until three o'clock in the morning. With those American crooners and all that sadness. It was the most beautiful Christmas of my life."

In contrast to the life and family which Gérard was now actively creating for himself around town and among the Americans, school made him feel listless and passive. His teacher during two of these years was a stern, humorless man everyone called "Le Père Durand," Father Durand. He was not a priest, but behaved like one, and Gérard took an immediate dislike to the man. Le Père Durand, in turn, had no heart for Gérard and his swaggering ways. The spirit of Le Père Durand's class was nothing like Gérard's. Each day began with a *leçon de morale,* in which Le Père Durand would take a newspaper crime story, or some other public notice of transgression, and use it as a way of highlighting various precepts of right and wrong. "We would read an article and Le Père Durand would say, 'See, you shouldn't steal,' or 'You shouldn't cheat,' " says Serge Dubreucq, one of Gérard's pals at school. Le Père Durand practiced what he preached. In the best of times, he would go to his geography charts, pick up a pointer made of bamboo, and put it to good use at the blackboard or the map of France; in the worst of times, when someone was caught cheating or acting up in class, he used it to deliver sharp whacks across the tips of a student's fingers. What was often worse than the pointer was the sting of public humiliation. Serge and Gérard were far from being class intellectuals, and one of their worst ordeals was the Wednesday poetry recital. On Mondays, Le Père Durand would assign the class a poem to learn by heart, and on Wednesday afternoons he would call on students to go to the front of the class and recite. "This Wednesday lesson was worrisome," Serge recalls, "because there was no way to ask your neighbor for help."

But Gérard and Serge excelled at recess and on the soccer field. Both boys were big and strong, and on the athletic field they were both leaders and protectors of the smaller kids. At recess, they would organize games of marbles and pickup soccer. After school in the fall, they played on the school soccer team, which had matches against other local schools on Thursday afternoons (the day when French students had no classes after lunch). Serge was a star. His father was the coach of the town's top amateur team, Les Berrichons, and Serge himself, built like a tree, would go on to play professional soccer for ten years. Gérard started out as center forward, but later he was made goalkeeper, because he was quick and fond of sliding in the mud.

"Gérard had a strong combative spirit," Serge recalls. "Even then you felt in him a strength the others did not have."

Gérard also had a spirit for profitable mischief. Each year, as part of a school charity drive, Le Père Durand would distribute booklets of souvenir stamps for the students to sell. One two-franc booklet might contain ten stamps, worth twenty centimes each, and the kids were supposed to sell the stamps at face value and turn all the money over to Le Père Durand, who would give it to charity. But Gérard and Serge turned those booklets into a small industry. Instead of hawking the stamps in their neighborhood, they would sell them to Americans they found by canvassing the G.I. bars and other hangouts. "The G.I.'s or their wives would give us five or ten francs for a two-franc booklet, and we would keep the difference," Serge says. "We would pay other kids to give us their booklets and ask Le Père Durand for as many booklets as he had. It was our own way of picking up a little pocket money." Everybody else profited too: Serge and Gérard always sold scores of books, and Le Père Durand received the correct sum due from each book.

Just as he did at home, Gérard led a kind of double life at school. He was joyous and happy out in the schoolyard, and sullen in class. By the late 1950s, though, as Gérard approached adolescence, he became rebellious and unruly at school. In fact, he became so disruptive in class that Le Père Durand moved Gérard to a seat right in front of him, the better to keep him under control. In the face of such discipline, many boys would have fallen into line, but Gérard was not about to be tamed. His behavior deteriorated, and so did his marks. School now became a battle of wills between Gérard and Le Père Durand. To bring the boy into line, the teacher turned increasingly to his weapon of last resort: his bamboo pointer. Gérard took his raps, on the fingers and sometimes alongside the head, but it only stiffened his resistance, and he escalated the war with covert mischief.

According to Roger Lucas, one day when the teacher wasn't there, Gérard sneaked into Durand's classroom and broke the pointer. Then he added a cunning twist: he glued the pointer back together, so that it looked like new. The trick worked. The next time Le Père Durand rapped him with it in front of the class, the pointer snapped and hung limp in his hand. "Durand was furious," Lucas recalls. Furious, but not finished. Come the end of the year, Le Père Durand flunked Gérard, not just in one class, but across the board, so that he could not pass on to the next grade. Gérard's response was equally dramatic: he tore up his report card and stuffed it right back into Durand's mailbox.

Le Père Lucas also played a role in Gérard's demise at school, through one particular incident that still makes Gérard bristle. At the end of the year, each class took up a collection to buy a present for Lucas, the principal, whom the children referred to as Père Lucas. Each student contributed five francs. One morning, the collection box was found empty. "I was accused of stealing the contributions to Le Père Lucas," Gérard says. "Lucas called me into his office. He closed the curtains. Then *pof! pof!* He hit me twice with his hand. Then I pushed him back. Afterward, he called the classes together on the playground and told everyone I was in quarantine. Anyone found speaking to me would be punished. This was a shock and a complete humiliation—especially because I was being punished for something I didn't do."

This episode was one of the main reasons he was flunked at the close of the 1950s, Gérard says. Over the summer, he confronted the boy he suspected of pulling off the crime. The boy confessed, but Gérard would never tell on him, as a matter of honor and pride. But the episode hardened him into a defiant rebel at school. "I took this blow right in the face," he says now. "It vaccinated me against school." So Gérard withdrew even further into his emotional shell. He would finish school with a reputation as a poor and unruly student, and with an accusation of theft hanging over his head.

In the spring of 1962, Gérard did earn his grammar-school diploma, what the French call the *certificat d'études.* According to Lucas, Gérard had started school a year early for his age. As a result, flunking the one year may have been an embarrassment, but he still finished at the age of thirteen, in line with his age group. Lucas says that if Gérard had taken the test to get into the *lycée,* he probably would have passed. But the minute he had the *certificat* in his hand, Gérard never wanted to set foot in another school. His frustration and anger are understandable. Throughout his many years at the Ecole de l'Omelon, no one seemed to suspect for an instant what professors and doctors would discover just a few years later: that this deeply troubled youth harbored amazing intellectual and artistic gifts, including a near-genius level of intelligence and an almost photographic memory.

Toward the end of his schooling, and in keeping with his rebel attitude, Gérard began hanging out with a fellow outcast, a young tough named Jacky Merveille. He was nearly three years older and lived three blocks away in Omelon. Jacky's parents were not blue-collar; his father was a manager at the local branch of a national bank. But Jacky was by no means a proper bourgeois son. Like Gérard, he was big and strong and said very little. Among the kids, Jacky had charisma and status, but adults considered him a real troublemaker, *un voyou,* a young punk. For Gérard, surrounded by men who offered him little strength or example, Jacky was a French youth he could look up to and emulate. And as he entered adolescence, such a role model was enormously important for Gérard. By now, for reasons which are unclear, Dédé had lost his job as a sheet-metal worker, and he had begun a decline that would see him end up sweeping the shop-room floor. To feed their six children, Lilette still depended on welfare checks, and the family now carried an additional financial burden: Alain had moved on to a *lycée* in the region, to study design and prepare for a career in architecture. The school was in another town, and Alain's room and board there put a further strain on the family budget.

By now, there was another troubling line of demarcation running through the Depardieu home. Alain, Hélène, and Gérard had been born within a period of three years, then six years later came Catherine, Franck, and Eric. "The kids came in two very separate vintages," Alain says. "The three of us were very close, but I barely knew my younger brothers and sister." Gérard says the exact same thing, and today the different "vintages" remain distant, more like cousins than siblings.

At the time, Gérard never expressed his turmoil and estrangement with anyone, inside the family or out; he was governed by his own code, his own personal law of silence. Some of the people who were close to him sensed his problems, but what they mostly saw was his high-spirited, mischievous exterior. Roger Lucas and his wife lost sight of Gérard after he left school. Several years later, though, the Lucases were out walking in Omelon one day, and suddenly there was Gérard, back on a visit from his new life in Paris. He was huddled on the curb, and in a terrible state. He was disheveled, depressed, and evidently very drunk. Le Père Lucas was shocked. The man in charge of Gérard's entire grammar-school experience was suddenly confronted with something he had failed to see for six or seven years.

"He looked a wreck sitting there," says Lucas. "And we stopped and said, 'Oh, Gérard! What is this! What's the matter?' " Then, for the first time in all the years they had known him, Gérard drew back the veil, for an instant, on the secret turmoils of his childhood: "The memories here are just too painful."

7

Cutting Free

At the start of the 1960s, Châteauroux was entering something of a golden age, albeit with an American accent. Along with supplies of Elvis Presley, hamburgers, and Coke, the Americans were pumping in massive supplies of capital, energy, and technological know-how. Some five thousand Frenchmen were now working at the NATO base, and many of them were helping to service some of the most sophisticated airplanes and machinery in the world. Business throughout the town was prospering, and the initial tensions between the French and American communities had by now melded into a peaceful cohabitation, cemented by scores of Franco-American romances and marriages. Even the insular peasants of Le Berry were changing their ways. They were no longer using mules and horses to plow their fields; just like farmers in the American Midwest, they were now tilling their fields with big tractors bearing the logo "John Deere."

France as a whole was prospering as well. Despite the shakiness of the leadership of the Fourth Republic, the nation was entering an era of unprecedented industrial expansion, a boom accelerated by the creation of the European Common Market. In 1958, General Charles de Gaulle returned to power. Many Frenchmen regarded him as the hero of World War II and the savior of the nation, and de Gaulle had wide support when he consolidated his authority with a new constitution, creating the Fifth Republic. The new president was determined to cure France's postwar malaise and restore the nation's self-confidence and pride. Toward that end, in 1960 France reasserted itself on the world

With friend Jacky Merveille, early 1960s

stage by detonating an atomic bomb and joining the exclusive circle of nuclear powers.

But even de Gaulle, with all his stature and charisma, could not stop the crumbling of one cornerstone of France's former grandeur: its colonial empire. In 1954, after a grueling eight-year war against the nationalist leader Ho Chi Minh, the French had been forced to pull out of Indochina. Now de Gaulle's only exit from a disastrous war with Algeria was to grant independence to all of France's former colonies. Along with the collapse of its far-flung empire, other political upheavals would rock France during the 1960s, including a rupture with NATO and a dramatic student rebellion in Paris. As always, little Châteauroux would find its fate buffeted and shaped by the roiling currents of French history and international conflict, and so, too, would Gérard.

In 1960, Gérard was eleven years old and entering a tumultuous adolescent rebellion. He could not articulate his inner turmoil, but his behavior, his acting out, spoke for itself. He was rebelling against the resignation and passivity of Lilette and Dédé. He was rebelling against the small-town gossip and snootiness of his neighbors in Omelon. He was rebelling against Le Père Durand and Le Père Lucas and all the humiliations he had endured at school. He came away from his schooling with one conviction about education, and he holds to it today: "The only good education is to love and to try to instill confidence in children."

By the fall of 1962, Gérard had left school and the only education he wanted now was out in the street. At the age of thirteen, he was ready and eager to strike out on his own. Left to his own devices, he had been forced to grow up quickly, and now he was a powerful man-child, weighing 155 pounds and standing nearly six feet tall. At thirteen he could pass for seventeen, and in bars and at Joe from Maine he stood shoulder-to-shoulder with his G.I. pals. That September, at an age when many youths would be starting high school, Gérard went to work, as an apprentice at the Centre-Presse printing plant in a section of town called Contamines. Gérard liked the work, and he liked the smell of the ink and the camaraderie inside the plant. He still had speech problems, and he still talked in short, choppy sentences, but among the printers this was no handicap. Indeed, Gérard now found a strong satisfaction in setting words into clear, legible type. Gérard had an additional source of pride as well. When he worked the night shift, one of his duties was typesetting *The CHAD News,* the newspaper of the NATO base. "I considered this a noble calling," Gérard says.

Dédé and Lilette were relieved to see how well Gérard had settled into his apprenticeship. This seemed a fine road for their strange and troublesome son to be following. He was learning a quality trade, he was earning a little pocket money in the process, and for a boy they felt had such limited potential, who could ask for more? Gérard was also relieved, but for different reasons. He was free of the tedium of school, and he was free of Le Père Durand, Le Père Lucas, and their oppressive *leçons de morale.* And he was free to indulge his own natural curiosity. While he gave his parents the impression he was keeping to the straight and narrow, away from work Gérard was exploring the nightlife of Châteauroux, roaming the bars and the nightclubs, and acting not thirteen but twenty-one. Soon he was drifting into a life of kicks and risks, and his nightly escapades often began right at the railroad station in Châteauroux.

"We would say, 'Meet us at the station, at such and such an hour,' " Alain says. Then Alain, Gérard, and their pal Jacky Merveille would meet in the late afternoon, at the station bar or in the cafés of the Faisan or the Berry hotels. Gone were the days when they would order a Vittel *menthe* or a Coke with lemon. Now, like the G.I.'s, and like their own fathers, they would order a beer or a shot of wine or, for a real wallop, a double pastis. Never mind that they were still minors; the local bars were wide open, and run in a spirit of anything goes.

By sundown, the peaceful little square in front of the railway station, with its humble Sainte Solange church, would start pulsing with the evening parade. G.I.'s and air force pilots coming off work at the base would pull into town in their big Buicks and Chevys, or in little MGs and Triumph Spitfires, their car radios tuned to the Armed Forces Network and blaring the latest hits and golden oldies of Buddy Holly, Elvis, or the Everly Brothers; soon would come the Beatles and the Rolling Stones. The way Alain and Gérard describe it, the scene in Châteauroux by night was akin to the rock and roll era depicted in George Lucas's *American Graffiti,* but with all the teenage innocence siphoned away. *Les boys* would park their cars, have a few drinks, and then begin a wild night of cruising the bars and strip joints, with Gérard and his buddies not far behind. Gérard would still go to Joe from Maine for burgers and milkshakes, but this was just to get primed for a night of drinking and hell-raising, of make-it-up-as-you-go.

In the rough bars and strip joints which had earned Châteauroux its reputation as a little Havana, brawling was an intrinsic part of the male code. It was a way for young soldiers to blow off steam, to impress the ladies, to earn status and respect inside the G.I. family. As a boy, Gérard had loved everything physical; he loved to wrestle and scrap with his pals, on the soccer field or in the schoolyard. Scrapping was like playing goalie in soccer—it was healthy combat, on the grass or rolling in the mud. Real fistfights were a more serious matter. In the G.I. world of Châteauroux, violence was an everyday fact of life, for a boy or for a man, and as part of his going out on his own, Gérard took up boxing.

Being big and strong beyond his years, Gérard was able to join a boxing club at a local gym, and he trained under the knowledgeable eye of a no-nonsense Polish immigrant named Jablonski. Gérard lacked technique and finesse in the beginning, but right away he proved very tough in the ring. During one of the workouts, he got his generous Gallic nose knocked sideways, to his right, and with this battle scar his reputation soared among his friends and within his family. Boxing now became one of the main outlets for his monstrous energy. The local gym where he trained was dark and dank, like in a Hollywood B movie, but Jablonski organized bouts at the NATO base, and again Gérard was struck by the dramatic cleavage between life on the French side of Châteauroux and life on the American: "At La Martinerie, the gym was so clean, so beautiful. Where I was training was like a cave. There was no air. There was no anything."

Some of what Gérard could not express in words he could express with his fists, and under Jablonski's guidance he matured into a very skilled fighter. He became the preferred sparring partner of many of the local boxers, including one fine young American fighter who was training at the base. Alain, with a bit of fraternal romanticizing, began to call his kid brother "The Terror of Châteauroux," but the truth was less glamorous. Put him in the ring for a formal bout, in front of an audience, and Gérard would be struck down by a terrible case of stage fright.

"I was an ideal sparring partner," Gérard says. "I knew how to train a boxer, hit here, hit there. Fighting gave me a sense of equilibrium. But come a formal bout, I would lose everything. . . . In sports, I always had trouble competing in public. I was terrified by competition. I was a good swimmer, and in races at the municipal pool I won the fifty-meter race. But I was so scared, I couldn't swim straight. I kept veering around the pool. Later, on the stage, it was just the opposite. Everyone else was scared. Not me. Acting calmed me down. Because someone was finally giving me the words I never had."

He may have crumpled in formal bouts, but boxing layered Gérard with muscle and with adult confidence and a bit of swagger. Now to his jeans and T-shirts he added a new touch: he started rolling the sleeves up to the shoulder, to show off his biceps. He also let his hair grow long, and he took to wearing a leather flight jacket, just like the U.S. Air Force aces at the base. With his broken nose as a badge of courage and a Gitane cocked in his lips, Gérard no longer cultivated the look of a young James Dean; he more often cultivated the look of Brando in *The Wild One,* dressed in black leather and riding a Harley. All this set Gérard apart and boosted his stature among the kids of Omelon; yesterday's *enfant terrible* was now a full-grown hellion. The boy who used to dazzle his friends by riding his bike into the swimming hole now borrowed cars from older friends and took his friends on joy rides. "He had no license. Nothing," says Monique Dagaud. "And he still had no fear."

Impressing the kids of Omelon was one thing; impressing the G.I.'s was quite another. But now Gérard moved right into the rough, bare-knuckles night life of Châteauroux. In this atmosphere of heavy drinking and hell-raising, Gérard did not pick fights, but with all his boxing skills, he was not afraid to test his stuff. "He wasn't a thug, but he was a *provocateur,* and he would get into his share of scraps," Joe Gagné recalls. "But I would tell him, 'Gérard, either you calm down, or I'll throw you out!' And he'd calm down."

For Gérard, these scraps, in the ring and in the bars, were an important rite of passage, and they were a constant lesson in rough justice. "I never fought for the sake of fighting. I always fought to defend myself or to defend someone else," he says. "But in those bars and clubs there was always someone looking for trouble, and if you frequented this milieu, brawls were unavoidable. I would never be the one to punch first. In a street fight, the one who punches first is the one who is afraid. If somebody was trying to pick a fight, I would always see to it that he swung first, and I would make sure the blow was too far away or too close in, and I would fend it off. That way, the other guy discharges his anger and his energy. And then I could take him."

In this ritual combat, Gérard discovered that there was a code of honor strictly adhered to by the Americans. "With the G.I.'s, I was very surprised that each time we fought, afterward we made up. With the French, at least in Châteauroux, when a fight is over, it is out of the question to exchange a single word; you go over to the other side of the street. With the Americans, you shake hands, have a drink together, and you pay for each other's drinks. It's very 'fair play' and typically American. It's like entering a fraternity."

While he fought to prove himself among the G.I.'s, Gérard approached his sexual rite of passage in a much more delicate way. He was very timid and shy around girls and always had been. When he went to kindergarten at the Ecole St. Denis, he fell in love with a little girl named Odile Lacote. "She had a luminous smile, and I worshiped her," Gérard says. "But she never knew. I could never say a single word to her." Appropriately enough, his first real sweetheart was American, a black girl named Ronnie whom he had met while roller-skating at the NATO base. "Ronnie was a terrific roller-skater, and to me she was very exotic," Gérard says. "When Berrichons saw a black person, it was like seeing a god. We had never seen blacks. Ronnie was superb: tall, my age, and yet bigger than me, and I was big for my age. She had this magnificent mouth. I was madly in love with her, and, oh, I wanted to kiss that generous mouth."

They would skate together, holding hands and striding to the music, and there, surrounded by American kids and with Ronnie at his side, Gérard found a sense of happiness and equilibrium he had never known before. "We would skate for a while, then stop and have a Coke, and for me these were magnificent moments. It was truly another life, and there I had the impression of being—almost—an American, a real American teenager."

At the end of roller-skating, Gérard would take Ronnie behind the rink for a moment and they would kiss, sweetly, innocently. "I was terribly shy. Her lips were so soft, and I could see a shine in her eyes, and I knew what I felt was love. But it was impossible to communicate to her my feelings. I could not even communicate such feelings in my own language. I did not even have the means to say, *'Je t'aime.'* "

Through Ronnie, Gérard confronted his first experience of racism. One night after skating, he and Ronnie were outside necking when an American boy named Billy came up to them. " 'Never do that, Gérard,' he told me, wagging his finger. 'Black is black, and white is white.' This was the first time I understood what racism is. In the depths of the French provinces, I never saw racism as I saw it among the Americans."

His actual sexual initiation came with a very different accent. During his nightly roamings, he was befriended by two young French girls, Irène and Michèle. They became his sexual tutors, and he became their mascot. Sometimes he would join them at the Hôtel Berry, by the station; other nights he would stay with them at the apartment the girls shared at Lac de Belle Isle, a picturesque lake and forest north of town. The girls became like sisters to him. Michèle gave him his first tattoo, a star on the back of his hand, which became a permanent reminder to follow his own star. He later added more tattoos, including a small heart, half empty and half colored in, seemingly representing some sort of emotional split.

In Gérard's eyes, Irène and Michèle were not prostitutes; they were lonely rebels, just like him. The girls hung around the bars and clubs, and, in the reigning small-town atmosphere, they knew most of the G.I.'s and French youths by their first names. The Parisian pros who came in for the weekend turned tricks as fast as they could. Not Irène and Michèle. "They were middle-class girls who, to revolt against their families, said, 'Hah! I'll do this!' " says Gérard. "They ran away from school and became easy women for the Americans. The G.I.'s would give them a little money or buy them dinner. Like the G.I.'s, they were nineteen, uncomplicated, and full of life."

Whatever the nuances separating "prostitutes," from "easy women," and whatever the moral ambiguity about trafficking in cigarettes, Gérard soon crossed the boundary into what he knew was crime. "We used to steal big canisters of gasoline from the base," Gérard says. "We sold the gasoline and then cut the canisters in half, to make miniature boats for swimming or fishing." He and Alain now turned to trafficking in riskier booty, sometimes reselling provisions that had been pirated from the PX. During this period, a few episodes of public drunkenness got Gérard hauled off by MPs. They turned him over to the French police, and after a night drying out he was released without charge; in such cases, the French authorities treated minors with a large degree of tolerance. "Several times I had to get Gérard out of overnight detention," Alain says, "but he was never charged or convicted." When minors were put in overnight detention for drunkenness, they were held in an annex of the post office, not in jail, and they were almost always released without charge.

But Gérard did run into more serious trouble. One night a French customs team stopped a car and seized a trunkload of contraband. The arrested driver, hoping to lighten the charges against him, implicated Gérard, claiming he was an accomplice. Gérard says that he was in no way involved, but the police came and searched his parents' house. They found nothing, and while they had no substantive proof of any kind, they wanted to send Gérard to reform school anyway. But Dédé stood in their way; he refused to sign over custody of his son. So a local magistrate put Gérard on juvenile probation and required him to check in with the authorities one Thursday every month. When he first became a star and had to face scores of press interviews, Gérard tended to aggrandize these youthful transgressions, and some newspapers reported that he had spent time in jail. This was an exaggeration. Though he did have a celebrated encounter with the local police in 1968, Gérard never went to prison.

Still, he did have his share of violent experiences. On Saturday nights, especially in the summer, Gérard and Alain would meet up with Jacky Merveille and often they would wangle a car or thumb a ride out to Le Père Jean, a country tavern and dance hall located on the main road south to Lyons. The tavern was situated beside a very dangerous intersection, and Saturday nights at Le Père Jean had led to some terrible auto accidents. But risk and kicks were part of the attraction. Le Père Jean drew a rough crowd: G.I.'s looking for action, heavy French drinkers from the surrounding farms and villages, and plenty of women out to kick up their heels.

The place was equipped for trouble. Father Jean, the proprietor, was a tough, smart operator who worked as his own bouncer, and his place could accommodate big crowds. The tavern was built around a big open courtyard with a fish pond in the middle, and in the back was a spacious dance hall. Central to the thrill of Le Père Jean on Saturday nights were the women. These were not proper bourgeois girls, or wide-eyed country girls; these were prostitutes and easy women the G.I.'s had picked up at Le Crazy or the Rodeo Bar, or who had just drifted in on their own. Sometimes, on a hot summer night, a married woman or two would stray into Le Père Jean, women eager to share a few liberties with a tattooed G.I. or slum with a young Frenchman from the wrong side of the tracks.

At Le Père Jean, the music included some mournful Piaf, but the dominant beat was rock and roll, often featuring the songs of two French rockers with an American sound: Johnny Halliday and Eddie Mitchell. With the scents of booze and sex in the air, and with everyone writhing to the music, the dance floor at Le Père Jean was a real show, and for the price of a few beers, Gérard and his pals could find any kind of thrill they were looking for. For the additional price of a cigar, they could sit in a corner and imagine they were Jean-Paul Belmondo, the way he was in *Breathless.* Godard's film had come out in 1959, and it had created a sensation; Gérard and everyone else in France had seen it. With the same outlaw energy of Brando in *The Wild One,* Belmondo played a wily, insouciant punk. He steals a car in Marseilles, kills a cop, and makes his way to Paris. Exuding rough Gallic charm, he seduces an angel-faced child of a woman, an American played by Jean Seberg, a girl straight from the corn fields of Iowa—a girl very much like Ronnie and the other Americans Gérard would see when he went roller-skating at the NATO base right outside of Châteauroux.

For Alain and Gérard, these Saturday nights at Le Père Jean also carried a whiff of *Rebel Without a Cause,* Nicholas Ray's stunning look at disaffected American youth. When it was released in 1955, the film became a huge hit in Châteauroux. James Dean plays Jim Stark, a lonely, confused high school student who at school feels he is an outcast and at home feels misunderstood and alienated from his parents. His father is well-meaning but bumbling and ineffectual; his mother is remote and preoccupied with keeping up social appearances. To her, Jim is a good-for-nothing, an embarrassment. Neither of his parents understands Jim, and neither can give him the emotional sustenance and moral guidance he craves. The boy is desperate for some lesson, some example, about how to be a man. Brawling is the favorite activity of the high school group he wants to belong to, and while Jim doesn't like brawling, he doesn't want to back away from a fight, to "chicken out." In his eagerness to be accepted by the group, to feel their approving embrace, he accepts a dare, a rite of initiation that will lead to tragedy, in an auto accident. The film opens with Jim in juvenile detention for public drunkenness, and a fatherly officer encourages him to open up and vent his turmoil and frustration:

"Things pretty tough for you at home?"

"It's a zoo. . . . Boy, if I had one day when I didn't have to be all confused, and didn't have to feel I was ashamed of everything, if I felt I belonged someplace. . . ."

One night, Gérard drove out to Le Père Jean with some American friends, and as they neared the tavern they witnessed a horrible accident, two cars in a head-on collision. "It was a catastrophe," Gérard says. "There were three dead. In one car were some American friends of mine, and I had to close the eyes of one of them. The other car was a Peugeot 403, parents with two small children. I wound up with a little girl in my arms crying, 'Mommy's dead! Mommy's dead!' "

Experiences such as this, along with the trafficking in contraband, the brawling, the Saturday nights at Le Père Jean, the initiations with Irène and Michèle—all these engraved themselves deeply in Gérard. Just as he had watched his mother give birth, he took everything in, never averting his eyes, absorbing every detail. But at the same time, he was totally incapable of understanding or releasing the storms of emotions such experiences generated. He had careened abruptly from boyhood into manhood, with little to cushion the blows. Everything went inward, and little came out, except via alcohol and brawling. He fantasized about a different life, living in an adopted American family. That was his anchor: being accepted by the G.I.'s, feeling a part of their world and their extended family. Being with the Americans gave him an exhilarating sense of freedom: with them, his identity was in no way linked to Lilette and Dédé, to Omelon, or school or anything exterior to his own wit and humor. He could make everything up as he went along; he could constantly change languages and cultures, masks and roles. He was free to act.

"I led two lives," Gérard says. "Days I spent with American teenagers, and nights I spent with G.I.'s who brawled. I had the rare privilege of playing during the day with the kids and then drinking at night with their fathers. At Joe's or Jimmy's or La Grenouillère, you often had sergeants, with four bars on their sleeve, and they'd be dead drunk. I knew them all, I would play with their kids during the day, and in the bar at night they'd clap me on the back and say, 'Hey, Jerrrrrrard. Har you?' "

Part of him thrilled to this wild existence, but another part of him shrank from the bars and the brawling and the rudderless life of crime he was drifting into—not out of fear, but out of revulsion: "What disturbed me was the violence of it all. I grew up thinking violence was the norm." His home life was filled with arguments and shouting—verbal violence. His life at school had been charged with various forms of discipline, coercion, and physical violence, from bullies picking on little kids at recess, to Le Père Durand using his pointer to rap knuckles. Growing up, Gérard absorbed this stark lesson: when you go out into the world of men, out to the bars, or even to a family-run eatery like Joe from Maine, you had to be ready for violence; it could hit you at any time. You had to learn to handle all sorts of violence, from verbal to brawling. You didn't take up boxing because it was fun, like soccer, or because you liked getting pummeled or having your nose broken; you took up boxing to build your body, boost your confidence, and learn self-defense. In essence, a boy took up boxing to help forge himself into a man.

"My dream was never to be a gangster," says Gérard. "This was the dream of many people out to get back at society, and it was the dream of many of the kids I grew up with. But to me this is the dream of an idiot. This dream finishes in prison or with a bullet in the head. Belmondo in *Breathless* was far too violent, too crude for my taste. The dream I had was different: to make something of myself, to do good.

"But when you grow up in a place like I grew up, violence is a central fact of life, whether you like it or not. I don't care if you're in Châteauroux or Paris or Los Angeles, the fact is that if you grow up in a ghetto or a poor neighborhood, or if you grow up in a rough milieu as I did, you face violence every single day. And either you get out or else at some stage, in some form or other, you are going to suffer violence."

Gérard already knew his choice: to get out. As a child, many of his happiest times had been when he was away from Châteauroux, beginning with his summers on his aunt's farm in rural Berry. In the late 1950s, Gérard spent part of his summers with Grandma Denise, Dédé's mother. Denise was warm, maternal, and uncomplicated, and she adored Gérard, even if he had stuck a pea in her ear when he was three. In her cottage just south of Paris, Gérard had room to breathe and unpressured time to himself. He loved to work in her garden, pruning, turning the soil, tending the beets, leeks, carrots, radishes, and fruits she planted every spring.

When he was only eleven, Gérard found a way to do what Dédé had always talked of doing and had never done: he went to the sea. The local soccer team was playing a match in Monaco, and Gérard wangled himself onto the bus carrying fans down to the game. "It was a great trip, the bus smelling of red wine, eggs, and garlic sausage," Gérard says. "I didn't care about the game. The bus was cheap and I wanted to see the sea. I was the first person in my family to do so." He loved the openness of the sea, the smell of the salt air; another summer he went to the beach with a family from Omelon, and he stayed a month in Arcachon, on the Atlantic coast.

In June 1964, after the second year of his apprenticeship in the print shop, Gérard was ready to set out traveling on his own. He packed a small bag, went out to the main route south, and stuck out his thumb. He had no precise destination in mind, only a general direction: the Riviera. In his brief trip to Monaco, Gérard had loved what he had seen of the south of France, and he knew Cannes from newsreels and from Lilette's *CinéMonde* magazines. Cannes was that magical place where every May scores of French and American movie stars gathered for the annual Cannes Film Festival. To Gérard, the south of France also meant St. Tropez, the sun-dappled port where Brigitte Bardot and her blazing, naked sexuality had left Jean-Louis Trintignant seduced and abandoned in Roger Vadim's *... And God Created Woman.* The film had come out in 1956, and it had been pure elixir to the imagination and lust of every adolescent boy in Châteauroux, and most of France.

Gérard enjoyed the kick and the challenge of hitchhiking, and often when he jumped in a new car he would make up a new identity to amuse himself and fool the driver. This was a private psychological game and a form of education. "When you hitchhike," he says," "if you have a sour face, no one stops. But if you do it for a while, you learn how to be accepted by strangers and all sorts of other people."

Long before he ever stepped onto a stage, Gérard was putting on new identities and creating his own reality, and this was just what he did when his last ride finally landed him on the Riviera. He went looking for a job as a *plagiste,* a beach boy. The *plagistes* work at the posh beaches on the Mediterranean, putting out the umbrellas and lounge chairs, serving as busboys and lifeguards during the day and raking the beach clean at night. With unerring instinct, Gérard found his way to one of the most exclusive spots on the Riviera, the Bay of Millionaires, just down the coast from Cap d'Antibes.

Even to the most jaded eye, the Bay of Millionaires is a visual splendor, a feast for the senses; to a kid of fifteen from the sticks of Châteauroux, this looked like paradise: the pristine blue of the sea, with sailboats leaning in the wind; the palm trees and promenades, freshly swept and smelling of jasmine and coconut; the villas sitting regally on the hill, sunlight shimmering on their terra-cotta roofs and whitewashed façades. Nestled discreetly behind immaculate hedges were five-star resorts with silvery names like Hôtel du Cap, and in their driveways were sleek Mercedes-Benzes and Rolls-Royces, with liveried chauffeurs polishing the chrome. In the heat, Gérard walked along the sea-front promenade in a kind of feverish dream, looking at the sea, watching the waves come rolling up onto the rich white sand, up and up until their foam licked the toes of young women stretched out on the sand, their bodies lithe and languid, their legs and their torsos tanned and oiled and glistening in the morning sun.

Gérard went to the far end of La Garoupe, to a private beach club called Chez Joseph. It was an idyllic spot, with green and white cabanas, matching parasols, and neat rows of lounge chairs facing out across the bay to Nice. One section of the beach club had a bar and shaded table set with freshly ironed tablecloths, sparkling silverware, and big silver ice buckets to chill the white wine to be served with the seafood specialties Chez Joseph served at lunch.

Somewhere along the way to Chez Joseph, Gérard had been befriended by two fashionable older women. He walked into the beach club with them, ordered drinks, and after the women left, he presented himself to the manager, a cheerful little fellow named Loulou. Shyly and politely, Gérard told him he was looking for a job as a *plagiste.* Though they chatted only briefly, Loulou was impressed and gave him a job. Gérard struck Loulou as handsome, poised, and strong, and for some reason, Loulou was convinced Gérard came from a cultured, aristocratic background.

"He arrived with two older women, two very elegant women, and I'll tell you a little secret: I'm almost positive he called himself Gérald," Loulou says. "Most of the summer I thought of him as Gérald, and to the ears of a poor fisherman like me, the name 'Gérald' reeked of nobility."

Gérard swears he never told Loulou his name was Gérald, but he was certainly trying to make a good impression, as this was just the kind of place where he wanted to spend this first summer completely out on his own. In any case, the two elegant women disappeared, and Loulou took this newcomer and instructed him in the ways of a Riviera beach. Gérard proved to be very friendly and able around Loulou's upper-class clientele, and this further convinced him that Gérald—or Gérard—came from a rich family. Every year, rich families came to the Riviera and found summer jobs for their sons, those pampered boys who needed sun and rest from the travails of the *lycée* and studying for the *baccalauréat,* the exam that would determine their next level of grooming for a place among the French elite.

Loulou had spent his life right here on this beach, catering to the rich. He had just taken over Chez Joseph following the death of his father, and he was trying to keep the same clientele that for years had been coming to the Bay of Millionaires and Chez Joseph. And what a clientele it was. General Eisenhower, when he was commander of NATO forces in Europe, used to stay at the nearby Villa Sous-le-Vent, and he would come here to swim and have lunch. Loulou himself had given mats and towels to Churchill. And in the 1920s, this was one of the favorite Riviera hangouts of Ernest Hemingway; Loulou has his photo in a family scrapbook. Gérard, of course, had never seen anything even remotely resembling this kind of privilege, but Loulou says he immediately fit right in: "He was shy and discreet, and he was very thin and muscular. Right away you could see he had a human touch. Everyone adored him, and he made a lot in tips. He had a feeling for people."

Gérard put in long hours and slept right there at the beach, in an old fisherman's shack where mats and rakes were stored along with the sails from the skiffs which Loulou rented out daily. "The shack smelled of salt and the sea, and all summer Gérard slept there alone in a sleeping bag, and he always told me how happy he was there," Loulou says. Gérard was indeed happy: "For me, this was another world. And I didn't even have to talk. All I had to do was smile at people and bring them drinks, and they would give me big tips. I made a good bit of money, and I sent some home to Lilette and Dédé."

One source of his contentment that summer was Loulou's mother, Jeanne, a large jolly country woman who ran the kitchen. She took Gérard into her family, fussing over him and cooking for him. One night she even bandaged him after he got into a brawl in a bar in Cap d'Antibes. Lilette had rarely showered him with this kind of maternal warmth, and according to Loulou, Gérard just soaked it up. "With my mother, he found a family. We all felt that very strongly. She gave him moral support, and he, in turn, revered her."

With the sun browning his body and bringing out the blond in his hair, Gérard was one of the most attractive young men on the beach. "Women were drawn to him. You could see it," Loulou says. But all summer, Gérard remained polite and reserved with these elegant, glistening sunbathers. They were wealthy bourgeois women, and they were very intimidating to Gérard. He never imagined women like these could have any interest in a rough, uncultured kid from the streets of Châteauroux. Still, here under the Mediterranean sun, some of the class distinctions he had grown up with seemed to melt away. Take Loulou: He was short and heavy, and he had the same peasant hands as Gérard, with the same thick, rough fingers. His speech was awkward too, thick with the twang of the Midi, which gave words endings like *raaannggg* and *maaaannng*. Even a simple, everyday word like *pain,* bread, from

Loulou's lips came out *paaaannnnggg.* And yet Loulou moved in this world of class and money with a definite status and confidence, and not just because he was the boss, *le patron.* No, in dealing with people, Loulou had a definite touch, an ability to connect. And among these rich people he didn't pretend he was invisible, the way Lilette and Dédé always did. Loulou's example gave Gérard encouragement.

By the end of the summer, Gérard was not eager to go home; his time at Chez Joseph had given him real pleasure and a new awareness. When he arrived on the Riviera, with all its luxury and wealth, he never dreamed he could be accepted into a world like this—not with his background, not with his awkward speech and his lack of language. To be accepted into this world, he assumed, your family name had to have an aristocratic *de* in front of it, and it would be a lot easier if your first name had a distinctive ring, like Frédéric, Jean-Christophe, Charles, or François-Valéry. Or even Gérald. Just by changing one letter, his name could have a wholly different ring; imagine how liberating it might be to change identities altogether, the way actors do.

At the same time, this summer on the beach stripped away any mystique the rich might have held for Gérard. Yes, they had lots of money, but under the sun, with their clothes stripped off, many of the distinctions that wealth bought magically vanished. Under the sun there was a great equality; flesh was flesh. And if a man had the touch, he did not have to traffic in cigarettes or set type to earn money and win approval. If he had a little humor, and an ability to connect, why, he could do nothing more than serve drinks and arrange umbrellas, and people would shower him with affection and tips. And if he could do all this with enough humor and panache, a fellow could even work up his courage and say a few words to one of these golden girls, one of these dream *parisiennes.*

After such an intoxicating summer, Gérard came home with fresh eyes and different dreams. But nothing had changed at his house. Nor at the print shop. Nor at Joe from Maine. Nor among his friends in Omelon. The town was still dominated by coarseness and violence, and now that his dreams were elsewhere, Châteauroux, and his life in it, seemed unbearably drab and suffocating.

In the fall of 1964, Gérard returned for the third year of his apprenticeship as a printer, but now he was working at a shop which labeled packing cartons, a job with none of the appeal of putting out *The CHAD News,* and none of the nobility. This was grunt work, and Gérard was becoming fed up with it. But what else could he do? So he stuck it out, as always turning his frustrations inward and not confiding them to a soul. At about this time though, he made a new friend: a shy, serious, and soft-spoken young man named Michel Pilorgé. Michel was three years older than Gérard and came from a privileged background. His father was a prominent doctor in town, and the Pilorgés lived on an estate in the surrounding countryside. These two very different young men first met by chance one evening in the fall of 1963.

"I was sitting on a doorstep in front of the girls' *lycée,* waiting for a girlfriend," Michel recalls. "And along comes this guy with a pair of boxing gloves slung over his shoulder. You could see he had just come from a workout. The street was otherwise empty, and I watched him approach. As he walked along with a friend, he must have found my glances annoying, because he stopped and said: 'You want my photo?' "

Soon thereafter, Gérard and Michel ran into each other at one of the local cafés. They discussed the music of Jacques Brel and Georges Brassens, they had a snack together, and soon after they would often meet at the café of the Hôtel Faisan and go for cheeseburgers or omelette sandwiches at Joe from Maine. Gérard had never had a friend like Michel. He was a proper bourgeois son, studious and able at his *lycée,* respectful to adults, a young man in every sense *bien élevé,* well brought-up. Like every young male in town, Michel had tried his hand at trafficking in cigarettes, but he had quickly shied away from the risks. On the face of it, Michel and Gérard had little in common, but the two young men intrigued each other, and they became good friends. Before a night on the town, Gérard would have Michel meet him at his house, and Michel got to know Lilette and Dédé. He liked them both: he found them warm and genuine—certainly a far cry from his patrician parents. Dédé liked Michel right away and called him "Mimi." Lilette, always fretting about class distinctions, called him "Monsieur Pilorgé," and she could never understand what a fine young man like him could see in her Gérard. Lilette would even hold Michel up as a shining example of how Gérard ought to behave.

By now, though, everyone around his age, male or female, rich or poor, was fascinated by Gérard. Even at fifteen, he had charisma and magnetism. Some youths were drawn to his tough, exuberant, free-spirited exterior; Michel was drawn to what he sensed was hidden inside. "He wanted to be loved by everybody. Gérard has often been catalogued as being a borderline thug, but to me that always seemed false. God knows I was very far removed from that milieu, but he seemed comfortable frequenting both shady milieus and a privileged milieu like mine. He wanted to belong to all the groups; he wanted to win everyone over."

He did not succeed though, at least not with the golden girls Michel knew. For all his bravado and swagger with men, Gérard was still painfully shy around women, especially women from bourgeois families. With an ease Michel could never hope to match, Gérard could befriend "easy women" like Irène and Michèle, and other women from his own social background. But around a sophisticated young woman from Michel's milieu, Gérard remained awkward and tongue-tied.

Meanwhile, many of Gérard's friends, almost all of whom were older, were falling in love and pairing off. The G.I.'s, with their dashing convertibles and their pockets full of dollars, were the kings of Châteauroux. "French women adored the G.I.'s," Gérard says. "I often introduced French girls to my G.I. friends"—always the *entremetteur.* But Gérard remained emotionally unattached. By now, Ronnie had moved on with her military family, and when it came to courting those French girls whom he found attractive, Gérard could not compete with the G.I.'s. At night he would see them driving women around in their convertibles, taking them to the base for ice cream or an American movie. Gérard could also imagine the couples at the end of the evening, cuddling in the back seat, the G.I.'s telling their French honeys all about the land of opportunity, a place filled with penny loafers and peanut butter and ranch houses with big stoves and refrigerators, a place just perfect for raising a family.

"There were scores of local girls who ended up marrying *les boys,"* says Maurice Croze. "And most of the marriages worked out pretty well. But we always heard of a few local girls who thought they had married engineers, but when they got to America they discovered that their engineer was only an auto mechanic or a fireman."

During this period, Gérard commanded enormous respect among his pals, but he remained a loner. "We hung out together, with Jacky and others, but Gérard was never a member of a gang," says Alain. "He was always independent." Gérard could fit in almost anywhere, and he had scores of friends, but he had yet to find a real home, or even a real sense of belonging. Now he grew restless and increasingly disenchanted with his life in Châteauroux, and he gave up his printer's apprenticeship without finishing the critical third year, the one which would have earned him the certificate he needed to get a job. This exasperated Lilette and Dédé. Now they were sure he would amount to nothing. Gérard started drifting, working at odd jobs, hitchhiking around France, giving himself new names and new identities with every new ride. When Gérard did come home, his friends found him withdrawn and increasingly volatile, especially when he drank. "You always felt in

Gérard this sense of rebellion, this need to breathe," Alain says. "And you never knew what would come out of him next."

Neither did Gérard. But one day in the late autumn of 1965, when he was sixteen, he was hanging out at the railroad station, aimlessly, and along came Michel Pilorgé. Gérard hadn't seen his pal Mimi in quite some time; Michel was going to school in Paris now. Michel's father had wanted his son to follow in his footsteps and study medicine, but Michel, like so many kids of the sixties generation, was determined to go his own way. And now he was completely swept up in a single dream: to study theater and become an actor.

"Mimi! What're you doing here?"

"Going back to Paris."

"Oh. And the theater? How's it going?"

"Fine, thank you, Gérard. And what are you up to?"

"Ouff. Nothing."

Maybe it was Gérard's tone of voice, or the look on his face, but Michel acted on impulse. "Nothing? So come up to Paris with me. I'm sharing an apartment with my two brothers, and we have plenty of room. Come on, Gérard, come to Paris."

Gérard just laughed and waved good-bye. But later he started to think. Mimi leaves for Paris, just like that. He takes up acting, just like that. Imagine: becoming an actor, just like that.

Three days later, Michel was alone in his apartment on the Left Bank, trying to memorize some lines from a play, when there came a knock at his door. Michel opened the door and there he was.

"Non!" Michel exclaimed.

"Si," Gérard said.

"Alors," Michel said, clapping him on the back. *"Bravo."*

Gérard had come to Paris with one small bag and no return ticket to Châteauroux. He had no money in his pocket and no idea how he was going to live. All Gérard knew was that he had finally made his escape. He had cut himself free.

PART 3

Paris

Upon arrival in Paris

8

La Crème de la Crème

Gérard was ecstatic to be in Paris. To his eyes, Michel's apartment looked like heaven. It was located in a quiet neighborhood of the Left Bank near the southern rim of the city, on the rue de la Glacière. The apartment was by no means extravagant, but it was spacious and sunny, and it looked out over the rooftops of Paris. Michel's two older brothers were serious students, and each had his own room in the rear of the apartment. Michel camped in the living room, and Gérard happily settled into an opposite corner.

Like so many earlier generations of students in Paris, the Pilorgé brothers lived a bohemian existence, eating at university canteens or cheap local cafés and couscous joints. Their apartment was near several Parisian schools, including the prestigious Lycée Henri IV and the Ecole Polytechnique, one of France's elite *grandes écoles.* Michel frequented a neighborhood café called Le Polytech, a familiar meeting place for Castelroussins who had come to Paris. With Michel as guide, Gérard toured the *quartier* and immediately felt at home. And he took it as an auspicious sign that the owner of Le Polytech was a jovial, big-hearted soul everyone called Dédé.

This was not Gérard's first time in Paris. He had been to the city with Grandma Denise, so he had some sense of its look and feel: the Eiffel Tower, the Arc de Triomphe, the way the Seine cut the city into a Right Bank and Left. But just as he had arrived on the Riviera two summers before, he arrived in Paris with a head full of romantic notions, many of them coming right out of the movies. In his imagination, Paris was filled with people of glitter and refinement, people who would have no interest in a hayseed like him. Paris, in his imagination, was also filled with golden *parisiennes* like the ones he had catered to at Chez Joseph on the Bay of Millionaires—women who would find nothing attractive, he was sure, in a rough, uncultured dropout from Châteauroux. From the movies, Gérard also knew that Paris had a tough underside, the Paris of Les Halles, of Jean Gabin, Jean-Paul Belmondo, and Edith Piaf. That is where he figured he might fit in; perhaps there he could find a gym and make some money as a sparring partner.

But Gérard was also intrigued by this acting business, and as soon as he arrived he started quizzing Michel. What exactly did it mean to study theater? What did you learn at these acting schools, anyway? A dropout from a poor family in Châteauroux would have no chance, would he? "His main anxiety centered on who these people were studying theater," Michel recalls. "What were their backgrounds? To get in, did your parents have to have money?"

To answer all of Gérard's questions, Michel invited him to come along to his next acting class. Gérard had sworn never to set foot in a classroom again, but this he wanted to see. The class was across town, so they took the Métro from Glacière, and it was a direct ride to Trocadéro. This particular class was held in the evening, and when the two young men walked up out of the Métro station, across the Seine from them stood the graceful Eiffel Tower brilliantly illumined against the night sky.

The drama school where Michel was studying was called the Cours Dullin, named for its late founder, Charles Dullin, and it was an offshoot of the Théâtre National Populaire, the National Public Theater. The class met at the Palais Chaillot, in a rehearsal studio with a small stage. Michel led them in, chatted with some of his friends, and introduced them to Gérard. With his acute radar, Gérard scanned the room and sized up the students. They smelled of money all right. The young men were neat and clean, and some wore blazers and ties. The young women were well groomed, with sparkling teeth, and more than a few wore fancy earrings and necklaces and freshly pressed pleated skirts. Almost everyone looked to be about three years older than Gérard, and with one glance he knew that most of them had graduated from *lycée,* and were probably going to the Sorbonne, or its equivalent, during the day. But Gérard looked as mature as everyone else, and he was bigger and stronger, and as he sized up the students and absorbed the feel of his surroundings, for some reason he immediately felt right at home. And instead of feeling that he had to remain "invisible," as he always did at school in Châteauroux, to keep away from trouble, here he had the sense he could let go and be himself. "I had the impression I was a student, too," he says. "And I felt very alive."

Tonight the class was going to work on improvisation techniques, under the direction of a professor named Lucien Arnaut. As Michel explained to Gérard, this was now an important focus of their work. Students would volunteer to go on stage and act out a theme. The other students would then try to guess the theme, and the professor would critique the performance. This will be interesting to watch, Gérard was thinking, and then Professor Arnaut walked into the class. "What happened then was incredible," Gérard recalls. "As soon as he walked in, the professor turned to me and said, 'You, it's time you took the stage.' And I had never even been there before. Michel had been there for months, and he had never gone on stage."

Gérard knew nothing about acting; what could he do? What kind of theme was he supposed to act out? Was he going to be ridiculed? Michel felt panicky: What have I gotten Gérard into? But when his turn came, Gérard went straight into action, pretending he had been in the class for months. "He went right up on stage and began to mime," Michel says. "Within moments, the entire hall was in stitches."

On stage, Gérard just followed his instinct, drawing upon his own array of youthful experiences. "I was up there on stage, in the light, and I had with me all my background from Châteauroux," Gérard says. "It was like being in front of the police, and the only way to come out all right was to smile. So I started to smile, and I could feel a crazy laugh welling up inside me. I didn't say a word, but everyone saw I had this strange smile on my face, and they started to giggle, and then out of me came this hysterical laugh, and everyone joined in. I didn't have to say a word."

His theme, of course, was to make everyone laugh, and Professor Arnaut applauded Gérard's performance. "Now *that* was improvisation," he told the class.

"Gérard has a laugh that naturally generates laughter in others," Michel says. "And from then on he could always get the class to laugh, by mimicking or just by coming out with one of his onomatopoetic grunts or rumbles. . . . By the end of this first session he was already one of the stars of the class—just like that. It was incredible."

The first session was pure oxygen to Gérard, and from then on, he started coming regularly to class, sitting in without paying. There were about one hundred students in Michel's class at the Cours Dullin, and Gérard continued to earn their applause and respect. The class met three times a week, and after most sessions, many of the students would go to cafés and keep right on memorizing texts and working on scenes. Gérard was happy to go with them. These students came from wealthy, cultured families, yet they accepted Gérard as he was, without the painful snubs he had experienced in Omelon. Their approval did wonders for Gérard's confidence and self-esteem. Just as he had earned the embrace of the G.I. family, now he sensed that he could earn himself a niche at the theater school, among these children of the Paris elite.

The acceptance delighted him, but it was the work itself which really excited Gérard. Typsetting had been physically demanding and tedious; acting was by contrast child's play, and it seemed to come very naturally to him—as long as he was not called upon to speak. "In a very short time, I realized that acting suited me perfectly. It gave me a feeling of health and balance. I couldn't speak; by now I was completely blocked. But with improvisation, I didn't need to. I only had to laugh." Within just a few weeks, Gérard was dazzling his professors and his classmates. Michel saw what his friend could do on stage, he heard the other students talking, and soon the verdict was in: Gérard may have been a school dropout, and he may have looked like a brute, but when it came to acting, this unusual kid from Châteauroux had natural talent.

"The acting classes were very easy for Gérard," Michel says. "It was exactly what he already knew how to do. But even if it was easy, it was nonetheless extraordinary that a guy who had never before even approached the phenomenon of the theater could do it just like that. And with no hesitation. . . . I don't want to make him out to be some sort of mythic being, but it is hardly my fault if Gérard was someone who stood out as exceptional, right from the beginning."

Curiously, though, when he was only a few weeks into this new experience, Gérard abruptly stopped coming to class. This perplexed Michel, especially as his new roommate said little about it. But the truth was that Gérard found his sudden change of life overwhelming; Paris and the acting classes had upended his world and his sense of self. In his first sixteen years, he had always been painfully shy about his distinctive head and build; in acting class he discovered these could be assets, for they helped him to attract and hold people's attention. He had grown up embarrassed about the odd, disjointed way he talked; in class, he was still too timid to talk much, but he saw that the strange patter he had picked up from Dédé could also be turned to his advantage. In the eyes of these cultured Parisians and professors, it seemed fresh and expressive. Instead of being a source of embarrassment, his patter could make people laugh.

He also saw that in an artistic world which prized spontaneity and originality, these Parisians from bourgeois families—with their polished manners and reticent demeanors, with everything about them impeccably *bien élevé*—they often came across on stage as timid, conformist, and constrained. By contrast, Gérard was elemental and free-spirited, and his raw, volcanic temperament gave him something else many of the Parisians lacked: dramatic flair. Unencumbered by formal language and intimidated by words, he had turned to his instincts and his body for guidance, and that, too, seemed to work on stage.

Still, Gérard did not know what to make of it all. It was as if he had passed through some disorienting looking glass and come out into a world where everything was the exact opposite of Châteauroux. Here at drama school men would never dream of brawling, and the professors urged the students not to shut up but to open up. These young men and women came from bourgeois families, but he felt no class antagonisms dividing the students. After sixteen years of living under the oppressive belief that "the shame is upon us," Gérard felt that maybe, just maybe, he had some sort of potential and worth. The realization came as a profound shock.

"I suddenly saw that my lack of education could actually be a stroke of good fortune," Gérard says. "I had been to a play only once in my life, a Molière, a production of *Don Juan* that came to Châteauroux. The other students were cultured. They knew how to read and write, and they know how to express themselves. I, too, wanted to go to school and become educated and cultivated, and yet now I realized there were advantages to the fact that I had done everything my way, according to my choices and my pleasures, even if much of it had been difficult to stomach."

As always, Gérard kept all his internal confusion to himself. He did not confide in Michel; Alain was off studying architecture; and Gérard had virtually cut himself off from Lilette and Dédé. It was the mid-1960s, but his parents still had no phone, and Gérard refused to write them so much as a postcard. As always, what Gérard relied upon was gut instinct, and his instinct now was to withdraw even further into himself and stop going to class. He was plagued by doubts and insecurities. Yes, he told himself, there were advantages to having done everything his way, but everyone else knew so much more than he did. They read, and they had been reading all their lives. You'll never catch up to them, he told himself. Give up this folly.

"I was at a terribly difficult age, between sixteen and eighteen, and it was hard being alone in a city like Paris, and being among students who could recite verse and classical texts," Gérard says. "Michel gave me texts to recite, but most of the time I could not even understand what I was saying. When I first arrived in acting class, I had never even heard of the names 'Pyrrhus,' 'Hippolyte,' and 'Andromaque.' I thought they were the names of dogs."

During this period of turmoil, Gérard bunked at Michel's and ate on the cheap. For his coffees and drinks he hung out at Le Polytech, where Dédé extended him credit. Michel Mouilleron, one of his buddies from home, came up to Paris and moved into a nearby *chambre de bonne,* a tiny maid's room. Two other pals from central France came to town as well, Michel Demoule and Michel Arroyo, the son of another prominent doctor in Châteauroux. Soon Alain came to Paris, after finishing his studies in architecture and design. He took a job as a draftsman at an industrial design studio, and he joined Gérard as a regular at Le Polytech. As Alain was earning money, and staying with Grandma Denise in her cottage by Orly airport, Alain periodically paid off Gérard's tab at the café. Even though they rarely talked, Alain could see what Gérard was going through.

"When he first came to Paris, Gérard was in bad shape. Very bad shape. He was searching, trying to see where he could fit in. To us, Paris was a different world. When a kid from the provinces comes to Paris, he has trouble for a year or two. It's like a guy from the country in America going to New York, knowing no one. There are many people, but people in Paris are very hard. You feel completely alone."

With their usual flair for small-town gossip and belittling, many Castelroussins who had heard that Gérard had taken up acting ridiculed the very idea of it. A school dropout, from a family like that, take up acting! Who ever heard of anything so preposterous? Lilette and Dédé figured it was all nonsense as well. At this time, Michel Pilorgé was dating a proper young Castelroussine, whom he would soon marry, and he often went home to see her on weekends. On one of these trips, he bumped into a shopkeeper named Chudi, who knew Gérard well. Chudi ran a clothing shop on the rue de la Gare, and Gérard had often done odd jobs for him. Now Michel eagerly told Chudi about Gérard's impressive debut in acting school. Aghast, Chudi scolded Michel and told him he was doing Gérard a terrible disservice: "You're going to make a fool out of him," Chudi told Michel. "What an idea, leading a guy like that into this kind of artistic adventure. In no time, he is going to fall flat on his face."

In his bleaker moments, Gérard saw himself doing just that. All right, so he could screw up his face and make people laugh—so what? In his few weeks at the Cours Dullin, what he had tasted was just froth, a game for rich kids; what did a bit of improvisation have to do with the real work of acting? That demanded words and language and recitation, that demanded education and culture, and he had none of these. Look at Michel and his two brothers. They were avid readers, and had been all their lives. Even at home they spoke a language Gérard could barely follow, much less fathom or hope to emulate. To become an actor, Michel was immersing himself in plays by Molière and Racine, and often at night he listened to a recording of Edmond Rostand's *Cyrano de Bergerac,* set forth in tongue-twisting verses. To Gérard, such classical texts seemed like insurmountable barriers. Growing up, he had never been a reader, and he certainly had never tackled anything even remotely resembling Molière or Racine. Poetry had been crammed down his throat at school, and reciting in front of Le Père Lucas's class had been a painful ordeal; how in the world would he ever learn Molière? No, there was no way to overcome such handicaps. This whole idea of becoming an actor was ridiculous.

Plagued by doubts, Gérard roamed the grand boulevards and back streets of Paris. For a while he took up with a Dutch girl, in one of his many brief, passionate flings. He hung out at Le Polytech, and sometimes he paid surprise visits to his friends from Châteauroux. Michel Arroyo, like Michel Pilorgé, had come to Paris to study theater against the wishes of his doctor father. Arroyo had found himself a small room in the north of Paris, in the Place Clichy, near where Henry Miller used to live. He was renting on the cheap in exchange for a couple of hours of baby-sitting per week. One morning very early, when Arroyo was still asleep, Gérard showed up at his door, unexpectedly of course.

"He came for breakfast," Arroyo recalls. "The problem was, I had only one bowl for coffee. So I gave him five francs and sent him down to a local store to buy another bowl. Ten minutes later, he came back with a new bowl, and he gave me back my five francs. I said, 'How'd you do that?' Gérard just shrugged: 'There was nobody there to make you pay.' "

Arroyo was studying in a private class run by a professor named Jean-Laurent Cochet. Michel told Gérard that Cochet was the most esteemed professor of theater in the whole of Paris. Over coffee and *tartines,* Arroyo also told Gérard about Cochet's approach. Unlike Dullin and its most populist spirit, Cochet was extremely selective about whom he would take on, and he taught classical *déclamation,* an approach emphasizing formal recitation. This was the tradition of the Paris Conservatory and the Comédie-Française, two of France's most prestigious institutions, and two places where Cochet had both acted and taught. In style, Cochet was a *personnage,* a true character, and as a teacher he was brilliant and demanding; his classes were small, rigorous, and cutthroat. Cochet rarely suffered fools; if you did shoddy work, you faced the sting of his waspish wit. Still, in the world of theater, this was it, *la crème de la crème;* if you wanted to know whether you had the makings of an actor or if you wanted to see if the very notion was only a ridiculous pipe dream, then Cochet's class was the place to come strut your stuff.

Gérard was impressed by what he heard, but he was not ready to test his mettle in Cochet's class. In fact, Gérard soon put Cochet out of his mind. He turned seventeen that Christmas, and throughout the spring of 1966, he kept close to Michel Pilorgé and Alain and continued to roam the city. That summer, instead of going back to Châteauroux or hitchhiking down to the south of France alone, he and Michel decided to go together to the Riviera. They took the train. ("I remember," says Michel. "I paid for the tickets.") Gérard had never before had a friend like Michel. Shy, serious, and with a gentle, self-deprecating humor, Michel was good company, and yet he knew how to cut loose. He was also handsome, in a boyish way, and he certainly knew how to flirt with bourgeois women. They found jobs as beach boys in Cannes at the Plage des Sports, a private beach club like Chez Joseph. For Gérard it was familiar, pleasant work. Michel enjoyed it as well, and they became tanned and relaxed. Again, Gérard was surrounded by golden *parisiennes,* swimming or stretched out in lounge chairs and sunning themselves in micro-bikinis. Topless bathing was also starting to come into vogue.

"There was one girl who came to the beach every day," Michel recalls. "She was an absolutely magnificent creature, with fabulous blue eyes, and clearly she was coming there for Gérard. But he could never, ever believe that." Gérard still could not dream that any woman who came from a background of culture and privilege might find him the least bit attractive. His timidity did not stem from any lack of desire, but from what Michel knew to be a painful embarrassment: Gérard's worsening speech problems. Now he was constantly tongue-tied. "He was stuttering terribly. He could not finish a sentence," Michel says. "He could express himself by sound, often perfectly well by sound, but his formal language was very primitive."

As he had with Loulou and his family at Chez Joseph, Gérard soon developed close bonds with the club's owners. Ever the *entremetteur,* Gérard brought Alain around to meet the proprietor and his family, and Alain wound up marrying the boss's daughter. By that summer, Gérard had lost some of his taste for brawling. He and Michel were given the responsibility of guarding the private beach at night, and they slept right in the bar of the Plage des Sports. One night a group of rowdy punks paraded through the beach—just the kind of provocation that once would have propelled Gérard into action. Now, though, he and Michel prudently stayed inside the bar, neither of them eager for a fight. The two young men had a fine summer, putting out the mats and beach umbrellas, serving drinks, raking the sand, collecting handsome tips, and swimming in the early morning and after work. Gérard still had an irresistible thirst for mischief, but Michel now saw in his friend a new maturity and balance.

At the end of the summer, Gérard went back to Paris tanned, fit, and with his mind made up: he was going to test himself against the master, Jean-Laurent Cochet. One day that fall, in 1966, along with Michel Pilorgé, Michel Demoule, and Michel Mouilleron, Gérard went to Cochet's headquarters at the Théâtre Edouard VII, a small jewel of a theater located next to where the legendary Jean-Louis Barrault had his theater troupe. Gérard may have wanted to make a strong first impression on the most esteemed acting professor in Paris, but he was not about to put on any airs. He arrived in his usual garb: jeans and a T-shirt, with the sleeves rolled up to the shoulders, showing off his biceps and his tattoo.

The arrival of these four characters came as a bit of a shock to the prim, refined Professor Cochet. "The class had just begun, in a rehearsal hall, and who do I see sail in but four strange characters, including one huge, long-haired fellow I took to be a woodsman," Cochet recalls. "I had no idea where they had come from, or where they were going. They looked like they had just stepped out of a Sergio Leone western. For a moment, I thought they must be looking for the cellar. But no, they said they had come to sign up for my course."

Cochet shooed them in the general direction of his office, hoping it was all just a silly mistake. But soon his secretary came rushing in to him, in a terrible tizzy. With a touch of panic in her voice, she whispered into the professor's ear: "These people you sent me—what do you expect me to do with them? They're young thugs and they scare me. And the big one, well! He has the strangest laugh." Cochet calmed her down, and the four prospective students submitted their applications.

Soon thereafter the professor put them through a standard audition, in front of the entire class, and he suspected that this would end the entire adventure. Cochet patiently watched as three of these provincial rustics read or recited from memory texts they had prepared. But even as the others read, it was the fourth one who kept attracting Cochet's eye: the woodsman. Finally, Gérard took the floor.

"He had learned, I have no idea where, a text by Claudel, or maybe it was Jules Laforgue," Michel Arroyo recalls. "In any case, it was not an easy text, the role in no way fit Gérard, and when he delivered it in front of the class, it rang impossibly false. His recitation was completely out of synch with the words of the text. The students, aspiring actors of a horrible ferocity, all started laughing, and the scene was supposed to be sad. It was a disaster. A true disaster. But here we saw that Professor Cochet was no idiot. He did not laugh at all during the audition, and when it was over, he took Gérard aside and said, 'You can come back.'

" 'But your class,' Gérard replied, 'it costs.'

" 'Yes.'

" 'Well, I have no money.'

" 'Hmmm,' Cochet said. 'Okay, you can come back anyway.' "

This encounter proved to be crucial. At the outset, Cochet still expected this unusual young man to last only a few months in class, but Gérard quickly became a fervent, dedicated student. To Cochet's utter amazement, Gérard also revealed a delicacy and sensibility that were the exact opposite of his rough-hewn exterior. To Cochet's further surprise, this hulk of a young man, with his rude tattoos and bulging biceps, proved extremely docile in class. He listened to every word of advice and quickly applied them to his work on stage. Working with texts from Molière and Racine, he made rapid progress and seemed to catch fire. From this point on, Gérard plunged into the craft of acting with a hunger and zest that delighted the uncompromising Cochet.

"The success of this miraculous adventure was sealed almost as soon as Gérard began listening and watching with those gigantic eyes and ears of his," the professor recalls. "In working with the texts [of great authors], he discovered, first and foremost, the real happiness, the pure sensual pleasure of words and of all the ideas and feelings they could convey."

Using the classical French repertory as a foundation, Cochet put his pupils through the fundamentals of the craft. Once students had developed their memories and mastered the craft of recitation, improving to the point where they could recite long scenes with fluidity and freedom, Cochet would shift his focus to teaching these aspiring actors how to free their minds and bodies and their emotions. His aim was to enable the students to respond naturally and spontaneously to the chemistry of a scene, and then to respond to the chemistry of an entire play. Cochet believes, and teaches, that the true essence of the craft of acting is emotional liberation. Acting should not be mental work; it should be physical and emotional, almost as spontaneous as a child's game of make-believe: "From the moment you know how to reinvent a situation, to open up your imagination and really 'play' a comedy, you no longer need teaching or improvisation or cerebral effort. These are all compromises."

Within the first months, Gérard demonstrated everything Cochet wanted to see in an acting student: the presence, the voice, the ear, and most of all, the will to work and work and work. One day Gérard and three fellow students came to class with a project they had been developing on their own. While other students were content to prepare one scene from a play, these four had prepared a long section of a very difficult play by Alfred de Musset: *On ne badine pas avec l'amour* (Don't Trifle with Love). They were two men and two women, and they played out several major scenes, revealing the flow and continuity of the entire play. Gérard was clearly the driving force behind the venture, and Cochet was ecstatic. "This was the first time that a student had the idea, the drive, and the flair to present this kind of work," he says. "Another thing that was extraordinary about Gérard was that as soon as I would mention this or that play or book, it would be written in his head, and then he would obtain the book. He was consumed by passion, by desire, but he always remained just who he was. He was a gourmand, ingesting whatever he could to learn and become cultivated."

During this period, Gérard started taking classes in physical self-expression from Odette Laure, a famous French actress and teacher. Her approach was Oriental in inspiration, using yoga-style breathing and body movements to generate what she called a "corporal awakening." The course was difficult for Gérard. He was built like a lumberjack, and his idea of physical movement was playing the goal in soccer: lunging for a ball, blocking it with his fist, and then giving it a good boot. Grace and elegance of movement were not his forte. According to Cochet, Odette Laure was not impressed with Gérard. He was physically awkward and ill at ease, and while clearly he had talent, she was not sure he would be able to work through his many handicaps. On one occasion, she took Cochet aside and asked him why he was so enchanted by this young brute. Cochet was unbending:

"To my mind," says Cochet, "Gérard's look was so typical of the young people of the period that he seemed to me symbolic of his generation. So when Odette asked me, 'What do you expect us to do with a guy with that? What can he become?' I replied, a bit dramatically to make the point: 'I think he can become the premier actor of his time.' "

As Gérard moved deeper into the craft of acting, his friends began seeing subtle changes in his behavior outside of class. His usual ebullience and volatility were still lurking just under the surface, but now Gérard's cut-loose antics took a theatrical turn, often in scenes that would eerily anticipate his role in *Les Valseuses* a few years later. Late one night, Arroyo, Gérard, and Michel Demoule were heading home on the Métro, and they entered a car that was empty except for one old man. "Naturally, Gérard went and sat down right next to him," Arroyo recalls. "We sat opposite. Gérard took his Métro ticket, folded it, and pop!, stuck it in the old man's shoe. The old man was terrorized, of course, being all alone in the car. Gérard then turned to him and said, 'I'm going to eat your ear!' " After this very unpleasant introduction, Gérard soothingly told the man that it was all in fun, they were just acting students, no offense intended, have a very pleasant evening, *bonne nuit.* The old man may have been somewhat appeased, but it is a safe bet he took a close look over his shoulder as he headed out of the Métro.

By now, Gérard had no more doubts about the course he intended to pursue, and he pursued it with ferocity. The following summer, in 1967, Cochet was on vacation with a group of students in the south of France. One afternoon, out of the blue, Gérard showed up at the front gate, clad only in a bathing suit, as though he were just coming back to the house after a swim. Cochet had left him no address, but Gérard had nevertheless found a way to track him down; this was a family to which Gérard desperately wanted to belong. He moved right in, eating his way through the refrigerator and emptying a communal bottle of pastis. Once, he and his mentor talked all night long, to the irritation of everyone who was trying to sleep.

Gérard was now eighteen. It had been less than two years since he had left Châteauroux, but his entire life and frame of mind had radically shifted. After a boyhood of failure at school and believing that he may indeed be a dunce, here was the most esteemed drama professor in all of Paris grooming him and believing he had enormous talent. The work was exciting, he was being accepted and respected by the sons and daughters of the Paris elite, and in this milieu he did not have to brawl or constantly keep up his guard. He still could not speak very well, and next to the intellectuals in the class he felt hopelessly uncultured. But it seemed that all he had to do to please everyone was let go of some of what he had bottled up inside him, even if it in no way corresponded to the codes he had learned growing up in Châteauroux.

"What always struck me most about Gérard was his tenderness," Cochet says. "If I had just one quality by which to define him, it would be that, contrary to his appearance."

From this point on, Cochet and Odette Laure took full charge of developing every aspect of Gérard's talent. They taught him how to dress on stage, they fussed with his hair, and they moved him rapidly into the most demanding steps of an actor's apprenticeship. Cochet gave him difficult texts to prepare, starting with Musset, and the more they pushed Gérard, the more he seemed to thrive. But there was one imposing obstacle with which they made little or no headway: Gérard's agonized difficulties with speech, language, and delivery. They worked intensively to improve the quality of his voice, trying to make it less guttural and heavy, and they tried to teach him to modulate his speech patterns and to make them more rhythmic and lyrical. But for all their efforts, they produced poor results. "He had little vocabulary," Cochet says. "And while his speech was not completely blocked, it was harsh and lacked fluidity." The professor was convinced that buried inside Gérard was a knot Cochet could not untie. Gérard had more raw talent than Cochet had ever seen in a young man of eighteen, but he feared that unless that knot could be untied, all of Gérard's talent and potential would go undeveloped. And this, he felt, would be a tragedy of major proportions.

When Cochet realized that there was nothing more he could do about Gérard's speech problem, he turned to Dr. Alfred A. Tomatis, a controversial speech therapist and researcher. Cochet had worked with Tomatis for years, and he regularly sent him students for examinations of their hearing and speech. Tomatis had begun his career as a physician, first as a general practitioner and then as a specialist in the ear, nose, and throat. Then he turned his attention almost exclusively to the ear and to treating problems of hearing and speech. His theories about the ear and voice were unconventional, but many people in the arts community, especially singers at the Paris Opéra, considered Tomatis a true genius. Cochet was an unabashed believer, and he felt sure that if anybody could find a way to untie Gérard's knot and free up his voice, it would be Tomatis. So one morning, Professor Cochet recalls, he went into his private office and picked up the phone:

"Alfred, I won't give you the details; those you will see for yourself. But I have a young man here who is truly exceptional. To my mind, he has in front of him an extraordinary future. But he has serious problems. Very serious problems. I don't know where they come from, or what he may be missing. But please, Alfred, treat him. Take this young man and prepare him for his future."

9

Dr. Mozart

Gérard was apprehensive. He trusted Professor Cochet, and he was desperate for help, but he knew nothing about this Dr. Tomatis, and he figured that no one could fix the embarrassing speech problems he had been suffering his entire life. What could anyone do, replace his tongue? Still, nervous though he was, Gérard took the Métro to a stop near the Arc de Triomphe and then walked to a stately residential building just across the street from the Parc Monceau.

To Gérard's provincial eye, the building seemed the epitome of Parisian refinement. It housed a law firm and very fancy apartments, the brass in the entryway was freshly polished, and in the center of the hallway was a majestic staircase spiraling up like a freeway to the sky. This was not the kind of building you found in Châteauroux. The Centre Tomatis occupied an entire upper floor, and when Gérard walked in, he could scarcely believe his eyes. He was expecting to find a doctor's office, smelling mildly of disinfectant, but what he found was a lobby stylishly decorated with paintings and sculpture. Coming off the lobby were two big rooms filled with people wearing headphones. In one room, everyone seemed to be daydreaming, swaying to music, or looking out the window onto the lush greenery of the Parc Monceau. The other room contained brightly colored study carrels, and at each carrel someone in headphones was sketching or drawing or painting with watercolors. Between these rooms was a sophisticated sound studio, lined with electronic equipment and huge tape decks, their reels slowly turning. The atmosphere was hushed, reverential, and what was that exuberant music Gérard could just faintly discern escaping from all the headphones?

Dr. Alfred Tomatis

Mozart.

Totally bewildered, Gérard presented himself at the reception desk, and soon he was ushered in to see the august doctor himself. Professor Tomatis (pronounced Toe-mah-teese) greeted Gérard with his usual cheerful good humor. Then they sat down to talk. Physically, Tomatis was tall and self-assured. His hands were huge, his head was large and perfectly bald, and he had an engaging gap-toothed grin. Though Tomatis no longer practiced medicine, his manner remained that of an experienced physician: gentle, reassuring, fatherly. Despite his apprehensions, Gérard warmed to him right away, and as they talked, Tomatis could see that this young man was extremely troubled.

"He was very shy, very closed off," Tomatis recalls. "He wanted desperately to become an actor, and he thought he had it in him, but he feared he just could not accomplish it." And Tomatis could clearly see the source of Gérard's fears. "In size, he was already the giant we know today, with a fabulous musculature, but he was crippled by a voice which would not come forth. Very little came out. And worse, the harder he tried, the less it worked."

After their talk, Professor Tomatis sent Gérard for a series of seemingly simple diagnostic tests. In a soundproof booth, a lab technician fitted Gérard with headphones and began testing his hearing. First, tones were sent into his headphones, and Gérard had to signal as soon as he could make them out; each ear was tested separately. Then the technician repositioned the headphones, not on the ears, but one on the temple and one on the back of the skull. This was to measure how well Gérard's bone structure was resonating sound to his ears. The next phase of the testing measured how well Gérard could distinguish relative tones; he was to signal if the tone fed into his ear was higher or lower than the one before. Next came eight other checks, again deceptively simple. Point to an ear, to an eye, to the tester's eye. Look through a tube. Throw a ball. Kick a ball. Trace a square with one foot. Throw a punch. These were to determine if Gérard favored his right hand and foot or his left. Finally, to record the power and patterns of his voice, Gérard was told to speak for two minutes into a microphone.

Immediately after the tests, the results were mapped onto a graph, producing what Professor Tomatis calls a "hearing curve," a visual imprint of the functioning of Gérard's ears. Studying this hearing curve, Tomatis was able to conclude a first level of diagnosis: Gérard's hearing was completely out of kilter, and his right ear was severely damaged. "Gérard's right ear permitted him no regulation of incoming sound," Tomatis says. "Even when he spoke softly, what he heard was very loud."

Tomatis was not trained as a psychologist or a psychiatrist. But from the hearing curve, and from thirty years of treating similar speech problems, he was able to conclude a second level of diagnosis: that the cause of Gérard's ear damage was not physical but "purely psychological." He also concluded that Gérard's damaged right ear was disrupting two other domains of cerebral activity: memory and concentration. Tomatis was certain that this young man was caught in a tangle of emotional and psychological problems that made his life a nightmare. "Among young people, those who are overflowing with aggression and can no longer express themselves, somewhere they are wounded," the professor explains. "Gérard's was an extreme case. He had a terrific strength, he was capable of becoming very aggressive, and he could not express himself, which made things even worse. The most striking thing about his case was that when he wished to talk, he strangled himself. And when he tried to learn a text, he could retain nothing. He had no memory." Gérard knew this was true. When he started in with Tomatis, memorizing was agony for him, and even when he learned texts, he could not retain them for very long.

Tomatis did not explain his diagnosis to Gérard; he simply told the anxious youth in a very clear, simple way that he would put him into a program of treatment that would relieve his speech problems and allow him to pursue his interest in acting. What sort of treatment? Gérard asked. Surgery? Medication? Speech therapy? No. What Tomatis outlined to him was of an entirely different nature: "For the next several weeks, I want you to come here every day for two hours and listen to Mozart."

"Mozart?"

"Mozart."

"Ummm. . . . Do I have to pay?"

Tomatis just smiled. He realized the youth had no money. But he decided to take him on free of charge. "No, you don't have to pay."

Gérard left totally mystified. How in the world was listening to Mozart going to cure his speech problems? What was this bizarre treatment, witchcraft? Despite his doubts, the next day Gérard began coming to the Centre Tomatis for a daily two-hour dose of Mozart. Through his headphones, Gérard did not hear pure Mozart. The music was fed to him through a series of filters. Some days the filtering was minimal, and Gérard would hear a Mozart concerto with little distortion. But at other times the filtering was so thick that what he heard was little more than rhythmic scratchings. The whole business was strange and puzzling, but after just three or four sessions, Gérard started to notice marked changes in his physical and mental activities. His sleep pattern started fluctuating wildly, and so did his appetite and the level of his mental energy. And while the initial two-hour sessions were not exactly joyous, he found himself eagerly looking forward to each fresh injection of Mozart. Gérard sensed he was undergoing a momentous experience, even if he had no clue where it would lead.

What was this strange treatment, and where was it leading? Was it science, or was it, as Gérard first wondered, just witchcraft? To many specialists in the French medical and psychiatric communities, there is no doubt: Professor Tomatis and his ideas and treatments add up to only intriguing theory, with very little substance that has been scientifically proven. His vast array of critics, both inside and outside the medical community, insist that Tomatis is an eccentric, although an eccentric with a gift for self-serving public relations. Now in his seventies, Tomatis has been enduring such attacks throughout his professional career, and he has written a half-dozen books elaborating and defending his extensive theories and their scientific underpinnings. Today he operates more than one hundred and fifty centers across Europe, to treat disorders of the ear and speech. And despite the criticism he has taken,

Tomatis has not wavered in his core, defining conviction: that he has found an almost magical key for opening the mind's powers of language and speech, and also its powers of memory, concentration, and creativity.

In light of what happened to Gérard Depardieu through his course of treatment, Tomatis's ideas and methods demand precise and thorough examination. The specific way in which he treated Depardieu also requires a detailed recounting.*

The clearest way to enter the complex ideas of Alfred Tomatis is by following the evolution of his life and work, as the impetus for his medical career and research can be traced back to his own childhood traumas. His mother was Italian, his father French, and Tomatis was born in Nice in 1919. He was born prematurely, six and a half months into his mother's pregnancy, and when he emerged from the womb, his family believed he was dead. He weighed under three pounds and showed no signs of life. As Tomatis recounts in his autobiography, *The Conscious Ear,* while everyone else in the family plunged into anguish and began consoling his sixteen-year-old mother, he was revived by a perceptive grandmother. The incident engendered in him a lifelong commitment to studying science and medicine. It also inspired in him a particular interest in life inside the womb, an important part of his research.

Tomatis's research stemmed also from another childhood trauma. He grew up in a home where the common language was the insular dialect of the Midi. French to him was a foreign language, and he spoke it poorly. In school this proved to be a terrible embarrassment—and also a potent incentive. With great effort, Tomatis overcame his weakness with French, completed his studies in Nice, and, intent on studying medicine, went to Paris and enrolled at the Sorbonne. World War II interrupted his studies. Tomatis was drafted into the army, and he served in the light infantry until he was taken prisoner by the German Army. He managed to escape, and when France surrendered, he returned to medical school in Paris.

During the years of Nazi occupation, Tomatis studied general medicine and neurology, and he became intent on specializing in the ear, nose, and throat. When the Allies landed in Normandy and the bomb-

* For this biography, and with Depardieu's permission, Professor Tomatis agreed to talk extensively about his own work and about this particular case. To illustrate his unusual approach, Tomatis also suggested that the author undergo a process of diagnosis and treatment similar to that of Depardieu. The author agreed. What follows is based on interviews with Tomatis and his staff, on a reading of Tomatis's books, on talks with Depardieu and other former Tomatis patients, and on the author's own two-week immersion in the Tomatis methodology and treatment.

ing of Paris intensified, like most medical students he began treating the wounded. After the war, he went into private practice, and he also became a consulting physician to the Army air corps, treating men whose hearing had been damaged by exposure to gunfire, explosions, or roaring jet aircraft. This proved key to his later work. Using an audiometer he imported from America, Tomatis began testing these men with damaged hearing, and he began studying how their occupational deafness was also disrupting their motor skills and their general psychological stability. He saw a pattern: Damage to the ear often led to damage of the mind and other parts of the body.

Now Tomatis's primary focus became the human ear. At the same time, he became intrigued by problems of voice and speech. Umberto Tomatis, his father, was an opera singer, and in his private practice the son now began treating professional singers with voice problems. At one stage, two of his father's colleagues, both baritones, came to him with the same complaint: they could no longer hit particular notes. At that time, the accepted medical wisdom was that all voice problems originated in the throat and larynx. As Tomatis wrote in *The Conscious Ear* (quoted here from the English edition): "According to the prevailing theory, vocal quality was under the strict control of the larynx, which had to be regarded as a musical instrument." But when Tomatis examined the singers, he could find no evident damage to their throats or larynxes. So Tomatis wondered about their ears. How was their hearing?

He tested the singers with the same audiometric equipment he was using with the air corps, and the results were clear: The "hearing curves" of the ailing singers proved to be strikingly similar to those of airmen whose hearing had been damaged by roaring aircraft or explosions. The baritones had suffered hearing loss. But what had caused the damage? Using his audiometric equipment, Tomatis now carried out a series of experiments. He placed a gauge a meter from the singers' lips and had them sing just as they would in rehearsal and at performances. As a cross-check, he tested the voices of many other singers. Tomatis's findings were dramatic:

"Good professional singers were emitting 80 to 90 decibels when singing at half-strength. At the full extent of their powers, they easily reached 110, 130, even 140 decibels. At a meter's distance, 130 decibels represents 150 decibels inside one's skull," he wrote. This was an ear-shattering level: some jet engines of the period, turning at ground-level speeds, registered only 132 decibels. The singers therefore had the equivalent of jet engines reverberating inside their heads. No wonder their ears might be susceptible to damage.

But the singers' impaired hearing did not explain why they were unable to sing particular notes. Tomatis set forth a startling hypothesis: The voice can produce only those notes the ear is able to hear. If a singer cannot properly hear a note, then he cannot reproduce it with his voice. In singers with ailing voices, the trouble was often not in the larynx but in the ear. To encapsule his premise, Tomatis set forth this maxim: "One sings with one's ear."

To test his hypothesis and explore its implications, the professor now studied the voice quality of the legendary Italian tenor Enrico Caruso. Though Caruso had died in 1921, there existed many recordings of his performances, and these Tomatis tested with his sound equipment. He found that from 1896 to 1902, the quality of Caruso's voice was impressive but not dazzling. But after 1902, his voice quality suddenly improved, exhibiting all the purity and majesty for which he became so famous. Tomatis could hear the change, and his tests also showed a quantifiable improvement in voice quality. "Below 2,000 hertz there was always a drop of at least 18 decibels per octave toward the low notes. It was as if Caruso had benefited from some sort of a filter which allowed him to hear, basically, high frequency sounds rich in harmonics, as opposed to lower frequency fundamental sounds."

But what had caused this filtering and this sudden improvement in voice quality? Looking for clues, Tomatis read several biographies of Caruso, and in one of them he discovered that in late 1901 or early 1902, the tenor had undergone an unspecified surgical operation on the right side of his face. "The author said nothing more about it, but I imagined what might have happened," Tomatis wrote. "His Eustachian tube was damaged, causing a partial deafness that resulted in his transformation from a gifted singer to the greatest vocalist in the world! Following his operation, Caruso no longer heard the lower frequencies. He sang so remarkably well because he could no longer hear except in the singing range."

Now Tomatis began to see a whole new field opening up for his focus on the ear. If the ear, not the larynx, controlled the voice, could voice and speech disorders be unraveled and cured by treating the ear? And if the quality of Caruso's voice had soared because he was hearing music through "some sort of filter," could a damaged voice be cured by hearing music through another form of filter?

To test these ideas, Tomatis developed a crude prototype of what he calls the "electronic ear." In simplified terms, this device was designed to feed filtered music into a patient's ears, via tapes and headphones. The filtering forced the ear to adjust itself to a range of unaccustomed frequencies. Inspired by the techniques of Pavlov, Tomatis felt that if this readjustment could be imposed on the ear over and over for two hours per day for several weeks, a person's entire pattern of hearing could be re-educated. That, in turn, could help to rehabilitate a damaged voice. Put simply, Tomatis believed that if he could cure the ear, he could cure the voice.

Initial research with the electronic ear convinced Tomatis that his theory held promise. But how could he entice patients to sit through two hours of intensive ear re-education every day for weeks and, in more serious cases, for months? Enter Wolfgang Amadeus Mozart. In experimental testing, patients told Tomatis and his staff that Mozart was enchanting to the ear, and his musical oeuvre was so rich and diverse, they rarely got bored. Tomatis also favored Mozart's music because it was especially rich in high-frequency tones, a problem area in many speech disorders.

By similar research and testing, Tomatis developed his primary tool for diagnosing a patient's hearing problems and evaluating his progress in treatment: the hearing curve, the visual imprint of an individual's hearing pattern. According to Tomatis, these curves are like fingerprints; everyone's hearing curve is distinctive. Through diagnostic tests—the same ones Gérard went through—Tomatis and his staff produce two hearing curves. One is a person's ideal hearing curve, showing which frequencies and tones he should be able to hear, and how well. The other shows how the person's ear and hearing are actually performing. The ideal hearing curve usually shows one smooth arc. The real one is often filled with jagged ranges of distortion, and sometimes even breaks, at frequencies where a patient with damaged ears hears no incoming sound at all. By comparing the two curves. Tomatis and his specialists can pinpoint and measure ear damage, in precise or broad ranges of frequencies.

It is the distortions or breaks in the curve that lead Tomatis and his specialists to the underlying problems affecting a patient's speech, whether these problems are physical or "purely psychological," as in the case of Gérard. Indeed, Tomatis and his staff can read hearing curves as though they were comprehensive charts of physical and psychological health. At Tomatis's center in Paris, after the initial diagnostic hearing tests new patients meet with Dominique Cavé, a psychologist and one of Tomatis's chief supervisors since the time he treated Depardieu. First Cavé studies a patient's hearing curves, then she asks the patient a series of questions. In one case, for instance, Cavé studied the patient's two hearing curves and she opened her questioning this way:

"How long have you had trouble with your lower back?"

"What?"

"How long have you had these lower back problems?"

"Uh, since college. You can see those on the chart?"

"Of course. Now, I see that you had a serious illness at the age of seven. Do you recall what that was?"

"What? You can see *that* from a hearing test?"

"Of course. Now, I can see that you have had a long and very deep interest in painting, and that when it comes to music, you have a fine feel for harmony, but rhythm is a problem. . . . I also see that your digestive system is too acidic. We'll have to work on that."

How does all this emerge from a hearing test? And from a test that appears no more complex than what children might get from the school nurse? The answers are to be found in the importance of the ear in relation to the rest of the body and the brain. Through his research, Tomatis became convinced that the ear plays a far more important role in the way the body works than most people suspect, including many doctors. It is accepted medical wisdom that the inner ear controls balance and verticality; people with ear infections often suffer dizziness or motion sickness. Tomatis notes that an ear disorder can disrupt everything from posture and digestion to physical and even mental equilibrium. He also believes that the inner ear and its hypersensitive vestibule together control "the entire musculature of the body." Tomatis draws a sharp distinction between what the ear physically receives and the messages the brain actually decodes and "hears." There can be physical problems in the ear itself, or problems in the linkage of the ear to the brain, he says.

According to Tomatis, the ear is vital to the functioning of the brain. As he explains in *The Conscious Ear,* zoologists have shown that the ear supplies energy, in the form of sound waves, to the brain. Indeed, he says, one of the ear's primary functions is to flood the brain and central nervous system with sound waves and energy. High-frequency sounds transmitted harmoniously, as in the music of Mozart, are especially beneficial in stimulating the brain and its multiple activities, Tomatis believes. Through his own research and physiological tests carried out by other scientists, Tomatis found that the ear transmits sound waves and energy to the brain and central nervous system according to a specific pattern. In basic terms, higher frequencies move to the uppermost reaches of the body and the brain. Lower frequencies resonate to lower regions of the body. In effect, each frequency "massages" a precise part of the body. If a damaged ear blocks sound waves coming in at a particular frequency, a corresponding part of the brain or body will suffer; it will not receive its proper "sonic massage." Ear damage at one frequency might lead to back problems; damage at another sound frequency might lead to stomach trouble.

This is how Tomatis's hearing curves turn into fingerprints of a patient's physical and psychological health. If Cavé sees a distortion or a break in a particular frequency, that may lead her to ask, "And how long have you had these back problems?" A break in another part of the hearing curve might suggest that the liver or the digestive tract is not receiving its proper massage. Similarly, a break in the higher frequency levels might suggest that the uppermost parts of the brain are not receiving their proper sonic massage, with the result being disruptions in language, speech, and memory function. Such breaks or ranges of distortion suggest that there has been trauma, either physical or psychological. Utilizing a deeper level of analysis, Tomatis and Cavé can even find indications of the exact age at which the patient suffered the trauma.

Now the governing principles of the Tomatis course of treatment come to the fore. Using the hearing curve as a map, Tomatis filters the music of Mozart in ways that will target "sonic massage" to the damaged ranges of a patient's ears and hearing. Repeated daily, these sonic massages force the ear to readjust and reopen itself to the full range of incoming frequencies. As the ear opens, the body as a whole then receives its proper sonic stimulation. Once the body and the central nervous system and vital organs are properly stimulated, the full system regains its proper harmony, equilibrium, and energy flows. In a conception of the body similar to that of traditional Chinese medicine, Tomatis believes that when the ear regains its full capacity to funnel energy to the brain and body, and when this energy flows properly throughout the central nervous system, the body's own internal power of healing will naturally relieve problems of the back, posture, sinuses—and even speech.

For more than three decades now, Tomatis has been using this unique system to treat stammering and stuttering, with results that he, and many patients, say are excellent. He also treats problems of memory and concentration, and other learning disorders, including dyslexia. Using a similar approach, Tomatis has also tried to treat other disorders, including schizophrenia and autism, but here he has had only very limited success. Tomatis has written up his work in several volumes, but the French medical establishment complains that it has never had a proper chance to evaluate his casework or verify his success rate. In 1992, his work came under another barrage of criticism in the French press.

Against this background, how did the Tomatis method work in the specific case of Depardieu? In his diagnosis, Tomatis found that Gérard's ears, and especially the right ear, were so badly damaged that he was incapable of regulating the intake of sound. Instead of acting as a filter, the ear was like an open valve, allowing too much sound to rush into the brain and central nervous system. As a result, Gérard was constantly flooded with in-rushing sound. His brain was flooded and overwhelmed with noise, way beyond his capacity to decode the meaning of what he was hearing. "When you have someone who can no longer decode sound, he becomes incapable of defending himself against noise," Tomatis explains. "He hears badly, and all sound now assaults him. He receives too much noise, all at once. And that becomes very painful."

This flood of sound broke down the linkage between Gérard's ear and voice, and that breakdown, in turn, crippled his ability to speak. With the collapse of his means of self-expression, Gérard's psyche became like an inward-exploding bomb. "If someone has psychological problems, he stops listening to his body, and he cuts himself off completely. He enters into a state of alienation. Everything implodes. His life becomes a nightmare," Tomatis says.

This implosion of distorted sounds and energy provoked even graver damage, Tomatis says. "Gérard was not able to distinguish between what was real and what was not. The world appeared to him as if he were seeing it through a glass that distorts everything," Tomatis explains. "That meant the brain was obliged constantly to try to re-establish a true image—a huge effort. When somebody said something to Gérard, he had trouble knowing if this was real or not. That might be okay for one sentence. But after three sentences, or ten, it becomes fatiguing and debilitating. Worse, when he tried to speak, he had to pass back through this distorted glass. It was terrible."

But how can the ear itself become damaged by causes that are "purely psychological," as Tomatis contends? "Suppose that in my life," Tomatis explains, "I had heard voices which were harsh and hurtful. As a means of self-protection against hurtful voices, the ear literally shuts down, tunes out. And it does so selectively, at that precise place in the hearing curve, to protect the psyche from assaults coming in at that particular frequency. . . . This I call 'selective closing.' If a father's voice is extremely warm, it will lead us toward sociability. If it is harsh and aggressive, if it throws at us all sorts of nasty names, we cut off the sound right there. But we also cut off the relationship with that person. Someone who is constantly assaulted verbally, or whose mother is always on his back, his ear will crash. If you have a father who verbally assaults you every day and a mother who does not love you, what do you do? You slam down the curtain."

Slam down the curtain. This is a phenomenon Tomatis has observed and treated with opera singers, with troubled children, and with soldiers suffering wartime trauma. Soldiers who had been exposed to bombings, gunfire, and engine roar suffered hearing loss for purely physical reasons but also because their psyches in effect slammed down curtains to protect themselves against incoming noise, Tomatis says. He insists that the voice of a parent can be just as damaging as an exploding bombshell. The hearing curves of troubled youths like Gérard can thus be read as a detailed psychological profile. The lower registers of the hearing curve usually correspond to the range of a father's voice, and a break in these registers often suggests that the patient had a problem with his father. A break in the higher registers would suggest a tuning out of the mother's voice, and therefore of the mother herself. In treating young children suffering with speech problems, Tomatis often has the mother record her voice on tape, and then these tapes are used with the Mozart in the course of the treatment, to gently re-educate the child to accept his mother's voice.

Tomatis never questioned Gérard about the traumas of his childhood. But from the hearing curves, and his own intuition, Tomatis divined the broad outlines of Gérard's emotional turmoil with Lilette and Dédé, and of the frustrations of family life with six children living in very cramped quarters. Having grown up struggling to speak French as a second language, Tomatis also knew what Gérard had suffered in school with his stuttering and stammering. Classical psychologists and psychiatrists might have established a course of therapy in which Gérard would revisit his early childhood traumas. But Tomatis avoids anything resembling Freudian analysis. While he does receive referrals from psychiatrists and psychologists, in his own framework of theory and treatment Tomatis keeps his focus on re-educating the damaged ear and hearing functions, and removing any distorting blockages. He believes that with a full nourishment of Mozart and sonic energy, the brain and psyche regain their natural balance and heal themselves.

"The electronic ear gives you the euphoria of listening," Tomatis explains, "and above all, it restores the ear to its full, deep functioning—a functioning completely forgotten even by most doctors. If you have many problems, I have the good fortune to furnish your brain with enormous energy. And when I light up your brain, it is intelligent. It will look at those problems, put them back into proportion, and the result will be healing."

In Gérard's case, Tomatis prescribed a typical first phase of treatment: sixty hours of listening to filtered Mozart. The selections generally include *A Little Night Music*; symphonies number 40 and 41; the youthful symphonies number 1, 8, 9, 29, and 33; and various concertos for piano, flute, and violin. The individualized filtering Gérard received on any given day depended on his hearing profile and the precise stage in his treatment. During his sessions, Gérard, like most patients, was told to refrain from intellectual activities such as reading and writing. Sleeping is permitted, as Tomatis believes the effects of "sonic massage" can even work when the mind is not fully awake.

In addition to the almost immediate and profound shifts in his sleeping and eating patterns, Gérard also reported improvements in his posture and levels of energy. All these are typical reactions, according to Tomatis and Cavé. In some cases, the first days of treatment can plunge the patient into a state of lethargy and fatigue; if so, he is encouraged to sleep as much as he likes, in order to give his sleep pattern a chance to readjust. As treatment progresses, the patient's sleep often becomes deeper and shorter. This, too, happened with Gérard, with lasting effect. Always an early riser, he can now function well on three or four hours of sleep a night.

During his sessions with Mozart, Gérard was urged to engage in unstructured creative activity, especially sketching or painting. Tomatis prizes visual expression; the paintings and sculpture in his lobby were given to him by his patients, many of whom had never before shown creative interest or talent. In their first days of treatment, some patients use their Mozart sessions as a pleasant interlude in their work or school day, a welcome pause for sorting through this problem or that. But after a few days, and especially when sketching or painting helps a patient to put all thinking aside, the patient begins to experience the "euphoria of listening" that Tomatis described. For some patients, this euphoria is reminiscent of happy childhood memories of drawing or doing watercolors or making model ships or planes. Cavé encourages this childlike joy by steering patients away from trying to sketch anything figurative or highly intricate; that demands too much cognitive and intellectual effort. Instead she urges patients to allow the music of Mozart to flow out into color. This emphasis on visual expression is designed to help patients break free of the barriers of rational thought and language—French in particular.

"French is a rational language," Tomatis explains, "and if you venture too far into rationality, you become alienated. Rationality leads you to believe only in reason. True thinking was killed by Descartes, because Descartes locked us into a system of rational thinking. With Cartesian analysis and synthesis, you are operating within a framework that is mechanistic and systematic. Einstein was intuition. He listened in the manner of a great singer."

In the case of Gérard, his hearing damage and speech disorders were so acute that his treatment took several months longer than with most patients. He also required additional exercises to re-establish the proper harmony between his ear and his voice. These included reading into a microphone and hearing the playback of his own voice in a set of headphones, but with a brief delay, in order to jolt his ear and stimulate its re-education. Gérard also listened to many hours of Gregorian chants, to help restore his hearing in the lower, "paternal" registers. As the treatment unfolded, Tomatis and his staff monitored a series of marked changes in Gérard. His mental energy increased, and his powers of memory and concentration improved radically. As his psychic tension eased, some of his very disturbing aggressiveness seemed to drain away. As his treatment progressed, the curve showing Gérard's actual hearing smoothed out. The cumulative effect was a progressive restoration of his innate powers of hearing, speech, and memory.

"We were lucky with Gérard," Tomatis says. "As we re-established his proper ear and as we liberated his mental energy, the improvement was stark; he refound his voice and his memory."

From the beginning, Tomatis sensed that Depardieu was an exceptional case, and, like Cochet, he never charged a franc for the months of care he gave Gérard. But Tomatis was still very surprised by what surfaced during the course of treatment. Once Gérard's physical and psychological blockages were cleared away, and once his innate powers of speech and memory were allowed to surface, Tomatis and Cochet both could see that Gérard possessed astounding gifts and capacities: an extraordinary creative intelligence, a near-photographic memory, and an ear with perfect musical pitch—all in a youth whose performance at school had been so lackluster. How to explain it?

Though Gérard was surely born with unusual capacities, Tomatis is convinced that, paradoxically, the same childhood traumas that had crippled Gérard's speech actually wound up enriching his imagination, his consciousness, and his mental prowess. In simplified terms, all the monstrous trauma and emotions he had absorbed throughout his early years, but could never express, kept imploding, enriching his dreams, his fantasy life, and his creativity. "We are midwives," Tomatis says of himself and his staff. "We cannot give anyone intelligence; we can only help someone find his intelligence and exploit it, to the maximum of his potential. . . .

"Ironically, the more troubles we have as a child, often the luckier we are. If you look at Depardieu, everything came from inside him. He had all the troubles on earth—as an infant, a child, and later. And that is part of what makes him a great artist: He understands everyone else. He had so many problems and so many obstacles to overcome that at a certain point there was a conversion, and those problems became a vast archive, storing what he needed to know to understand others."

The results of Gérard's treatment flowed directly into his work with Cochet. Tomatis suggested that Gérard read aloud his required texts so that his ear, his eye, and his voice would all be engaged simultaneously. When Gérard applied this technique, memorizing ceased being an epic struggle. And now when he took to the stage to recite a passage or perform a role, Gérard no longer suffered a panicky, choking feeling. Now he found he could perform long passages of even the most complicated texts with ease and fluidity. It would take him much more work with Cochet to develop his acting technique and prowess, but with his new freedom of speech, Gérard was no longer flooded with anxiety, and his confidence began to grow rapidly.

Part of the credit for this, Gérard believes, belongs to Mozart. Whatever the difficulties of growing up in Châteauroux, Gérard never entered into the rigid schema of the French language, with all its formality, its rules, its socializing diktats, and its subservience to Cartesian logic and reason. Gérard feels that Mozart taught him a whole new language: the language of music, poetry, intuition, and the emotions. "With so little schooling, I grew up with no inhibitions regarding language," Gérard says. "And when I started working with Tomatis and Cochet, I saw each word with its own visual image. And when I read Racine and Molière, I heard the words as music."

This was key: hearing the words as music seemed to magically unlock all Gérard's powers of memory and concentration. Like a musical prodigy who could hear a melody once and remember it forever, Gérard now found he could read a poem or a scene only once, and if he was drawn into its internal harmony and rhythms, he could remember complete passages without a single flaw. The discovery of this gift was a joy and a relief for Gérard. Just yesterday, or so it seemed, he was an embarrassing failure at school. Now he might not be the *petit Mozart* his Grandma Suzanne had foreseen, and he was still a long way from envisioning himself playing Cyrano de Bergerac. But now Gérard had a strong sense of hope—hope that one day he could overcome some of the educational and cultural handicaps that just a few months before he had believed to be insurmountable.

His fellow drama students saw Gérard's transformation, and so did Cochet: "Gérard had found a passion, a desire. He plunged into books, grooming himself and accumulating knowledge. People imagine that it's simple to master the craft of acting. You have a good physique, you have temperament, and *hop!*—you learn lines and play a role. Of course, it is the exact opposite. Mastering the craft of acting is as demanding, as complex, and as subtle as learning music or any other art form. Acting is almost an exact science, and Gérard was now determined to master all of it."

The transformation was even more apparent to the friends who had known Gérard back in Châteauroux. "All at once with Gérard there was what I would call an illumination," says Michel Arroyo. "Everyone could see it." Alain Depardieu believes the transformation probably saved his kid brother. "What Gérard discovered inside himself was a raging talent, and I have always said that if Gérard had not gone into the theater, he probably would have wound up in jail, if he had survived at all."

Michel Pilorgé, along with several other students in Cochet's class, also went to Tomatis to improve his ear and his voice. He was so impressed by the results of his own treatment that later in life, after a psychological trauma, he would go back to Tomatis, and he sent his children to him as well. Still, Michel was frankly awed by Gérard's transformation. He had known Gérard as an aggressive, tongue-tied punk in Châteauroux, as a shy, well-mannered beach boy in Cannes, and now as the star of the most prestigious acting course in Paris. As he watched Gérard's hidden gifts emerge, Michel knew he was witnessing a stunning event: the birth of an artist.

"In one of our first assignments for Cochet, I worked with Gérard on a poem by Jules Laforgue, and he had no memory at all. But in less than a year, he developed a prodigious memory. And he started nourishing himself with everything he could read or get hold of, anything that would enrich his mind and his talent," Michel says. "He seemed able to integrate whatever he learned into his very being. Inside of a year, he became someone completely different and yet completely the same. He acquired the language he didn't have, all the while keeping the originality and the freshness he had had in the first place."

In the fall of 1965, when he left Châteauroux and came to Paris,

Gérard had vowed to remake his life. By the summer of 1967, less than two years later, he had done just that. Through a series of remarkably fortuitous encounters, he had discovered his talent for acting. In the theater community of Paris he had found a family of kindred spirits who gave him warmth and acceptance. He had met the most esteemed drama professor in Paris and made him his mentor, and after suffering years of humiliating speech problems, he had found relief from one of the most prominent voice specialists in all of Europe. With the help of Cochet and Tomatis, he had gone through a profound awakening, almost a rebirth. In terms of art, literature, and the theater, he knew he was still a primitive, and he still believed he would never be worthy of the affection of a golden *parisienne*. But for a dropout who had arrived in Paris without a centime in his pocket, Gérard knew he had come a long way—further than he could have possibly imagined on that fateful day when he had seen Michel Pilorgé coming into the railway station in Châteauroux.

"Jean-Laurent Cochet opened for me the craft of acting, and Alfred Tomatis opened me up to language," Gérard says. "Before Tomatis, I could not complete any of my sentences. It was he who helped give continuity to my thoughts, and it was he who gave me the power to synthesize and understand what I was thinking. But Michel Pilorgé was also key. Michel showed me that there could be another route, another itinerary. Through him, I encountered another world, a world where I saw hope. I saw it was possible. You can. Whatever it is you want, you *can* seize it."

As a drama student in the late 1960s

10

Le Képi

On March 8, 1966, the townspeople of Châteauroux were quietly going about their business when stunning news arrived from Paris: General de Gaulle was ordering American troops off French soil. In a dramatic rupture with its Western allies, the French government announced it was cutting its military ties to NATO, pulling all French troops out of the NATO command, and ordering the closure of all NATO bases in France. By unilateral decree, de Gaulle was also ordering the NATO high command to fold up its headquarters outside Paris and leave France. The communiqués from the Elysée Palace set forth this dramatic decision in more diplomatic terms, but in Châteauroux the message was heard loud and clear: Yankee Go Home! Now!

"It was a stunning blow for the town," says Joe Gagné. "No one had ever imagined the base could close overnight."

But close it would, and at what most Castelroussins considered to be a very inopportune moment. For the first time since the war, and really for the first time in its history, the town was enjoying real prosperity, almost a golden era. Most of the initial tensions between the French and American communities had been bridged or erased. Some ten thousand Americans were living in town and pumping massive quantities of dollars into the local economy. The French population had swelled to fifty thousand, some five thousand Frenchmen were working at the base, and thousands more were working in related industries or services. The postwar gloom of high unemployment and lack of investment had come to an end, as new businesses opened and catered to the bustling base at La Martinerie. The *quartier* of Omelon was typical of the new prosperity. It had become a thriving middle-class enclave, with its own small shops and amenities, and its own microeconomy. Dédé and Lilette Depardieu were on a more solid footing as well. Gérard was in Paris studying theater, Alain was at the *lycée* studying industrial design, Dédé had a steady job, and Hélène was busy going to school and working at two part-time jobs to help support the family. After the birth of their sixth child, Dédé and Lilette even had the means to move the family into a home of their own, two blocks away. Their new house was a pleasant, functional little two-story structure with plenty of room for a garden out front, more room in back, and ample space for the family inside. The house was also ideally located just across the street from the Ecole de l'Omelon, thus easing Lilette's daily burdens in keeping track of her three youngest children.

In other parts of France, de Gaulle's decision to close the bases was applauded as a masterful stroke. But as a result, in part, of their new prosperity, the people of Châteauroux became incensed at de Gaulle's decision. What was going to happen to the five thousand Frenchmen working at the NATO base? What would the base closure mean for the rest of the Castelroussins? What would happen to their shops and businesses, which for the past fifteen years had boomed thanks to American trade? Was Châteauroux now destined to sink back into economic depression and decline? No one knew, and again the town felt itself hostage to international politics. Like so much else that happened to their town and their lives, all the power of decision making remained in the hands of Paris and came down to them in unilateral decrees. And the specific target of their anger now was the same target chosen by millions of Americans who were shocked by the decision: General Charles de Gaulle.

But once the general had made up his mind, and made up the mind of his government, there was no stopping the closing of the NATO bases around France. Out on the huge runways and in the cavernous hangars at La Martinerie, the Americans packed up all their materiel and shipped it to U.S. bases across West Germany, still the front line in the cold war. Planes, radar equipment, machine shops, and office supplies were crated and shipped, and so were all the fixtures of the American community that had grown up around the NATO base and its military mission. Families packed up and moved out of Brassioux and Touvent. The PX closed its doors. The American high school and all its books and desks were boxed and shipped to England. And in a touch of efficiency—and pique—that would remain legend in Châteauroux for decades to come, the Americans dismantled the golf course they had built at the base, and they even dug up the greens and sent the sod to a U.S. base in West Germany.

"I remember the night when the last of the Americans said their farewells to the Castelroussins out at Belle Isle," wrote the journalist Maurice Croze. The setting sun struck the town's lone skyscraper and colored its walls red, then blue. "Rapidly, the whole town became blue like those walls," Croze wrote. "Châteauroux realized that the American soldiers, who had brought us an ephemeral prosperity, were about to cross the Atlantic. This was one of the last nights when the town saw the full illusion of streets bustling with cars gleaming with American plenitude. In the nightclubs, the Blue Moon and Le Crazy, those whom chance alone had brought together now drank a final round. Good-bye, Rocky. Good-bye, Joe."

Those clubs soon disappeared, and most traces of Americana were quickly erased as well. Before the last Americans were gone, the price of real estate collapsed, though not at the former American enclave of Brassioux. The French company running it was flooded with bids for the American ranch houses with the big refrigerators and the American sinks and faucets. The French Army took over La Martinerie, including its advanced facilities and its massive three-kilometer runways. As France was rapidly becoming one of the world's largest exporters of military hardware and technology, the base would remain a hub for the French military and arms industry for years to come. In the late 1960s, South Africa trained pilots there. Throughout the 1980s, the air base would be the principal loading zone and point of embarkation for the tons of arms and materiel France was shipping to one of its biggest clients in the Middle East: Iraq.

Joe Gagné had been there at the creation of the NATO base, and he was there at the end. He and his wife stayed on and retired to a cottage outside town. Their daughter and her daughter today are keeping the family business going, but for Joe it is all history: his hamburgers and Budweisers, his anti-brawl fire extinguisher, and his legendary Ford Fairlane convertible. "De Gaulle's decision was the end of an era," Joe says, sitting in his living room by the old stone fireplace. "Now I'm the only one left."

After the closure of the base, Gérard rarely came back to Châteauroux. He was now preoccupied with becoming an actor and remaking his life in Paris. When he did return, it was not a happy time, and sometimes it was downright miserable, such as the day in 1968 when he came back for the funeral of Jacky Merveille. To the bourgeoisie of Châteauroux, Jacky was a wild young thug, but to Gérard and his friends, Jacky had been a charismatic rebel and a loyal friend. Even Hélène, who often did not approve of her brother's friends, had liked Jacky. "He was a tough guy," she says, "but he was not a real hoodlum." His fate had not been pretty. Jacky got drunk one night, stole a car with a friend, and wound up driving off one of the town's bridges and drowning in the Indre River. Search parties spent two days looking for the bodies; Jacky's was finally found wrapped around a pylon.

Gérard was a wreck at the funeral. All of Jacky's friends were there, and Gérard wailed and wailed at the gravesite. To him, Jacky meant *les quatres-cents coups;* he meant rebellion, kicks, freedom, and a hearty "Up yours" to the town's oppressive caste system and suffocating provincial ways. When Jacky was lowered into the ground, it was like burying a period of Gérard's own life, burying his last days as Pétarou. Gérard says that a strange thing happened as he watched the coffin lowered into the ground. For a long moment, he could see Jacky hovering above the lid, looking at Gérard with a devilish grin.

Gérard came back to Châteauroux another time in 1968, and this was not a happy visit either. During this period he was in Paris studying with Cochet and he was in treatment with Professor Tomatis. He was nineteen, and his main concern was educating himself and filling in the awful gaps in his knowledge of theater and literature. But all around him was a rising political rebellion, generated by a small, merry band of self-styled revolutionaries headquartered at the Sorbonne. In terms of background and upbringing, Gérard felt little rapport with these students from privileged Parisian families; he often felt they had no idea how fortunate they were. Gérard also had no time for politics, be it student politics, French politics, or international politics. By instinct, he was a rugged individualist with a streak of anarchy; he suspected that all politicians were a bunch of phonies.

But there is no escaping politics in Paris. As the capital of France, and with all its machinery of government, administration, and finance, Paris and its daily life are permeated with politics, from fixing parking tickets to the elections of grammar-school PTAs, and to getting your child into the day-care center of your choice. Politics is also woven deep into the fabric of the cultural and intellectual life of the city, and the entire country. The minister of culture holds one of the most powerful positions in France, and in the realms of art, theater, film, dance, museums, and schools for the arts, he wields influence unmatched in any other country. Be it the André Malraux of the de Gaulle era or the Jack Lang of the 1980s and early '90s, the minister of culture can shape the cultural life of the nation and literally change the face of cultural Paris.

With the approval of the President of the Republic, he can construct a museum in the center of the city, and he can put a post-modern pyramid in the courtyard of the Louvre. France, more effectively than any other country in the world, has also made culture a primary element of its foreign policy, setting for itself the mission of trying to civilize the world through the radiance of French culture and the French language.

Gérard understood none of this when he first came to Paris, but the student rebellion in May 1968 gave him a crash course. Inspired by the example of such intellectuals as Jean-Paul Sartre and Simone de Beauvoir, many of the Parisian students surrounding him in drama class saw political activism not as an adjunct to their studies but as a central requirement for their intellectual and cultural development. To Gérard, though, political activism seemed alien and abstract, a luxury for the rich, and when thousands of students and workers took to the streets and shut down the Sorbonne in the famous uprising now known simply as "May '68," Gérard remained immune to the fever.

"For me, May '68 was not very interesting," he says. "It was not a revolution. It was an event for the bourgeois—people who had nothing in common with me. People who were cultivated, who knew how to read, who knew how to write, who knew how to speak."

Still, Gérard could not escape the upheavals, as the student and worker rebellion reached right into the worlds of art and theater and cinema. The New Wave film directors Jean-Luc Godard and François Truffaut took the revolution down to the annual Cannes Film Festival, and in Paris the protesters shut down most of the theaters and drama schools. Some professors might have wanted to teach, but their pupils were in the streets. Gérard had further reason to feel estranged from the student radicals: their uprising cut short his very first role on the stage. Cochet was putting on a small production of *Boudu Sauvé des Eaux* (Boudu Saved from Drowning), a play drawn from the 1932 movie by Jean Renoir starring Michel Simon. "It was his first time on stage, and it was only a small role," says Cochet, "but Gérard was delicious. As a student he was shy and discreet, and on stage he was charming and unaffected."

When the student rebellion closed down the play, and Paris was paralyzed by day and locked in street fighting by night, Gérard and Michel Pilorgé went south to Châteauroux for a breather. As he liked to do on these rare trips home, Gérard went to meet his old buddies at a tavern next to the city hall, an English-style place known as The Pub. The details have now become obscured, but a brawl broke out in The Pub, and the police were called in. Soon a paddy wagon roared up and a band of policemen came in wielding billy clubs. They rounded up several of the brawlers and pushed them into the paddy wagon, but Gérard was in no mood to be incarcerated. Ever since his trouble with the law over contraband, and his narrow escape from being sent to reform school, Gérard had had an inordinate fear of the police, and now he refused to go quietly into the paddy wagon. Powerful as Gérard was, two, three, and perhaps as many as five policemen joined in the scuffle, trying to wedge Gérard into the wagon. Of course, this only inflamed Gérard and increased the fury of his resistance. Finally he was subdued, but in the scuffle it turned out that one of the officers had lost his *képi,* one of the distinctive round hats worn by French gendarmes and many branches of the military, and in the melee a heel had come down and crushed the *képi.* No one knew for sure if it had been Gérard's heel, but he wound up formally charged with a rather unusual offense: crushing a *képi.*

To some of Gérard's friends, the charge seemed comical. But the local authorities charged with maintaining public order treated it as a serious offense, perhaps not punishable by the guillotine, but close. Gérard was released provisionally, and a court date was set for him to appear before a local magistrate. On the day of the trial, Gérard's friends and family packed into the small courtroom in what was a rather tense atmosphere. The events of May '68 had jarred law-enforcement authorities; the old order in France was under siege, de Gaulle himself was in the cross hairs of the revolt, and here in court was what looked to be a long-haired radical hippie from Paris, the fountainhead of national dissent, revolution, and violence. Worse, the accused youth had been in trouble with the law before. Gérard's entourage feared the prosecution would show no mercy. Or humor.

But Gérard's lawyer waged a clever argument, along the following lines: Your Honor, you have no doubt seen all the violence and turmoil sweeping the streets of Paris. We are witnessing a period of drama, high tension, and explosive political conflict. Passions are running high and threatening the very foundations of our country. But, Your Honor, my client is a peaceful soul, a quiet student of the theater in Paris, and the minute violence erupted in our fair capital, he did the proper and the prudent thing, *bien élevé* as he is: he rushed home to Mama and Papa. Home to his beloved, tightly knit family in Omelon. And, Your Honor, when my sweet, innocent client was doing nothing more than having a beer and rekindling the warmth and camaraderie of his youthful friendships here in his beloved Châteauroux, he was caught in the middle of this unfortunate and lamentable incident. To prosecute him now for crushing a *képi* would be a gross miscarriage of justice, a tragedy of the first order, and it would serve only to further undermine the confidence which the youth of this nation have in our entire system of government. . . .

The magistrate, embodying all the legal authority and moral suasion of the Fifth Republic, was no doubt faced with a difficult decision. Looking at the accused man before him, he saw an ill-kempt, long-haired student with dubious marks in his background in Châteauroux. In getting drunk in front of city hall he had offended the public morality; he had challenged the public order by resisting arrest; and, with one ill-placed foot in a *képi,* he had sullied the honor of the French police and the forces of law and order. The man had to be punished. An example had to be set, especially in the present environment of anarchy and violence.

What the magistrate could not have seen, of course, was the irony of the case, and Gérard did not see it fully either. Gérard may have viscerally detested politics, and he may have wanted nothing to do with the May '68 rebellion. But in a naive and uncomprehending way, he incarnated many of the social and generational conflicts at the very heart of the uprising. For what was on the surface a battle about politics and university reform was, in many ways, a deeper, inchoate uprising against the politics of caste. Workers from auto factories and steel mills were in the streets as well, right beside the Parisian students from bourgeois families. These workers felt suffocated and oppressed by different branches of the same caste system that had made Gérard choke in Châteauroux. Also in the ranks of the rebellion—or at least, sympathizing with it from a safe distance—were millions of common citizens who felt powerless and victimized by policies laid down in Paris, often by presidential fiat. Many Frenchmen at the time felt they lived under a patriarchal regime that was inflexible, uncaring, and preoccupied by Parisian politics and by an overweening desire to recapture and refurbish the grandeur that once was France.

In his head, Gérard may have wanted nothing to do with politics, but his heart for years had been wrenched by the confusions and anger underlying the May '68 rebellion. Politics and social conflict were to him faceless abstractions. But when bourgeois neighbors snubbed his family and made him feel like a contaminating pest, he felt it. When Le Père Durand ran his class in the same rigid and patriarchal manner as the French government ran France, Gérard felt it. And when his friends and neighbors in Omelon, and even his parents, were one day prospering and the next day faced with economic ruin, all because of a presidential decree from Paris, Gérard felt it and shared their anger. His intellect may have grasped little of politics, but in some deeper way he incarnated the social upheavals at the heart of May '68, and it was perhaps no accident that six years later, through the revolutionary film *Les Valseuses,* Depardieu would emerge as an international symbol of the entire sixties generation, with all its outward rebellions, its internal torments, and its moral confusions.

The magistrate, out of infinite wisdom—or perhaps out of some spineless desire not to offend either the police or this scruffy, volatile rabble-rouser standing before him, accused, in essence, of sullying the honor and authority of France—found a compromise that appeared to please all sides. Jail would be excessive, the magistrate said, and no one wanted to see this young man branded a criminal. So Gérard was convicted of the destruction of a *képi* and sentenced not to Devil's Island but to pay a fine of 300 francs, about 50 dollars. Gérard and friends and family were relieved at the verdict, and Gérard was even more relieved by the denouement: Michel Pilorgé paid the 300 francs. "What else could I do?" Michel shrugs. "Gérard was penniless."

Justice was served, the honor of France was preserved, and one might even envision General de Gaulle approving the verdict, with a faint nod of his own distinctive and imperious *képi.*

11

Elisabeth

By the autumn of 1968, Gérard was again deeply immersed in mastering the craft of acting. With his powers of speech and memory unlocked, he now set out to make up for his years of cultural and artistic deprivation. With a ferocity that amazed everyone around him, he continued to spend countless hours reading. Whether he was alone in Michel's apartment or on a break from Cochet's class, Gérard had his nose in a book. He read plays, he read novels, he read science fiction, and he loved to read biographies of artists. To really understand a play or a novel, he needed to have a clear sense of the author, he needed to sniff the creator's flesh and blood. Only then could he enter into the skin and spirit of the work of art.

When he was not reading or attending acting classes, Gérard was out roaming the streets of Paris. The City of Light is, of course, a celebration of physical and aesthetic pleasures, and what Mozart was to Gérard's ear, Paris was to his eye and nose. With the same conviviality with which he had roamed the streets of Omelon as a child, befriending colorful local characters, Gérard now roamed the Left Bank and the gathering places of the Parisian artistic elite, making friends along the way. In a nightclub frequented by actors he met Pierre Brasseur, one of France's most prominent stars of the stage and screen, and they ended up drinking and talking through the night. In a bourgeois salon he befriended an elderly woman who had an apartment filled with paintings by Bernard Buffet. She was a true matron of the arts, and Gérard shared with her one of his newest passions: poetry.

In this period, Gérard became enraptured by the poetry of Alfred de Musset. The sensuality and voluptuousness of language were fresh and exciting to Gérard, and in Musset he found a kindred spirit. In the mode

Elisabeth Guignot

of Keats, Shelley, and Byron, Musset was a grand nineteenth-century romantic; indeed, his *Confession d'un Enfant du Siècle* is considered one of the classics of French Romantic literature. Musset also had a strong link to Gérard's own roots: for a time he was the lover of George Sand, Le Berry's most celebrated cultural figure. Sand divided her life between Paris and her country house in Nohant, where friends like Chopin, Liszt, Balzac, Delacroix, and Musset would come to stay with her for weeks of fun and mutual inspiration. These artists and their epoch constituted one of the richest veins of French culture, and through Musset, Gérard could enter directly into their spirit.

Michel Pilorgé was also an admirer of Musset's poetry, and in the beginning he was a bit skeptical about Gérard's ability to take on such a complex writer. Gérard, after all, had no grounding in French literature, and not so long ago his idea of kicks had been brawling and a Saturday night at Le Père Jean. Wasn't jumping into Musset perhaps a bit premature? As always, though, Gérard amazed Michel. "Gérard was not really ready for Musset, but he plunged in anyway, straight into the sea. And before long, he was reciting Musset like no one I had ever heard."

The words and the lyricism of Musset seemed to give Gérard wings, and Gérard, in turn, gave the poet breath and made him come alive. "It was in no way a classical reading, but Gérard had such a love, such an evocative force inside him, that it was truly magnificent," says Michel. So magnificent that even now, some twenty-five years later, Michel can still hear Gérard reciting Musset, especially one brief romantic passage, a passage oddly prophetic of Depardieu's next formative encounter:

L'amour, vous savez,
C'est une peine extrème
C'est un mal sans pitié
Que nous infligeons nous-mêmes

Love, you know,
Is a wretched punishment
It's a hurt without pity
That we inflict upon ourselves

By now, Gérard had established himself as one of the stars in Cochet's drama class. He combined the brawn and power of a prizefighter with the delicacy and hypersensitivity of a romantic poet. Watching him on stage or playing scenes with him, many of the women in the class found Gérard both intriguing and disturbing. At times he was shy and withdrawn; at other times he was volatile and emotionally excessive. He was a young man of chaotic extremes, and women were at once drawn to him and eager to keep their distance. In the eyes of one young *parisienne,* though, Gérard stood out as a source of constant fascination.

"He was completely different from all the others," recalls Elisabeth Guignot. "In every way, Gérard was a man apart."

In Cochet's class, Elisabeth Guignot was a woman apart. She was a shade older than most of the other students and already had extensive training as an actress. She had studied with Tanya Balashova, another eminent professor of drama in Paris, and she had spent several months on the road with a theater troupe. She was studying psychology at the Sorbonne and working on a *doctorat du troisième cycle,* comparable to the final stage of a Ph.D. in the United States. During her *lycée* years she had spent five months in New York, and she spoke very good English.

"She was already a woman, more mature than we were, and she was already accomplished as an actress," Michel Pilorgé says. "She always kept herself a bit apart, but she knew what she wanted."

Physically, too, Elisabeth was very attractive. She was tiny and shapely, with fiery blue eyes and long, shimmering hair the color of burnished gold. She carried herself with poise and self-possession, on stage and off. By any standard, Elisabeth Guignot was a golden *parisienne,* right down to her family's aristocratic credentials. Her mother was an Amat-Dupeix, a family from Grenoble whose noble lines traced back to the eleventh century. Her father, Jean, had a distinguished career in the highest echelons of the French civil service, as one of the chief directors of the Paris Métro.

With such breeding, and with a very different turn of spirit, Elisabeth would have been a perfect wife for a brilliant young graduate of one of France's *grandes écoles,* one of those best and brightest destined to make minister, or at least *chef de cabinet,* a minister's chief of staff. She could move effortlessly among the privileged circle of Parisians who played tennis at the Racing Club, skied at Val d'Isère, and raised their families in the posh apartments of Neuilly or the seventh or sixteenth arrondissements, areas of Paris comparable to New York's Beekman Place or San Francisco's Pacific Heights. But beneath her polished veneer, Elisabeth was anything but a bourgeois princess. At heart she was a rebel and a poet, with an artistic temperament given to restlessness and emotional storms. "An adventurer," was the way she viewed herself, and the love affair she began in Cochet's class would be enough to engrave that title permanently on anyone's private coat of arms.

"I was not drawn to Gérard immediately," Elisabeth explains. "But he was a man who intrigued me. I watched him; I followed him closely. Everything about him was unusual. There was no artifice to him, not a breath of falseness. He was brute authenticity."

In terms of background and physical presence, it would be hard to imagine a more unlikely couple. When they first met, Elisabeth was twenty-five and Gérard eighteen. He was a rough country boy with fists like meat cleavers and tattoos up his arms; Elisabeth, as delicate and refined as an orchid, was barely five feet tall, and the only way she would weigh one hundred pounds would be with Gérard's hand resting on her shoulder. Their powers of language also marked them as coming from different worlds. Maybe it was genetic, or maybe it came from her training as a psychologist, but Elisabeth possessed a precision of observation and language that could cut through flesh and go right to the bone; Gérard at that stage was still working with Tomatis and was in the process of emerging from his linguistic shell.

"There were times when he could not get a word out of his mouth," Elisabeth recalls. "There were other times, by contrast, when what came out of him was a veritable verbal diarrhea; he just could not stop talking."

Gérard also had the habit of recounting all sorts of stories about himself, and never telling them the same way twice. Elisabeth was never quite sure where the truth lay in Gérard's tales, but she understood that he was compulsively re-creating his own background and reality, embroidering on a past of which he was not particularly proud. At the same time, Elisabeth found in him what she felt was a more important kind of honesty: "There was an emotional truth about Gérard, an emotional honesty," she says, "and despite our very different backgrounds, I think that was exactly what I was searching for."

The two of them circled each other for months, and finally in 1968 their attraction became irresistible. For Gérard, the moment of realization came when he was doing a scene with Elisabeth in a play called *La Lune Est Bleue* (The Moon Is Blue). "In the light, I saw your two blue eyes, I saw all sorts of blue," Gérard wrote to her in *Stolen Letters*. "Your dress was blue, with a touch of white. And I thought, 'She's petite, it's beautiful a petite woman.' I was moved by the perfection of your form, your trembling body. Your voice was poised, despite the emotion, the stage fright. Jean-Laurent Cochet, usually severe and authoritarian with his pupils, spoke to you with great respect. You evoked extraordinary feelings, by your femininity, your courage, your sense of fantasy."

When she met Gérard, Elisabeth was involved with an Irishman, a painter, but once she started seeing Gérard seriously, the Irishman was swept from her life. From the outset, Elisabeth knew this was not going to be a short burst of passion with Gérard, but the love of her life. "Very soon it became clear we were going to live together," Elisabeth says. "For me, Gérard was like the last piece of a puzzle."

This was no simple puzzle either. Elisabeth was born during the course of World War II, and she grew up in Bourg-la-Reine, a fashionable suburb of Paris. She was one of four children and, like Gérard, she was the third-born. As in many upper-crust families in France, her parents were very reserved and formal in the way they treated their children, and to Elisabeth they were both emotionally aloof. "I come from a family where showing emotion was considered bad form. Emotions were painful in our house, and we did not speak of them, we hid them. We were governed by propriety."

By nature, though, Elisabeth was emotionally volcanic, and when she erupted, it both embarrassed and worried her parents. They told her to hush up, or to put a smile on her face, or to find a distraction—anything but give free expression to her bottled-up feelings. "In adolescence, I would have these emotional outpourings, and everyone would be afraid I was crazy," Elisabeth says. "My outbursts made everyone very tense. People were always telling me, 'Calm down. Do this. Do that.' No one understood me."

Her family was not wealthy, but it was privileged and cultured, and Elisabeth grew up in a milieu which appreciated literature, music, art, and the theater. She may have been emotionally turbulent, but she also had a lucid, organized mind, and she was an insightful judge of character; psychology seemed an ideal field of study. Mime and the classical theater also intrigued her; she considered them both to be pure psychology with a theatrical mask. In working first with Madame Balashova and then with Professor Cochet, she came to fully realize what she had always sensed: that the emotions were vital to an individual's strength and creativity, and that emotional intensity was at the very root of artistic expression. Central to this realization was young Gérard.

"On stage, it is the emotions which bring forth beauty, it is emotional pain and suffering which bring forth a quality performance. And when I saw Gérard, this huge bundle of emotions, when I saw him convey what he conveys on stage, I told myself, 'Of course. There it is.' I was right to allow myself to be invaded by emotion. For emotion was at the heart of his power. When I was growing up, the emotions were presented to me as a source of great disturbance, never really as a source of creation. When I saw Gérard, it was as though, out of the blue, someone tells you, 'See, you were right.' "

At first they intimidated each other, but once they broke through their mutual reticence, Elisabeth and Gérard discovered they were emotional twins. Both of them had grown up in emotional isolation, and along with the myriad other pleasures of falling in love, they now brought to each other a profound sense of relief: they were not freaks; *someone* understood their unusual temperaments and ways. "Our encounter came as an immense comfort to me," Elisabeth says. "I was completely reassured by Gérard, because he was like me. When I would erupt emotionally, and no one else could understand me, Gérard always understood."

Before Elisabeth came into his life, Gérard believed real love would always be beyond his grasp. "I had given up on the idea of love. I expected only to go with women who liked to screw. I never thought a woman could love me, given—and this comes from my mother—given that I was not desirable. As a child, I was not desired; therefore, I was not desirable." He found everything about Elisabeth reassuring, a validation that, in fact, he was attractive, even to a golden *parisienne*. Their opposite traits and their emotional congruity made for an interlocking fit, one that finally made him feel complete. Above all, he found that in almost every situation, no matter how excessive his mood, Elisabeth *understood* him. "Right away I felt good with you. I had no idea why, because then I knew nothing about feelings," he wrote in *Stolen Letters*.

"You spoke to me in a way whereby I heard everything. I stopped being deaf and closed off. At the movies, by your side, I understood everything, I understood everything because we were together. After that, we could not leave each other's side. I found my road, I found my voice."

As usual, Michel Pilorgé was close at hand, witnessing another phase of Gérard's transformation. Michel went to the movies with Gérard and Elisabeth, he recited lines and rehearsed scenes with them, and in their presence Michel often felt a tinge of jealousy. For he, too, was enamored of Elisabeth, and he envied the intensity and totality of their passion. Before his eyes, Gérard and Elisabeth seemed to fuse and give each other strength. "Elisabeth was deeply, deeply in love," Michel says. "She and Gérard were living something truly extraordinary. The rest of us, off on the sidelines, watched it, envied it. This kind of love was so beautiful that we all said, 'Shit, I too want to live a love like that.' "

At the time, Elisabeth was living in a tiny apartment on the rue Lepic, at the foot of Montmartre, and Gérard began to spend more and more time there. The apartment was bright and cheerful, with a view onto a garden out back. Everything about the place was dainty and elegant: the plants and the paintings, the fabrics on the throw pillows, the knickknacks on the dressing table. The feel of Elisabeth's world was very different from that of the Pilorgé brothers, and it was, of course, light-years away from the drab, cramped home in which he had grown up. Elisabeth's was a world of femininity and good taste, and as she became Gérard's constant companion, she also became a valuable guide in his quest for knowledge and culture. She took him to Paris's art museums and to the small galleries along the rue de Seine; they went to plays in out-of-the-way theaters; they prepared scenes for Cochet; and in Elisabeth's arms, Gérard learned a new sensibility and a new language: the language of love.

"Before Elisabeth," Gérard says, "I never knew how to talk to a woman. Before her, I never had the feelings, and I certainly never had the words to express them."

Right from the beginning, Elisabeth's aptitude and training as both a psychologist and an actress proved invaluable to Gérard. He was a natural, a born artist, but he moved in a mental haze, with no clear idea what to make of his gifts. From her dual perspective, Elisabeth understood the artistic temperament, and she understood the creative process, and she could clearly articulate both to Gérard. In several ways, their romance and love evoke the story of *Pygmalion,* with Elisabeth taking a rough-hewn force of nature, grooming and polishing him, and leading him into a sophistication of language and taste quite distant from his origins. "Elisabeth played *My Fair Lady* in reverse," Michel Pilorgé says.

"She had the capacity, the will, the background, and the talent. And she really helped Gérard. Cochet and Tomatis helped a lot, and I did my part, in my own way. But it was Elisabeth who was the guide who lifted him out of the washbasin. She was the most important."

Elisabeth does not see their relationship in any Pygmalion-like mold of master and student. "In the beginning, Gérard had some striking deficiencies, and, of course, I explained certain things to him. But we complemented each other perfectly, and Gérard brought me new understandings as well. He is extremely permeable, he opens himself to everything, and he impregnates himself with everything. He approaches the world in a spirit of animism, in which nothing is out of bounds. . . . With me or without me, he was going to progress very rapidly in his drive to make himself cultivated."

Gérard could learn about artists and their natures and craft by reading biographies and studying their works, but Elisabeth was uniquely trained and placed to help him understand that artistic gifts were not the sole province of Parisian intellectuals and cultured sophisticates; indeed, an untutored youth from a poor family in Châteauroux might, in fact, be better equipped to bring originality and force to an art form such as acting. In essence, and whether by design or not, Elisabeth gave Gérard clear, knowledgeable eyes through which he could see himself in a much more positive way.

"When I first met him, Gérard was someone who hated himself," Elisabeth says. "He detested his corporal envelope; in his eyes he had no contours or edges. He didn't know who he was. He didn't know if he was handsome or ugly. He knew nothing. He had no center."

Having no center, and no clearly defined self-image, might be a terrible handicap in most people, but Elisabeth saw these seeming deficiencies as potential strengths for an actor and artist like Gérard. "The fact that Gérard had no contours also meant he had no constrictions, no limits. He could just plunge. Not having a mother who said to him, 'You're fine like this, you're not fine like that,' gave him a freedom from restraints. And this, too, I see as rather positive in the development of an artistic gift. When you know no limits, you give everything."

Plunge, and give everything, Gérard now certainly did, both with Elisabeth and in his increasingly demanding work with Cochet. He was now studying and preparing scenes and plays of Corneille, Marivaux, Camus, and Chekhov. Gérard's grasp of his craft was such that he was able to enter deep into the skin and spirit of the characters he was portraying—so deep he would often lose all sense of self; the line of demarcation between actor and role would wind up a blur. Who am I?

Where am I? Often Gérard would not be sure. In most people, such a lack of mental lucidity, even for a brief period, might be a terrible strain; for an actor like Gérard, Elisabeth saw, it could be a strength. "Lucidity is not always what an actor wants," Elisabeth says. "When an actor is too lucid, he has trouble transforming himself into his fictional character. Lucidity for an actor like Gérard is a burden. It's a shackle. He needs to plunge and stay submerged."

In his writings, Keats frequently examined the ability of an artist to lose himself totally in the beings he creates, a gift Keats referred to as "negative capability." In "Ode to a Nightingale," the poet "becomes" the nightingale, able to see and feel as the bird does on his distant branch. Elisabeth could see this same gift in Gérard and his ability to "become" a created character. In her own work on stage, Elisabeth felt this impulse toward complete immersion and self-negation, but she could rarely let go as fully as Gérard, and it became even more difficult after their marriage. "I plunge," she says, "but with me there is always a small light which draws me back. I have a family, and two children, and I want to know where they are, what they're doing. Like many women, I place love and motherhood above all else. When I do a play, I plunge, but I always pull back. Gérard, by contrast, always stays submerged."

Like Elisabeth, Professor Cochet understood Gérard's moods and excesses, and he, too, saw that one of Gérard's greatest assets as an actor was his freedom from conventional restraints. With a talent as rare as Gérard's, Cochet acted on the belief that it was best to give him wide latitude, instead of trying to hammer him into some preconceived mold. "Cochet did not treat Gérard the way he treated the others," Elisabeth says. "Cochet is a very rigorous man, very persnickety, and I liked him very much. He was always kind to me. At times, though, he could be irritable, over the smallest things. But with Gérard he was magnificent. And he always left him his freedom. For example, Gérard was the only one who had the right to leave class to go smoke a cigarette in the hall. Cochet would explain, 'He can't help it. He can't help it. That's just the way he is.' Cochet took a big risk with Gérard."

Cochet considered Elisabeth a very capable actress, and he often gave her some of the choice roles in his productions. "She was very cute, bubbly, tiny, and very intelligent. A charming girl," he says. But he also sensed that the very breeding that made her refined and discreet might prove to be a constraint on her further development as an actress. In fact, Cochet believes Elisabeth's greatest role in the theater may well be the one she has so admirably played in real life: being midwife and wife to Gérard and his gargantuan talent. "I know she helped Gérard enormously, and few people had her ability to do so," Cochet says. "But I suspect that in helping Gérard, she also paid a price in terms of her own life and career."

That observation would certainly prove true over the course of their tempestuous marriage. Elisabeth would become Gérard's wife, the mother of his children, a sounding board for his projects, his co-star in two movies, and she even wrote a series of songs which Gérard sang on a popular record sold in France. But one of the primary reasons he could plunge, why he could make four or five movies a year, why he could spend most of his life on the road, being a husband and a parent from afar, was Elisabeth. She understood and accepted his creative needs. With his volatility, and with the totality with which he would invest himself in his movies and his roles, Gérard's existence would become a perpetual hurricane; Elisabeth would always be there, holding the center.

In the beginning of her romance with Gérard, Elisabeth also had to hold her own with her parents. She understood Gérard's unconventional ways, but what would happen when she brought him home to meet her very traditional upper-crust parents? Gérard and her parents came from two opposite poles of French society; would her father think she had lost her mind? On his first encounter with Elisabeth's parents, Gérard arrived in jeans and a T-shirt, and with his usual long hair and hulking presence. The Guignots received him in the drawing room of their sumptuous villa at Bourg-la-Reine. "My parents were extremely surprised," Elisabeth says. "It was as though I had brought home a savage."

Still, her father soon came to see that whatever his appearance, Gérard possessed a rare honesty and force, two qualities Monsieur Guignot valued highly. He also saw that his daughter, no matter how tempestuous her nature, had sound reasons for losing her heart to such a young man. "On important matters, my father is marvelous; he is among that tiny group of people who always rise to the occasion," Elisabeth says. "Ultimately, he had confidence in me, and he knew I would not bring home an idiot, as different as Gérard was from my parents."

On April 11, 1970, Gérard and Elisabeth were married in Bourg-la-Reine (a town which, ironically, is believed to be the birthplace of the name Depardieu). Gérard and Elisabeth were married by a magistrate at the town hall, and then her parents held a lovely reception in the garden of their villa. Elisabeth was radiant in a gown of elegant simplicity, and she had taken Gérard in tow and had him outfitted in a proper suit. Being allergic to neckties of any variety, Gérard wore a stylish turtleneck of white silk.

Michel Pilorgé served as best man, and as chauffeur for Lilette and Dédé, who had taken the train up from Châteauroux. Michel picked them up at the Gare d'Austerlitz. Dédé got off the train dressed in a rumpled suit that looked thirty years old, with the frayed cuffs of his shirt dangling out the sleeves. Lilette wore a flowered print dress, and she seemed very ill at ease about the idea of watching her son marry the daughter of such an eminent family. They were running late; Michel rushed toward Bourg-la-Reine and got lost on the way. Gérard's sister Hélène was already on hand, fretting about her parents' arrival. Finally, the best man and the groom's family arrived—just as the ceremony was about to begin.

Monsieur Guignot, tall, distinguished, and always the perfect gentleman, greeted the groom's father with great dignity, with Pilorgé at their elbow. "*'Ouaff, bof, ooof!'* was about all Dédé could get out, he was so nervous," Michel recalls. "And from there on, he stuck to me like glue. And he had a problem: he was in desperate need of a glass of red wine." The reception after the ceremony featured champagne and whiskey and all sorts of liqueurs, but there was not a bottle of red wine in sight. So Michel took temporary leave of his duties as best man and rushed Dédé out to a neighborhood café for a few hits of *vin ordinaire.*

When they returned to the party, Michel lifted a glass of champagne to toast the newlyweds. For Gérard and Elisabeth, this was the culmination of a passionate courtship and the beginning of a new life together. For Michel, it was more the end of something, as both of his friends would soon be going places where he would not follow. From here, Michel would move into the theater and the movies, and he would marry, twice, and have children. But he would watch Gérard and Elisabeth mostly from afar, as they rose and became stars. Today, Michel sees Gérard and Elisabeth only rarely, but he still admires their romance and their enduring marriage, however turbulent it may be. In his eyes, theirs remains a unique love story, as poetic and poignant as any evoked in the verses of Alfred de Musset.

"Elisabeth passed him her spirit," he says, "and Gérard was the one man who knew how to annex that spirit and make it his own."

For Gérard as well, the marriage was the end of something: the end of his long campaign to remake his life and remake his family, his way. In his mind, he had done the impossible: he had won the heart of a golden *parisienne,* and with Elisabeth he had discovered a love and a sensibility he never knew existed. And Elisabeth felt the very same way. Whatever she may have felt she was giving up, she gave up willingly, and she was perfectly happy to pass her spirit to Gérard, for the feeling of fulfillment he gave her in return.

"We completed each other, marvelously so," Elisabeth says. "We made of our respective lacks a plenitude."

With Patrick Dewaere and Miou-Miou in *Les Valseuses*

12

Les Valseuses

From the beginning, married life for Gérard and Elisabeth was a creative adventure, without maps. Elisabeth's apartment in Montmartre was too small to contain Gérard comfortably, so soon after marrying they moved to a larger apartment near the Porte de Vanves, on the southern rim of Paris. To furnish it, they began spending weekends and free afternoons hunting antiques and knickknacks at neighborhood flea markets, including the small one right at Vanves. Gérard had a good eye for spotting quality, but in the beginning he let Elisabeth be his guide. She had taste, knowledge, and a seemingly unerring instinct for enlivening a nest.

Elisabeth became Gérard's guide in other domains as well. Growing up in Châteauroux, and coming of age among the G.I.'s, Gérard had lived in a world dominated by men; now Elisabeth guided him into the language and sensibilities of women. During the formative stages of his career, some of Gérard's most important encounters would be with leading women in French literature and cinema, including Marguerite Duras and Jeanne Moreau. "I always turned toward those women—mothers of language, I'd call them—who could lead me, step by step, into everything which makes women different from men," Gérard says.

The first of these encounters was with Agnès Varda, one of the most original *auteurs* in French cinema, and it was Elisabeth who arranged the encounter, long before they were married. In 1967, Elisabeth's agent sent her to see Varda, the creator of *Cleo from 5 to 7,* and *Le Bonheur.* Varda was planning to do a short film about three disillusioned young people in Paris, and Elisabeth was interested in playing one of the leads.

At the suggestion of Cochet, Elisabeth had shortened her last name to Guy, to give it a crisper ring and more marquee appeal, and that is how she presented herself at Varda's charming little house on the rue Daguerre, on the rim of Montparnasse. Varda is tiny, warm, fiercely intelligent, and a bit dotty; you can readily imagine her playing someone's eccentric aunt in a BBC drawing-room comedy. Varda's living room is just like she is: filled with books, scripts, sunlight, and such a clutter of furniture that the room resembles a neighborhood flea market. In the midst of the clutter, Varda and Elisabeth sat down to talk, in what amounted to an informal audition. The interview went very well, but Elisabeth, so dainty and elegant in appearance, and so regal in her bearing, was not what Varda had in mind.

"She was a very agreeable young woman, and very intelligent," Varda says, "but she was too refined for the role." Varda wanted raw street characters, real down-and-outs, and Elisabeth hardly fit that description, no matter how talented an actress she might be. Still, Elisabeth impressed Varda as being a very perceptive young woman, and Varda asked her for a bit of help. She had already found one of the male leads for this short film, but she was having a devil of a time filling the other role, that of a rough-looking beatnik she had named Igor. Did Elisabeth know any young actors who might look like a beatnik and fit the name Igor? Yes, Elisabeth told her, she knew a perfect Igor, a young man in Cochet's drama class. On the strength of Elisabeth's recommendation, Varda arranged to have Gérard pay her a visit. This was before Gérard had begun his speech therapy with Tomatis.

"He was an angel," Varda says now, curled on a sofa in the same living room where she first encountered Gérard. "Handsome. Bearded. Hairy. Thin. A feverish desire. Wild eyes. And the look of a dropout."

Varda gave him the part of Igor, and she shot several minutes of film in the streets of Paris, but she ended up shelving the project. However, she did not shelve Gérard. He became something of a regular at her house, dropping by for supper or spending time there during the day. This strange young man from the provinces made a strong impression on Varda and on her husband, Jacques Demy, the brilliant creator of *La Baie des Anges,* with Jeanne Moreau, and *The Umbrellas of Cherbourg,* the film operetta that launched Catherine Deneuve. "Gérard was very unusual," Varda says. "He was very violent in what he said, and he stuttered terribly. Yet he had about him a profound sweetness."

Varda was not troubled by Gérard's rough-hewn appearance and hulking presence, but her husband had his doubts. One night, Agnès and Jacques went out for the evening, and they left Gérard to look after their daughter Rosalie, who was then about eight and down with some typical childhood malady such as chicken pox. Midway through the evening, Demy turned to his wife and asked, "Do you think it was wise to leave our Rosalie with that guy? We don't even know where he comes from." Agnès reassured him, and when they got home, Rosalie was not only fine, she was elated. For hours, Gérard had sat at the foot of her bed, reading her stories. "He was very fragile," Rosalie recalls. "He was nothing like his image today."

During this period, Cochet put on a French adaptation of *The Boys in the Band,* about gay men, and he wanted to cast Gérard in a central role, as the surprise gift at a birthday party. But when the producer saw Gérard, he was repulsed. "That head! That face! Never!" Still, Cochet was adamant. "It's him or me," Cochet says he told the producer. Gérard got the part, which did not call for him to do much speaking. The play was a success and it had a run of fifty performances. "Gérard was wonderful, and he got very good reviews," Cochet says. "He had a way of looking, of listening, and of laughing from time to time. He was at once a beast and a great actor. And from this role on, he was capable of playing anything."

Gérard's name now started circulating around the Parisian theater community, and he landed some bit parts in several plays and television dramas, often as nonverbal thugs. When he had time, he also did a bit of comedy improvisation at the Café de la Gare, a zany club that would become the launch pad for several of France's finest young comedians. Such was his hunger for exposure and experience that Gérard also did some routines at a late-night club on the rue de la Gaîté, in Montparnasse. One night at the club, in 1969, he received a visit from Claude Regy, a highly respected drama teacher and director with a taste for the English playwrights Harold Pinter, Tom Stoppard, and John Osborne. Regy had heard about Gérard, and he was looking for an actor to play a young hoodlum in Edward Bond's violent play *Saved,* which Regy was going to put on at the Théâtre National Populaire. Gérard impressed him. Regy took him on and the two men ended up working together for the next three years.

"You did not have to be a genius to recognize he was a most exceptional being," Regy says. Where Cochet had immersed Gérard in a purely classical theater training, Regy now plunged Gérard into the contemporary avant-garde, in terms of both training and productions. In his workshops, Regy put his new pupil through months of exercises based on Stanislavski and the Method. Under Regy's guidance, Gérard would portray rich boys, thugs, mental cases, dreamers, and characters of several different shades of sexual orientation. In one exercise, Regy had Gérard imitate an alcoholic at a café table. Gérard sat immobile for what seemed like hours, lost in some distant fantasy world, his face a shimmering canvas of mood and feeling. Regy found the work stunning.

"I was having him imitate his father, his mother, whores—exercises to reconnect the actor to his own life and his own emotions. We all could see that Gérard had a touch of genius. All you had to do was look at him with his fishing pole, fishing, in the middle of a rehearsal studio. I auditioned many people that way, and nothing happened. With Gérard, you could see his dreams, his ideas, his passions. He understood that an actor has to use everything he has—his feelings, his memories—in order to have an imagination that is completely free. In two years, he displayed such a richness of possibilities that I had the impression his talent was limitless."

Limitless, but also troubling. For Regy saw something else in Gérard: acting for him was not just a craft or an art form, it was a form of psychological stabilization. "He always knew, perhaps unconsciously," says Regy, "that he was on the verge of being a murderer, that he was on the verge of being a mental case. He had the obscure notion that the craft of acting could serve as some sort of cure. Acting would be a way for him to avoid madness or prison."

Working with Regy in the early 1970s, Gérard earned a living and was exposed to some of the most accomplished and original actors and writers in France. At the Espace Cardin, Pierre Cardin's theater by the Champs-Elysées, Regy would put on experimental sketches using such actors as Jeanne Moreau, Delphine Seyrig, Semi Frey, and Michael Lonsdale. Now Regy brought Gérard into the circle. Many of the sketches Gérard did with them were intellectual, abstract, and very demanding, including works by the eminent French writer Nathalie Sarraute and the German expressionist playwright Peter Handke. Gérard also did David Storey's *Home,* translated into French by Marguerite Duras. Regy was an admirer of Duras, and of her novels and unusual work in film, and she often came to see Regy's plays. One night Duras came to see Regy's production of *Saved,* and she was intrigued by the new addition to the troupe. Duras was then casting a new movie, *Nathalie Granger,* and she needed an actor to play the role of a washing-machine salesman. Duras discussed Gérard with Regy, and after the performance, Regy took his young star aside: "Listen, Gérard, Marguerite Duras wants to see you. She may have a role for you."

Duras, of course, was one of France's pre-eminent novelists and experimental filmmakers, and one of the *grandes dames* of intellectual and artistic life in Paris. Gérard knew little about her, but the following afternoon he set out to meet her. Gérard was now getting around Paris on a motorcycle, and he rode over to Duras's apartment on a bustling little street in St. Germain des Prés, the heart of literary Paris. "I rang the bell," says Gérard, "and a voice summoned me to the second floor. It was winter, and I was wearing a big coat and my motorcycle helmet. The door opened, and before me was this tiny woman. I introduced myself: 'Gérard Depardieu. Claude Regy told me you wanted to see me.' She stepped back from the door and then retreated all the way back across this huge apartment, finally stopping only when she was backed against a wall. 'Come toward me!' she demanded. I was totally confused, but I walked toward her, and I just kept coming at this tiny woman until I was right up against her, towering over her. Finally she cried out, 'Stop! It's good; you scare me. You can have the part.' "

Up to then, Gérard had played relatively small roles in a number of very forgettable movies and some TV dramas. Working with Duras was an entirely different experience. For his role as a washing-machine salesman, Gérard was given neither a script nor a story line; he was just told to come out to Duras's country house in Neauphle-le-Château, a village west of Paris that a decade later would become the headquarters of the exiled Iranian holy man the Ayatollah Khomeini. Depardieu was baffled, but he made his way into the countryside outside Paris, riding his motorcycle along the tree-lined avenues leading to the village, and at the appointed hour he pulled up at Duras's door.

"It was early morning," he says. "The door was open, and so I just went in and did what I would do naturally. I walked around and poked my head into individual rooms. In one room there was a beautiful woman sleeping. Suddenly she woke up and looked at me as if I were some sort of monster. '*O, pardon,*' I said, and backed out of the room. I poked into another room, and there was Jeanne Moreau." Of course, a Duras cinematic experiment was well under way, and Depardieu was forced to play the entire film purely by feel, by following his nose. The film was not a thundering success, but it was fine training for Gérard, and it suited both what he had been learning with Regy and his own instinctive approach to acting. After *Nathalie Granger* he made three more movies with Duras: *Baxter, Vera Baxter, La Femme du Gange,* and *Le Camion* (The Truck). When he worked with Duras, Gérard did not only act; he pitched right in on her makeshift sets, working the lights, setting up the camera, and even laying out lunch. This was filmmaking family-style, on a tiny budget, with a small group of very talented actors. For Gérard, this was part of his initiation into French cinema in one of its purest incarnations: working with an *auteur* whose intent was literary and artistic and in no way commercial: This was cinema as *le septième art.*

Odd couple though they were, she a Parisian intellectual and he an untutored peasant from Châteauroux, Duras and Gérard became fast friends. If she sometimes treated him like a factotum, he was still enchanted to be a part of her quirky movie family. And Duras was a true original and a constant surprise. One summer in the early 1970s, they both spent time at the seashore in Trouville, Gérard with Elisabeth, and Duras with her husband, Anthelm, who had been taken prisoner by the Germans during World War II, only to be later found in a concentration camp by a young French officer named François Mitterrand.

Some mornings Gérard would bicycle over to Duras's summer house and, riding up, he would call out, "Marguerite! Marguerite!" On one such occasion, Duras stuck her head out a window and called, "Ah, Depardieu! Good! I need you. Come!"

Gérard parked his bicycle, went in, and there was Claude Berri, just arrived from Paris. Berri was already one of the most respected producers and directors in France, and Gérard was dazzled to be in his presence. Duras introduced them, and she explained to Gérard that Berri had come from Paris expressly to see her. Now they were going to hold some very important discussions.

"Gérard, you can render me an indispensable service."

A service? Gérard's imagination took immediate flight. Marguerite Duras is meeting with Claude Berri and she's turning to me! For guidance? Or is she proposing me for a role in a Berri movie? *"Oui,* Marguerite, anything you want."

"Wonderful! You see, my dear Gérard, my toilets are all clogged up, and I desperately need you to repair them!"

For Gérard, Duras was an education in and of herself. Through her novels, Duras had established herself as one of France's literary giants. The cross-cultural love story she had written as the scenario for *Hiroshima, Mon Amour* was regarded as a masterpiece. As a filmmaker, Duras never earned the same acclaim as Godard, Truffaut, Claude Chabrol, or Eric Rohmer, the founders of France's New Wave, but her films had an intimacy and originality which set her apart from other *auteurs.* In the spirit of Sartre, Camus, and Simone de Beauvoir, Duras situated herself at the vortex of art, literature, and political history, in much the same way that Paris situates itself at the vortex of international cinema. Through the Cinémathèque Nationale—the national film archives—and a number of independent theaters which specialize in screening rare films from abroad, Paris offers film lovers a far greater selection of movies than even New York and Los Angeles. And this has been true since the early part of the century, when Russian émigré filmmakers used to meet at Fouquet's, the famous café on the Champs-Elysées. Now Gérard entered into this cosmopolitan conception of cinema and into Duras's rarefied world, and he somehow managed to fit right into both. At first, Gérard had felt intimidated by Duras and her intellectual and cultural prowess, but then he came to feel a strong kinship with another aspect of her complicated being: her poetic sensibility.

"Poetry is not words and books, it is an approach to life," Gérard says. "Poets do not necessarily have the gift of words; they have inspiration. A poet is someone who goes to the depths of his being, even if he is not sure who he is. A poet is someone who dares to be who he is, who has no inhibitions, and who stays aloof from the herd. A poet lives on the edge, with his art, and with his special way of seeing things. At the risk of shocking or wounding, the poet remains authentic. Duras is a poet; she transcends words."

Working with Duras, seeing her approach to life and art, Gérard came to a startling realization: he saw a confluence between Duras and Dédé. In his own approach to life and to the craft of hand-tooling sheet metal, Dédé, too, was a poet, though with no powers of language. "He believed you had to work the metal by the full moon, and that is poetry. Dédé had no need for language, because he had only to communicate with his family and his craft. He was a mute poet." The *grande dame* of French letters and Dédé Depardieu, linked by the same poetic spirit. For Gérard, seeing this connection was illuminating. Elisabeth was right: culture and language did not guarantee access to the gifts of a Duras. Art and creativity did not have their roots only in wealth, privilege, and a Parisian education; they could have their roots in sheet metal, and in a mute poet like Dédé or a suffering soul like Lilette. This realization helped reconnect Gérard to his own roots. For years he had seen his family and his background as a source of shame; now he realized they could be a source of strength and pride. This was an enduring lesson for Gérard. As he had already learned with Cochet and Regy, what an actor needed to convey on stage was authenticity and purity of feeling; roots were key to both, and an actor who cuts himself off from his roots does so at his peril. Later he would try to pass on this same lesson to his son, Guillaume, when he took up the craft of acting in *Tous les Matins du Monde*.

"I told him to avoid the temptation so many actors succumb to," says

Gérard. "They want to project a certain image, and then work to project it. Better to accept whatever image you naturally project—accept it and then work within it. Your roots are your strength and force. They keep you natural and authentic, instead of artificial. With actors and with people in general, it is just as it is with wine. Some soils are rich in clay, others are gravelly, and the vines can be very different as well. But you have to work a wine in keeping with the true elements of its roots and nature. This is essential to wine making, but it is also a philosophy of acting, and it is a philosophy of life."

Gérard also learned lessons in authenticity and generosity from Jeanne Moreau. Through films such as Truffaut's *Jules and Jim* and *The Bride Wore Black,* Moreau had established herself as one of the finest actresses of French and world cinema. On screen she had a mesmerizing presence; her face was infinitely subtle and filled with nuances of emotion. By any standard she was a great star—by any standard, that is, except ego. Moreau was not impressed by fame or the trappings of success; ego trips were for Hollywood and for starlets parading their wares in Cannes. Watching her work, in Regy's sketches, or in Duras's improvisational films, Gérard saw a quiet and poised professional who detested hierarchy and never put on airs. Moreau was the real thing, and everyone who worked with her knew it. With Gérard and other young actors, she did not so much give advice as exude it. Their craft was her craft, their spirit was her spirit; all the rest was either artifice or beside the point.

During the period when Gérard was working with Duras and doing bits in movies and TV dramas, the core of his attention was still focused on the theater, and at the start of the 1970s he landed a small but very promising part in a new play in Paris: *Galapagos,* starring one of France's most singular characters, Bernard Blier, Bertrand's father. Short, rotund, and distinctively bald, Blier was a menacing presence, on stage or in person. He made for an ideal gangster, and one of his greatest roles was in the 1957 film version of Victor Hugo's *Les Misérables,* in which he played the pitiless Inspector Javert, who tracks down Jean Valjean, played by Jean Gabin. Among his fellow actors, Blier was no Jeanne Moreau. He was a man of volatile, unpredictable moods, and he had a scowl like a hatchet. In fact, depending on his mood and the role he was playing at the time, he could be a tyrant, and everyone in the world of French theater and film knew it.

During the rehearsals for *Galapagos,* Blier quickly lived up to his reputation. He ran roughshod over the director, the crew, and the rest of the cast, including Gérard and Nathalie Baye, who was playing the part of a young journalist. Before long, Blier managed to have the director fired, and he was tormenting one of the actresses. "The rehearsals were agonizing," Baye recalls. "His behavior split the entire cast."

Baye had never seen anything quite like Blier, even though she came from a background rich in complex artistic temperaments. Her father was a gifted painter whose drawings had the clean, simple lines of Matisse. Nathalie spent most of her childhood in Paris, playing in the Luxembourg Gardens and going to school at the prestigious Ecole Alsacienne. But then her family moved to the Midi. Nathalie had a talent for dance and became a serious student of ballet. Apart from a year's break, when she worked in New York as an au pair, she studied at the Paris Conservatory, where she moved from dance into the dramatic arts. Nathalie is in some ways like Gérard. She can be at once very tough and very fragile, and she, too, had grown up with learning problems: she suffered from dyslexia. But where Nathalie was irate at Blier for his odious behavior, Gérard took a posture that at first infuriated her. "The cast was split," she says, "and Gérard was on our side. But he was also sufficiently clever and crafty and intelligent to bring Blier jars of *confit de canard.* That's Gérard."

At first, Natalie took those jars of preserved duck to be high treason. But Gérard, like the peasants she had known in the Midi, turned out to be even craftier than she had imagined. "In fact, Gérard wound up defusing the situation with Bernard. By catering to him in all sorts of ways, including with *confit,* he wound up making Bernard much more pleasant and docile. Gérard was operating not as a traitor but as a great orchestrator."

With immense fanfare, *Galapagos* opened in Paris, at the Théâtre de la Madeleine, and because of Blier's presence it attracted many of the most influential people in French theater and cinema, including Jean Carmet and Jean Gabin. For Gérard and Nathalie this was a major opportunity, their first big break, and, of course, Gérard rose to the occasion with a choice bit of creative mischief. In one scene he and Nathalie had to pick up a body and carry it across the stage. This was to be a sober and solemn task, but there was a complication. The actor they had to haul night after night exuded a body odor that was rather pungent. So night after night, just as they got the body to center stage, Gérard would inevitably grunt or sniff or flare a nostril—anything to provoke Nathalie into a fit of the giggles.

To anyone outside the world of theater, such a prank might seem puerile, but Baye saw the method wrapped in Gérard's mischief: he was keeping her nervous and off-balance, he was trying to inject a jolt of excitement and unpredictability into their nightly routine. And his mischief paid off: the play was a flop, but he and Baye gave outstanding performances.

"Gérard is a genius," Baye says, "but he can also be awful, diabolical and sometimes downright odious." Baye later co-starred with Gérard in *The Return of Martin Guerre* and *Rive Droite, Rive Gauche,* and she knows his mischievous side. She also knows his dark side: his frequent blindness to other people, including his family, and his tendency to overeat, overdrink, over-everything. But she feels that his emotional excess and extravagance, as well as his mischief, are key to what he generates on camera and to an audience:

"As awful as he can be, you cannot stay mad at him, because he is always so generous. When Gerard gives, he gives more than anyone else. He overflows in every direction. With him there are never small emotions or small angers, only grand emotions and grand angers. That's why working with him is so marvelous. He is so passionate about what he is doing that the very fact of being with him carries you along and gives you wings."

Both Carmet and Gabin, close friends of Blier, were deeply impressed by Gérard's performance. He played the part of a brutish customs officer, with an imposing uniform and his hair cut short. It might have been a minor role, but Gérard turned it into an effective showcase for his talent. "He was stunning," Carmet says. "Even at twenty he thoroughly commanded the stage, just as he does now. Gérard is a painter's or a filmmaker's dream. Wherever he is, that's where the show begins. 'Depardieu in front of the fireplace.' 'Depardieu in the vineyard.' 'Depardieu in a chair.' It's amazing. In his mouth, even the worst banalities become poetry. From the very beginning, we all knew."

Away from the stage and the camera, Gabin, Carmet, and Blier formed a jolly triumvirate, and they now brought Gérard into their circle, introducing him to fine wines and cuisine and to their own spirit and ethics of the craft of acting. In effect, they became Depardieu's godfathers in cinema. Another person who was impressed by Gérard in *Galapagos* was Bertrand Blier, the actor's son and the man who would launch Depardieu into international film stardom. The younger Blier was in many ways the exact opposite of his father, though they shared the same caustic wit: he was shy and introverted, and behind his mask of wry humor and bourgeois manners he was painfully sensitive—and a bit uptight. His father and Carmet would go on raucous drinking binges; Bertrand would vent his inhibitions on paper, later composing

Marcel Depardieu, Gérard's paternal grandfather. He died in 1931, when Gérard's father was only seven.

Dédé Depardieu, Gérard's father, was a big, strong man who grew up in rural France. He could barely read or write, but he was a skilled craftsman and metallurgist.

Dédé (center) rarely spent time at home with his wife and children. When not working, he loved to fish, hunt mushrooms, or go drinking with his pals.

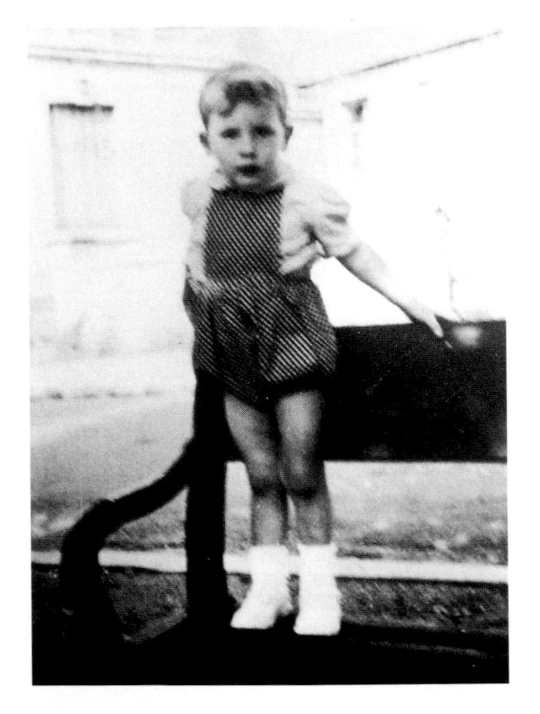

Gérard at about three. Because of his high spirits and antics, he was nicknamed "Pétarou," Little Firecracker.

Gérard (right) was the third born, and he was more impish than his brother Alain and his sister Hélène. Circa 1951.

Gérard (back row, center) went to kindergarten at the Ecole St. Denis, near the family home in the Omelon section of Châteauroux. Lilette took the children to school on her bicycle, with Alain and Hélène running alongside and Gérard tucked behind in her basket.

Gérard (second student in front of the teacher) completed grammar school at the neighborhood Ecole de l'Omelon. Not a great student, Gérard had speech problems and later became bored and rebellious at school.

At thirteen, Gérard finished school and began working as a printer's apprentice. He also took up boxing and became the favorite sparring partner of an American boxer at the base. But come a formal bout, Gérard would suffer terrible stage fright.

American Joe Gagné and his French wife, Janine, ran Joe from Maine, a popular haunt for homesick G.I.'s. Joe's featured hamburgers, milkshakes, Budweiser, and the occasional brawl. Gérard and Alain became regulars there, serving as translators and mascots for the G.I.'s.

At fifteen, Gérard hitchhiked to the Riviera and found work as a beach boy at Chez Joseph, a posh beach club once favored by Churchill, Eisenhower, and Hemingway. In 1966 (above), he returned to the Riviera and worked as a beach boy in Cannes.

Gérard, now a young man, with Michel Pilorgé. Michel later went to Paris to study theater, and through him Gérard discovered acting.

Ever since his days as a beach boy on the Riviera, Gérard had been fascinated and intimidated by cultured Parisian women. He never dreamed they could be attracted to a tongue-tied hick from Châteauroux, but then he met Elisabeth Guignot, a brilliant student of psychology and the theater. They were married in April 1970.

Grandma Denise, Dédé's mother (left), with three of her grandchildren—Gérard, his younger sister, Catherine, and his younger brother Franck. Elisabeth has Guillaume at her knee, and she is pregnant with Julie, her and Gérard's second child.

In the mid-1980s, Gérard's parents went into physical decline. Dédé and Lilette both died in 1988, just a few months apart.

As a young actor of enormous promise, Gérard was taken in hand by three godfathers from French cinema: Bernard Blier (left), Jean Carmet (right), and the legendary Jean Gabin. Blier's son Bertrand wrote *Les Valseuses,* the movie which launched Gérard into stardom. This is a scene from Bertrand Blier's *Buffet Froid*.

After *Les Valseuses,* Gérard went to Rome to make *1900* with Bernardo Bertolucci (left). In this epic look at Italian history, Gérard played a caricatural pure-hearted peasant who fights against the corrupt, exploitative ruling class.

In 1977, Gérard again teamed up with Patrick Dewaere (from *Les Valseuses*) in another Blier comedy sensation, *Get Out Your Handkerchiefs.* Baffled by his melancholy wife (played by Carole Laure), Gérard recruits a total stranger, Dewaere, to be her lover. It won an Academy Award as best foreign film.

In 1980, Châteauroux put on a film festival to honor its most famous native son. Gérard was on hand and visited one of his favorite restaurants with Dédé (center) and Patrick Bordier, his brother-in-law and business partner (second from left).

Throughout the 1970s, Gérard played a daring range of thugs, punks, and sexual misfits, and the public often confused the actor with his violent roles. But in 1980, he encountered an *auteur* who would reveal Gérard's more sensitive side: François Truffaut, seen here with Catherine Deneuve on the set of *The Last Metro*.

In 1981, Gérard made *La Chèvre*, an uproarious comedy in which he played straight man to Pierre Richard (right). This was the first of three hit comedies they made with director Francis Veber, many of whose comedies have been remade in America.

In 1986, Gérard won acclaim for his portrayal of a naive hunchback in Claude Berri's *Jean de Florette.* Then he played a tormented priest with Sandrine Bonnaire in *Under Satan's Sun*, directed by Maurice Pialat, with whom Gérard also made *Loulou* and *Police*.

In 1988, Gérard portrayed the renowned sculptor Auguste Rodin in *Camille Claudel*, co-starring Isabelle Adjani. The film, a salute to the artistic spirit and the difficulties of creation, earned Adjani an Academy Award nomination as best actress.

Gérard's portrayal of the classic French hero Cyrano de Bergerac earned him a César and an Academy Award nomination as best actor. The film sealed his reputation as the most gifted actor in Europe today.

In 1990, Gérard came to Manhattan to make *Green Card*, his first major movie in English, with the Australian director Peter Weir (next to Gérard). To help him through, Gérard worked with his favorite French sound team, Pierre Gamet (with beard) and Bernard Chaumeil.

As Gérard's following in America grew, he won an award from U.S. distributors as the most popular foreign actor. Michael Barker (far left) and Tom Bernard have distributed a dozen of Gérard's movies, first at Orion Classics and now at Sony Classics.

It was a $45 million Hollywood-style extravaganza, and Gérard did win some acclaim for his portrayal of Christopher Columbus. But *1492* was not a commercial or a critical success. The experience reaffirmed Gérard's belief in the traditional European way of making movies, with *auteur* directors and highly original scripts.

In 1993, Gérard made *My Father, The Hero,* the English-language version of a warm, intimate comedy he had made in French. He portrays an absentee father on vacation with his American daughter (played by Katherine Heigl), who is no longer the little girl he wants her to be. Disney hoped it would be an even bigger hit than *Green Card.*

Acting, for Gérard, is not a career or a profession—it is a creative need and an obsession. In the mid-1990s, he furthered his artistic exploration by making movies with Jean-Luc Godard and with Giuseppe Tornatore, director of the Academy Award–winning *Cinema Paradiso*. This is a scene from Tornatore's *Une Pure Formalité.*

some of the most ribald dialogue ever written for the French screen.

Gérard would become Bertrand Blier's alter ego and foil, acting out whatever the *auteur* dared to put on paper. But when Bertrand first saw him on stage, in *Galapagos,* he did not believe Gérard would become a serious dramatic actor; he was too gifted at comedy. At the time he first saw Gérard, Bertrand was in a creative funk. "I was in a black period," he recalls. His main interest was in making documentary films, in the style of "cinema verité," but he had had little success. Starting at the age of twenty, he had also tried his hand at feature films, making *Hitler Connais Pas* and *Si J'Etais un Espion* (If I Were a Spy), a sendup of James Bond. Neither was a success. Worse, Blier's fresh attempts to write screenplays had only left him more depressed. He wanted to cut loose, break free, but he was not sure how.

Living in the shadow of his mercurial father only made matters worse. The elder Blier was bad enough on stage; at home he was often a monster. "In one stretch, lasting more than a year, he was portraying an assassin, and when he came home at night, I can tell you, it was terrifying," Bertrand says. Years later, when Bertrand had become a director, neither his father nor his father's legend had mellowed, but now Bertrand had found ways to turn both to his advantage. "One day, when Bertrand was making a movie, someone on the set became furious with his directing," recounts Nathalie Baye. "The man screamed at him, 'If you continue to give me shit, I'll come back here with my dog!' and Bertrand replied, 'Fine! And I'll come back with my father!' "

To break away from screenwriting, and to distance himself from the Parisian film and theater worlds in which he had grown up, Bertrand now made up his mind to write a police thriller. But when he actually started writing he found himself veering into a different genre: the picaresque novel. The story flowing from his pen told of three French youths off on a wild, inchoate quest for adventure and kicks. For inspiration during this period at the end of the sixties, Blier did not have to do any extensive research; all he had to do was roam the streets of Paris, or read the newspapers, or sit in any bourgeois parlor in Paris and listen to the talk about May '68 and frustrated youths, these hippies and flower children demanding liberation and revolution.

Blier absorbed this mood, stripped away its political rhetoric, and set his story in the French provinces, in a town as dispiriting as Châteauroux in its grayest mood. The result was *Les Valseuses,* a wild picaresque novel tracing the misadventures of two punks out on an extended joy ride, consequences be damned. The story was told in a jaded first-person voice, and the tone and language were fresh and corrosive. Part of the brilliance of the book rested on Blier's ability to have his punks pull outrageous stunts, but to pull them with such charm that they would end up seducing their victims, and the reader. These two young men had no interest in the future; they lived for right now, and their "up yours" spirit was encapsulated in the title. Literally, *les valseuses* means "the waltzers," evoking a prosaic image of the 1940s, but in Parisian argot, the expression colorfully translates as "balls." The novel became an instant best-seller. Many critics and readers felt that it accurately captured the feel of an entire generation: the rebellious, anarchic sixties generation.

Blier was now flooded with offers for the screen rights, but he decided to take a gamble and adapt it himself into a movie. From the beginning, he faced one key question: Who to play the young hellions? To find just the right actors and chemistry, Blier began what would be a six-month search. One of the places he looked was the Café de la Gare, the Left Bank theater known for burlesque comedies, merriment, and sometimes brilliant improvisation routines. The fun began right at the door. In the entryway, the club held a lottery for all the customers, and winners were allowed in free. The losers paid to get in, but got a free bowl of soup. Like many of the comedy clubs in New York and Los Angeles, the Café de la Gare was considered a first-rate training ground and launch pad for young comedians, and Blier found three strong prospects there, including an adorable pixie with the unusual name of Miou-Miou. In his novel, Blier's two punks drag off a waifish hairdresser, seduce her, and make her part of their merry band. Miou-Miou seemed to fit the role perfectly.

Along with Miou-Miou, Blier auditioned two other young French actors from the Café de la Gare. One was a crazed, fast-talking, Italian-born nightclub comic who went by the name of Coluche, and the other was a young actor named Patrick Dewaere, a long-haired, doe-eyed dropout who came from a family of Parisian actors. After an agonizing series of auditions, Blier finally chose Dewaere to play one of his two male leads. Coluche went on to become France's zaniest comedian and political activist. With a humor reminiscent of Lenny Bruce and Mort Sahl, Coluche did nightclub acts and movies, and in 1981 he made a riotous run for the French presidency, an escapade that made the entire French political establishment squirm. Later he had a daily show on French radio and it became a sensation. From that platform, he launched a highly successful radio phone-in campaign to raise money to feed the poor and the homeless, in makeshift kitchens known as "Restaurants of the Heart."

To round out his trio, Blier considered Depardieu, but he did not seem to fit the part. "With Gérard I had a problem. Among professionals he was well known already, and everyone knew he was an exceptional actor, but no one knew yet how to use him. Up to then he had done only small movie roles, nothing important."

But Gérard began waging a full-scale campaign for the role of Jean-Claude, clearly the "older brother" of the two punks. "I was looking for an actor who was more fragile," Blier says."Depardieu was thin at the time, but he still had a quality of the farm about him. The punk I had in mind was not that. But Gérard was not to be stopped. He sensed I didn't want him, but he had read the novel and he desperately wanted to do the film. So he came to see me every day, at my producer's office at the Invalides, and tried to impose himself. Every day he would sit down in front of me, and he just would not move. And each time he would be dressed differently. One day he would show up *très chic,* dressed in a blazer. The next day he would be in jeans, and the day after that he would come in dressed as a bum. It was very funny. And when it became clear that the other actors we were considering just did not have his power of personality, we took Depardieu. And, of course, the results were extraordinary."

The chemistry took right from day one of the shoot. Blier feels the best actors always get totally swept up into their on-screen characters, as his father did, and his trio did not disappoint him. In fact, they got so swept up into their roles as wild punks that at night, after a day's shoot, they could not turn it off. Spirits flying, they would sail into bars and bistros and reel into trouble. At times they started drinking champagne during the lunch break, and Blier had all he could do to channel their wild, anarchic energy onto the set, for the cameras to capture it. As an admirer of *cinéma vérité* and of the improvisational style of John Cassavetes, Blier liked the way the chemistry was working, and soon he sensed his movie was turning into a major cinematic event. Along with his cinematographer, Bruno Nuytten, Blier kept his lighting and choice of shots extremely basic and traditional; the anarchy was all in the acting. While Blier did allow improvisation of movement, he insisted the actors adhere to every word in his script. Like Claude Berri, and so many other French directors, Blier's was essentially a literary, not a visual, intelligence; if the words of the script were right, the feelings would be right, and the proper physical movement of these fine young actors would naturally follow.

Gérard in particular had trouble turning off his on-screen punk. One night he got into a drunken fistfight in a restaurant; the resultant charges would take two years to resolve. Blier did not know whether to be delighted or appalled by his three young actors. He was in no way a part of their gang, and he rarely joined them for drinks or dinner. Indeed, the trio saw Blier as a stuffed shirt, a killjoy, and Miou-Miou often felt angry and exploited, convinced that the director was using them, literally stripping them naked, to act out his own fantasies and to shock the moviegoing public. As Gérard recalls it, during the shoot Miou-Miou would often ask in wonderment, "How could *he* have written that novel?"

The film itself opens with a startling image: a full-grown man rolling down the street in a shopping cart, his face radiating all the glee and intensity of a five-year-old hellion ready to strike. Depardieu. Wheeling the cart was Dewaere, and the two of them seem to roll out of some dream or fable, as if Tom Sawyer and Huck Finn had sprung back with a whole new wave of escapades and mischief. But this was Tom and Huck stripped of any semblance of innocence; these two pranksters were clearly out to rampage through the avenues and malls of the bourgeoisie. Gérard's character, literally hell on wheels, turns his radar on a priggish old woman walking down the street carrying a box from the bakery. She is snooty and walks with a waddle, the very picture of bourgeois propriety, and when that cart sidles up behind her, the viewer's intellect prepares for an outrage—or a treat; the suspense comes in not knowing which. One instinct in the viewer says "Leave her alone!" Another yells, "Steal her cream puffs!" The hellions trail Madame to her door, pin her to the glass, steal her sweets, and when everyone in the theater expects this oh-so-proper woman to cry "Police!" she just subsides into a smile of secret delight; she clearly has not felt such shivers in years.

As read in cold print, and as judged by anyone's standards of how to treat women, what the characters Depardieu and Dewaere were portraying got away with was downright outrageous. For from this opening scene, the two punks move on to a wave of petty crime—stealing cars, jumping a train, and harassing characters played by Miou-Miou, Jeanne Moreau, Brigitte Fossey, and Isabelle Huppert, who turns in a wonderful performance as a young bourgeois virgin who insists on being deflowered. The challenge for the actors, and Blier, was to find a tone whereby the mindless, nihilistic punks could be shocking and outrageous, and at the same time endearing enough not to lose the audience's sympathy. In part, Blier managed to do this by setting the punks' getaways to the cheerful music of Stéphane Grappelli, but the real key was found in the ingenuity and chemistry of his three principal actors.

"Our rapport was extraordinary," Miou-Miou recalls. "We got along so well together that the result was very strong. We lived an entire film right next to the real film. The entire ambiance during the shoot was exactly like what came out in the film, and it was like that right from the moment we had coffee together in the morning."

Though Blier was the director of the movie, he relied on Gérard to catalyze and maintain the necessary on-screen chemistry, a mode of operation many other directors would later adopt with Gérard. "As an actor, Gérard can do absolutely anything, his interior palette is so rich," Blier explains. "This gives the director an ease and a confidence he might not have with another actor." The rapport Gérard and Patrick had off screen was just what they had on screen: Gérard was the dominant, protective older brother, and Patrick in many ways looked up to him. "Gérard knows how to seduce women, and certainly he has many friends who are women," Miou says. "But he is also very appealing to many men; he incarnates a force many of them do not have."

To set the proper tone for the launch of the film, Blier's team came up with a daring poster for the marquees and the advertising campaign. The poster was filled with greenery and sunshine, and in the middle was a country lane with the three merry pranksters sauntering along, Depardieu and Dewaere wearing straw hats and rakish grins, and Miou with a case of the giggles—and her dress ripped open down to her navel. Both the poster and the film proclaimed a new era in French cinema.

When the film was released in 1974, the Catholic Church in France declared it a scandal. Its frontal assault on conventional morality and values deeply offended many conservative quarters in France, and like Blier's novel, the film became a *succès de scandale.* There was even talk of seeking legal action to ban it, a move that would only have elevated the film's stature to something akin to Henry Miller's *Tropic of Cancer* or D. H. Lawrence's *Lady Chatterley's Lover. Les Valseuses* also sparked a fury of debate in the French press, and not purely along predictable liberal and conservative lines. *Le Figaro,* the voice of traditional France, worried that "these joyous and dishonest anarchists could invite imitators, especially among viewers who might be mentally vulnerable." *Libération,* the voice of the sixties "revolution," also condemned the film's moral implications, but from a feminist viewpoint: its critic deemed the film *phallocratic,* a French description of male chauvinist bias. The only unanimity was on the quality of the acting: the French critics agreed that the film's three young actors were fresh, unconventional, and outright brilliant.

"In the theater, as in the cinema, Gérard Depardieu is the revelation of the year," wrote Jean de Baroncelli in *Le Monde. "Les Valseuses* is going to thrust him to the top."

What Godard's *Breathless* had done at the end of the 1950s, *Les Valseuses* now did in the early 1970s. It signaled the arrival of a new tone, a new freshness, a new generation, and a major break with the French cinema of the past. Among young actors, the film was hailed as the beginning of a whole new style of behaving in front of the camera. "Suddenly, every young actor in France wanted to be Depardieu," says Jean-François Perier, a political scientist who became an outstanding character actor in French theater and cinema. Tchéky Karyo, a Turkish-born actor who grew up in a blue-collar neighborhood in the north of Paris and later starred in *La Femme Nikita,* sees *Les Valseuses* as both defining and inspiring his generation: *"Les Valseuses* was a landmark for us. It captured the spirit of our generation. It was real. It was us."

In America, or at least in New York and in other urban centers where French film can be seen and is appreciated, *Les Valseuses* was hailed by many critics and by a large public extending beyond the usual "art house" crowd. *"Going Places* [the American title] is brimming over," said the New York *Daily News,* not usually a fan of French movies. "It is funny, tragic, gentle, brutal, erotic, pornographic, clever, crude, romantic, misogynistic, charming, immoral, lyrical, grim. It's extravagant but exceptional—a film of rare energy and artistry."

For all of America's purported puritanism, *Going Places* provoked little controversy on this side of the Atlantic. This was not because America had suddenly become as libertine as Paris, but because, in part, the film did not go into wide circulation. Also, America's viewing tastes were now being stretched by other provocative films, such as Bernardo Bertolucci's *Last Tango in Paris* and Stanley Kubrick's *Clockwork Orange,* drawn from Anthony Burgess's novel of renegade youth in a Britain of the future. Several American films of the time also reflected the free-spirited ways of the sixties. The music of the period and the love-in at Woodstock were being celebrated in the play *Hair* and the movie *Alice's Restaurant.* The sexual revolution of the sixties became a central theme of a string of Hollywood movies, and the sixties counterculture, with its drug use and slide into violence, was depicted in one of the emblematic movies of the period, *Easy Rider.*

Going Places did have its detractors in America. Paul D. Zimmerman, a film critic at *Newsweek,* found it a sad commentary on the May '68 generation and its "revolution." He pointed out that General de Gaulle may have been toppled, but he had been replaced by Georges

Pompidou, a de Gaulle cohort not likely to listen to John Lennon or Bob Dylan, Coluche or Jacques Brel. *Going Places,* he said, "speaks of a new generation so desperately alienated that its members prize vulgarity for its supposed honesty, seize upon constant motion and change as the only way to outrun corruption, and view sexual satisfaction as the only human response worthy of trust. Like it or not, this film expresses—in an extreme but uncompromising way—the feelings of many of the best and brightest young people in France today."

Blier was surprised by the generally positive response his film generated in America. Indeed, when he first brought the film to New York in search of a distributor, Blier feared no one would agree to take it. When he first screened the film for Donald Rugoff, head of the Cinema Five distribution company in New York, Blier expected Rugoff to hate the film. Rugoff was a faithful promoter and distributor of French films in America, but Blier felt the film would be too raw for his taste. Rugoff loved the picture, though he did see a problem with the ending. "The original ending had the trio being killed in a car crash," Blier explains. "But Rugoff said to me, 'You have to change the ending. You can't let these kids die, they're much too sympathetic.' " Blier decided that Rugoff was right about the ending, and he changed it before the film was released in France and America. He is now thankful that he did. An unhappy ending would have changed the entire tone of the movie, and it would have turned an "up yours" satire into a tragic morality play.

As it turned out, *Les Valseuses* established Blier as one of the most daring and original *auteurs* in France, and it launched his trio toward international standing. It also made them into symbols of the sixties generation. For Gérard, the success of *Les Valseuses* crowned his own personal transformation, and it did so in a fitting way. In fundamental ways, he had always been a child of his times. In the 1940s, he was born in a town devastated by World War II and the Nazi occupation, and he was born in a year that made him part of the baby-boom generation. In the late 1950s, he came of age in a subculture dominated by G.I.'s, Americana, and Elvis Presley, and he belonged to a rock-and-roll generation that transcended national boundaries. In the late 1960s, he was drawn into the political upheavals of his time, and in his hometown, during the episode of *le képi,* he was even portrayed as a symbol of the May '68 student rebellion. Now, in the 1970s, thanks to a brilliant novel and the growing power of cinema in our popular culture, Depardieu became a movie star and an international symbol of his generation.

Still, Gérard was not an unqualified hero in his hometown. In Châteauroux, the movie's reception was decidedly mixed. Many of Gérard's old pals were delighted that a real celebrity had come from their milieu, and several young women suddenly broke years of secrecy and publicly declared—from fantasy, not foundation—that they had been Gérard's childhood sweetheart. But in the more conservative quarters of town, people were appalled. *La Nouvelle République* ran a story along the lines of "local boy stars in scandalous comedy." At the Ecole de l'Omelon, Le Père Lucas and his wife found the content of *Les Valseuses* to be distinctly distasteful; indeed, both of them must have been sorely tempted to use the movie as the basis for a morning *leçon de morale*. Many upstanding Castelroussins feared that the scandal and Gérard's involvement in it would tarnish the image of the town and corrupt its young people.

Everyone in town, though, turned out to see the movie. It played at the Apollo theater, one of the cinema halls where Castelroussins had once hissed Pétain and Pierre Laval, and where Gérard's mother still went every Wednesday with her friend Memmette. Both Lilette and Dédé went to see the film. Dédé rarely set foot in a movie theater, and while he was very proud of his son, he did not know quite what to make of him behaving on screen like the town's bad boys. Lilette, ardent movie fan that she was, should have been delighted to see that her son was now being compared to the cinema giants she adored: Jean Gabin, Michel Simon, Raimu. But when she came out of the theater that night, she was anything but happy.

"He was up there completely naked!" she moaned to her neighbor Josette Croze. "I'm so ashamed!"

13

The Godfather

On April 7, 1971, a year after she married Gérard, Elisabeth gave birth to their first child, Guillaume. He was a handsome baby, and he would have Elisabeth's eyes and some of the delicacy of her features. Gérard was more than thrilled by the baby's arrival; he was deeply moved. For much of his turbulent life, Gérard had dreamed of remaking his family, his way, and now Guillaume sealed the new life he was creating with Elisabeth.

Gérard felt comfortable around babies and young children, as he came from a household with three younger siblings, and now with Guillaume he was a doting father. He loved to make faces and play the clown to amuse the baby. As Gérard might have put it, Guillaume and he were kindred spirits; they both lived in the "primal, prelanguage world of *ahhhh!*" But while Gérard was the entertainer, it was Elisabeth who organized and guided the baby's daily care, and she blossomed under the charge. She had no intentions of permanently giving up acting or her interest in psychology, but she had every intention of devoting herself completely to her children, at least while they were in their critical first years of growth and development. Elisabeth was by no means a conventional French woman—no woman who dared marry a being like Gérard could ever be described as conventional—she just wanted to enjoy every minute of the experience of motherhood. And having grown up in a household where her own parents were emotionally distant, Elisabeth felt an especially strong need to be close to her children.

Gérard took his responsibilities as a father very seriously. In the first

Gérard, Julie, Elisabeth, and Guillaume

years of their marriage, his daily existence was already a frenzy of plays, films, rehearsals, and squeezing in a comedy-improvisation stint when he had a moment's spare time. This was not conducive to maintaining anything like a traditional household, but Gérard did try to be helpful with Elisabeth and the baby whenever he was home. When he was not home, Gérard tried to keep in close touch with her via the telephone—a practice he has maintained ever since, even when he is making movies in far-flung reaches of the world. Elisabeth knew when she married him that Gérard was a troubadour at heart, and she also understood the ferocity with which he plunged into new roles and pursued the art of acting. She accepted his physical absences because the two of them retained a strong emotional closeness.

"I know that when Gérard is submerged in a role, he is not completely whole, and I have to tell myself that for a while I cannot totally count on him," Elisabeth says. "But at the same time, he always has the good will to want to be with the family, no matter what. He also has a strong desire to take on the very real responsibilities of being the head of a family."

On June 18, 1973, two years after Guillaume was born, Elisabeth gave birth to their second child, Julie. She, too, was an adorable baby, and she would have a beautiful face and a gentle, quiet nature, both as a child and later as a young adult. With two small children, Gérard and Elisabeth decided they wanted to move to a house in a country setting, somewhere on the outskirts of Paris. After a long search, they found a house in Bougival which suited them perfectly. It was like an old country farmhouse, what in the south of France is called a *mas,* and yet its interior was gracious and elegant. Its many rooms offered the family plenty of space, and yet its labyrinth of rooms and hallways gave the house all sorts of different moods and a general feeling of intimacy. They bought the house in 1975, in part with Gérard's earnings from *Les Valseuses,* and over the next several years, they would prowl the flea markets to make it into the home they envisioned.

For a young family, the house also had other advantages. It had a pleasant garden out back, ideal for toddlers. It was on an isolated street with little traffic, and it was near good public schools. Guillaume and Julie would go to primary and secondary schools right there close to home. The house also had a bonus for Gérard: cellar space. When he began taking a serious interest in wine, and had the means to begin collecting, he built himself an elaborate wine cellar and began stocking it with a selection of fine wines. As Gérard's movie success expanded, so did his enclave and his wine cellar. He eventually bought two adjoining houses, whose wine cellars he promptly stocked. He later converted these houses into living quarters for Guillaume and Julie.

Gérard also took on wider familial responsibilities. With his first earnings from acting, he bought Lilette and Dédé their first television set, and after they moved into their new house in Omelon, he helped them pay off the mortgage. Ever the go-between and orchestrator, Gérard also tried to organize the life of his sister Hélène, with whom he had been very close since childhood. Industrious, soulful, and a bit shy around men, Hélène had finished a degree in accounting and for several years had managed the office of a psychologist in central France. But in 1974 she quit and came to Paris, uncertain of what she wanted to do next. Gérard had his own ideas for her and he set them in motion.

In late 1974, Gérard went to Rome to work on Bertolucci's *1900*. Elisabeth and their two toddlers were going to join him there for at least six months, and Gérard asked Hélène to come along and give them a helping hand. She did, and she has been indispensable to them ever since. Hélène serves as Gérard's aide-de-camp, office manager, appointments secretary, and the anchor of his chaotic international switchboard. But Gérard did not stop there. At the flea market at the Porte de Vanves, he and Elisabeth had befriended a tall, handsome antique dealer with roots in Burgundy: Patrick Bordier. Gérard arranged for Hélène to meet Patrick, the chemistry immediately took, and Patrick and Hélène not only married and had two children, they settled into a house across the street from Gérard and Elisabeth.

Gérard also had other plans for Patrick. One day in the early 1970s, Gérard needed a driver to take him to the set of a film he was making with Marguerite Duras. Gérard asked Patrick to drive him out to the set, and by about noon of his first day ever on a movie set, Patrick had made himself a part of the crew. ("It was really quite simple," Patrick says. "Marguerite had no one else to manage the production.") Patrick was a quick study, with an organized and efficient mind, and he soon became a highly respected movie production manager. In hiring crews, scouting locations, and managing a shoot, Patrick needed a competent partner. He found one in Alain Depardieu. Gérard's older brother had tired of industrial design and was already working as a production manager. For several years he and Patrick would work on films with Gérard, and also independently. Alain later became a production chief at Ciby 2000.

Gérard also had a way of drawing his closest friends into his extended family circle. During their days of mischief on the set of *Galapagos,* coping with Bernard Blier and trying to turn the play into their first big break, Gérard and Nathalie Baye had become enduring friends. When Gérard and Elisabeth moved out of the rue Lepic, the apartment was a jewel not to be given up, and Gérard arranged for Nathalie to rent it. She stayed there six years. Nathalie would have some fabulous highs in her career: she would win a César for her performance as a victimized streetwalker in Bob Swaim's *La Balance,* and one of her biggest successes would come in playing Gérard's wife in *The Return of Martin Guerre.* But Nathalie also went through some serious dry spells, and when her spirits got low, Gérard would sense it and visit her at the rue Lepic. If he knew she was out of work, he would try to get her parts in movies he was doing. Like Elisabeth, Nathalie is strong yet very feminine, and Gérard respects her. When they work together, Nathalie is one of the few people who dare to tell Gérard that his performance is off the mark or over the top. She is also one of the few people who dare to tell him to stop drinking. "It is very strong between us," Baye says. "When we work together, we never discuss our roles; there is usually nothing we need to explain. Everything is already understood."

In a similar way, Gérard maintained his bond with Michel Pilorgé. When he made *Les Valseuses,* Gérard introduced Michel to Blier, and Michel then earned himself a small role in the film, as a well-to-do youth with a new motorbike. In fiction as in real life, Gérard was the more rude and aggressive: in the film he pushes Michel away and steals the bike. Gérard and Elisabeth see Michel only rarely, but he remains in their circle of confidants. With Michel, Gérard can stay out of touch for months at a time, and then he has an uncanny way of calling out of the blue and picking up a previous conversation right where they left it off.

Gérard built his film family with the same charm and cunning with which he built his extended family. At the start of the 1970s, when Gérard and Elisabeth began creating their family, and when Gérard was stalking his first big break, Jean-Louis Livi was already one of the hottest young agents in France. He was smooth and erudite, with a keen eye for talent, and he had a calm, unflappable manner. In Paris, as in Hollywood, agents perform two very different roles. One is glamorous: managing movie stars, cutting deals, lunching at first-class restaurants, and commanding a suite at the Majestic or the Carlton during the fifteen-day carnival of the Cannes Film Festival. But agents also have their grunt work: playing nursemaid to spoiled prima donnas with eggshell egos and pretensions to grandeur. Livi loved both sides of the job.

His introduction to Gérard was memorable. By inclination and by professional necessity, Livi often went to the theater in Paris, and one night in 1971 he went to the Théâtre de la Madeleine to see Bernard Blier in *Galapagos.* As always, Blier proved to be an imposing, monstrous presence on stage, but what kept drawing Livi's eye was the customs officer being played by Gérard. Livi had seen the young man in an earlier play and had found him interesting; now he found him absolutely captivating. Here was a young actor with raw magnetism, but his appeal was more complex than that: he had a mysterious mix of power and fragility. Livi left impressed—not with the play, but with young Depardieu.

A short time later, the director Claude Sautet came to Livi with a problem. Sautet was then casting a movie called *César et Rosalie,* starring Romy Schneider and Yves Montand. In a masterful script by Jean-Loup Dabadie, Schneider and Montand play an adoring married couple, the picture of familial stability and bliss—until the day Romy is swept off her feet by a charismatic young lover. Schneider and Montand promised to be magic on the screen, but Sautet was now stumped. Which young French actor could plausibly outcharm Montand and seduce Schneider, probably the most beguiling and sensual woman in the whole of European cinema? Sautet had considered several actors to complete the love triangle, but none seemed right. Livi was deeply implicated in this venture: he represented Sautet, and he had just taken on the management of his uncle Yves. But Livi, too, was stumped. Then he remembered Depardieu. True, he was a virtual unknown—this was before *Les Valseuses*—and playing a lowly customs officer was a long way from seducing Romy Schneider. But Livi was intrigued by the idea, and he called Depardieu into Artmédia for an exploratory conversation. As usual, Gérard made an indelible first impression.

"He arrived dressed bizarrely," Livi says, "all in leather, like a motorcyclist, and he had a motorcycle helmet under his arm. I didn't recognize him."

Gérard was, of course, the very antithesis of the fabled French lover. He was not suave, cultured, elegant, or eloquent. He bore no resemblance to Alain Delon or Louis Jourdan or Charles Boyer or the young Maurice Chevalier. He was in the roughneck mold of Belmondo and Gabin, but he lacked the jaunty insouciance of Belmondo and the polish of the young Gabin. In fact, as Livi could see, Depardieu was sui generis, a pure original. But Livi felt sure that Gérard could generate plenty of heat in a love triangle with Schneider and Montand, and he presented the idea to Sautet. "I told him, 'Listen, you are going to be surprised by him, but I want you to take a look at a young actor named Gérard Depardieu.' " Sautet met Gérard and was impressed, but he wound up choosing the smooth, handsome Sami Frey for the role of Romy's lover.

A few days later, Gérard called Livi at Artmédia. At this stage, Gérard was only a struggling young actor and Livi was one of the premier agents in France, but Gérard was not going to be slowed down by any hierarchical protocols. *Voilà,* he said to Livi, "I was very impressed with the way you conducted those talks with Claude Sautet. I would like to know if you would be willing to represent me."

Livi was amused, and impressed, by Gérard's directness and his seeming lack of guile, and he agreed to take him on at Artmédia, a decision he was not destined to regret. "This proved to be one of the three or four most important encounters of my life," Livi says. The encounter would prove to be equally fortuitous for Gérard. Livi would become his agent, his business manager, his adviser, his trusted confidant, and eventually his partner in various movie deals, from producing and distributing French and foreign films to putting on extensive retrospectives, as they were to do with the work of John Cassavetes.

Livi was involved with *Les Valseuses* from its inception. Bertrand Blier was one of his clients, and had been since the days when Blier was having trouble writing screenplays. But one day, during one of his darkest periods, Blier brought Livi a few pages of a novel he was writing, a story tentatively entitled *There's No Point in Being Nice.* Livi read the pages and immediately knew what he was holding: a potential best-seller and maybe even a hit movie.

"I was so blown away by the tone and the quality of the story," Livi says, "that I went out and found Blier the money he needed to finish the novel." This seed money came from Paramount's wing in France. But because of an internal upheaval, Paramount gave Blier no further funding. Once Livi had Blier's finished book in hand, and before it was published, he tried to cut a deal for the screen rights to what was now called *Les Valseuses.* But with no initial success.

"With all the success *Les Valseuses* later enjoyed, one central truth has been forgotten: nobody wanted to make this film," Livi says. He went to producers and bankers throughout the movie industry, and all of them found Blier's script too raw, too abrasive, and with too little commercial appeal. And Blier had no *auteur* credentials by which potential backers could hope for at least a *succès d'estime.* Finally, Livi put together a deal that called for Blier to wrap the shooting in eight weeks. Blier started work, and when he again ran behind schedule, the bankers exploded—at Livi. Using all his diplomatic skills, Livi negotiated an extra two weeks for the shoot, but he had to go to Blier with an ultimatum from the bankers: wrap this movie by the tenth week or we close you down. Impossible, Blier countered. I need at least twelve weeks, and probably thirteen, to finish. Livi agreed to seek more leeway from the bankers, but he laid out a cold warning to Blier: "Listen, Bertrand, it's simple. You can either succeed with this film and continue to make movies, or you can fail with this movie and face terrible difficulties." Blier finished in thirteen weeks and, of course, delivered a success far beyond the bankers' expectations. For Livi, *Les Valseuses* was a triple success. Blier was his client, Livi had played a key role as midwife, and the result proved to be an ideal launch pad for his new client, Gérard.

For Livi, working with Depardieu would not only be an adventure, it would be an education, for Gérard was completely different from any actor he had ever known or seen. "The problem with Gérard and with understanding him is this: he is not an actor; he is an artist of genius," Livi says. "In him, you find none of the things you fear you will find in an actor. Most actors find a niche and then shrink from any possibility of expanding their talent. They stop developing. Gérard is the opposite. He is on a perpetual search, a perpetual exploration."

While Gérard enjoyed having both money and ego satisfaction, these were never among his primary concerns. In 1976, he co-starred with Isabelle Adjani in a film called *Barocco.* Before the launch of the film, Livi called Gérard into his office to show him the poster for the film. Gérard looked at the poster and shook his head. "It's a handsome poster, but it's wrong. I'm listed in the credits before Isabelle."

"That's right," Livi said. "That's the way it's set out in the contract."

"Contract or no contract, it's wrong," Gérard replied. "A woman should always be listed before a man." The poster was changed.

Gérard now had the beginnings of his own film family. In Blier he had found a director who was a kindred spirit with a gift for language, and in Livi he had found an agent and business partner with perfect contacts and credentials. In Gérard's eyes, both Livi and Blier could operate in bourgeois circles, and yet they both also had a touch of the peasant and the poet. For all his urbane polish, Livi was the son of an Italian immigrant and had spent his childhood in the alleys of Marseilles. Blier, despite his Parisian bourgeois upbringing, "knows how to fart," as Gérard had so colorfully explained it. Fittingly, Gérard and Livi sealed their rapport with a familial gesture common to their French and Italian roots: Livi asked Gérard to be the godfather of his son Victor. Livi, in turn, became Gérard's *consiglière.*

"We form a couple," Livi says. "I am his feet on the ground, and he, in a way, acts out my dreams."

As Livi points out, Gérard is on a perpetual exploration, and the roles he took on in the mid-1970s pushed him in difficult directions. In *Vincent, François, Paul, and the Others,* Sautet's follow-up to *César et Rosalie,* Gérard played a boxer who takes some terrible punishment. In Barbet Schroeder's *Maîtresse,* he played the boyfriend of a perverse, domineering madam whose brothel is a kind of living museum of sadomasochism and sexual debasement. In *Barocco,* he played a dumb but goodhearted boxer whose conniving girlfriend, played by Isabelle Adjani, lures him into a scheme to smear a local politician: for a fee, Gérard publicly—and falsely—claims to have had a homosexual love affair with the politician in question. In Marco Ferreri's *The Last Woman,* Gérard falls in love with Ornella Muti, one of Italy's steamiest actresses. However, this was not exactly a romance in the Hollywood mold. One night Gérard winds up in a drunken stupor and amputates his penis with an electric carving knife (an effect simulated with an artificial penis filled with animal blood, for any film enthusiast curious about such ghoulish special effects).

Given Gérard's penchant for totally immersing himself in his roles, this run of movies did little to enhance his psychological stability or his image with the viewing public. In fact, Gérard was in desperate need of a professional hand to manage his public image and his dealings with the press. With his spectacular success in *Les Valseuses,* Gérard had been thrust in front of the world press without a script and with little guidance, and some of his first interviews with the press were rather maladroit, to say the least. In keeping with the rebel spirit of Blier's punks, Gérard would regale reporters with highlights of his youthful delinquency and brushes with the law. His hypersensitive side, his family problems, his speech handicaps, all the raw matter of his artistic awakening—this Gérard was not about to parade in public. Any semblance of that part of his nature vanished; now he was a renegade and an outlaw, born and bred. He had grown up on the wrong side of the tracks in Châteauroux, and he had come of age in a milieu dominated by G.I.'s and hard-bitten whores, and by brawling and trafficking in U.S. Army contraband. As he now projected himself, Gérard had not been a self-protective loner who was painfully shy around middle-class women; he had been the leader of the pack, a wily con artist who had trouble with the law, a notorious hell-raiser with scores of women clawing at his leather jacket and begging for rides on the back of his Harley.

None of this was pure fiction; it was just exaggeration and embroidery, an amateurish rendering of a Hollywood-style image to fit the role he played in *Les Valseuses.* Of course, this image was cut right from the cloth of the Bad Boy Mystique, the same cloth that had once garbed

James Dean and Marlon Brando, but it played well in France. And anyway, what else could the star of *Les Valseuses* give to the press as a capsule cliché of his upbringing? A *petit Mozart*?

"Gérard had no identity of his own," Elisabeth says. "At the time, the rebel, the wild one, was part of the imagery of the period, and it was the only image Gérard could take for himself. He felt it was his only solution."

With Gérard's help, and with the laxity of a celebrity press that rarely lets accuracy interfere with sex and glitz, Depardieu's bad-boy image grew into legend—a legend that later would come back to haunt him. For a time, though, that image served its purpose. In the French imagination Depardieu became a phenomenon: the outlaw who had been saved by the movies, the wild child with a heart as big as the Arc de Triomphe. In 1979, after a decade of playing punks and thugs and sexual outlaws, Gérard made *Loulou* with Isabelle Huppert, a highly acclaimed film written and directed by Maurice Pialat, who is as iconoclastic and irascible an *auteur* as Jean-Luc Godard. Judging from the script and Gérard's character, it seemed that Pialat was holding up Gérard's bad-boy image as a faithful representation of the seventies generation in France. Janet Maslin of the *New York Times* perfectly summed up the image Pialat put on the screen: "Loulou (Gérard Depardieu) is a scoundrel, and women adore him. He is carefree, irresponsible, sexually rapacious, and a big baby."

For writers and directors, Gérard was of such malleable material that he could be shaped into almost any form they needed; he was the incarnation of an amorphous character in search of an author. Bertolucci tried but could not find the right resonance for Gérard. In *1900,* his epic look at seventy years of Italian history and social conflict, Bertolucci cast Gérard opposite Robert De Niro, and he loaded them both with political baggage and symbolism. He tried to paint Gérard as the noble peasant, the force of nature who grows up to be a selfless union organizer and a dedicated Marxist. The congruency of actor and role seemed promising enough, but for all the subtlety and complexity Bertolucci had demonstrated in *The Conformist* and *Last Tango in Paris,* and would later confirm in *The Last Emperor,* he made Gérard look like a comic-book hero. De Niro did not fare any better. He came out a comic-book aristocrat and Italian Fascist: decadent, self-indulgent, wicked, prone to sexual perversion, and secretly impotent. The result was a Tom-and-Jerry view of Italian history, and a cinematic flop on a colossal five-hour scale. Not even the gifts of De Niro and Depardieu could save Bertolucci from a critical pounding.

"The film begins beautifully, uproariously, as a realistic, three-generation, the-mansion-and-the-shanties family saga," wrote Vincent Canby, chief film critic of the *New York Times,* "and then slowly congeals into the overblown attitudes of a political pageant, so positive and upbeat it's difficult to believe it comes from a land whose problems are a tiny bit more complex than those of Oz. . . . Once the film moves into the 1920's, only Mr. Depardieu's character maintains interest and identity. Mr. De Niro behaves as if he were making up his character as he went along, doing busy, Actors' Studiolike things that suggest he is sending up both the character and the film."

From the making of *1900* on, De Niro would hold a fascination for Gérard; the American, in all his power and versatility, would serve as a point of reference for Gérard's own artistic development. In Gérard's eyes, both he and De Niro were heavyweights, prolific actors who could play everything from light comedy to epic drama, and both had a flair for taking quirky characters and making them poignant and universal. In physical appearance, Gérard was more like Nick Nolte or Jeff Bridges, and he admired the work of Dustin Hoffman and Tom Cruise and adored the films of Woody Allen. But De Niro was the actor Depardieu most carefully circled, for De Niro could play brutes in *Taxi Driver* and *Raging Bull* and then play a quiet, touching dropout unable to read in *Stanley & Iris*. In *1900,* Gérard also worked with one of his idols, Burt Lancaster, who portrayed an aging Italian patriarch.

Donald Sutherland was in *1900* as well, and many a night he and Gérard would wind up together at the bar after a long day's shoot and a long night of eating Italian food. On one particular night, in the lounge of a hotel in Parma, Sutherland was in a very bad way. That day on the set, Bertolucci had somehow talked him into doing a stunt in which he ran headfirst into a wooden telephone pole, all in the interests of getting an unusual camera angle of his head splitting open. Sutherland was convinced he had come away from the stunt with a concussion, and now he and Gérard were commiserating about it over several glasses of Italian brandy. In the lounge with them was an American salesman, and to dramatize the misery of the episode to him, a tipsy Sutherland decided to re-create the scene.

"I ran headfirst toward an aluminum pillar holding up the lounge ceiling," Sutherland says. "I tripped and crashed into it with my head. It wasn't aluminum after all; it was a mirror. Now a shattered mirror. I was turning around and around trying to find where the blood was coming from. A shard, a big shard, had guillotined my ear."

Gérard jumped into action. "He lifted me off my feet and, with a hand at the scruff of my neck, the other holding my ear together, he propelled me to the hospital, laid me on a gurney, ordered doctors into the room, covered my face with a dark-green cloth, and frightened them into sewing my ear together. There were no doctors there, just students and male nurses. They didn't know anything about anesthetics, local or whatever. Gérard said it was okay, he would hold me down." And Gérard did, for seventeen stitches.

Needless to add, Sutherland came away from the shooting of the film with a rather vivid set of impressions about the young French actor. "I remember the tattoos, and the eating," Sutherland says. "And the exuberant 'show me, show me' as the world revealed itself to him. Unlike so many of us carting around mummified visions and revisions, he always seemed to be visited by new ones, or revitalized old ones, looked at from such a different perspective that they were as good as new."

Along with playing heavies and Marxist heroes, Gérard in the 1970s also starred in a string of comedies. One was *René La Canne,* a farce set in Nazi-occupied Paris. He plays a small-bore criminal who gets arrested, pretends he's crazy, goes to an asylum, and winds up trafficking in stolen goods out of an American PX. The script, written by Francis Girod, fit Depardieu like a glove. Then, in *Les Chiens,* Gérard starred as a man trying to work through a paralyzing fear of dogs. This script, too, resembled an episode from Gérard's life. Earlier on, when Gérard was doing a play in Lyons with Claude Regy, he had been brutally attacked by a police dog and had suffered bites and lacerations all over his body. Badly shaken, Gérard was placed in the hands of a local psychologist. Later he had three sessions in Paris with Jacques Lacan, one of the pre-eminent figures of French psychiatry.

Even this early in his career, Gérard was cast in romances with some of Europe's most enticing women. In *René La Canne* he was in the arms of Sylvia Kristel, the sexy Dutch-born star of the *Emmanuelle* soft-porn movies. In *Loulou,* it was Isabelle Huppert; in *Barocco,* Isabelle Adjani. In *The Last Woman,* he falls for Ornella Muti. But none of these movies portrayed Gérard as a typical leading man. *Les Valseuses* had made him a symbol of the sixties—the era of the pill and the sexual revolution. In the 1970s, many directors seemed intent on turning Gérard into a paradigm for a seventies generation of men marked by the rise of feminism and the collapse of traditional sexual roles and attitudes. Indeed, in terms of sexual orientation on the stage and screen, Gérard was the decade's man for all seasons. In one of his first appearances, he portrayed a homosexual in *The Boys in the Band.* In *Les Valseuses* he played an amoral woman-hunter who, when the mood strikes him, assaults his pal Patrick Dewaere from the rear. In *The Last Woman,* Gérard was cast as the prototypical male chauvinist pig.

Whatever the merits of these movies, and whatever the validity of the viewpoints being expressed through Gérard, they all give rise to one persistent question: How many actors would dare to experiment so openly on the screen, with such potential danger to their public image?

In France, if there was one film that managed to combine popular appeal with a semiserious exploration of the sexual confusions of the 1970s it was *Get Out Your Handkerchiefs,* again from the pen of Bertrand Blier, and again starring Depardieu and Dewaere. In the lexicon of Hollywood, this might be called a sequel to *Les Valseuses,* but for Blier it was more of a continuing meditation on the themes of love, sexual liberation, and the mysteries of women. In the first movie, Miou-Miou plays a hairdresser who doubles as the mistress of her boss, but in sexual terms, she is getting no kick and no satisfaction. When Gérard and Patrick heist her boss's car for a joy ride and then get caught returning it to him afterward, they end up grabbing Miou-Miou as a hostage as they make their getaway. Miou finds them charming, winds up in bed with both of them at once, and still finds no satisfaction. This elicits an exasperated conversation between the two would-be studs, who belittle her for her sexual unresponsiveness. Blier has been accused of being a misogynist, but his point of departure is that these two would-be studs are actually louts, with no clue how to please a woman, or even how to talk with her. When she has her first orgasm, it is not with either of them; it is with a bumbling young man with no apparent sex appeal whatsoever. Men are Neanderthals, Blier is saying, and women are both irresistible and unfathomable. Who can figure them? Surely not men. This is the point of departure for *Get Out Your Handkerchiefs.* Now Blier's same two punks have grown older, but they are no wiser in the ways of women. Worse, Gérard, the sixties rebel, has slipped into a conventional marriage with a woman he simply cannot understand. Or sexually excite. Or impregnate. All she wants to do is knit woolens for the baby he cannot produce. Exasperated, frustrated, his manhood under siege, Gérard nonetheless is now a sensitive, enlightened seventies male, eager to please his wife no matter what the cost to himself. So he goes out to recruit her a lover. Lo and behold, he finds Dewaere sitting morbidly in a café. In keeping with the setting of urban sophistication, Dewaere is no longer a punk in the provinces; he is a fanatical fan of Mozart, a man in touch with the realms of art and culture, and presumably in touch with his own finer, feminine side. At Gérard's insistence, Dewaere reluctantly follows Depardieu home and climbs into bed with Gérard's wife—with equally poor results. Even the New Man, with his consciousness raised and pulsing with sensitivity and enlightenment, cannot arouse Madame. In this movie, the personification of Woman is the Canadian actress Carole Laure, and Woman is as unfathomable as in *Les Valseuses*. And this time the improbable instrument of her sexual fulfillment is a thirteen-year-old boy at a summer camp. Ah, women, Blier seems to be saying. Who can figure them?

Get Out Your Handkerchiefs elicited some very heated responses. Through Depardieu and Dewaere, Blier was mocking, satirizing, and eviscerating the image of the French lover. His intention was a wry, bemused reflection on the hollowness of the sexual revolution and the still-impenetrable barriers separating men from women. In some ways, the film today seems almost a precursor to the 1990s American bestseller *You Just Don't Understand,* which brilliantly illustrates what the French take to be self-evident: that men and woman do not speak the same language, and that they imbue the same words with wholly different meanings. But many viewers did not take the movie as a satire. In America, *Get Out Your Handkerchiefs* was pilloried by many feminists. Janet Maslin of the *New York Times,* a perceptive and usually mild-mannered film critic who writes from a feminist perspective, hated Blier's movie with a virulence that surprised even her:

"I have trouble looking at the light side of Bertrand Blier's *Get Out Your Handkerchiefs,* a comedy with a heroine who isn't altogether funny. Here is a woman who barely speaks, never thinks, spends most of her time scrubbing and knitting, is completely available (and indifferent) to any man who wants her, and will be happy only when she is at last made pregnant. She has so little will of her own that a thirteen-year-old boy can persuade her to have sex with him by pointing out that he'll 'have to wait five, six years for another chance like this.' Arguably, she is an object of mystery. But by the same argument, so is a shellfish or a goldfish or an ashtray."

Many other American women were also outraged by the film, and when Blier came to New York for its opening, he was subjected to a rain of invective that made him feel like the Boston Strangler. As always in his movies, he had set out to touch nerves, but he never expected a response with this degree of hostility. Also, as with *Les Valseuses,* he viewed his tale as a fable, not to be taken at its most literal level. David Denby, the film critic of *New York* magazine, took issue with Maslin and the feminists: "This courageous and subversive movie has attracted widespread critical support, including a surprise award as best picture of the year from the National Society of Film Critics. However, many people seem to be circling around the film uneasily. 'I hear it's *sexist,*' several friends have said to me, as if this dread possibility placed it beyond the pale. But isn't it about time we dropped this naive habit of grading works of art in terms of sexual ideology? (Most of the great art of the past wouldn't stand a chance.) It's depressing to think that thousands of New Yorkers live in mortal fear of coming out on the 'wrong' side of a feminist controversy."

Pauline Kael of the *New Yorker,* an admirer of French cinema and the doyenne of American film critics, had loved *Les Valseuses,* and in her review of it she captured Blier's guiding intent and spirit as he expressed them in both films. "Blier's explosively funny erotic farce is both a celebration and a satire of men's daydreams. It makes you laugh at things that shock you, and some people find its gusto revolting in much the same way that the bursting comic force of the sexual hyperbole in Henry Miller's book *Tropic of Cancer* was thought revolting. The crude energy of the two young roughneck protagonists is overwhelming, grungy, joyous. They're outsiders without jobs or money who want to satisfy their appetites. So they snatch purses, steal cars, swipe things from shops, make passes at almost every woman they get near. It takes a half hour or so before a viewer grasps that the two pals are guileless raw innocents and that almost everything they do backfires on them. They're cavemen who give women what in their exuberant male fantasies women want."

Blier could not have explained himself any better. In fact, he is a man who, like so many Frenchmen, adores women and sees them as the fount of art and culture, of civilization itself. Women to him are muse, mystery, motherhood, and romance, the very perfume which elevates daily existence above the grubby and insipid clutches of men. For some American feminists, it has long been a source of frustration and perplexity that in France, there has never emerged a women's movement as vocal and vigorous as the one in America. Blier, in these two movies and later in *Too Beautiful for You,* puckishly suggests that equality of the sexes is a comical notion. Why in the world would any woman yearn for equality, he seems to ask, when woman is so clearly superior to man in every single domain pertinent to true human development? In the face of natural feminine superiority, of course men are reduced to behaving like frustrated, uncomprehending boors—just the way he portrays Dewaere and Depardieu.

In transatlantic film circles, how differently American and French audiences react to the same film is a source of constant wonderment, and

Get Out Your Handkerchiefs serves as an amusing case in point. In a nation with feminine role models as powerful and as intelligent as Simone de Beauvoir, Duras, Simone Weil, Moreau, Deneuve, and Elisabeth Badinter, a prominent writer and political activist, Blier's meditation on the shifting gender roles of the 1970s generated little interest and almost none of the controversy of *Les Valseuses.* In America, Blier's movie, trashed by the *New York Times* and vilified by feminists, was applauded by the general public for its satire and raucous humor. The result was a strong commercial run, even in areas of Middle America where French films are not usually well received. Then in 1978 it won the Oscar for best foreign film.

In Gérard's mind, his movies naturally separate themselves out into definite periods, roughly parallel to the decades in which he has worked. The 1970s were what he calls his "mad dog" period. But at the close of the seventies, he began to meet several writers with a very different sensibility. One *auteur* in particular would lead Gérard into his next important phase of creative and artistic development. "Throughout the 1970s, I made films in which I mutilated myself, *films noirs,* harsh films, provocative films," Gérard says. "And then, at the beginning of the 1980s, I met François Truffaut."

PART 4

Wings

With Catherine Deneuve on the set of *The Last Metro,* 1980

14

Truffaut and Deneuve

Depardieu is a man in perpetual motion, and during the early years of their marriage, Elisabeth went along with the whirl. When Guillaume and Julie were still small, she would pack them up and follow Gérard to wherever he was shooting a movie. With Hélène there to help, this kept the family together, and it also provided Gérard with a steadying influence.

He certainly needed it. For by the mid-1970s, he was already making four or five movies a year, and in every aspect of his life he was moving at maniacal speed. Consider just the broad outlines of what he had accomplished by 1978, after thirteen years in Paris: he had learned acting, cured his speech problems, taken the world of theater and cinema by storm, married the golden *parisienne* of his dreams, and he had fathered two children and established a home in Bougival. He had transformed himself from a wayward son into the hero of his family, and he had turned himself from a stuttering dropout into one of the most gifted actors of his generation. He had made one landmark movie, starred in a half-dozen major successes, and starred in a movie that had won the Academy Award as best foreign film, an honor no French film would secure for the next fifteen years. Gérard was not living life; he was consuming it with ravenous abandon. He seemed intent on ingesting, in real life or through the stomachs of the fictional characters he inhabited, every form of human emotion and experience. His credo seemed to be an Oscar Wilde witticism he surely had never read: "Moderation is a fatal thing. Nothing succeeds like excess."

Elisabeth, and sometimes only Elisabeth, could slow him down, and she did her best to try. On weekends, and on the long summer nights Paris is known for, the family would often go on bicycle rides around Bougival or in nearby forests. Each summer Elisabeth organized two-week holidays with the children in August, and then she tried to rope as much time with Gérard as she could. When the kids were small, the family explored Normandy and the Midi, and for three or four summers they spent time at a small *pensione* in Corsica, which had a private beach. The family loved to go to the beach, but often it was just impossible; Gérard was so well known that he would be instantly surrounded by fans, autograph hunters, and people who just wanted to gape. Obviously, this was no vacation. Also, with Gérard's demanding schedule, there was almost always a last-minute change of vacation plans or dates. Elisabeth would adapt to whatever the hassle, but it was often a strain.

"Sometimes I would get mad and tell him that the next time I would marry a teacher," Elisabeth says, laughing. "At least I would know at what time he was coming home, at what period during the year we were going to go on vacation, and at what hour we were going to eat."

But while some part of her longed for a bit of predictability in their family life, another part of Elisabeth's being loved the adventure of a marriage in which so much was spontaneous and improvised. Also, when they were together, that made up for all the hassles.

For many years, Gérard had desperately wanted to share with Elisabeth some of what he had grown up with in Châteauroux and Le Berry. After many visits with his parents, she knew his hometown but not really the environs. So in the summer of 1975, Gérard lined up a camper that would sleep the whole family and stocked it with provisions. Then one morning he and Elisabeth loaded in Guillaume and Julie and set out from Bougival, bound for the back country of La France Profonde. They wound their way through much of Le Berry and went looking for the aunt Gérard had stayed with as a small boy on the farm where he had unwittingly scratched that cow's eye. All along their meanderings they camped out, had picnics in the countryside, and slept either under the stars or all four in the camper. For anyone seeking family closeness, this was it.

"For me, it was a nightmare," Elisabeth says, laughing. "I never worked so hard in my life. But it was one of our best trips, and I think it was very important for Gérard."

Elisabeth always got along pretty well with Gérard's family. She and Hélène became especially close, and Elisabeth admired Lilette and

Dédé's simplicity and lack of pretense. During their camping trip, Gérard took the family around Châteauroux, told the kids about the big American air base that had been on the outskirts of town, and even had one of his grandmothers give Elisabeth a look at some of the milder forms of the local witchcraft. Elisabeth felt that in some way Gérard was still trying to reconcile his new life in Paris with his childhood in Châteauroux.

On these trips, Gérard was always great with the kids. He was attentive, physically demonstrative, and an irrepressible clown. "Gérard is very good with little kids," Elisabeth says. "But with children ten to eighteen, he is less sure of himself, as many fathers are." In fathering, as in almost everything else in his life, Gérard had few effective role models from childhood to help guide his way. So he relied on Elisabeth to anchor the child rearing.

By the end of the 1970s, Gérard's life was becoming more and more consumed by his movie projects. By now he was one of the biggest box-office draws in Europe. At any given moment, he would have several films in the works and a dozen directors would be pounding on Livi's door or sending him draft scripts and treatments. In 1980, one of these directors was François Truffaut. He wanted to see Gérard about a major role in a movie he was writing about life in Paris during the Nazi occupation. Depardieu and Truffaut had been circling each other for more than a decade, and it was probably inevitable that these two giants of French cinema would work together, especially since their backgrounds and temperaments in so many ways converge.

Truffaut was born in Paris in 1932. His father was an architect; his mother was a secretary. His grandmother raised him for the first eight years, and his boyhood and loss of innocence were nearly as turbulent as Gérard's. In the 1950s, Truffaut was discharged from the French Army for "psychological instability," just as he was about to be shipped off to war in Algeria. A decade later, Gérard was rejected from military service for what he said was a psychological condition known as "hyper-emotivity," meaning a debilitating overabundance of emotion. As was a common practice at the time, Gérard's exemption was organized by a friendly doctor, in this case a psychiatrist who was a personal friend of Michel Pilorgé's father. The doctor extended the same favor to Michel. In his early years, Truffaut had worked as an assistant to Roberto Rossellini, a spiritual godfather to many of France's New Wave directors; in the early years, Gérard had worked with the Italian directors Bernardo Bertolucci, Marco Ferreri, Luigi Comencini, and Mario Monicelli. By temperament, Truffaut and Gérard were both hypersensitive, and they shared a reverence for women and for elegance of language.

Still, at the start of his career, Gérard had had mixed feelings about working with Truffaut. He had loved *The 400 Blows,* Truffaut's semi-autobiographical account of his youthful escapades and traumas. In Truffaut's young hero Antoine Doinel, growing up in an unhappy home in working-class Paris, Gérard had seen himself growing up troubled in Châteauroux. But by 1968, when Gérard was studying drama in Paris, he was not identifying with what Truffaut was putting on the screen. Movies such as *Stolen Kisses,* recounting Doinel's later romantic adventures as a young man, left him cold.

"What put me off was the way this little boy of *The 400 Blows* had turned," Gérard says. "He had become a bourgeois. That drained away some of the earlier passion I had had for Truffaut."

Truffaut had heard of Gérard's work in Cochet's drama class and had expressed an interest in working with Gérard as early as 1968. But Gérard refused even to see him, mostly because he lacked the confidence to meet France's most celebrated *auteur.* "He sent word he wanted to meet me," Gérard says. "But in the late 1960s, what did I have? I was in drama class. I had nothing."

Now Truffaut again sought out Gérard, this time via Gérard Lebovici, the head of Artmédia. Truffaut was casting a movie he had written about a theater troupe in Paris during the Nazi occupation, and he wanted Depardieu to play the part of a member of the troupe who becomes a hero of the Resistance. Lebovici relayed Truffaut's intentions to Gérard, but again Gérard was not sure, either about Truffaut or about his own readiness to work with him.

"You really think Truffaut is for me, with the kind of films he's making these days?" he asked Lebovici. "I mean, his work's a bit *bourge,"* he said, meaning bourgeois.

"Listen, Gérard. It's worth seeing him and talking."

Unconvinced, Gérard went to see Jean-Louis Livi, who told him he thought Truffaut's story would make for a fascinating movie. He also urged Gérard to seize the chance to play a romantic lead with Catherine Deneuve, who had already agreed to star in the film. Still unsure, Gérard went to see Jeanne Moreau. She was a close friend of Truffaut, she had starred in his classic *Jules et Jim* and in *The Bride Wore Black,* his bow to Alfred Hitchcock. Gérard trusted Moreau and her judgment, and she told him not to hesitate.

"She told me François was someone extraordinary, and that he had a special energy and poetry," Gérard says. "From what Jeanne Moreau said, you could feel all the romanticism and everything else which had brought the New Wave to French cinema. And something more: the love François had for Hitchcock and some of the great American directors." So Gérard went to see Truffaut, and the encounter would be one of the most important of his creative searchings.

Truffaut was not at all what Gérard expected. He was slender, disheveled, and whimsical, and he seemed to burst with a childlike energy and enthusiasm. But what impressed Gérard most was the look in his eye. "I met a man with a regard that was extremely lively and perceptive," Gérard says. "Only great artists have a regard like that; it was sharp but on the lookout for everything."

Truffaut recounted the story of the film he wanted to make, and Gérard found both the man and the subject irresistible. Truffaut's tale told of actors and artists caught at the vortex of politics, culture, and history, and in exploring the issues of resistance and collaboration, Truffaut was going to probe core themes of classical theater: cowardice and courage, loyalty and betrayal. Up to now, the Occupation had been a period of French history that seemed remote to Gérard; now Truffaut, ever the lover of books and the written word, suggested a number of works for Gérard to read, starting with *Moi, sous l'Occupation* (Me, Under the Occupation), by the popular French playwright Sacha Guitry.

When Truffaut finished telling Gérard about the movie, he added a surprising twist, which gave Gérard an instant insight into the way Truffaut worked. " 'Because this is a film about the Occupation,' he told me, 'this must be a secret film. And because you will be a hero of the Resistance, you have to keep everything to yourself. We have to do everything to put ourselves back into the context of the Occupation.' "

This touch of childlike make-believe amused Gérard, and it proved to be just a foretaste of what it would be like to work with Truffaut. Most of the movie was shot in an abandoned factory outside of Paris. The place felt like a cellar, and the ambiance on the set was that of a secret world, as if purposefully shut away from the probing eyes and the hostility of the Nazis and the Gestapo lurking outside. The story is centered inside the Théâtre Montmartre. The theater's eminent director, Lucas Steiner, is Jewish, and he has been forced into hiding to escape deportation to Hitler's concentration camps. In his absence, the theater is being run by his gentile wife, Marion, a star of the Paris stage, regally embodied by Deneuve. Gérard plays Bernard Granger, a woman-hungry

Grand Guignol actor looking for his first big break in the legitimate theater. The entire theater troupe believes Steiner went south into the underground in an attempt to escape from the Gestapo. Only Marion knows the truth: Lucas is hiding in the cellar of the theater, and is trying desperately to keep alive his theater—and maintain his sanity—by continuing to direct the troupe in a major new play. To do it, Lucas is using Marion as his secret link to his stand-in director. Through a duct coming down from the stage, Lucas can listen to each scene and feel how the relationships and the play are jelling in the weeks of rehearsal leading to opening night.

On his set, Truffaut not only re-created the atmosphere of the theater and the secrecy of the Occupation; for added verisimilitude he directed the film in many ways as though he were Lucas Steiner. These multiple layers of make-believe turned the entire shoot into a creative adventure, and it quickly dispelled any lingering doubts Gérard may have had about Truffaut's genius. "François revealed himself to be the opposite of everything I had imagined," Gérard says. "I had imagined him to be a petit bourgeois. Now he revealed himself to be a great adventurer, with crazy love affairs and women everywhere. At the same time, though, he was extremely discreet. On the set he used the formal *vous* form with everyone, his women included." By "his women," Gérard was referring to Truffaut's many girlfriends, past and present, on the set.

The director used *vous* with everyone except Gérard; between them it was always the more informal *tu.* As usual, on the set Gérard peppered his conversation with bawdy tales, and his antics often bordered on the piggish. But Truffaut loved Gérard's peasant earthiness; it provided comic relief inside the sealed world of the set, and such behavior was perfectly in keeping with the way Truffaut had scripted the role of Granger. Instinctively, Gérard was merging with his role, and he was generating the kind of chemistry Truffaut wanted to capture on film.

The love story at the heart of the movie unfolds through a story within a story. In the play that Lucas's troupe is rehearsing, the character Marion plays is powerfully drawn to the character being played by Granger, the brutish newcomer. But Marion is drawn to Granger off stage as well. Lucas, listening at his duct, follows the course of the two parallel romances, and he can feel that the play's romantic chemistry is drawing his wife and Granger into a "real-life" attraction. In order for these two levels of attraction to work in the movie, Truffaut knew that the chemistry between Deneuve and Gérard would have to be as electric as that between the characters they were portraying. Truffaut was not disappointed.

Gérard had first met Catherine some fifteen years before, when he was doing Peter Handke's play *La Chevauchée sur le Lac de Constance,* with Jeanne Moreau, Delphine Seyrig, Michel Lonsdale, and Sami Frey. Catherine at that time was with Marcello Mastroianni, the father of one of her children, and Gérard would meet them at the theater and in related social settings. In Gérard's eyes, and in the eyes of many French men and women, Deneuve was the embodiment of Parisian sophistication and the ideal romantic heroine of French cinema. Still, Gérard found her surprisingly warm and unaffected, and he came to regard her as a sister. But when he met her on the set of Truffaut's movie, the chemistry changed.

"This time when we met, I had a flash, a very sweet flash," he says. "Together we discovered an extraordinary complicity." Growing up, Gérard had idolized and idealized sophisticated and elegant *parisiennes,* to the point where he sometimes could not utter a single word in their presence. And now here he was, playing in a Truffaut film in which the script called for him to seduce Deneuve, the very embodiment of all he most revered—and feared—in women. Naturally, Gérard loved the role; he adored Catherine's beauty, her delicate presence, and her professional toughness. "She is the man I would like to be," Gérard has often been quoted as saying, and by that he means he admires her discipline and her lack of cant and frivolous sentiment. On the set Deneuve is a pro, but without ever losing her femininity and grace. Just being next to her was for Gérard an inspiration.

"I loved working with Catherine," he says. "I was proud of her beauty. . . . I was happy to be beside her."

Deneuve, for her part, now discovered in Gérard a gentleness and richness of feeling she had not fully appreciated before. As rough as he usually appeared, and as violent as his language could be, she saw that his exterior was a form of self-protection. "In situations where Gérard becomes violent, in truth it is because he lacks confidence in himself," Deneuve says. "In fact, he is very gentle, and he is someone who needs softness around him. That is why he is so complicated: he needs softness, but he also needs to embark on great voyages."

Deneuve had long been intrigued by Gérard. In the mid-1970s, she was co-producing a film with Claude Berri, and the two of them, looking for an actor to play one of the lead roles, screened *L'Affaire Dominici.* They were supposed to be looking at a different actor, but Catherine found her eye constantly drawn to Gérard. "I kept noticing this young man who was absolutely incredible," she says. "I was intrigued by his presence and by the particularity of his presence. He had an unusual sensibility, and I found it very striking."

To allow the chemistry of *The Last Metro* to build naturally, Truffaut shot his story in chronological order. In the first stages of the script, Gérard's Granger chases after several women in the troupe—all of them "easy" women, from his own blue-collar background. He seems to pay no attention to Deneuve's majestic Marion. As the wife of the famous theater owner and the queen of the Parisian stage, Marion is clearly from the upper reaches of Parisian society, and Granger never seems to imagine for a moment that a woman like that could find him appealing. But, in fact, Marion is attracted to Granger, perhaps for the same reasons Catherine was drawn to Gérard on the set: he could reach beneath her carefully constructed public façade of bourgeois manners and propriety.

"Gérard is not at all conventional," Catherine explains. "I admire him as an actor because he is completely generous in his work. In his attitude, he is totally positive. He helps people, and not just his female partners; he helps everyone on the set. When he is there, at one stroke the humor and ambiance are jacked up a notch. He is constantly forcing people to wake up. He stops everything from becoming routine. He takes risks. He takes risks."

So does Granger. He "borrows" a gramophone from the theater, and a few days later a Nazi colonel is assassinated—by a bomb hidden inside a gramophone. In the Théâtre Montmartre, Marion is surrounded by Frenchmen of refinement and culture, but some are effeminate, some are homosexual, and some try to please both the Nazis and an all-powerful French theater critic collaborating with the Nazi regime. Bernard Granger is a man apart. In Truffaut's script, he is portrayed as rough and sometimes uncouth, yet courageous and willing to take risks for what he wants, be it freedom or, finally, Marion. In sum, Granger is like Depardieu: real, tactile, authentic. Marion likes that in a man, and so does Deneuve; such men free her up; they let her drop her tough, masculine façade; they release her pent-up femininity and bring forth her own emotional force. The way Catherine describes herself, beneath her cool, regal exterior there beats the volatile, impassioned, quixotic heart of a gypsy.

"I may have the appearance of a bourgeoise, but I am a false bourgeoise," Catherine says. "Unmarried, two children born out of wedlock and not baptized—this is not exactly what you would call the bourgeoisie. In Gérard's mind, I was certainly more bourgeois than he was. But once he got to know me, he saw differently, and for that reason we could have a true rapport."

Truffaut's story builds into a triangular romantic intrigue, with Bernard and Marion being drawn to each other off stage as well as on, and with Lucas Steiner following the intersecting romances by listening to the rehearsals through the duct leading from the stage down to his hideout. Just by listening to the way Bernard's voice intermingles with Marion's, he can sense the growth of their still-undeclared passion. Lucas closely questions Marion about Bernard when she sneaks down to see him, after everyone else has left the theater. On some of those sneak visits, Marion and her brilliant, bookish, acerbic husband make love, but so subtle is Truffaut's screenplay that even before Marion acknowledges her growing heat for Bernard, she is less and less inclined to curl up with her husband.

The fictional Lucas was staging his play as an act of love for Marion, and Truffaut wrote *The Last Metro* specifically for Deneuve, in what many insiders said was a burst of passion for her. So just as there was a triangle in the film among Bernard, Marion, and Lucas, there was an unstated, even more subtle triangle among Gérard, Catherine, and François. In this triangle, Truffaut was acting not as a rival to Gérard but as his accomplice, and as the shoot unfolded, Gérard and François forged an almost brotherly rapport. This, too, facilitated the on-camera chemistry between Gérard and Catherine.

"I found that Gérard was very different in *The Last Metro* from the way he had been in almost every film up to then," Catherine says. "When he is impressed by a director, Gérard becomes an actor of incredible sweetness and docility. He's very animal, Gérard. If a director puts him in a position of distrust or fear, he pulls back. With François, he was receiving admiration and reassurance, and so he really let himself go. He entered totally into the character."

The filming took nine weeks, and it built toward a climactic love scene between Bernard and Marion—a scene in which both Gérard and Catherine let go with an animal abandon. For this consummation of their passion, and of the film, Truffaut chose to direct the scene the way Lucas was following the course of the play: by listening to it only. "François did not want to see us," Catherine says. "He had an audio feed sent into an adjoining room, and he followed us through a set of headphones. He directed the entire scene only by listening to our voices; he could not bring himself to watch us in person. It was very strange."

Perhaps Truffaut could not bear to watch Deneuve, the source of his inspiration for writing the movie, succumb in passion to another man. But

Truffaut had another reason to stay away: by nature, the three of them—Catherine, Gérard, and François—were all terribly shy, and Truffaut felt that his presence behind the camera would only spoil the chemistry between Gérard and Catherine. "Actors are a mixture of timidity and fear of not being up to the task," Catherine says. "In love scenes, it is always best to shoot them fast, even love scenes which are discreet. Because in a love scene, all of a sudden you are no longer an actor. As soon as there is physical contact, carnal contact, you are in the realm of emotions. And sensitive directors know you can't trifle with that."

This may have been an unusual way to shoot the scene, but the results were sublime. The climactic love scene was a combination of violence and tenderness, and the electricity Deneuve and Depardieu generated on screen helped turn *The Last Metro* into one of Truffaut's most successful movies. For his performance, Gérard won his first César, and for Deneuve, the star of so many great European movies, the film was a triumph. She won the César for best actress, and critics around the world hailed her performance. "It's not since *Tristana* that Miss Deneuve has had a role to match that of Marion Steiner, a woman of intelligence, backbone and the kind of beauty that, you believe, would have made her a star of the Paris stage," wrote Vincent Canby in the *New York Times.* "With her hair done up in a style I associate with Danielle Darrieux, Miss Deneuve is elegant without being frosty, grand without being great lady–ish. It's a star performance of a star role."

The film immediately established Deneuve and Depardieu as the premier couple in French cinema, and for Gérard it did far more. "*The Last Metro* and the encounter with François were the opening of the second part of my life as an actor," Gérard says. "François made me more supple as an actor, and he eased some of my complexes." So did his rapport with Deneuve. In Catherine he found a woman who, like Elisabeth, understood him. She gave him confidence, and she guided him into a new way of expressing himself with a woman, this time in front of the camera. Catherine talked with Gérard about his childhood and about his problems with language, and she smoothed away many of his remaining rough edges. Her responses to him were as accepting and articulate as Elisabeth's.

"Gérard is extremely bashful, and the fact that he doesn't like himself physically only reinforces his natural physical modesty," Catherine says. "I think that when you are raised in a family in which no one talks, there are many things people don't tell you. And I think there are things about love, and physical love, you just don't learn. I don't think Gérard ever saw his parents touch each other or kiss. I think that makes his own emotional relationships rather difficult. But perhaps that is precisely what makes him so strong on another side. He is so insecure about expressing his personal emotions that he can completely expose himself as an actor."

Through Gérard, Catherine and Elisabeth forged their own bonds of friendship and mutual admiration. Deneuve feels that Elisabeth was probably Gérard's salvation. She took a man-child of eighteen, emotionally fragile and unable to speak, and guided him to emotional strength and incredible powers of self-expression: "Elisabeth is the person who calmed Gérard and taught him how to reveal himself through language.... Gérard is someone who needs words and language. He had imploded. Growing up, he lived with people who loved each other, no doubt violently, and very secretly, without being able to speak to each other. For certain sensibilities, this is terrible. Gérard speaks of his parents in an extraordinary way. But at the same time you feel that his upbringing weighed on him terribly, aggravated by the fact that he was unable to express himself. Language for Gérard is a cage. A cage. If he doesn't have the language he needs, he is like a caged gorilla."

As intense as her own feelings for Gérard were during the shoot, Catherine felt that he belongs to those rare spirits you can grasp but never hold. She knows: she is exactly the same way. "Actors tend to believe we are all one big family. That's false. We are more like a family of gypsies. We're everywhere. We meet for a moment, we throw a party, and we make a movie. That's all. Then we refind our solitary paths and maybe find each other again later, farther down the road."

Though she did marry once, one reason Deneuve never remarried was that she feared marriage would interfere with her career. But she also says that her itinerant, gypsy life is in some ways a form of emotional self-protection. In this same vein, Catherine knows that Elisabeth curtailed her own aspirations as an actress in order to anchor her family life, and Deneuve admires Elisabeth for that decision and for the way in which she has carried it through. In a subculture that breeds careless, whirlwind love affairs and shattered marriages—affairs which so often prove destructive for the lovers themselves and even worse for any children involved—Elisabeth and Gérard have managed to maintain some degree of stability, a feat for which Deneuve gives full credit to Elisabeth. "It is very difficult being the wife of Gérard Depardieu," Catherine says. "It takes enormous courage."

Indeed it does. As Gérard's fame grew, so did the offers for his acting talents. These were fine for his professional life, but it did not make his family life any easier. Gérard was now on the road for months at a time, and often he was away from his wife and children for eight or nine months a year. In effect, he was leading two lives, and he was depending on Elisabeth to be the selfless anchor of their marriage and parenting. Every night, wherever he was in the world, Gérard would faithfully put in a call to Elisabeth, and there were many times when Elisabeth grew exasperated by their long-distance marriage. Still, she tried to remain positive: "When he was home, we had a very definite harmony. I just took life day by day, and I lived our marriage as a love story with no conventions."

For the American premiere of *The Last Metro,* in the fall of 1980, Deneuve, Depardieu, and Truffaut gathered at the New York Film Festival. The film was chosen to close the prestigious festival, in a gala event at Avery Fisher Hall at Lincoln Center. The hall was jammed with twenty-seven hundred American critics and cinephiles, and in the crowd was a young cinema whiz named Michael Barker. At the University of Texas, Barker had managed a student film program, and he was a great admirer of European cinema, especially the films of Truffaut. After college, he had come to New York and gotten a job in the film business, and by 1980 he was about to join a new division of United Artists that handled the distribution of quality foreign films in America. Barker had never been to the New York festival before, his mother was in town, and when he saw that a new Truffaut movie was closing the festival, he paid hefty scalper's prices and went to the closing gala. The tickets would end up being worth whatever price he paid, and then some.

"François Truffaut was introduced, and the reaction was just tremendous," Barker recalls. "To this huge crowd, Truffaut told the following story. 'I love New York; you can touch and feel things here you cannot touch or feel anywhere else in the world. When I first came to New York, I went to the Museum of Modern Art and they were showing *Birth of a Nation.* I was watching the movie and at one stage the Confederate army knew the Union army was in the distance, but it wasn't sure where. The Confederate colonel told his aide to put his ear to the ground, to see if he could hear the incoming army. The aide gets down, puts his ear to the ground, and all of a sudden the whole theater started to shake. I learned only later,' Truffaut told the crowd, 'that it was the D train going by under the museum.' "

Truffaut then introduced Deneuve, Depardieu, and Truffaut's cinematographer Nestor Almendros. Like almost everyone else in the hall,

Barker had loved *The Last Metro,* and afterward he went backstage with his mother and shook hands with Gérard, whom he had never met. Soon thereafter, Barker met with the head of the new United Artists division, Tom Bernard, another young connoisseur of foreign films. Like Barker, Bernard had run an eclectic film program, at the University of Maryland, and had moved to New York to get into the film business. UA had put him in charge of this new unit with one set of instructions: find new ways to locate, distribute, and promote classy foreign films in America. At Barker's urging, UA took on *The Last Metro* as the first film in the new division. They picked up the film's U.S. distribution rights for $125,000.

Bernard and Barker handled Truffaut's film differently from the way most of his films had been handled in the United States. Instead of putting it into the distribution networks of the big studios, Bernard and Barker went city by city, choosing the art house most appropriate to the film. Truffaut involved himself in every aspect of his films, including their marketing and international distribution. Once he flew in from Paris on the Concorde just to meet with United Artists and approve the ad campaign and posters they had created for the American launch. The film proved to be a major hit in America, and it was nominated for an Academy Award as best foreign film. From then on, first at UA and later when they moved to Orion Classics and then Sony Classics, Barker and Bernard enjoyed privileged relationships with many of the leading European directors. They handled many of Gérard's most important movies, including *Jean de Florette, Too Beautiful for You,* and *Cyrano de Bergerac.* Barker and Bernard in effect became an American branch of Gérard's film family, giving him advice and counsel about how to handle the press and his growing fame and reputation in the United States.

Gérard also developed close ties to Truffaut's main liaison to foreign film markets, Alain Vannier of Roissy Films. Vannier had worked with Truffaut since the 1950s, when he sold U.S. rights to *Jules et Jim* for what was then a considerable sum for a French film: $40,000. Vannier also had close ties to Gérard Lebovici and Jean-Louis Livi at Artmédia. Vannier's associate in the United States, Tom Sternberg, who had handled the foreign sales of Francis Coppola's *Apocalypse Now,* took *The Last Metro* to United Artists. Gérard would use this same network when he co-produced Blier's *Too Beautiful for You* and brought it to America at the end of the decade.

After *The Last Metro,* Gérard had a smaller role in *Je Vous Aime,* a Claude Berri movie featuring Deneuve, Jean-Louis Trintignant, Alain Souchon, and Serge Gainsbourg, with music by Gainsbourg. Gérard then played Public Enemy No. 1 in *Inspecteur La Bavure,* starring Coluche, the comic who had discovered Miou-Miou. Coluche had become a quixotic star in France, both on radio and in movies. He had long since broken up with Miou-Miou, and she had taken up with Patrick Dewaere, who had edged out Coluche to play in *Les Valseuses.* Gérard also played a hoodlum in Alain Corneau's *Choice of Arms,* with Yves Montand and Deneuve, in a dark thriller about the French underworld.

On April 1, 1981, just before François Mitterrand and his Socialist party swept to power in France's presidential elections, Gérard began his second film with Truffaut: *The Woman Next Door,* the story of an unbridled, adulterous passion between Gérard and Fanny Ardant, a tall, stunning, and very talented actress who was the latest leading lady in Truffaut's private life. Here Gérard plays another Bernard, a rather dull and settled husband living in pleasant domesticity outside of Grenoble—until the day he runs into Ardant's Mathilde, with whom he had had a stormy love affair several years before. They become next-door neighbors and are inexorably drawn back into their overwhelming passion.

"Some people say that in today's world you can no longer live a passionate, romantic love affair," Ardant says. "François wanted to show that even in the framework of modern everyday life—at the supermarket or in the parking lot—you can know the same passion as Madame Bovary."

Ardant brought great beauty and a quirky humor and intelligence to the romance, as well as an unusual background. She had studied political science and diplomacy in Paris and was planning on a career in the foreign service. In fact, she might well have wound up a cultural attaché in some French embassy around the world except for her inability to be on time during a training tour she had spent at the embassy in London. "I was always late," she says, "and so they let me go. That was my big break." Once free of all notions of becoming a diplomat, she turned to the theater and very quickly became a star on a television series called "Les Dames de la Côte." Truffaut spotted her there, sent her an enthusiastic note, and within a year she was in Grenoble, shooting Truffaut's new movie, which thrust her into the arms of Gérard. In Ardant's view, Truffaut saw Gérard as a sort of alter ego: "They both had a difficult childhood, a rebellious childhood, a lonely childhood. And they both became self-made men, men who all alone had remade themselves."

While many critics adored *The Woman Next Door,* the film received a mixed response in France and abroad, and no one will recall it as Truffaut's best. But in terms of Gérard's evolution, the film again demonstrated how far he had come from his "mad dog" days. Indeed, for all the grand passion of the adulterous love affair he carries on with Ardant, the role Gérard played was that of a genteel suburban bourgeois—precisely the kind of person he had been mocking and terrorizing a decade earlier in *Les Valseuses.*

But if Gérard was an adaptable child of his times, his pal from *Les Valseuses,* Patrick Dewaere, was not. As gifted an actor as he was, Patrick never seemed to shake his screen role of the disaffected sixties rebel. By 1982, Dewaere and Miou-Miou had gone their separate ways. Dewaere—whimsical, emotionally fragile, and as passionate about music as the character he had played in *Get Out Your Handkerchiefs*—drifted in and out of drugs, and by the late 1970s he was caught in a downward spiral of drugs and depression. In 1982 he was found dead, killed by his own hand. For many of the sixties generation in France, Dewaere's death seemed to be the end of an era, closed with a tragic punctuation mark. Born in the baby boom year of 1947, Dewaere was exactly thirty-five years old when he died, a fact that eerily echoed a bit of dialogue from Blier's *Handkerchiefs.* Patrick was talking about his idol Mozart and his untimely death:

"The poor guy, he died at the age of thirty-five! Thirty-five! Do you realize the loss? What an era of jerks!"

After *The Woman Next Door,* Gérard made *La Chèvre,* the first of three hugely successful comedies in which he played the straight man to Pierre Richard, one of France's wackiest slapstick comedians. The film was written and directed by Francis Veber, whose flair for farce and zany comedy is such that Hollywood has bought or remade a dozen of his scripts, including the classic *The Tall Blond Man with One Black Shoe.* The plot Veber had written for *La Chèvre* was slender, and he knew that the entire film would rest on the interplay he would be able to generate between Depardieu and Richard—an interplay that began the first time Veber brought them together in Paris, over a proper French lunch, of course.

"We met at Le Bernardin, which at that time was on the Quai de la Tournelle," says Veber. "I put my couple facing each other, and the effect was wonderful, because when Pierre eats, he sprays food in every direction. He dirties himself, but he ruins your suit as well. As he was talking to Depardieu, and trying to convince Gérard they would be very good together on screen, Pierre was sending tomato soup all over Depardieu. By the end of the meal Gérard was covered, and I was watching all this and laughing. At the end I said to them, 'You know, you two are wonderful together.' I had my clown and my straight man."

In France, *La Chèvre* drew nearly one and a half million people into the theaters after it was released in December 1981, making it a huge hit in France and Gérard's biggest box-office success ever. Veber then sat down and wrote two sequels, *Les Compères* and *Les Fugitifs,* the latter of which Veber remade in English as *Three Fugitives,* starring Nick Nolte in Gérard's straight-man role and Martin Short as the zany slapstick. Like Colline Serreau, the author of the original *Three Men and a Baby,* Veber writes scripts that are so original, Hollywood usually cannot resist remaking them. He now shuttles between homes in Paris and Los Angeles, where he remains under contract to give original scripts to Disney.

During the shooting of *La Chèvre* in Mexico, the rapport between Gérard and Pierre Richard on the set was just as it had been at their first lunch. "Pierre had a new girlfriend. She was very young, and he was very excited about her," Veber recalls. "Pierre and Gérard were sharing a trailer and sometimes that caused problems. For while Gérard was there getting his makeup put on, Pierre would be in the back of the trailer with his girlfriend. The trailer would bounce up and down so much that the makeup girl kept getting her brush in Gérard's eye. 'Stop already!' he'd cry. 'Enough! *Merde!*' "

Be it in France or America, Mexico or Italy, all film sets are worlds unto themselves, with actors, writers, directors, assistant directors, makeup people, wardrobe people, sound experts, cameramen, electricians, construction hands, stunt men, producers, accountants, paymasters, and apprentices and groupies of every stripe all thrown together for several months, forming an itinerant family with only one real common bond: the movie they are making and their love of cinema. But as similar as movie sets appear, European and American actors tend to be very different, in both their attitude and their approach toward their common craft.

"I must say the differences astound me, now that I have met American actors and have seen how bitchy they can be, for very mysterious reasons," Veber says. "They are treated like gods, and many of them behave like shit. Gérard is completely the opposite. He is like Mastroianni. He never complains."

To illustrate his point, Veber tells a story about Mastroianni talking about his life as an actor and about how royally he is treated on film sets in Italy. Veber, with his celebrated comic flair, does his own exaggerated rendition of Marcello's description of a hard day on the set. " 'You arrive at the studio at six in the morning. You have a makeup artist who takes you and makes you look fifteen years younger in half an hour, and she's interested in you. Usually it's the same one who's been with you for ten or fifteen years. She's like a mother. She says, "How's the *caca*? Did you go today?" And if you didn't, she gives you a little pill. They give you a coffee, they bring you onto the set, and they say, "Sit down." So you sit down. The director says, "We're not ready for you," so you go back to your trailer. They feed you. They give you more coffee, cigarettes. At the end of all this, you are very richly paid and you can even make love to the producer's wife. Now I ask you, why should I be a pain in the ass?' "

As Cyrano de Bergerac, 1990

15

Cyrano

By the mid-1980s, Guillaume and Julie were entering their teenage years and going to the local schools in Bougival. Elisabeth was returning to her work in acting. She starred as Gérard's wife in *Jean de Florette,* she played opposite him on the stage in *Tartuffe,* and she also wrote a group of lovely songs for Gérard, which he turned into a popular recording.

Elisabeth was now giving acting classes a few times a week in Bougival, and one season she had her students prepare a whimsical play titled *Toute Différente et la Langouste.* While the project started out modestly enough, Elisabeth and her students began getting excited about the idea of putting on a full-scale production for the village of Bougival. They found a local hall, put together their costumes, and started rehearsing. Soon word of the project started to spread in the small Paris theater community. By opening night, the village was lined with big Peugeots and Citroëns and Mercedeses from Paris, as the opening of Elisabeth's play had become an intriguing event for Paris theater insiders, and anyone eager to curry favor with the Depardieus. And when the crowd poured into the hall, who should all these Parisians see up on a platform, manning the lights and lending moral encouragement? Gérard. He was delighted that Elisabeth was again working on stage, and he was eager to lend a hand. Her play later had a limited run in a theater in Paris.

For several years, both of Gérard's parents had been in declining health, and in 1988 Lilette died. Just a few months later, Dédé, heartbroken, died too. Lilette, who had always dreamed of traveling the world, died in an ambulance en route to the hospital. Dédé, who had spent much of his life traveling in his mind without ever leaving Châteauroux, died in a Paris clinic filled with elderly Moslems. Gérard, who had acted out his mother's dreams of travel and had pursued her passion for cinema, had never really shared his feelings with Lilette. And Gérard, who had acted out his father's dream of seeing the sea and had pursued Dédé's passions for wine and poetic whimsy, had never really shared his feelings with Dédé either. So that same year, when he wrote his memoir, *Stolen Letters,* Gérard said in public what he had never been able to tell them in private. The first letter in the book is written directly to Lilette.

"You sacrificed yourself for us," he wrote. "You were a woman of charm, like Catherine Deneuve, you transformed yourself, without understanding it, and without realizing it, into a childbearer. You gave me everything, discreetly. To the point of exhaustion, almost to the point of death. So now you cannot stop me from saying what all your noise and yelling tried vainly to stifle. That taboo phrase, that minuscule phrase that our cries so long contained, that phrase of which we were all afraid, I write you now, my Lilette, simply: '*Je t'aime.*' "

The next letter Gérard wrote directly to his father. "Surprise, Dédé. In spite of yourself, you were a model for me. Oh, sure, you never told me one night, in a private moment, looking me in the eye, your hand on my shoulder, 'You will be a man, my son!' You never imposed anything on me, I never received lessons or advice. I would not have wanted them anyway. . . . If you were pressed to teach me a lesson, it was to say I did not know how to hold my fishing rod. About that you'd scream. . . . One thing you left me with, my Dédé. I never saw you judge anyone, or ever once badmouth anybody. At the very most, I would sometimes hear a great sigh: *'Ouaff!'* And never another word was said."

In writing his memoir, part of Gérard's purpose seemed to be to achieve a final reconciliation with Lilette and Dédé, and with the turmoils of his childhood. And it was typical of Depardieu that he would carry forth this very private communion in the full glare of the public eye. Most actors struggle to keep their private lives private; Gérard has a different urge. He does not want his family, and, above all, his children, subjected to public scrutiny because of his fame. But at the same time, he sometimes feels a compelling urge to throw open his own heart for all the world to see. Why?

When Gérard says that he feels he is a "medium," he is not talking mysticism and claiming that he is in touch with divine spirits. He is saying that as an actor and an artist, he absorbs all sorts of forces and feelings, and then seeks to communicate them and share them with the public, through his art. In his mind, this is near to the essence of what cinema is all about. Why do people go to the movies? To be entertained, certainly. But also to find people on the screen who feel the same way they feel, who share their worries and their insecurities, their hopes and their disappointments. In Gérard's mind, some people may go to the movies only for thrills and chills, but many others go in search of an emotional transaction, a bonding, and an actor is there to facilitate that bonding, to reach out and free up the emotions of his friends in the audience, to help them laugh when need be, or to help them cry when need be. And when it came to the death of Lilette and Dédé, he felt a compelling need to explore what he felt, to bring his emotions to the surface and share them with his public. If by sharing his emotions through the medium of a book, as he constantly does through the medium of cinema, and if those emotions can somehow reach out and touch readers, even resonate and move them, then he feels he has served a useful and even noble purpose. And if readers in turn applaud his book, the way people applaud his movies, that irrefutable sign of affection will give him the sense of satisfaction and fulfillment he constantly craves.

In the mid-1980s, Gérard entered a particularly fecund period of work. Miou-Miou describes Gérard as "a force cut free," and that certainly is reflected in the fluidity and abundance of his creative production during this period. Now he seemed able to take on new roles and shed them with the same ease that he pulled on his jeans, or his medieval robes in *The Return of Martin Guerre,* or his wig and skirt in Blier's *Ménage,* or his hunchback's hump in *Jean de Florette.* He helped to lead the French Revolution in *Danton,* played Rodin in *Camille Claudel* with Isabelle Adjani, and incarnated a tormented priest in Maurice Pialat's *Under Satan's Sun.* His range and relentless drive awed many critics around the world, and many of his peers as well. When Hollywood remade *Martin Guerre* in the early 1990s under the title *Sommersby*, with Jodie Foster and Richard Gere, Gérard's role was first offered to Tom Cruise. "I was intrigued by the idea," Cruise says, "but then I went back and screened the original. And when I saw Gérard, I said no way am I going to do this picture. There is no way I can match what he conveyed on the screen. He was awesome."

"Gérard Depardieu is not only the greatest, most enthusiastic film actor in France, he is also the most generous," Vincent Canby wrote in 1989. "Since 1971, he has made 64 movies, good, bad, great and indifferent. Some people give time, bone marrow or blood to help their friends. Mr. Depardieu appears in their movies. Without him, there might be no French film industry."

As Canby underscores, Gérard was now more than an actor; often the whole of French cinema seemed to rest on his beamlike shoulders. His choice of roles, and his relentless pace, were dictated, to some extent, by the needs of his extended film family; he had become essential to the health of the French film industry. His presence in a film was now a guarantee of box-office success and therefore startup funding; if a young director could interest Gérard in a script—and dozens tried—it would be a virtual guarantee of a first big break. Like a peasant planting his garden and working his fields, Gérard was now generating script ideas of his own, and he was helping produce and distribute the films of friends. In this role, he was also becoming one of the leading matchmakers of French cinema, linking up actors with directors, directors with producers, and French friends with his extended film family in America. In the clannish world of French cinema, he was becoming the central switchboard and *entremetteur,* fulfilling a role he felt he had been entrusted by François Truffaut, who died in 1984. As Gérard wrote four years later in *Stolen Letters,* addressing his friend François directly: "It was you who told me to make sure that everyone in the world of cinema talk to each other and get together." Gérard did not intend to let him down.

But Gérard's matchmaking did not always work. One of his most difficult cases was Maurice Pialat. Stormy and irascible, with the temperament of a great painter, Pialat was both a brilliant director and a celebrated pain in the ass. Naturally, Gérard considered working with him a first-rate challenge, and together they made three fine films: *Loulou, Police,* and *Under Satan's Sun.* But with Pialat, nothing was easy. One day, while shooting a scene for *Loulou,* Pialat went into a snit and stormed off the set. Gérard calmly took over, called *"Moteur!"* and shot the scene himself. "Maurice told me later it was the best scene in the movie," Gérard says with a laugh. Gérard came to adore Pialat, in part because, as he puts it, "we're both out of the Middle Ages and we both love to eat." During the shooting of *Under Satan's Sun,* every day they would take their lunch break together and sit down to huge mounds of frogs' legs. Soon both men saw their weight shoot up, and their blood pressure as well. Finally, the shoot had to be halted for three weeks to give them a chance to recover.

One night, out of some fiendish impulse, Gérard invited Pialat to a dinner party he was throwing in a Parisian restaurant. (Gérard at this moment was trying his hand at singing, in a very successful show at the Zenith Theater with Barbara, one of France's most popular and original singers.) He also invited Marguerite Duras, and he arranged for Pialat and Duras to sit facing each other at the table. The two were giants in their fields, and they both had giant temperaments as well. "There they were, two monsters," Gérard says. "And Duras says to Pialat, 'Is it true that in making one movie you dug up your dead mother?'

" 'Well,' said Pialat, 'I didn't want to dig up anybody else's!' "

With *Jean de Florette* in 1986, Gérard's international reputation was sealed. In Claude Berri's adaptation of Marcel Pagnol's novel about La France Profonde, Gérard plays a naive, hunchbacked city slicker who inherits a family property and moves to the country to become a farmer. But two wily peasants, played by Yves Montand and Daniel Auteuil, want his property, so they plug up his only water source, a natural spring, in order to drive him from their realm. In this epic production, Elisabeth played Gérard's understanding and sympathetic wife, a woman unable to wean her husband from his insane labors and his folly about "going back to the land." At the outset, the city slicker does pretty well in the country, planting his crops, raising rabbits, and integrating himself into the closed village society. But then a terrible drought sets into the south of France and starts ruining all the fruits of his labor. In a valiant effort to save his crops, and his dreams, Gérard hauls in water from wherever he can find it, carrying the buckets on an ox's yoke he balances across his hump. Meanwhile, the two greedy peasants watch his plight with growing delight. Gérard prays for rain, and a storm appears on the horizon. But when the storm blows off in another direction, Gérard is a broken man. He slumps to his knees, and with tears in his voice he waves his fist at the sky and cries: "There's no one up there! There's no one up there!"

It is one of the most moving scenes of his career, and it is just one of the reasons why *Jean de Florette* became an international hit. In America, the film broke out of the usual art-house circuit and became a success in mainstream theaters as well, competing against the big blockbuster action pictures that by then had become the rage in Hollywood. "*Jean de Florette* worked in Middle America like no French film of its kind," Michael Barker says. "People felt such sympathy for Gérard and his character."

In 1989, Bertrand Blier came back with another of his romantic triangles in *Too Beautiful for You,* written, as usual, with Gérard in mind. After it premiered in America at the Telluride Film Festival in 1989, it opened the New York Film Festival, again at Avery Fisher Hall. Nine years after Gérard had stood on that same stage behind François Truffaut, here he was with Blier and Carole Bouquet, who plays Gérard's wife in the movie. Gérard was planning to stay in the background, behind Blier, and he was totally unprepared for what happened next, again in front of twenty-seven hundred people.

"Blier came out to introduce the film," Barker recalls, "and after telling a few jokes about it, he said, 'And now I would like to introduce not only my actor, but my brother: Gérard Depardieu.' "

Gérard received a thundering ovation and it lasted several minutes. He was overwhelmed and speechless; he had no idea how popular he had become in America. "My heart is beating so hard," he told the crowd, in English. He pointed to the ground and said, "Just nine years ago, Truffaut was right here with me. I can say nothing else." The ovation went on for several minutes more.

For Barker and Tom Bernard, this confirmed what they had been hearing from their theater contacts around the United States: Gérard had achieved a stature in America rarely, if ever, reached by a foreign actor, especially one not speaking English. *"Martin Guerre, Jean de Florette,* and *Too Beautiful for You* put Gérard in that dimension of fame that very few foreign actors have ever had in America," Barker says. "Mastroianni had it in the sixties. Charles Boyer had it in the thirties. One reason these pictures worked was that women really felt romantic about Gérard as a persona."

For Gérard, the warmth of the reception he was receiving from American critics and the American public thrilled him. Growing up among the G.I.'s in Châteauroux, he had idealized and romanticized America. American movies had seized his imagination, and in his mind there was little difference between the reality of America and the America he had seen projected on the screen. Now here he was, at the age of forty, in the adoring embrace of the land he had vowed, as a child, to seduce and conquer. And he probably never suspected for a moment that celebrity in America always carries inside it the seeds of comeuppance and betrayal.

At the close of the 1980s, Gérard embarked on a new movie project: *Cyrano de Bergerac.* Written in 1890 by the poet and playwright Edmond Rostand, *Cyrano* holds a unique place in French literature and in the French imagination. The story, set forth in intricate alexandrine couplets, is drawn loosely from the life of Savinien Cyrano de Bergerac, a seventeenth-century satirist, dramatist, scientist, and intellectual rebel. This Cyrano was a Renaissance man who started out as a soldier and wound up as a free-spirited poet and creative thinker. As portrayed by Rostand, Cyrano embodies two opposite poles of the Gallic spirit: the swashbuckling warrior and the romantic poet. With an artful sword, Cyrano the warrior slays men; with an artful pen, Cyrano the poet seduces women. Rostand's Cyrano has all the makings of a Nietzschean superman, were it not for the undisguisable emblem of his vulnerability and humanity: a grotesquely large nose. Both sides of Cyrano's being yearn for the joy and salvation of a woman's touch and approval. And not just any woman: Cyrano's heart has been captured by the beautiful Roxane, a distant cousin and a kindred romantic spirit. But, shamed by that nose of his, Cyrano the great warrior cannot find the courage or the words to tell her of his love. In her majestic presence, Cyrano is tongue-tied and speechless, certain that a beauty and a spirit as fine and delicate as Roxane's could never be charmed by a face as uncomely as his. One fateful day, Roxane confides to Cyrano that she is attracted—wildly, miserably—to a member of Cyrano's own regiment, the handsome Christian de Neuvillette. Roxane is in a complete romantic swoon, and she fears for Christian's safety in battle. Would Cyrano, indomitable warrior that he is, help to protect the man of her dreams? Cyrano, a romantic to his core, seeing Roxane so upset and wishing desperately to please her, agrees to come to her aid with Neuvillette. Yes, he will serve as her go-between, her trusted *entremetteur.*

Many French schoolchildren read *Cyrano de Bergerac,* and so do many American college students. Theaters around France revive the play from time to time, and in 1950 Hollywood made a thoroughly agreeable *Cyrano* starring Jose Ferrer. Jean-Paul Belmondo played Cyrano on the Paris stage, and so did Jacques Weber. Gérard came to *Cyrano* through the interlocking relationships of his extended film family. The project originated in 1984 with the French production and distribution company Gaumont, when it was under the direction of Gérard's friend Daniel Toscan du Plantier. The first phase of the search was for a writer and director, and Toscan turned for guidance to Jean-Louis Livi, who had left Artmédia to become an independent producer. Livi liked the idea of a joint venture and he put in a call to Jean-Paul Rappeneau, one of France's most refined and meticulous *auteurs.*

"How would you like to make a *Cyrano?"* Livi asked him.

"For television?" Rappeneau asked.

"No, for a feature film."

The idea did not appeal to Rappeneau. "I don't know. Let me think about it. When do you need to know?"

"Tonight. Tomorrow at the latest."

Rappeneau was not a man to make abrupt decisions. He came from an old-line family in Burgundy. He had come to Paris to study law and had been drawn into the movies. He apprenticed and wrote screenplays with Louis Malle; he collaborated with Philippe de Broca on the screenplay for *That Man from Rio,* starring Jean-Paul Belmondo; and he was in his late thirties before he turned to directing. He did *La Vie du*

Château with Philippe Noiret, Catherine Deneuve, and Pierre Brasseur, then waited several years before doing his next film, *Le Sauvage,* with Deneuve and Yves Montand. In between, Rappeneau made publicity films, and he was content to do a feature film once every six years or so. He was a perfectionist, planning every detail of a shoot, and he wanted to leave nothing to chance or instinct. Tall, bald, and courtly, with a taste for fine wine, Rappeneau was the epitome of the gentleman director, and yet he came back to Livi with only one explicit demand: "If I were to do your film, and I am not at all sure I want to, the only man who would be truly interesting to do it with is Gérard Depardieu."

"Gérard?" Livi said. "Great idea! I'll call you back in twenty minutes."

Livi called back in five. "Absolutely. Gérard loves the idea." The word "hesitation" is not in Depardieu's vocabulary.

Rappeneau says he thought of Gérard because he saw in him the same two poles he saw in Cyrano. "Cyrano is someone who is weak and strong at the same time. In France there are few actors who can be weak and strong within the same role, but that is precisely Gérard's strength."

To collaborate on the screenplay, Rappeneau turned to Jean-Claude Carrière, probably the most talented and prolific screenwriter in France. Like Rappeneau, Carrière at first felt that *Cyrano* was outdated and trite, and frankly not worth the months and months it would take to make it into something cinematic. To assess the play more fully, the two men decided to go see a stage production of *Cyrano;* Jacques Weber was giving his final performance of it that very night. By chance, Depardieu had had the same idea: he was sitting in one of the front rows. The two writers watched the play with little enthusiasm. At the end, Weber received a huge final-night ovation. In a grand gesture of the variety Cyrano himself would appreciate, the actor yanked off his false nose and flung it into the cheering crowd.

"The nose landed right in Gérard's lap," Rappeneau says, and he and Carrière decided that this was sign enough to get to work. They tore into Rostand's text, blew off the dust, and found that the heart of the play had not aged at all. They began to see a reservoir of visual images they could weave into a screenplay. Both men now became impassioned with the idea of breathing fresh life into this venerable classic. But the movie was not to be—not yet. Toscan was ushered out of Gaumont amidst corporate financial troubles, and the project sat on the shelf for the next three years. Then Gérard came back into the venture, playing godfather and go-between. René Cleitmann, a friend of his, had just helped produce Blier's *Ménage,* and Gérard set up a meeting between

Cleitmann and Jean-Louis Livi to discuss potential joint projects. Livi mentioned *Cyrano,* Cleitmann agreed, and suddenly Rappeneau's phone was ringing again.

"Drop everything!" Livi told him. *"Cyrano* is back on."

Rappeneau envisioned a sumptuous production, and he knew a way to cut costs: shoot all the interiors in Budapest. Rappeneau had done a film there before, and he knew of a quality local crew and a well-equipped studio. He and Cleitmann went to Budapest and made the necessary arrangements. Then Rappeneau plunged back into the final draft of his script and the daunting process of casting. The primary difficulty in putting on a production of *Cyrano* is in the delivery of the alexandrine couplets. Rostand's classical, literary French does not roll off the tongue when read as prose; it takes special gifts to make it flow forth in rhyming couplets with twelve syllables to the line. Rappeneau knew he would have a terrible time assembling a proper cast, and in months of auditions he found that only classically trained actors and actresses seemed able to handle the language and the delivery. To play Roxane, Rappeneau did find just the woman he wanted: Anne Brochet, the brilliant young star of the Paris Conservatory. She had beauty, delicacy, passion, and a long, elegant neck reminiscent of Audrey Hepburn. She also had talent. To play her suitor de Neuvillette, Rappeneau settled on Vincent Perez, a classically trained actor who seemed to fit the part of a handsome but somewhat dimwitted soldier. But the deeper Rappeneau got into the complexities of Rostand's verses and the problems of delivering them, the more nervous he became. "I had a whole troupe of classically trained actors," he says, "but how was Gérard going to cope?"

Rappeneau was not encouraged by their first working session. Using a tape recorder, Rappeneau put Gérard through some of Cyrano's passages, and the reading did not go well. And Gérard felt it. But when Rappeneau suggested more such sessions, Gérard refused. Rappeneau's anxiety grew as the scheduled production date approached. One month before they were all to leave for Budapest, Rappeneau rented a large rehearsal studio and called in his top forty actors and actresses. He was nervous about this critical meeting—so nervous that he set all his thoughts out on paper beforehand. Then, with the elite of the Comédie-Française and the Paris Conservatory gathered around him, Rappeneau read his letter, outlining his planned procedure and his goals for the production, explaining how "we would find our own music in the verses."

Gérard took in Rappeneau's presentation with little reaction, and soon thereafter he and the rest of the cast gathered for several days of readings in Paris. Now Rappeneau's worries deepened. Some of the classical actors did well, but Gérard's readings were dry, academic, and off the mark. Worse, he seemed bored with the exercise, and occasionally he even seemed to doze off. At one stage, the Comédie-Française actors wanted to get some props and begin adding gestures and movement to their rehearsals. Gérard would have none of it. "He believes in those crucial, magical seconds when the camera starts to roll," Rappeneau says. "I was not so sure."

Fretting all the way, Rappeneau packed up his cast and crew and went to Budapest. But he felt better upon his arrival. This was the fall of 1989, the Berlin Wall was coming down, and the winds of freedom were blowing across Hungary and the rest of Eastern Europe. The local crew was excited to be helping with *Cyrano,* and the first week of the shoot went very well—without Gérard. He was not in the opening scenes and did not need to be on hand. Finally came the day of his first appearance as Cyrano. In the film, Cyrano enters in the middle of a theater production, and he is so appalled by its mediocrity, he cries out from a balcony in the theater and demands that the play be stopped. Rappeneau was shooting in chronological order, and so Gérard first appeared on the theater set just as Cyrano did—and just as dramatically. The hall was immense, and it was filled with four hundred actors in costume when Gérard appeared on the balcony to halt the performance.

"He launched into his opening monologue with a vengeance," Rappeneau says. "He was shouting, shrieking. And this was not at all as he had done it in rehearsal. I was panic-stricken. After these first few minutes, I took Gérard aside. 'Listen, Gérard, this is a bit strong, don't you think?' By the end of the first day I was asking myself, If we start here, where are we going to end up?"

But that night Gérard explained what he had felt making his entrance. "When I stood on that balcony, and I saw all those people below, and I saw the immensity of the hall, by instinct I felt I had to have this power, this force, if I was going to silence the entire crowd." Rappeneau, when he saw the rushes, knew Gérard had been right. "I had thought of everything—except the physical reality of that huge hall filled with people. Gérard saw it instantly."

Still, during the first days of the shoot, Gérard was not happy with the chemistry on the set. Then he realized why. Scores of the extras were Hungarian, and they had no clue as to what Cyrano was saying. Gérard, in turn, could not feel from them the response he needed. So he stopped the production and brought in a translator to explain, line by line, the day's verses and actions. Only then could he feel he was truly communicating with his fellow actors and his surroundings. "Gérard absorbs everything," Rappeneau says. "When he comes into a group, right away he can sense the tensions there might be between so and so, and everything that is simmering below the surface. He has an eye and, above all, an ear which are extraordinary."

A few days into the shoot, Gérard melded totally into Cyrano. The ear that Professor Tomatis had once found to be badly out of kilter now had perfect pitch. The memory that once had been able to retain nothing now catalogued every syllable and nuance of Rostand's play. Above all, there was his voice. The voice that throughout his childhood had been so blocked it could emerge only in choked fits and starts was now filled with the music of ancient French, flowing forth in the lilting rhythms of alexandrine verse. Gérard's fellow actors were stunned by his virtuosity and feeling, and so was Rappeneau, especially when he thought back to those first days of rehearsal among the elite of the Comédie-Française.

"During all our first readings," he says, "when Gérard was sitting there expressionless, sometimes even seeming to doze, in fact he was listening to everyone, he was ingesting their technique, and finally he took their technique, transformed it, and surpassed it. On their own terrain, he proved he was better than anyone else."

Cyrano's unrequited love for Roxane is the core of the story, and Gérard was most inspired during his scenes with Anne Brochet, his Roxane. Brochet found that Gérard demands that his fellow actors be very open and natural with him. "You have to be very simple," she says, "honest. As soon as you start to bluff or fake, he feels it. You have to be real. Happily, we found a certain harmony, even in the way our voices came together."

Authenticity, purity of flavor, generosity, emotional truths. The watchwords of Gérard's acting credo all came to the fore in the special chemistry of Rappeneau's production, and in Gérard's own symbiotic rapport with Cyrano and all he represents and evokes.

"Technique was forgotten, but the technique was there," Rappeneau says. "We were in the realm of pure emotion. That is what Gérard brought forth. In the beginning, during the rehearsals, I had been thinking only of technique. But Gérard was already beyond that. At some point he had assimilated everything, and he was going higher, to find the truth. He was making great art."

In France, in America, and around the world, audiences and critics reacted to the movie with a rare degree of fervor. "The glorious new *Cyrano de Bergerac* brings together the right man—Gérard Depardieu—at the right time of his life and career with one of the juiciest roles in European drama, one he was born to play. And with precisely the right nose," wrote Kevin Thomas of the Los Angeles *Times. Variety,* the bible of the American film industry, was equally exuberant: "A winner by more than a nose, *Cyrano* attains a near-perfect balance of verbal and visual flamboyance. Depardieu's grand performance as the facially disgraced swordsman-poet sets a new standard with which all future Cyranos will have to reckon."

"Mr. Depardieu brings astonishing humor and pathos to Cyrano," wrote Vincent Canby of the *New York Times.* "It is one measure of his mysterious grace as a film actor that he can play the manic, love-possessed homosexual lover in *Ménage,* the bewildered bourgeois husband in *Too Beautiful for You* and now the title role in *Cyrano de Bergerac* without missing a beat, or appearing to change his suit or even his nose." Andrew Sarris, one of the most knowledgeable American experts on French film, wrote of Gérard in the New York *Observer*: "He is more than flesh and blood, he is open wound and enraged vulnerability. The key to the dynamism of his acting is not in action but in emotion."

In Britain, the critic for *Time Out* also raved: "Unexpectedly light on his feet in the vivid action sequences, hauntingly tender in the love scenes, deftly shifting between comedy and tragedy, Depardieu breathes teeming, complex life into a fustily over-familiar character—and in so doing looks set to conquer, once and for all, the movie-going world."

In France, *Cyrano* silenced any remaining skepticism about Gérard and his awesome gifts. At Cannes he was named best actor; he won the César for best actor; and *Cyrano* won the César for best movie of 1990. Along with the rest of his work, *Cyrano* brought Gérard a "Super César" as the actor of the decade. Later would come more glory from America: *Cyrano* would be nominated for an Academy Award as best foreign movie, and Gérard would be nominated for best actor—a rare Hollywood honor for an actor in a foreign-language movie.

Beyond the awards and the applause, for Gérard, an actor in perpetual search of an author, Cyrano was more than a role—it was a final act of validation and self-definition. From this point on, the richness of Cyrano's story and the poetry of his language would still belong to Edmond Rostand, but the voice, the feelings, and the universal grandeur of *Cyrano de Bergerac* would now belong forever to Depardieu.

"What is beautiful in *Cyrano* is that we are all Cyrano," he says. "What is beautiful is his quest for love. He is not a man of small emotions; he is a man of big emotions. Cyrano is a role for all actors, not just me. To play Cyrano, you need heart. You need life. Joy. It is the opposite of ego; you just have to do it, and give it everything you've got inside."

PART 5

To America

The *Green Card* softball team

16

The Gift

What is the nature of creativity? What are its roots? Is it a natural gift? Or can creativity be taught? And if so, how?

The Australian director Peter Weir has been pondering questions such as these for much of his life, and he explored certain aspects of them in his highly acclaimed movie *Dead Poets Society*. In the film, Robin Williams plays an unconventional teacher at a stuffy prep school on America's East Coast in the late 1950s. Like the real teacher who inspired this story, Williams tries to lead his students into the realms of art, literature, and poetry by offering them a compendium of advice, almost a guide to enriching the creative spirit: Break out of your mental and physical habits! Stand on desks! See the world from fresh perspectives! Get back in touch with the sensory and the instinctive! Cultivate a free and open heart! Take risks! Take risks! *Carpe diem,* seize the day! And follow the credo of the poet Henry David Thoreau and "suck out all the marrow of life."

Weir brought to the film an unusual sensibility and background. His family origins trace back to Scotland, but he is a third-generation Australian. He grew up in Adelaide in the 1950s and sixties in a traditional middle-class home. But in 1965, when he was an impressionable young man, he took a trip to Egypt, Greece, Italy, and finally to France. For Weir, as for generations of students from Australia and all over the world, such journeys were not a sight-seeing vacation or a pleasant way to while away a summer break. They were part of a much deeper yearning. "In Australia, we tend to feel a bit dispossessed," he says. "There's no connection to the past."

Before he left, Weir sensed that momentous things would happen on the trip, and indeed they did. On the five-week boat trip to Egypt, he met a young Australian woman named Wendy. They became friends, then fell in love, and she would become his wife and the mother of their two children. At the Pyramids in Egypt, the temples in Greece, and the archaeological sites in Italy, Peter became increasingly excited with everything he was encountering. "It was a kind of classical education," he says. And then came France and Paris, the real or spiritual home of so many of the world's greatest painters and writers. "I had some sort of dream of France," he says, and he was not let down.

In Paris, Weir roamed the boulevards and cafés and the art museums, strolled along the Seine and through the Luxembourg Gardens. He and Wendy went home with an enduring love for France and for Paris in particular, and he returned to Australia with a heightened artistic sensibility.

From the beginning of his career in making movies, Peter managed to weave some very serious themes into high-class entertainment. In *Gallipoli,* a story with echoes of *The Red Badge of Courage,* he told of a young man coming face-to-face with the horrors and the random stupidities of war. In *The Year of Living Dangerously,* among the finest movies ever made about the life and work of a foreign correspondent, he tells the story of a young journalist facing political upheaval and repression in Sukarno's Indonesia. The year was 1965, the same year he went to Europe. "That was my year of living dangerously," he says. With the young Mel Gibson playing the lead, and seducing Sigourney Weaver in the process, the movie was acclaimed by critics and audiences around the world. With Hollywood backing, Weir then made two movies starring Harrison Ford, *Witness* and *The Mosquito Coast,* the latter drawn from the novel by Paul Theroux.

With *Dead Poets Society,* Weir again managed to tackle serious themes in a popular way. Through the character portrayed by Robin Williams, Weir raised troubling questions about traditional ideas of teaching and how we educate our children. Williams was terrific, and so were the young men who played his students. In America, the film became a must-see for parents, teachers, and many young people, and in France it became a sensation. For months it was the country's number-one hit, and it stirred a national debate about creativity, teaching, and the state of education in France.

After *Dead Poets,* though, Weir went into a creative lull. He was not blocked; he was just not thrilled or energized by any of the ideas he was considering turning into movies. He toyed with several story lines, but whichever way he turned, he could get no wind into his sails. "I was becalmed," is the way he puts it. In the middle of this post-*Poets* funk, he and Wendy went to see Andrzej Wajda's *Danton,* with Gérard in the title role, and they found him brilliant and exciting. As a leader of the French Revolution, he exuded energy, life, and creative fervor. "God, I'd love to work with him," Weir said coming out of the movie, and then Wendy gave him an idea. "What about adapting the story of that Englishman in southern California?" This was a draft script that had never quite jelled, either on paper or in Weir's imagination. It was the story of a foreigner who was having trouble securing working papers, what in America is referred to as a green card. In order to secure the papers, the Englishman was looking for a bride, a quick, temporary "paper marriage," a shady but common practice among immigrants in America and Western Europe.

By coincidence, Gérard at that moment came to Australia, on one of his marathon global tours promoting a movie, in this case *Les Compères.* In his interviews, Gérard was also telling the local press how much he admired the vibrance of Australian cinema, including the works of Peter Weir. Wendy suggested that Peter arrange a meeting with Gérard, but Weir demurred. In his mind, Gérard was now one of the greatest actors in the world, and if Weir went to see him, he would go with a script in hand. What he did instead was clip a photo of Gérard from a local magazine and pin it above his writing table, for inspiration, and he turned back to his fictive Englishman in California. Weir now saw the story as a light romantic comedy and a perfect vehicle for Gérard. He would play a Frenchman who comes to New York; this would be an ideal way to introduce Gérard and his gifts to a broad cross section of the English-speaking world. Now Weir felt both his imagination and his story catch fire. As he puts it, "My muse returned."

In writing a part he hoped Gérard would play, in entering his skin and spirit the way an actor does with a role, Weir came to see a side of Gérard that was far different from the violence and coarseness he had seen in some of Gérard's early roles. In his screenplay, Peter brought out Gérard's vulnerability and presented him as a struggling composer who was painfully self-conscious about his problems with English. But Gérard's character also has a primal force and a peasant instinct; in this cross-cultural romance he would not be susceptible to New York notions of political or gastronomic correctness. No, he would smoke unfiltered Gitanes, drink powerhouse black espressos, and eat plenty of red meat, blood-rare. Still, with women he would be very timid and respectful. As a struggling artist, he would be blocked; music would come from him only in fits and starts.

Once Weir had a strong draft of the screenplay, he took it to Hollywood, to Disney. The Disney executives loved it, and Weir finally took the project to his intended partner. Gérard had never done a major film in English, and so, as usual, Gérard was hesitant, analytical, and reflective. "Absolutely!" he cried at the very first suggestion of working with Peter Weir, in whatever language. The two men first met in Paris; then, in December 1989, Gérard went to Australia to work with Weir on the script. The man Gérard met was tall and slender, with freckles, reddish hair graying at the temples, and very gentle eyes. Right away, Gérard sensed that the director of *Dead Poets Society* was a kindred spirit. Gérard and Weir worked well together. As Gérard put it, "Peter did the writing; I knew about the lighting."

Weir speaks a bit of French, and at that stage Gérard spoke only a rough approximation of English, so their means of communication often bypassed language. This made for some frustrations but ultimately a stronger bond between actor and writer. "Peter is someone who listens beautifully, a bit like a father," Gérard says. When Weir made *The Last Wave,* he became close to an aborigine wise man, and they had a profound, mostly nonverbal communication. The aborigine language contains no past tense and no future tense, only the present. Everything is here and now—real, tactile. Weir found it was the same with Gérard, and he started thinking of him as a "white aborigine."

Ironically, Weir's observation echoed something Gérard had written in *Stolen Letters.* When he was growing up, Dédé and Lilette lived in a world where the past and the future were shuttered off. All that remained was what Gérard termed "the force of the present." "The present is the most violent thing there is, because it's there. It's *there,"* he wrote. "It's what we call life. With its odors, its discomforts. Happily, the present burns, it sizzles, it is a gigantic fire. It keeps us from stopping. To love the past is uncertain. I don't like to wallow in memories. The rule of my parents was time, the beating heart of a clock: 'Tick, tock. Tick, tock,' present time."

At the start of 1990, Gérard was very nervous about making his first movie in English. He was nervous that working in a language he barely understood, he would lose the spontaneity he needs to fly. "It was just like when I arrived in Paris at the age of sixteen, knowing nothing of my own language," Gérard says. "Then all I could do was repeat the words

I was reading, without really understanding them, and now twenty years later I was arriving in America in exactly the same situation."

For help, Gérard turned to Professor Tomatis, the man who had guided him through his initial speech problems. Tomatis outfitted him with a portable "electronic ear" and a series of tapes, to help accustom and train Gérard's ear to the specific frequency ranges of American English.

In March 1990, Weir began shooting *Green Card* in Manhattan. Gérard's arrival for his first major English-language movie merited two lengthy articles in the *New York Times.* And just like the unbridled Frenchman he was supposed to portray, Gérard arrived on the set and promptly proved himself to be politically incorrect. "You have superb breasts," he casually told one young woman. She was outraged, which only left Gérard confused and embarrassed. "It was a bit surprising, because I arrived as I am. I don't like to provoke people, but my face just provokes, and in France you can come right out and say, 'You have superb breasts.' Well, when I said that in New York, American women were completely shocked. And I would say, 'No, no, I don't mean to be insulting or even suggestive; it's just because I find your breasts truly lovely. That is the right word isn't it, breasts?' Which only got me in deeper. Afterward, and only after they really rapped my knuckles, I could say anything, even the most monstrous things, and everyone laughed. They would say, 'Well, it's okay, he's a *Frenchman.*' It's sad. You can't let morality kill all the joy of life."

For Weir, working with Gérard opened a new phase in his own explorations into the mysteries of creativity. He was intrigued by how joyous and childlike Gérard was on the set and by the fact that he seemed "to have no ego." Weir had decided to weave into the script some of the details of Gérard's real life, such as his tattoos and his youthful encounters with Irène and Michèle. By keeping Gérard's spoken lines simple and allowing him to speak in his natural, approximate English, Peter lifted from Gérard a great deal of anxiety and gave his intuition free play. "Peter never forces. You are never a victim of his story," Gérard says. "Bertrand Blier is a savage in his approach, whereas Peter makes films the way the Beatles made music."

As a counterpoint to Gérard in all his Gitane and red-meat vigor, the American actress Andie MacDowell seemed perfect, a gentle soul with a delicate, almost ethereal beauty. As usual, Gérard put himself in charge of on-set chemistry, starting with Andie. They established a good rapport, but Gérard was still frustrated. Andie was a fine actress, yet at the end of the day's shooting she would rarely join Gérard and Weir for a drink or dinner; she would go home to her husband and children. Gérard says he was not out to seduce her, but he wanted to establish a closer emotional harmony with her, to translate to the camera. On the other hand, Andie's on-screen character, Brontë, is supposed to be standoffish and emotionally torn. At the outset, she has a safe relationship with an archetypal eighties politically correct New York man: a sweet, sensitive, nonsmoking vegetarian who promotes feminism and ecology. Next to him, Gérard represents trouble. He is gentle with her, but in other ways he's like a caveman, and, damn him!, he stirs in Brontë some deep-seated and seemingly repressed wellspring of passion and compassion. Her head looks at Gérard and says no way, but something deeper wants desperately to say Yes!

"My character could not really like him," Andie says. "My idea was that she likes him and it bothers her; he was all wrong. She is so attracted to this guy, but he is just wrong. And she is so worried about always pleasing everybody. He is shabby, and her parents would never approve of him, and, oh, God, she just loved him."

Weir tried not to tamper with the couple's personal chemistry. He usually stayed in the background, allowing Gérard to "direct" Andie, to give her confidence and draw her out. "Gérard has a talent for making you feel good about yourself. He's very generous in that way," Andie says. "He is a very humble man. And I can't imagine him being anything but that. Working with him, you never feel in him a trace of ego."

During the shoot, Weir also felt an unusual harmony with Gérard. Despite their language differences, there were no arguments or misunderstandings on the set. Working with Gérard was also a welcome reconnection to a certain idea he had of France. Over the years, he and Wendy had returned to Paris, but they had never again found the same freshness of spirit or creative fervor they had felt on their first idyllic trip. In working with Gérard, though, Peter felt that creative fervor. "Gérard was more than an actor; he was an artist. And a very unique one," he says. "He somehow embodied the original feeling I had of France. Working with him, I felt, 'Ah, yes, this is it.' "

Jean-Paul Rappeneau, like many other directors who have worked with Gérard, came to see him as a "medium," able to absorb and transmit energy and messages, and even to divine what Rappeneau was thinking. Weir, too, sees Gérard as a medium, with an uncanny ability to communicate with everyone, no matter what their language or culture. "Gérard is Russian, Jewish, aborigine, Hindu, Arab, whatever," Weir says. "In making *Green Card,* I got to know *a* Gérard Depardieu, but I doubt I got to know *the* Gérard Depardieu. He has all sorts of people inside him."

One night during a shoot in Manhattan, Weir organized a dinner party. Among the guests were Gérard; Harrison Ford; Linda Hunt, the marvelous actress from *The Year of Living Dangerously;* and Oliver Sacks, the neurologist whose research was celebrated in Penny Marshall's *Awakenings.* Sacks is also a writer, and in his book *The Man Who Mistook His Wife for a Hat,* he discusses unusual neurological disorders whereby some interior spaces of a person's brain seem to get disconnected from other realms of mental activity. The dinner was convivial and stimulating, and the next morning on the set Weir thanked Gérard for coming. Gérard was effusive about the other guests. "I slept wonderfully, and they gave me very rich dreams," he told Weir. "And you know, Peter, at one time or another I've *been* all those people." The remark still fascinates Weir.

"There are creative people who are wonderful transmitters," Peter says. "Gérard both transmits and receives. His is a pure communication, not an intellectual communication."

In his creative process, Gérard does seem to rely on a touch of magic. He often notes that his two grandmothers dabbled in the gentler forms of witchcraft, and Dédé, in his own primitive way, believed in the powers of alchemy, in the need to work sheet metal by the light of a full moon. All these references to alchemy, magic, mediums, and creative "transmitters" may sound like metaphysical nonsense, but they do pertain to the way Gérard works as an actor. As explained earlier, he prepares a role via an interior journey, searching inside himself for the hidden shadows of characters, or archetypes, he believes are buried in his being and psyche. Through the words of scripts and his encounters and connections with other creative people, Gérard feels he can locate these buried archetypes and bring them to the surface of his consciousness, where he can explore them in front of the camera. This part of his creative process is mysterious, almost mystical, and now some of what Gérard has to say about his creative process bears repeating in a fuller context.

In Gérard's view, many actors, especially many American actors trained in the Method, often work too intellectually and analytically. This to him is artifice and unnatural, and therefore deadening to creativity. There are many American actors, trained in the Method, whom he admires; if that process works for them, fine. But he has to follow a more intuitive path. When Gérard says that playing Cyrano is "the opposite of ego," he is not talking in a light, pop-psychology way; he is talking in a serious way about his craft. Too much ego in an actor, he feels, is deadening; it kills emotional spontaneity. Too much rehearsal, like too much ego, kills the necessary effervescence and intuition. Given a script with the right words and language, and given the right on-set chemistry, Gérard believes that the body and the emotions will naturally respond the way they should. Thinking only disturbs the creative process. "On camera, you must never think," he says. "If you think, you stop. You block yourself. You just have to do it."

Gérard feels that the roots of creativity are within all of us, and that creativity blossoms forth most naturally and spontaneously in children. When Gérard jokes and plays the prankster on the set, he is on one level just cutting loose and having a jolly time, but this is also his way of trying to remain childlike. When the camera begins to turn, he wants to be free of all artifice and mental constraints; he wants his mind and body to be like a musical instrument, not a word processor. Gérard feels that his own creativity resides in a realm beneath the ego—in the realm of emotions, dreams, and fantasies. "I never interpret a role," he says, "I just allow myself to dream."

When he starts preparing a role, Gérard also searches for the correlating shadow, or archetype, in a realm somewhere beneath the clutches of the ego. He can read books about *Cyrano de Bergerac* and study the text, and this will stimulate his mind, but the process by which he melds himself into Cyrano is by no means a rational one. Indeed, he says that the real search happens in a realm of mental chaos and anarchy—a realm not easily accessible to the conscious mind. "The best research always begins in darkness and incoherence," he says. "To me, creating is trying to explore all those interior spaces that belong to me, but which I do not yet know or understand. Only in living them can I discover them."

In talking about his creative process, much of what Gérard says in conversation bears a striking resemblance to what Carl Jung has written about archetypes and his own scientific process as a psychologist and a student of primitive cultures and mythology. In *Memories, Dreams, Reflections,* Jung's account of his own interior journey of discovery, he writes that the real synthesis of what he was researching and learning intellectually happened in a realm beneath his consciousness. His most valuable insights, he wrote, came from the exploration of his own interior spaces, by bringing his dreams, and the shadows they embodied, into the full light of his consciousness. Jung felt that this process of interior probing was a way of reconnecting himself to natural, innate wellsprings of energy and understanding. His account begins: "My life is a story of the self-realization of the unconscious. Everything in the unconscious seeks outward manifestation, and the personality too desires to evolve out of its unconscious conditions and to experience itself as a whole."

Gérard has not read *Memories, Dreams, Reflections,* and he has only a distant knowledge of Jung's work. But intuitively, and through his work with Professor Tomatis and his encounters with drama teachers, psychologists, and psychiatrists, Gérard seems to have arrived at some of the same insights and understandings as Jung. Gérard describes his work as an ongoing journey of self-discovery. Through the roles he plays he is constantly searching to define his inner dimensions and his outer edges and limits. In making more than eighty films, Gérard has embodied a vast spectrum of characters, temperaments, and sexual orientations; making four or five movies a year, he seems almost compelled to explore and to manifest outwardly everything he has inside. Gérard rarely plays the same type of character twice; that holds no interest or challenge. Once he has explored one part of his being, Gérard is eager to move on to an interior region he has not yet explored. By the end of the 1980s, for instance, Gérard wanted nothing more to do with violent roles. He had already explored his interior capacity for rage and violence too much. He told friends that from then on, he wanted to do only roles that were positive and life-affirming. But these, too, lead him into deep interior exploration.

In his work, Gérard often seeks ways to disrupt and alter his usual frames of reference and patterns of thought. Like the teacher in *Dead Poets Society* who urges his students to stand on desks, to see themselves and the world from a fresh perspective, Gérard has a variety of ways he uses to see his characters through fresh eyes. Rarely will he come onto a set drunk, but Gérard does see alcohol, and even external emotional trauma, as a means of pushing himself toward the most inaccessible caverns of his psyche. One day during the shooting of *1492,* an American actor came to him and said he might not be able to shoot that afternoon's scene; he was suffering from a bad fever. "Use it!" Gérard told him. "Bring your fever; play with it. Maybe it will give you a different view into your character."

Much of Jung's pioneering work in psychology focused on the concept of archetypes. In studying several primitive cultures and their myths, and in working with schizophrenic patients, Jung came to the conclusion that the human mind has an immense capacity for creating images with universal themes and meanings. In their myths and fables, radically different primitive cultures often produced clusters of images that were remarkably similar. These clusters Jung called archetypes. He believed that these "archetypal images" were buried in the psyches of men and women from many different cultures, no matter how civilized or how primitive, extending back in time for centuries, and probably millennia. Much of this converges with the way Gérard describes his own creative process, and it is very similar to what he and Professor Tomatis refer to as mankind's collective "genetic memory."

One of the universal archetypes Jung found was the Trickster. The Trickster is a wild, disruptive being, irrational, breaking rules, and possessing a primitive, caveman energy. The Trickster has a dark, malevolent side and a humorous, positive side—a side which some psychologists and sociologists define as the Prankster. The Prankster is a jester, a clown, someone who makes people laugh and forget their troubles, who puts their minds at ease. Laughter being a universal language, the Prankster is a welcome go-between, an *entremetteur* who draws people together. The Prankster's realm is not logic or reason; it is the senses and the emotions. He is not there to make you think; he is there to make you laugh or cry. To do that, the archetypal Prankster generates a nonstop stream of childlike make-believe and creativity.

Archetypes like the Prankster are essential to myth and art. In his essay "The Spirit in Man, Art, and Literature," Jung explains why: "The creative process, so far as we are able to follow it at all, consists in the unconscious activation of an archetypal image, and in elaborating and shaping this image into the finished work. By giving it shape, the artist translates it into *the language of the present"* (italics mine).

A movie draws its artists and viewers together in a realm of make-believe and myth, and movies constantly bring us present-day representations of timeless, archetypal images. The ways in which archetypes are represented evolve with changing times and changing social and cultural values. Through the roles he represented on the screen, Gérard became a symbol of the rebellious sixties generation, and then he became representative of the confused male caught in the sexual upheavals of the 1970s and eighties. With *Cyrano,* Gérard returned to one of the most enduring romantic heroes of French literature and the French popular imagination, and his portrayal was acclaimed the world over. Now, in *Green Card,* Gérard again represented an old-fashioned romantic hero, but in a contemporary context. The result was a success beyond its creators' expectations. The film cost $13 million to make, and it grossed over $30 million in the United States alone. The Australians also loved the picture, and it ran for almost a year in London. The French, by contrast, were rather cool to it, perhaps miffed that their national treasure had chosen to take his talents to America and work in English. In America, the film expanded Gérard's popularity from an art-house crowd to Middle America. Again, his screen presence and the spectrum of emotions he stirred produced strong, positive reactions in many American women. "Depardieu has an almost indecent magnetism," wrote Sheila Benson of the Los Angeles *Times*. "Peter Weir wrote *Green Card* with what seems like a seismic understanding of the actor's warring qualities: brutishness and delicacy; elegance and scruffiness; innocence and worldliness; masculinity and femininity." Janet Maslin of the *New York Times* also found Gérard appealing in this role—almost mysteriously so. "Although Mr. Depardieu happens to be one of the world's most graceful screen actors, everything about his physical being argues otherwise. Bearish and barrel-shaped, with unkempt hair and a nose that cannot be made to look straight from any angle, he lumbers amiably through this film without making the slightest concession to garden-variety romance."

In Jung's view, artists are mediums and go-betweens through whom various social and psychological pressures surge and subside. In "The Spirit of Man, Art, and Literature," Jung writes that art and artists often serve their respective cultures and epochs in ways that are veiled, or not immediately understood: "Therein lies the social significance of art: it is constantly at work educating the spirit of the age, conjuring up the forms in which the age is most lacking. The unsatisfied yearning of the artist reaches back to the primordial image in the unconscious which is best fitted to compensate the inadequacy and one-sidedness of the present." It is through art and artists, Jung writes, that we are able "to find our way back to the deepest springs of life."

Whatever the inadequacy or one-sidedness of our present age, what is clear is that writers and intellectuals as diverse and as cultured as Peter Weir, Jean-Paul Rappeneau, and Bertrand Blier now see in Gérard a muse who can guide them back to their own inner resources and lead them to artistic fulfillment. How ironic it is that in a postindustrial era which prizes the rational over intuition and money over artistic inspiration, actors, writers, and directors in Paris and New York, in Australia and Hollywood, now take lessons in creativity from the Prankster from La France Profonde, that timeless, mystical realm so impoverished by today's standards of cultural and economic wealth, yet which was once so rich in primitive folklore, superstition, and myth.

"Knowledge does not enrich us; it removes us more and more from the mythic world in which we were once at home by right of birth," Jung wrote. "The more the critical reason dominates, the more impoverished life becomes; but the more of the unconscious, and the more of myth we are capable of making conscious, the more of life we integrate. Overvalued reason has this in common with political absolutism: under its dominion the individual is pauperized."

17

The *Time* Affair

At the close of 1990, Gérard was on a tremendous high. *Cyrano de Bergerac* and *Green Card* had become big international hits, and both movies were being warmly received in America. In January 1991, the prizes and honors began to roll in. At the Golden Globe awards, the annual selections made by the Hollywood Foreign Press Association, Gérard won the prize for best actor in a comedy, *Green Card* was named the comedy of the year, and *Cyrano* was named best foreign film. Then Gérard received one of the most coveted honors in the movie business: he was nominated for an Academy Award as best actor, for his performance as Cyrano. The film itself was nominated for five Oscars, including best foreign film.

"It's absolutely incredible," Gérard said after the Golden Globe award ceremony in Los Angeles. "The people of America have welcomed me with a warmth and an appreciation of my work that I frankly never expected. It's a dream."

But his dream was about to sour. After the Golden Globes, Gérard flew to the Indian Ocean island of Mauritius. There he was going to make a new comedy, *Mon Père, Ce Héros,* in which he was to play a divorced, absentee father trying to get back in touch with his teenage daughter. Gérard felt a special kinship with the role, as his own daughter, Julie, was in her teenage years, and he, too, had often been an absentee father. Gérard loved the script, written by the droll French cartoonist Gérard Lauzier, and the film was being produced by Jean-Louis Livi. After the strain of doing *Cyrano* and *Green Card,* Gérard was looking forward to doing a light French comedy and having a bit of a breather.

Receiving a Golden Globe award in Hollywood as the best comedy actor of 1990

But in its issue of February 4, 1991, *Time* magazine in America published a profile of Depardieu, during the run-up to the Academy Awards. The article, written by Richard Corliss, one of *Time*'s film critics, sought to portray Depardieu in all his Rabelaisian excess. Under the title "Life in a Big Glass," the piece opened in typically yeasty *Time* prose. "Gérard Depardieu, France's best and best-known actor, is a glutton for adventure. He eats with two hands, acts with both fists. On screen he radiates wild energy, acting from his capacious gut, whispering or raging as the role allows and the moment demands. He embodies the primal male caged in modern society, ever raising the ante on his own anarchic instincts."

In a passage describing Depardieu's background, Corliss wrote that "... his early years play like a more desperate version of his first hit film, *Going Places,* in which he was a petty thief and vicious womanizer. The son of an illiterate weaver in the nowhere town of Châteauroux, young Gérard stole cars and sold black-market cigarettes and whiskey to American soldiers at a nearby Army base. He carried a gun at school. 'But that was a child's game,' he shrugs. 'I just had the gun a week, to show it to my friends.' And what of his story that at nine he participated in his first rape? 'Yes.' And after that, there were many rapes? 'Yes,' he admits, 'but it was absolutely normal in those circumstances. That was part of my childhood.' "

These few lines, in which Depardieu appears to be avowing rape and doing so in a casual, unrepentant manner, were to trigger one of the most traumatic periods in Gérard's life. And those few lines would also trigger an international uproar. But had Depardieu really been a rapist at the age of nine? Did he really say that he had committed many rapes and that it was "absolutely normal in those circumstances"? After the *Time* story was published, Depardieu categorically denied that he had been a rapist at nine, or at any other age. He claimed that he had been misquoted and he threatened to sue *Time* for libel. In response, *Time* claimed that Depardieu's remarks were on tape, and *Time* claimed that those remarks had been reported "fairly and accurately." Amidst these conflicting claims, where was the truth? It would take me two and a half years to find the answer.

The uproar did not erupt immediately. When the *Time* story first appeared, there was no visible reaction from the public or anyone in the media. A month later, however, *Time* published a letter from a reader who was angry about Depardieu's seemingly cavalier attitude toward women and the issue of rape. On March 8, the New York *Post* picked up the story and published an article quoting prominent feminists and rape counselors as being outraged by the actor's seemingly casual confession of rape and his characterization of such behavior as "absolutely normal." One senior researcher at the National Center for Control and Prevention of Rape, analyzing Gérard through the *Time* article, was quoted as saying that Depardieu's comments were "absolutely callous. This man is showing the usual pattern of active denial."

The point of departure for the *Post* story was that Depardieu was a confessed rapist, and it repeated the damning quotes printed in *Time*. The *Post* also talked with Corliss. He said that Depardieu had first admitted to rape during a magazine interview back in 1978, and that he had acknowledged the rape again in a recent, tape-recorded interview with a *Time* correspondent. "He was no more apologetic than in 1978," Corliss told the *Post*.

The National Organization for Women, probably the leading group of feminists in America, was also infuriated by the quotes attributed to Depardieu and added its influential voice to the growing controversy.

NOW called on Depardieu to apologize for his past deeds and urged him to make a substantial financial contribution to a rape crisis center, in order to demonstrate his sincerity and remorse. In the following days, Judy Mann, a columnist with the Washington *Post,* took up the issue. In a March 20 piece headlined "How Do We Handle the Rapist-Turned-Heartthrob?" Mann wrote:

"M. Depardieu has a very sordid past. He trotted out more of it than he should have in a 1978 interview that was recently resurrected in *Time* magazine by Richard Corliss, who asked the actor about his gun-toting, thieving childhood." Offended by the remarks quoted in *Time,* Mann urged Americans to boycott Depardieu's movies, in order to "make it clear at the box office that there are actions and attitudes that they find too abhorrent to even tacitly endorse by their patronage." Mann concluded: "What we don't need is for the media to go on glamorizing an actor who started out as a rapist."

The "Depardieu affair" now became major international news. Newspapers and magazines in Europe picked up the controversy, and many of them reprinted the damning quotes from the original *Time* profile. London's *Daily Mail,* among others, sent two reporters to Châteauroux to investigate the childhood of Europe's leading actor. In extensive reporting in Gérard's hometown, the reporters found no evidence to suggest that Depardieu had been a rapist. Still, their report was published under a huge picture of him and carried a headline with the question many people were asking: "Is This the Most Famous Rapist In France?"

When news of the *Time* article and the resultant uproar reached Depardieu in Mauritius, he at first thought it was some sort of sick joke. As he said to friends in France and America, "A rapist at the age of nine? Who are they kidding? Where does such nonsense come from?" He adored women and had learned his most valuable lessons from women; how could anyone even think he could be a rapist? But his friends and advisers soon made clear to Gérard that this was no joke. In anxious telephone conversations, they told him that the uproar was a grave matter, with potentially disastrous consequences for his career and his reputation.

From their office in New York, Michael Barker and Tom Bernard got through to Gérard in Mauritius and discussed with him another serious aspect of the *Time* affair: its potential consequences on the Academy Awards. Barker and Bernard had left United Artists in 1983 and were now running Orion Classics, which was distributing *Cyrano de Bergerac* in the United States. The Academy Awards were a month away, and all this negative publicity was undermining their efforts to promote Gérard and the movie for Oscars. Barker and Bernard had known Depardieu for more than a decade, and neither one believed for an instant that he had been a rapist at the age of nine, or at any other age. Still, they urged him to hire a spokesman in New York and to issue a strong denial to the press. They also urged him to seek legal counsel, as did his other advisers.

"The second the New York *Post* article appeared, we put out the red flags and proceeded to draw the wagons," Bernard says. "We just knew the onslaught was coming."

Depardieu followed their advice. He hired Lois Smith, who is a publicist in New York, and he hired a lawyer in Los Angeles. Then, in New York and Paris, he issued a statement in which he "categorically denied" the *Time* account. He charged that *Time* had mistranslated and totally misconstrued the remarks he had made back in 1978 and what he had told *Time* in the recent interview. Still, Smith and Depardieu's spokespeople in Paris put out differing statements, and Smith was quoted in *U.S.A. Today* to the effect that Depardieu was "sorry" about the incident. The newspaper interpreted that to be an acknowledgment of rape by Depardieu and published an article to that effect. But Smith claims she was misquoted, that what she meant was that Depardieu was "sorry" about the way *Time* had misconstrued his remarks. All this only further confused the actor's position, and his vehement denials did nothing to quell the mushrooming furor.

In response to Depardieu's categorical denials of its story, *Time* issued a strongly worded statement: "This is not a question of whether *Time* stands by its story. It's a question of whether *Time* fairly and accurately reported the remarks by Mr. Depardieu. The interview with Depardieu was conducted in French and was tape recorded. So there can be absolutely no ambiguity about what was said and reported, we are making the following transcription available." Along with this statement, *Time* issued a transcript of the actor's remarks to *Time* about rape. But that transcript then came under fire from the French press, which took issue with the way some of Depardieu's remarks had been translated into English.

All this was terribly painful to Gérard, and he plunged into a state of anger and confusion; indeed, he felt utterly humiliated. "I'm wounded," he told *Paris-Match.* "I feel dirtied." In a phone call from Mauritius, Depardieu told me that he had no recollection of the 1978 interview and that he had never seen it in print. He had never raped anyone, he insisted, but he had *seen* the act of rape when he was growing up. He had grown up in a rough town filled with G.I. bars, strip joints, and prostitutes, and he had circulated in a milieu where violence was pervasive; this was a central fact of his youth. In his interview with *Time,* he said, he was trying to make clear that violence and rape weren't "normal" in the sense that he accepted or condoned them. What was normal was that anyone frequenting that milieu would *witness* such terrible violence. Violence, in fact, was one of the principal reasons he had fled Châteauroux, he said. This was what he had been trying to explain to *Time,* but he claimed that everything he said had been either twisted or misunderstood.

When headlines around the world began proclaiming him a rapist, Gérard started to drink, heavily. According to many people with him on location in Mauritius, Gérard did not drink on the set, but at night he went on colossal binges—mostly on wine and food, but later, as the furor intensified, on scotch, pastis, local rum, or whatever else was at hand. Gérard was able to work on camera, but he was not able to cope with this international crisis and the daily flood of inquiries from the press. Jean-Louis Livi took over in Paris, coordinating the damage-control efforts in Europe and America and shuttling to and from Mauritius. But while Livi was able to put some order into Depardieu's crisis management, even he could not calm Gérard down. Gérard binged and binged, and the more he drank, the more his weight ballooned and the deeper he sank into depression. His closest friends saw just how low he hit.

"It was horrible. And what made it worse was that there was so little we could do," one of his friends says. "If you tried to humor him, he saw through it right away. And if you encouraged him to stop drinking, he would turn and accuse you of moralizing. We all felt so helpless."

At home in Bougival, Elisabeth and the children were under siege from a French and international press clamoring for fresh interviews and reactions. Reporters and photographers were camped on their doorstep. Elisabeth was especially worried about the impact on Guillaume and Julie, not just from the daily media feeding frenzy, but from the horrible shadow the rape allegation could permanently cast over the family. At the same time, Elisabeth was very worried about Gérard and his physical and psychological stability. "I have never, ever seen Gérard like that," she said later. "He felt so hurt."

The French public reacted to the *Time* story with outrage and disgust. Depardieu a rapist at the age of nine? Their national hero, their Cyrano, a rapist? The French took this as an attack on their national honor. Jack Lang, the minister of culture, led the denunciations of the *Time* story and the American press, calling the entire affair "a low blow against one of our great actors." The "Affaire Depardieu" provoked heated denunciation of *Time* in France's National Assembly, which issued a formal resolution of solidarity with Depardieu. Jacques Attali, then a key adviser to President François Mitterrand, called the *Time* story a "vile defamation." Elisabeth Badinter, a writer, political activist, and one of the most respected women in France, wrote that the affair smacked of "a witch hunt." According to French diplomats in the United States, the French government even sent an official note of protest to the U.S. government about the attacks on Depardieu.

In Châteauroux, people who knew Gérard during his youth were shocked and confused by the *Time* allegations. Roger Lucas, who had been the principal of Gérard's school and his teacher when Gérard was eleven and twelve, was among the most outspoken in defense of Gérard. In a number of interviews with the local and foreign press, Lucas said that while Gérard may not have been a choirboy when he was growing up, he was surely no rapist. Gérard had edged into puberty right before Lucas's eyes, in his class, and that was two or three years after he turned nine. The very idea of Gérard being a rapist at the age of nine seemed to him ludicrous. Hadn't anyone at *Time,* he wondered, ever seen a nine-year-old boy? Lucas, like everyone else in Châteauroux, saw the charge as a vile smear on the town's most celebrated native son.

Many French people, especially those in the press and French cinema, suspected foul play and some sort of Hollywood conspiracy. To them, the timing of the affair appeared particularly suspicious: right in the middle of the film industry's annual lobbying for the Academy Awards. In the French press, several articles noted that *Cyrano de Bergerac* was considered the favorite to win best foreign film, and many articles underscored the fierce campaigns that the studios and distributors undertake to win Oscars for their films. They also underscored the financial bonanza reaped by most Oscar-winning actors and movies. The French press also pointed out that Time-Warner was the parent company of both *Time* magazine and Warner Brothers, the influential Hollywood movie studio. Would a French loss somehow be a Warner Brothers gain? This far-fetched scenario was lent credence in French eyes by the fact that Jeremy Irons was also nominated for best actor, for his performance in a Warner Brothers movie, *Reversal of Fortune.*

In an article written for *Le Figaro,* and then adapted and printed by the *New York Times* and the *International Herald Tribune,* Toscan du Plantier wrote an eloquent defense of Depardieu, and he also suggested foul play. Toscan claimed the Academy Awards were steeped in politics, and he recounted the many instances in which French films had been edged out at award time, especially in the category of best foreign film. "Of course," he wrote, "it would be wrong to be too paranoid about our disappointments in the United States." He then went on to highlight, accurately, the fact that America's most serious competition in the worldwide marketplace of cinema comes from one country: France.

In American film circles, Toscan's article and the broader French suspicions of some sort of Hollywood conspiracy were greeted with derision. The Academy of Motion Picture Arts and Sciences has some 4,600 individual members who cast secret ballots for each year's Oscars, and Hollywood insiders insist there is little way to influence large blocs of votes. Even Gérard's closest advisers in America belittled the suggestion that a conspiracy was afoot. They felt that Depardieu's nomination for *Cyrano,* like Isabelle Adjani's for *Camille Claudel,* was Hollywood's way of applauding his talent and accomplishments. But Gérard's advisers agreed that he had little chance of winning the Oscar over his four anglophone rivals: Jeremy Irons, Kevin Costner for *Dances With Wolves,* Robert De Niro for *Awakenings,* and Richard Harris for *The Field.* "It is almost unheard of for a foreign actor to win best actor or actress for a film that was not originally done in English," Michael Barker says.

Still, in the final week before the Academy Awards ceremony, the furor in America kept escalating. There were published rumors that women's groups might picket Hollywood's annual gala, right in front of the scores of television cameras that would be beaming the event around the world. Tammy Bruce, president of the Los Angeles chapter of NOW, told the press that some of her 4,000 members were urging the U.S. State Department to ban Depardieu from American soil, arguing that his "entry into this country should be restricted based on the many self-incriminating statements he has made." Bruce was quoted as saying Depardieu's denials were "baloney," and she stressed that he had hung himself, with his own words. She said, "He's made clear in several statements now that he has raped, talking about it as if it was normal," an echo of the remarks published in *Time.* "Because he's a public figure, he's being made an example of. And we will not let up. We will make things as miserable for him as possible. We want him to feel the repercussions of his actions and his attitude."

In the face of this firestorm of controversy and rage, Gérard decided not to accept his invitation to fly to Hollywood for Oscar night, an event which just a few weeks before had promised to be one of the greatest moments of his life. Now he did not have the stomach for it. The trip from Mauritius to L.A. would take nearly two exhausting days, and on arrival he would have to spend all his time fighting off mobs of reporters and photographers, and he would have to repeat over and over, in his approximate English, "I am not a rapist." Besides, he figured he had no chance to win the Oscar as best actor; he felt no French actor could. In his mind, it was honor enough just to be nominated.

So Gérard stayed in Mauritius and watched the Oscar ceremony on television. As expected, he was passed over for best actor; the prize went to Irons. The real stunning blow, though, was that *Cyrano* lost in the best foreign film category to a small Swiss movie, *Journey of Hope.* To Gérard's mind, this revealed just how political the Academy Awards were, especially in this category. He also felt miserable that his own trouble with *Time* seemed to have undermined *Cyrano*'s chance for an Oscar, thus depriving the film's creators and cast and crew of the international recognition he felt they deserved.

Film critics and writers across Europe had similar reactions, and they blasted the outcome of the Oscars, charging that the *Time* scandal had stripped *Cyrano* of the Oscar it merited. "Hollywood and hypocrisy go together, of course, but seldom so blatantly as at this year's Oscars," the *Guardian* wrote. "Gérard Depardieu is one of the world's great screen actors. *Cyrano de Bergerac* is the French film that, in both America and Britain, had cemented the ultimate triumph of subtitles over box-office prejudice. It was a huge, and justified, success.... What Depardieu did or didn't do when he was nine years old is a matter for the courts.... The matter for Hollywood is what on earth any of this has to do with *Cyrano.*"

The critic for the *Observer* in London put aside all nationalist considerations and supported Depardieu. "Jeremy Irons is a fine actor, but Gérard Depardieu is a great one.... The enraged French assume, and they're probably right, that the reason is an interview he gave to *Time* magazine which suggested that he started raping girls at the age of nine and had continued to do so for some years.... Not that rape is ever to be condoned. But I sense here that we are seeing the worst side of prescriptive American liberalism: the belief that nobody can be deemed acceptable in any way unless, throughout the whole of their lives, they have adhered rigidly to this year's tenets of American liberalism."

In the early days of the furor, Depardieu turned for legal help to E. Barry Haldeman, a lawyer in the Los Angeles firm of Greenberg, Glusker, Fields, Claman and Machtinger, which handles many prominent Hollywood actors, directors, producers, and writers. Haldeman brought into the case one of his partners, Bert Fields, who is considered one of the entertainment industry's leading authorities on libel law.

Haldeman and Fields studied the main documents of the case, Haldeman talked by phone with Depardieu, and they concluded that Depardieu's remarks had been mistranslated and misunderstood. They demanded that *Time* print a retraction.

Throughout the spring of 1991, however, *Time* publicly stood by its story and refused to run a retraction or an apology. On April 8, *Time* ran a follow-up story in its press section recounting the international brouhaha over what it headlined "L'Affaire Gérard Depardieu." In the article, *Time* took the opportunity to reaffirm its position: "The *Time* interview, which was conducted in French, is on tape. The Depardieu camp contends that his words were mistranslated and that he admitted only to having witnessed rapes. *Time* has refused the actor's demand that the passage be retracted." Robert Pondiscio, an official spokesman for the magazine, told the press that *Time* realized the volatility of the story, and he insisted, "We did our homework."

Time's refusal to print a retraction infuriated Depardieu. "When I see headlines like 'Oscar, Depardieu, Rapist,' it's bad, bad for my family, my wife Elisabeth, my children. It's bad because even if it's not true—and it's stupid—it stays in people's minds. It dirties me," Depardieu told the French press. "Really, do you think that at nine years old you can rape someone? . . . I don't acknowledge any of those things. I never said those things."

Haldeman and Fields now prepared to sue *Time* for libel, on the argument that the magazine had wrongfully portrayed Depardieu as a rapist and that what followed had caused grievous damage to the actor's reputation, his career, and his family. As London's *Mail on Sunday* had put it succinctly in a headline, "Rapist Tag Threatens Actor's Career." In terms of American law, the general understanding among journalists and lawyers is that for a public figure to establish that he has been the victim of libel, he has to prove that some form of malice was involved on the part of the newspaper, magazine, or other media outlet. But Haldeman notes that proof of malice can rest on either of two points: "knowledge of falsity" or "reckless regard for the truth." Given the seriousness of the accusation, they planned to argue that *Time* had published the charge without proper substantiation. "I think we had a very strong case," Haldeman says.

Elisabeth Depardieu was also eager for Gérard to sue *Time* for libel. In her eyes, her husband had been the subject of a public tarring and feathering; taking the case to court was the only way to remove the smear and restore the family honor. Like many noble families in France, Elisabeth's had a coat of arms, and it bore this inscription: *"Qui aime bien, châtie bien"*—He who loves well, punishes well. Elisabeth wanted to live up to that creed and see *Time* punished.

But Gérard had no idea what to do. In the space of a few weeks, he had gone from critical and popular acclaim in America, crowned by the Golden Globe awards and an Academy Award nomination, to public disgrace and total despair. If there was any consolation, from his point of view, it was that Dédé and Lilette had died in 1988 and did not have to endure seeing their son's humiliation. At the same time, Gérard had serious doubts about the wisdom of going to court. He had no clear grasp of American libel law, he hated courtrooms, and he certainly did not have the patience or expertise in English to immerse himself in the nuances of language around which a libel battle might turn. A court case would take years and cost him hundreds of thousands of dollars in legal fees. The trial would be a media circus, and all that time he would have to face the world media and keep repeating, "I am not a rapist, I am not a rapist." Besides, his emotional state was already fragile; what would he be like at the end of three or four more years of this?

"We had a team ready to go," says Haldeman, but he and Fields had their own reservations. Would repeating and repeating "I am not a rapist" for the next several years only further damage Gérard's reputation? "We were worried that we would win the battle but lose the war," Haldeman says. He and Fields were fully aware of Depardieu's drinking binges and general psychological condition, his fragile emotional state, and they were not eager to put him into a media feeding frenzy —or onto a witness stand.

After much reflection and anguish, Depardieu decided not to pursue *Time* in court. According to Gérard, part of his decision was based on the fact that he received a warm personal apology from Steve Ross, who was then the head of Time-Warner. (Ross has since died.) But Gérard got no apology from *Time* or any of the other publications that reprinted the damaging remarks. He simply hoped the entire nightmare would blow over and eventually be forgotten. Indeed, public attention did soon shift. William Kennedy Smith, a medical student from a new generation of Kennedys, was accused of raping a young woman at the Kennedy compound in Palm Beach, Florida, and the Depardieu affair faded from the news.

Given the very serious nature of the charges, and the dramatic impact the rape allegation had on Gérard's life, work, and family, I carefully followed the affair from the very beginning. Obviously, if Depardieu had been a rapist at age nine, this would have been an important formative element of his childhood and youth, and I would have had to explore the issue in writing his biography. In all my interviews with Gérard, and with his family and friends, and in all my reporting in both Paris and Châteauroux, I found nothing to suggest that Depardieu had been a rapist at nine or any other age. During the course of my reporting, I also interviewed many people with firsthand knowledge of the affair, its aftermath, and its profound impact on Gérard. Throughout the furor, I collected published documents relevant to the case and studied them thoroughly. The results of this inquiry proved to be very revealing. And so did a series of climactic interviews I had at *Time* magazine, with people directly involved with the initial story and what followed.

The affair actually traces back to a story about Depardieu published in a 1978 issue of *Film Comment,* a small, high-brow movie magazine based in New York. At the time, the editor of the magazine was Richard Corliss. The *Film Comment* story was written by Harry Stein, an American freelance writer and editor then working in Paris. In the story, which was titled "French Primitive," Stein recounts a raucous day he spent on a movie set with Depardieu. The movie being shot was *Get Out Your Handkerchiefs,* Bertrand Blier's follow-up to *Les Valseuses,* the film which created a scandal in France and launched Depardieu to stardom. This, of course, was also the movie which Gérard helped promote by portraying himself as the bad boy from Châteauroux.

In summarizing Gérard's wild youth, the *Film Comment* story said: "Depardieu's background is so improbably wretched, that even the most cynical press agent would hesitate to put it out. That tale, as told by the French press, generally goes something like this: Depardieu, the son of a destitute weaver in the backwater town of Châteauroux, misspent his youth engaging in petty crime and hustling for amoral American soldiers from the local Army base; at thirteen he left home; at sixteen, broke, without any education or visible prospects, he found himself in Paris; recruited for the stage, he instantly stunned critics with his raw power and went on to become the luminous star he is today."

With this "tale" as a lead-in, the writer then recounts an interview he had over lunch on the set with Depardieu. At the lunch, Stein reports, Depardieu is sitting with three other people, and during the course of the meal, Gérard eats two huge steaks, and the four of them consume three bottles of Beaujolais. According to the writer's account, toward the end of Gérard's second steak and the third bottle of wine, he made the controversial acknowledgment of rape. The article describes this crucial part of the interview as follows, first quoting Depardieu:

> "I was always the youngest, the one who had to be shown things. Like, for instance, it was my pal Jackie—he was sixteen or seventeen—who took me along on my first rape." He pauses, then adds as an afterthought, "He's dead now, Jackie." The incident occurred, Depardieu adds nonchalantly, in a bus depot; the girl, a brunette in her early twenties, was waiting for a bus when the teenager and the nine-year-old began teasing her. "One thing led to another and, hup!!"—Depardieu suddenly rises halfway out of his chair, like an animal bounding after prey—"that was that." He pauses. "It was normal. After that I had plenty of rapes, too many to count."

Depardieu is then quoted as saying, "There was nothing wrong with it. The girls wanted to be raped. I mean, there's really no such thing as rape. It's only a matter of a girl putting herself in a situation where she wants to be."

Depardieu's comments, as printed, appear outrageous, and from any point of view they sound morally repugnant and indefensible. But the anecdote that Depardieu recounts does raise some questions, beyond the issue of a nine-year-old boy's physical capacity for rape. The "Jackie" Depardieu refers to is surely Jacky Merveille, who was indeed dead by then. But according to his mother, Jacky was born in 1946 and was two and a half years older than Gérard. Depardieu is quoted here as saying Jacky was "sixteen or seventeen" at the time of the incident. That would mean that Gérard would have been fourteen, not nine as the writer states. And if this really had happened when Gérard was nine, as the story claims, then two boys of nine and twelve somehow managed to rape a young woman in her early twenties, in the middle of a public bus depot.

Clearly, something is askew here. But there is no indication in the story that the writer—or his editors in New York—went back to Depardieu later to make certain that they had understood correctly: a rapist at the age of nine? Nor is there any indication in the story that the reporter made any effort to cut through the French press's "tale" of Depardieu's background and to establish the facts. Indeed, even a cursory fact check, with the files of a respectable French newspaper or publicity agent, would have shown that Depardieu's father was not a "destitute weaver," as stated in the profile.

There is another question here: Even if this was an accurate rendering of Depardieu's words, was this really a serious admission of rape? Or was it just drunken grandstanding by a young actor out to create a stir and an image in the movie world? Interestingly enough, when the article appeared, the same issue of *Film Comment* carried a companion piece on Depardieu by Molly Haskell, one of America's most respected film critics. Under the headline "You Gérard, Me Jane," she writes about her own visit with Gérard on a movie set. She also addresses the question of Depardieu's apparent avowal of rape. Haskell has her doubts about the avowal, as is evident from the very first words of her article: "Every once in a while Cro-Magnon man comes out of his cave and waves his spiked club in the air, but usually if you look closely enough, you will see a press agent in the wings, or an intellectual guiding his movements by remote control." Later in the piece, she again suggests that Depardieu's avowal perhaps should not be taken literally: "I've been allowed a peek at the interview, kindness of the editors, so as not to look a perfect fool, a feminist rushing in with mash notes to a rapist," she wrote. "But discounting a certain element of bravado, I would be more shocked by the interview if I didn't assume more bullying ignorance on the part of the uneducated than we enlightened followers of panliberation would like to think. Moreover, when Depardieu talks of rape, I don't thank he means what we mean."

And what of this ardent, hard-headed feminist's reaction to meeting the purported rapist in person? "He was all there, playful, grinning; there were no barriers between us," she wrote. "He grinned at me occasionally between takes, and I grinned back. Possibly I blushed.... Depardieu is the new world, regeneration, hope, attraction, Eros.... The man is enchanting, a natural. He is—have I said it yet?—one of the most exciting and important new actors in the movies today."

Nearly thirteen years later, now as an influential critic for *Time,* Corliss wrote his own profile of the French actor. By now Depardieu was the biggest star in all of Europe, and through his sensitive performances in such films as *The Return of Martin Guerre, Jean de Florette,* and *The Last Metro,* he had left his bad-boy image far behind. And by now, many American newspapers and magazines, including *The New York Times Magazine* and *Newsweek,* had run comprehensive profiles of Depardieu, and they had recounted his wild youth in Châteauroux in more circumspect—and more accurate—ways than the *Film Comment* piece. For his profile on the eve of the Oscars, however, Corliss framed the piece with Depardieu's original bad-boy legend, and he returned to some of the same points laid out by Stein thirteen years before.

Throughout the profile, Corliss portrays Depardieu as a hard-drinking, wrong-side-of-the-tracks macho man, long on talent and animal magnetism but a bit short on brains. This characterization fits exactly how Depardieu was described in the lead: "the primal male caged in modern society." To close this portrait, Corliss quotes Depardieu as saying, "I don't need to be intelligent. There are moments when I am a complete idiot, and others when I'm less of an idiot. That's all." Then Corliss concludes: "*The Idiot.* Who wrote that book? No matter. Gérard Depardieu could play the part. He has the appetite for it."

It may come as a surprise to many readers, but in preparing this bylined, highly interpretative profile, Corliss did not personally meet or interview Depardieu. In what is a common practice at *Time,* he wrote the piece in New York, from background files and a fresh file sent to him by a stringer working for *Time*'s bureau in Paris, a freelance journalist named Victoria Foote-Greenwell. As stated in Corliss's article, she had an interview with Gérard over lunch at the George V hotel in Paris. Afterward, she filed an account of her luncheon interview back to *Time* headquarters in New York. Then Corliss wove her account into his final "Life in a Big Glass" story, which included the explosive Depardieu quotes that appeared to be a fresh avowal of rape.

Since the entire controversy was triggered by those quotes, and since Depardieu had alleged that he was misquoted, the precise origin of those quotes demands careful examination. So on October 27, 1993, I went to the Time-Life Building in Manhattan in search of some concrete answers about Depardieu's purported avowal of rape to *Time*. Had he been misquoted, as Depardieu alleged? Or had his remarks to *Time* been reported "fairly and accurately," as *Time* contended? At *Time* headquarters, I met first with Robert Pondiscio, the official *Time* spokesman who had put out the strongly worded statement in the aftermath of the affair. Though the incident was now two and a half years old, Pondiscio recalled the chain of events with clarity and precision.

Pondiscio said that when Depardieu claimed he had been misquoted, *Time* took that as a very serious charge. The magazine immediately instituted a thorough process of double-checking and verification, Pondiscio said. The tape of the stringer's interview with Depardieu was sent from Paris to New York, someone transcribed it, and Depardieu's remarks were then verified by *Time* staffers, at least one of whom was a native French speaker, Pondiscio said. Richard Corliss provided *Time* with a copy of the original piece that ran in *Film Comment.* Pondiscio said that *Time* lawyers had checked the initial story before it was published, and the lawyers later went back through the material in the light of Depardieu's allegations and the demands by his lawyers that *Time* print a retraction. At the conclusion of the review by *Time* editors and lawyers, Pondiscio met with senior editors at *Time,* he said, and they discussed how to respond. Then Pondiscio put out the formal statement to the public. Pondiscio said he had advocated a strongly worded statement, and that top *Time* editors had agreed.

"We had a tape. We had a transcript. We've got the goods. Why not just say that?" Pondiscio told me. "In this case, we now saw no reason to just blandly say we stand by our story."

So after the review and checking with top editors, Pondiscio put out the statement saying that Depardieu was not misquoted and that *Time* had "fairly and accurately" reported his remarks. And even when the controversy kept on escalating, Pondiscio said *Time* never felt moved to change its position. "We would not say something like this casually," he said. *Time*'s process of editing and fact checking was so thorough, Pondiscio said, that even when Depardieu's lawyers threatened to sue *Time* for libel, the editors and lawyers felt fully confident. "The concern around here was minimal," Pondiscio said. "We didn't put things in his mouth. We wrote down what he said. How could he sue? There was no gray area as far as I was concerned; we had it all on tape."

But did *Time* have it all on tape? I asked Pondiscio specifically if all the relevant quotes cited in the article were on tape. "The whole interview was on tape and transcribed," he said.

Pondiscio, a former radio reporter, said that he believed in a policy of "full disclosure" in such matters, and he offered to help me meet with key *Time* people involved in the story and the resultant flap. At my request, he also told me he would give me the official transcript of those parts of the stringer's interview pertaining to rape. He also said that he would try to get me a copy of the tape of that entire interview. Pondiscio also urged me to talk with both Corliss and Foote-Greenwell, and to facilitate my work, he gave me her phone numbers in Paris, at work in the Paris bureau of *Time* and at home. Then he personally took me to see Corliss, on another floor of the cavernous headquarters of the Time-Life Building.

Corliss is a tall, thickset, distinguished-looking man with a trim white beard and a taste for cigarillos. His background was mostly in film, he told me, both in terms of his university studies and his work experience. In 1969, he took over the editorship of *Film Comment,* and in the early 1980s, he joined *Time* as a film critic. Corliss said he reads French, but does not speak it very well. He also said that he had met Depardieu only briefly. They had shaken hands once at the 1990 film festival in Telluride, Colorado, and he had ridden in an elevator with him once or twice during the New York Film Festival. Corliss said he had long admired Depardieu's work as an actor, and he said that for years he had heard in film circles that off-screen as well as on, "Depardieu was a larger-than-life fellow." From there, with a tape recorder running, we went back through the entire affair, from the beginning in 1978, when he was editor of *Film Comment.*

I asked Corliss how he came to publish the Harry Stein piece. He said that he had not commissioned the story; he said he believed the piece was written for another publication. But when Stein gave it to him, he was happy to publish it. Stein was a respected writer and editor in Paris, Corliss said, and the story appeared to be well researched and well written. Stein later wrote for *Esquire* and now writes a column for *TV Guide.* I asked Corliss if Stein had tape-recorded the interview, and he said he did not know. I also asked him if, in light of Depardieu's apparent avowal of rape, he had gone back to Stein for additional corroboration and fact checking. The following exchange comes verbatim from my tape, as do all of the succeeding question-and-answer exchanges:

> Author: So when you got Stein's piece, you took it basically as is; you didn't go back and say, "Are you sure?"
>
> Corliss: No, I don't recall doing that. I can't say. At any rate, at *Film Comment,* which had an editorial staff of two, we did not have a policy of red-checking the stories. So I may have asked Harry, in the course of conversation, "Gee, this sounds strange." And if Harry had said, "Yes, well, I made it up," then I probably would have said, "Well, we shouldn't print it."

Corliss said that when the Stein piece came in, he asked Molly Haskell to write a companion piece, from a feminist perspective. I wondered if Corliss, when he saw Haskell's skeptical reaction to Depardieu's purported avowal, had any doubts about that critical passage in Stein's story. I asked, "Judging from Molly Haskell's reaction, what do you think Gérard was doing at that moment in the interview? Did you take it as a serious admission of rape?"

"I took it as a good story. That's what I was looking for," Corliss said. "*Film Comment,* unlike most magazines that made a real impact on film scholarship and film theory, was not a policy publication. We printed theoretical pieces, we printed *auteur*'s pieces, we printed personality profiles."

Corliss said that his own profile of Depardieu in 1991 was prompted by the fact that the French actor at that time had two hit movies playing in the United States: *Cyrano de Bergerac* and *Green Card.* In preparing his own profile, Corliss says he did use the Stein profile as part of his source material. "In researching this, I did go over a number of articles, including the Harry Stein piece," Corliss said.

In his article, Stein presented the broad brushstrokes of Depardieu's background not as fact but as media legend. He wrote: "That tale, as told by the French press, generally goes something like this: Depardieu, the son of a destitute weaver in the backwater town of Châteauroux, misspent his youth engaging in petty crime and hustling for amoral American soldiers from the local Army base." Corliss's profile repeated almost the exact same sentence, but now the basic elements of Depardieu's background were presented in the pages of *Time* not as a "tale" or a media legend but as established fact: "The son of an illiterate weaver in the nowhere town of Châteauroux, young Gérard stole cars and sold black-market cigarettes and whiskey to American soldiers at a nearby Army base." As in Stein's piece, Depardieu's father is described, erroneously, as a weaver.

To bring his file material up to date, Corliss said that he sent a one-page, single-spaced memo to the Paris bureau of *Time*. In that memo, he said, he included a specific reference to the rape issue set forth in *Film Comment*. He said that he even thought he had included the passages detailing Depardieu's purported avowal of rape at the age of nine. Foote-Greenwell, he said, asked Depardieu about that avowal in her interview and she put his quoted comments in her return file to Corliss. He, in turn, put those quotes into the story that was published in *Time*. So I asked Corliss this: "The quotes that were quoted in the magazine came directly from her file? Did they come out of her file as is?"

"I would say yes," Corliss said. "In rare occasions, we do condense it."

Corliss said that when he saw Depardieu's responses to the stringer's questions, he took them as corroboration of Stein's earlier story. After all, he said, Depardieu could have responded in several other ways. "I thought there were any of a number of reactions that he might have had to the question," he explained. "One would be, 'No, that's a complete lie.' Or, 'Yes, I said it at the time, but I was just pulling Harry Stein's leg and you know how the Americans are about the French.' Another was, 'It was at a time when I was playing roles of vagabonds, layabouts, and other kinds of miscreants, and I was speaking in character of the parts I was playing at the time.' Another would be, 'Yes, I did do it, and wasn't that horrible?' Another would be, 'Yes, I did do it, but you have to understand: everybody did it.' But I was convinced that we got it right."

I wondered now about the process of fact checking. I asked Corliss, "Given that this was such a sensitive issue, would you or anybody else have gone back and said, 'Can we see the verbatim transcript of the references to rape?' "

"I didn't know if it was sensitive to Depardieu or not, since my entire knowledge of whatever his experiences were as a lad were from the Harry Stein story and from this file," Corliss said. "And it seemed to me that he was corroborating the story that Harry had quoted Depardieu as telling before."

Corliss said that while he did not ask the stringer for a transcript, researchers and the senior editors in charge of the entertainment section of the magazine may well have. But he said that he could not recall any editor or researcher ever raising questions or objections about the rape quotes to him. "I don't recall that there was any particular flagging of these comments by the editors," Corliss said. "I don't recall that there was any editorial comment on that part of the story, you know, 'Really? Did he do that? Can we say that?' " Corliss is listed on the *Time* masthead as a senior writer, but he portrayed himself as a low man on the *Time* totem pole: "In this kind of pyramidal structure of authority and checks and balances, the guy at the bottom is just shlepping stones. But I think I would recall if someone had said, 'You can't print that.' "

When he wrote the story, Corliss said, he did not feel that the reference to rape was very important; indeed, he mentioned it not in the first few paragraphs of the story but only in the last part. "If we had thought it was sensational material, we would not have put it in the eighth paragraph or thirteenth," Corliss said. When the furor erupted, Corliss said, he and *Time* were even accused by some readers of burying the rape references low in the story, in effect minimizing or excusing the crime. But Corliss said he felt the references were given the exact import they deserved. "It was not only not the most important element in the story, it was not the most important element in Depardieu's life."

Corliss said that he did not have any particular qualms about writing a highly interpretive profile of a man he had never spent time with or interviewed. "I should say that I think of myself as well suited for the *Time* process of news gathering, because as someone who is primarily here a movie critic, I like to keep my distance from the people I write about," Corliss said. "I do not like to worry about whether their feelings will be hurt or they'll be flattered by a story. I like to think of them as fictions on the screen."

I asked Corliss if, outside of the *Film Comment* story, he had ever seen any other published reports in which Depardieu had avowed rape. "I didn't know when I sent the query, or for that matter when I wrote the story, whether this anecdote had appeared hundreds of times in the French press or in biographies, if there are any, of Gérard Depardieu."

After Corliss wrote his draft, he sent it to *Time* editors and fact checkers. After they edited and checked the story, the edited version was sent back to the Paris bureau for what is referred to as "C & C," a phase of comments and corrections. Corliss said that although the Depardieu profile did carry his byline, the responsibility for the accuracy of the material that was published was not his; it was Foote-Greenwell's in Paris. "The story sent back to the correspondent [for C & C] is in effect another query," he said. "The correspondent is ultimately responsible for the information presented in the story."

"But in this case," I said, "the correspondent was not a correspondent; it was a stringer."

"Well . . ."

"That's not a distinction that worries you. . . ."

"No," Corliss said. "I don't think it's the job of a writer, at *Time* magazine or anywhere else, to determine, based on title, the level of competence of other people who work at the magazine."

A few minutes later, Robert Pondiscio came into the office where we were talking. He gave me the official *Time* transcript of the portion of Foote-Greenwell's interview pertaining to rape. He also gave me a copy of the complete tape of the interview she had conducted with Depardieu. Pondiscio then left us, and I studied the transcript. It was in French, on one sheet of paper, and it set forth, verbatim, three questions from Foote-Greenwell and three answers from Depardieu. At the end, there was another answer from Depardieu, but there was no question preceding it. To me, the transcript raised very serious questions.

Just after the furor erupted, I had obtained a copy, from a reliable source, of what appeared to be the transcript of the crucial parts of the interview relating to rape; now I could see that in the official transcript handed to me by *Time*'s official spokesman, the French was exactly the same as in my copy. At this juncture, I took out the original article that was published in *Time,* with the explosive quotes, and I set it next to the official transcript. I then asked Corliss to examine the two documents. For a long moment, we both examined the French exchanges, which were set down without the French accent marks or other distinctively

French punctuation. The explosive quotes in the story which Corliss wrote and *Time* published read this way, verbatim:

> And what of his story that at nine he participated in his first rape? "Yes." And after that, there were many rapes? "Yes," he admits, "but it was absolutely normal in those circumstances. That was part of my childhood."

But where were those quotes in the transcript? I now went through the French exchanges with Corliss, looking for those explosive admissions. But a careful comparison of the two documents showed that there were several discrepancies between the official *Time* transcript and what was actually published in *Time* and attributed to Depardieu, inside quotation marks. The first exchange from the official *Time* transcript was this:

> Q: . . . *et que a neuf ans vous avez assiste a votre premier viol?*
> GD: *Oui.*

This exchange was translated and published in *Time* this way: And what of his story that at nine he participated in his first rape? "Yes." But right here several problems arise. Much of the controversy that ensued after publication focused on the meaning of the French verb *assister.* It can mean "to participate," as *Time* chose to interpret it and print it. But in common French usage, *assister* can also mean "to witness." In fact, many French language specialists say that when *assister* is followed by the preposition *à,* it usually means "to witness." In common speech, when French people are invited to a wedding, they say they will *assister* at the marriage, meaning they will be present for the ceremony; it does not mean they will participate in the marriage. In one of my interviews with Gérard, in an unrelated context, he said that as a boy of six, *"J'ai assisté à la naissance de ma soeur Catherine."* Meaning, he witnessed, or watched, the birth of his sister Catherine. Clearly, he was not saying that at age six, he *participated* in the birth.

So a very serious problem remains. *Time* chose to translate *assister* as "participate." But it was not Depardieu who used the word *assister.* The stringer used it in her question to him, and he responded only *"Oui."* So what was the question to which Depardieu responded? Did he understand the question to be "Did you participate in a rape at the age of nine?" Or did he understand the question to be, as he maintains, "Did you witness a rape at the age of nine?" Obviously, this is a crucial difference in meaning; indeed, it is the difference between admitting to the crime of rape or admitting you witnessed rape.

In the *Time* transcript on the table in front of us, there was no indication that the stringer had tried to clarify the potential ambiguity. I turned to the second question-and-answer exchange in the official *Time* transcript. Here it is:

> Q: . . . *et que apres cela, c'etait normal, qu'il y a eu plein de viols?*
> GD: *Oui, mais c'est absolument normal. Il n'y a rien d'extraordinaire la dedans.*

As published in *Time,* this exchange was translated this way: "And after that, there were many rapes? 'Yes,' he admits, 'but it was absolutely normal in those circumstances.' " This was the quote that really hung Depardieu in the eyes of millions of people around the world. Depardieu not only appeared to be avowing rape, he seemed to be saying that it was "absolutely normal," nothing to get excited about, it was just "part of my childhood." But this exchange, as set forth in the original French, also does not make clear whether or not Depardieu understood the stringer's line of questioning to be about "witnessing" or "participating" in rapes; all the question asks is if "there were lots of rapes." Moreover, was Depardieu really saying that it was "absolutely normal" and "nothing extraordinary" for a boy of nine to "participate" in lots of rapes? Or was he saying that it was normal, in his milieu, to "witness" rape? I turned to Corliss:

"Would Gérard at this stage of the game say that at the age of nine there was nothing extraordinary about committing rapes?"

"Would he say that at the age of nine there was nothing extraordinary about witnessing many rapes?" Corliss replied. "How many rapes can one witness? That seems hardly more normal to me."

Now I picked up Corliss's story and pointed to the crucial concluding part of the explosive quote.

> AUTHOR: Where here, in this French, is this sentence: "Yes, but it was absolutely normal in those circumstances. That was part of my childhood."

Now Corliss admitted that Depardieu's precise words had been changed.

> CORLISS: Well, you know that's what we added: "in those circumstances. . . ."

AUTHOR: Why did you put in, "in those circumstances"?
CORLISS: Kind of as a . . . perhaps as an explanation.

Corliss explained that the words were inserted into the quotes to help readers better understand the context in which the rapes happened, namely Depardieu's deprived youth. But *Time*'s millions of readers around the world had no way of knowing that Depardieu's explosive quotes had been in any way changed, or that words not even spoken by him had been inserted into the damaging quote. In the published quote, there were no brackets put around the words that had been inserted—a practice which is standard procedure for many reputable news organizations.

AUTHOR: Should it have been put in brackets, or should there be some indication to the reader that was not precisely what he said?
CORLISS: Possibly. Perhaps we should not have done him the favor.

Again I asked Corliss to show me where in the official *Time* transcript were the two sentences which formed the rest of that explosive published quote: "Yes, but it was absolutely normal in those circumstances. That was part of my childhood."

AUTHOR: So where, though, are those two sentences?

There was a long pause, as Corliss examined the official transcript. Then he said, "I don't see it right here. I don't see it right here."

AUTHOR: That's because they're not there.
CORLISS: Well, they're not on this page.
AUTHOR: Well, they are, actually.

I then took the official *Time* transcript and underlined for Corliss the two sentences that were quoted together in *Time,* inside the same quotation marks. One of the sentences came in response to the second question the stringer asked Depardieu. The second sentence came from the very last portion of the transcript, and it did not come in response to a question at all. Here is the complete text of the official *Time* transcript, with the two sentences which were quoted together set out in bold type. These are what I underlined for Corliss.

Here is how the conversation went, verbatim:
Q: . . . *et que a neuf ans vous avez assiste a votre premier viol?*
GD: *Oui.*

Q: . . . *et que apres cela, c'etait normal, qu'il y a eu plein de viols?*
GD: ***Oui, mais c'est absolument normal.*** *Il n'y a rien d'extraordinaire la dedans.*
Q: *Mais cela veut dire qu'il y a des enfants—des jeunes—aux Etats Unis, qui vont faire ca.*
GD: *Non, ils vont pas faire ca. Ca depend si c'est ecrit.*
GD: *Tout ca me fait rire.* **C'est des elements d'enfance.**

As is clear from the French transcript, the two sentences that were quoted together, inside the same quotation marks, came out of two different Depardieu answers from two different parts of the transcript. Beyond the words that Corliss said that *Time* decided to add—"in those circumstances"—there were also several other discrepancies between the official transcript in French and the two sentences published in *Time*. In both sentences in French, Depardieu is speaking in the present tense. But the published version has Depardieu speaking in the past tense. The shift in tense significantly changes the meaning of the first sentence, because it makes the verb refer specifically to past action, in this case a rape.

The second sentence quoted by *Time*—"That was part of my childhood"—comes from the very last passage on the transcript: *"Tout ca me fait rire. C'est des elements d'enfance."* Literally, this translates: "All this makes me laugh. These are elements of childhood." Here, Depardieu is talking about "elements," plural, and he does not seem to be talking specifically about rape at all. Again, he is speaking in the present tense. But the quote as published in *Time* is in the past tense and the phrase *"elements d'enfance"* is changed from plural to singular. The word "my" is also inserted, though Depardieu did not use it. With these changes, that sentence, when placed inside quotation marks after Depardieu's response to a different question, now appears to refer to one singular act in the past, namely, rape: "That was part of my childhood." I turned to Corliss for an explanation.

AUTHOR: I want to know where that quote comes from. Because these two sentences come from different responses from Gérard to different questions.
CORLISS: I don't know from this [transcript].

Corliss now said that he had never even seen this transcript of the French questions and answers pertaining to rape. He also said that he had never listened to the stringer's tape. Even after Depardieu claimed he had been misquoted, Corliss said, he did not go back to the original

French, either in the transcript or on the tape, to verify that what Depardieu had said was accurately translated and rendered in his story published in *Time*.

> AUTHOR: When the story broke, and there was this whole flap about the *assister,* and the possible mistranslation, did you then go back and see what the French looked like?
>
> CORLISS: No.

Corliss said that like every other file that comes in from the *Time* bureaus around the world, Foote-Greenwell's had come to him in English, with the quotes in English only. And that the English was all he ever worked with and wove into his story. It was not his job, he said, to verify the accuracy of the French.

> AUTHOR: So what you're saying is that it's the stringer's responsibility and not *Time* magazine's?
>
> CORLISS: No, I'm saying it's the correspondent who sent in the file from which I wrote the story.
>
> AUTHOR: So what was handed to you in English was what you worked with?
>
> CORLISS: Um-hum.
>
> AUTHOR: And the quotes that you put in the story were as they came to you in the stringer's file?
>
> CORLISS: Um-hum.

In the *Time* transcript before us, there was no specific reference to the 1978 *Film Comment* piece. So I asked Corliss if, in her questioning of Depardieu, Foote-Greenwell had made it clear to him that she was referring to a specific published account in which he appeared to avow rape.

"I don't know how I'll ever know. I wasn't there," Corliss said.

Corliss said that a month after *Time* published the explosive quotes, he was contacted by the New York *Post* and in the course of an interview he said that Depardieu's new remarks to *Time* showed that "he was no more apologetic than in 1978." I asked Corliss if the *Post* account was accurate, and he said it was. He also told me that after the furor erupted, he received a call from Judy Mann, the columnist at the Washington *Post* who called for a boycott of Depardieu's movies. He said he had an off-the-record conversation with her and that he supplied Mann with a copy of the original *Film Comment* piece.

On February 25, 1991, the European edition of *Time* ran a version of the Corliss profile that had appeared in America. But now the article was subtly recast, without the conclusion which had suggested that Depardieu was an idiot. The reference to rapes was included in the redraft, but this time with a small change in the translation. Now the key verb *assister* was no longer translated as "participate" in a rape but as "went along." In the view of Depardieu's lawyers, that tiny change suggested that *Time* was no longer comfortable with the way it had originally translated the explosive quote. Corliss told me he wrote the story that appeared in the European edition. I then asked him who had made that small but significant change in the verb *assister*.

"How that change came about I don't recollect," he said. "Whether it was a change I made, whether it was a change—refinement, shall we say—whether it was one that the new editor, that is to say, in the international edition, made, or by a Comments & Correction, by Victoria . . . Obviously, any of these are possible."

On December 2, 1991, ten months after the first *Time* story appeared, Corliss wrote an article for *Time* about the annual French film festival in Sarasota, Florida. Corliss reported that Depardieu was the star of the festival, and he again returned to the rape controversy, but this time in very different terms. "This was his first public appearance in the U.S. since last February, when a *Time* profile quoted some careless remarks Depardieu had made about sexual violence in his youth," Corliss wrote. So what *Time* had claimed on February 4 to be Depardieu's unrepentant avowal of rape now was characterized as only "careless remarks" about "sexual violence in his youth."

Throughout the furor, *Time* publicly insisted that the quotes were on tape, giving the public and other news organizations the impression that the quotes were accurate and verifiable. Corliss told the *Post* that the new interview was on tape, and in the story *Time* ran in its press section on April 8, the magazine affirmed: "The *Time* interview, which was conducted in French, is on tape." So after I left Corliss, I sat down and carefully went through the tape that Robert Pondiscio had given me. Now I discovered another discrepancy: the tape included the three question-and-answer exchanges that were cited in the official transcript. But the last two sentences quoted on the transcript—*"Tout ca me fait rire. C'est des elements d'enfance"*—were not on the tape at all. This was very important, since this last sentence provided the last sentence of the explosive quotes published in *Time*.

My examination of the tape raised other questions as well. The tape shows that Foote-Greenwell had a very convivial luncheon chat with Depardieu. They talked about wine, about what movies he was working on, about how he had liked working in English for *Green Card*. He talked about his emotional blockages as a child, about his ear problems, and about how reading had helped free his creativity. They spoke about literature for a very long time, about Cyrano, Musset, George Sand, and Dostoyevsky. They talked in detail about American cinema, about Woody Allen and Martin Scorsese, Hitchcock, Orson Welles, Truffaut. Depardieu mentioned how difficult it is for him to speak English, and Foote-Greenwell told him that she makes many mistakes in French.

Near the end of the interview, Foote-Greenwell went through a list of questions she had planned to ask Depardieu. Here is my own translation of one of the stringer's questions in French:

> Q: Also, at a given moment, I know that Richard Corliss said he had found in an American revue, it was, I don't know, in 1978, something like that, you were speaking of your youth, and that you spoke of your childhood as though you were, truly, what do you call it, a delinquent? [She looks through her papers.] Ah, yes, it was *Film Comment,* and in *Film Comment* you said that when you were at school you were in a gang, and that . . .
>
> GD: That I had a revolver, yes. One time, I had a revolver at school, yes. Like that. Because I had stolen a revolver and I was happy to be seven years old. But these are a child's things. Like tattoos. It's because you're in a gang; it's an identification.

At this stage, by way of explanation, Depardieu goes on to complain that his public image and reputation have become greatly exaggerated, and so has the way he is caricatured in many press accounts. He admitted that he drinks a lot, but he complained that people have labeled him an alcoholic and it is just not true. "They've given me the reputation of an alcoholic," Gérard told Foote-Greenwell. "But as you can see, I don't have the head of an alcoholic, nor the obsessions of an alcoholic. That comes from people who need to . . . Me, I said some things like that, and they thought that I always had a revolver. I had my revolver one week. I showed it to pals, like this, 'See this? It's a revolver.' But I didn't . . ." Here he is interrupted by another question.

What is clear from the tape is that Depardieu's remarks here came in the context of his complaint that in many press accounts, his youthful deeds have been wildly exaggerated, and he is using the story of the gun as a case in point. But his remarks were taken out of that context, and when published in *Time* they appeared precisely this way:

> He carried a gun at school. "But this was a child's game," he shrugs. "I just had the gun a week, to show it to my friends."

When Judy Mann picked up the reference to guns in her column in the Washington *Post,* it came out this way: "M. Depardieu has a very sordid past. He trotted out more of it than he should have in a 1978 interview that was recently resurrected in *Time* magazine by Richard Corliss, who asked the actor about his gun-toting, thieving childhood."

At this exact moment in her interview, Foote-Greenwell interrupted Depardieu's remarks about how the story of his revolver had been exaggerated to continue her line of questioning:

> Q: And now, they also said that you said that you, um, took [The verb she used in French was *prendre,* to take] cars and that you had friends who sold a lot of . . .
> GD: . . . of cigarettes and whiskey, *oui* . . .
> Q: . . . and that at nine years old you *assiste* at your first rape. . . .
> GD: *Oui* . . .

This is the beginning of the controversial passage about rape. But when Depardieu says *"oui"* throughout this exchange, he does not appear to be saying *"oui"* in the sense of confirming the truth of these purported deeds from his youth. Instead, he appears to be confirming only that he knows that such things have been written about him in the press, which the tape shows is the larger context of his responses. Nonetheless, Foote-Greenwell does not make any effort to clear up the ambiguity, at least not during the questions recorded on tape. In fact, the tape appeared to run out before she had completed her questions about the rape issue.

In search of further clarifications on these and other points, I now put in a call to Foote-Greenwell in Paris. On Saturday, October 30, 1993, I reached her at home and we talked for more than an hour. With her permission, I tape-recorded the conversation. Foote-Greenwell is an American who has been living in Paris on and off for the past seven years, she said. She works for *Time* on a freelance basis covering culture, especially theater and ballet. She said she writes for no other publications. She said she interviewed Depardieu on New Year's Eve day of 1990. I asked her what impression she had of Depardieu before she met him. "That I respected him as an actor," she said. "That's all I knew about him. I had read some stuff about him, but not much."

Before her interview, Foote-Greenwell said, she received a memo from Corliss with background on Depardieu and suggesting a number of questions to ask him. I asked her if Corliss's memo contained those paragraphs from the *Film Comment* story in which Depardieu appeared to be avowing rape.

"Um, I don't believe so," she said. "It seems to me that he said he had reason to believe that Depardieu had been involved in some kind of a rape or had committed a rape. . . . I was not really informed about what it was all about. But he did ask in the original file to ask about this incident."

"So he didn't put in anything specific?" I asked.

"No," she said.

"So then you conducted a series of interviews with friends and colleagues of Depardieu?"

"No, no," Foote-Greenwell said. "I just did an interview with him, because Corliss, I understood, had a lot of other information, and they just wanted to get some real feedback from him [Depardieu]. About a lot of other subjects, I should add. But the question of the rape, which became the issue, was really—certainly in my mind—a minor point. It was almost, practically for me a kind of last-minute detail to put in."

This "minor point" and "last-minute detail," of course, was whether or not Depardieu was an avowed rapist. The interview went very well, she said. They talked for about an hour and a half, and she said she liked Depardieu immediately. She found him generous and helpful, and that he even helped her with her tape recorder. In no way did she find him a brute, she said. "He was a really nice person; it was really fun to talk to him. I think that's one of the reasons that it was painful afterwards to feel that his basic good nature and positioning about life was being manipulated by a number of his press people, who got him to recant. They took a hard line about the whole thing."

After they had had such a convivial lunch and such a high-minded discussion about the arts, was it difficult to raise the issue of rape with Depardieu?

"It's not a cheerful topic," she said, "but I guess I figured it was just part of the job to ask him about it. As I said, I didn't have any real information about it. It had not been brought home to me that the [1978] article—I had not read it; I read it about a month or so afterwards—and yes, I guess I was shocked at the contents of the article. [At the time] I had not read it, so it was all rather abstract to me, frankly."

We discussed the ambiguity inherent in the word *assister,* and then I asked Foote-Greenwell if she took Depardieu's response to her questions to be a confession of rape.

"I felt he was admitting to me that he had *assisté,* yeah, *assisté,*" she said. "For me, as you know, a lot of this whole issue became the argument over *assister* and *participer.* And it's certainly true that in

French *assister* can mean 'in the sense of witnessing, looking on,' as opposed to actually being involved or participating. And the French press took it especially literally, because they said that he was talking about when he was a child of nine. Of course, it's obvious that a nine-year-old doesn't go around raping anybody."

This gave me pause. If it was so obvious that nine-year-olds don't go around raping, and if she recognized the significantly different meanings of *assister,* I wondered if Foote-Greenwell had gone back to Depardieu on this point, perhaps after the tape had run out.

AUTHOR: You didn't go back and say, "Am I understanding you right?"

FOOTE-GREENWELL: No, I did not say did you personally penetrate the person or whatever.

After the question turning on the word *assister,* in response to her next question, Depardieu seemed to be saying that the rapes were "normal." How did she interpret that?

"I interpreted that this was part of—and I think that this is what is really unfortunate about this whole case—is that the American press took this remark and just really misunderstood it," she said. "It seemed to me that it was clear—for me, and maybe not so clear in the article—that it was 'normal' in the context of what he had lived, and what he had lived was an extremely, profoundly deprived childhood and youth. And that that was the context in which these things happened—not that it was normal for men to go around raping women."

So on this very crucial point, indeed the very quote that suggested Depardieu was not just admitting to rape but condoning it as "normal," the reporter who conducted the interview confirmed that she did not think Depardieu was condoning rape. And she also acknowledged that this point was "maybe not so clear in the article." From the beginning, *Time* had said that Depardieu's remarks about rape were all on tape, and Pondiscio had been very specific in claiming that all the published quotes were on tape. But the final sentence quoted was not on the tape I had listened to. So I addressed this point to Foote-Greenwell.

AUTHOR: In terms of the tape, were his [Depardieu's] thoughts on the subject [of rape] complete on the tape?

FOOTE-GREENWELL: No. We went on and talked a couple of more minutes, I think, about it. The tape ran out and we talked a couple more minutes, and I believe I included it. Yeah, the last couple of words I jotted down, and then later, when I sent my report in, I put in what was on the tape and what I had jotted down.

Foote-Greenwell said that after the interview she filed a long memo to Corliss, some seven or eight pages, and she included long stretches of transcript from her interview. She also said she described the lunch and, to some extent, her favorable impressions of Depardieu. Then, later, in the process of Comments & Corrections, she saw a draft of Corliss's story. Given that she was aware of the ambiguities in the word *assister,* given that she had reservations about how in the story Depardieu seemed to be saying rape was "normal," and, finally, given that her own impression of Depardieu was far different from Corliss's portrayal of him as a brutish "primal male," I wondered if Foote-Greenwell raised any objections to the Corliss story, or its characterizations, or its handling of the rape issue.

"Um, I don't believe I raised any particular objections, no," she said. "In any case, it wouldn't be up to the reporter to raise objections, except if it seemed that it was really misrepresenting information that was sent."

AUTHOR: Before the story actually ran, did any of the editors in New York query you on the rape issue?

FOOTE-GREENWELL: It seems to me that they did, because when Corliss was going to write about it, they came back and said, "We're going to include this thing. We need to be sure about what was said." And I sent my transcript.

AUTHOR: In terms of the cross-checking on this particular point, was there a memo that came to you from New York asking for the transcript?

FOOTE-GREENWELL: No, I don't think that it asked for the transcript. It just said we want to be sure about this part of your reporting. So I, on my own initiative, sent my transcript of it.

AUTHOR: Did you tell them that all the relevant quotes were on tape?

FOOTE-GREENWELL: No, no. I told them that I reconstructed the last few remarks from my notes, because we ran out of tape and we ran out of time, too.

In the first days of the furor, I obtained a photocopy of an internal *Time* memo that matches Foote-Greenwell's description of the memo and the transcript that she sent back to *Time* headquarters in New York in response to a specific query about the rape quotes. The memo is dated January 11, 1991. It is addressed: Showbiz. For: Porter, which Corliss said was a shorthand reference to Christopher Porterfield, one of the senior editors in the entertainment and media section where Corliss works. The memo continues: "From Paris. By V. Foote-Greenwell. Slug: Depardieu." The memo then sets forth, in French, the exact same passages of Foote-Greenwell's interview that are included in the official *Time* transcript that I had received from Pondiscio. But preceding the transcript, Foote-Greenwell begins her memo with this advisory to the Showbiz section:

"The issue about the rapes is ticklish. The question was asked at the very end of the interview, and the last part of what he said was cut off by the tape coming to its end. Depardieu's last two remarks were written down afterwards, from memory."

Then the stringer sets down what she says is the verbatim transcription of that part of her interview dealing with the rape issue. The Foote-Greenwell memo contains both the original French and her own translations into English of her questions and Depardieu's answers. The official transcript has only the French. Interestingly enough, her translation of one of the key quotes that were later published in *Time* with the verb in the past tense has the verb translated correctly, in the present tense. After she sets down the three question-and-answer exchanges, Foote-Greenwell adds another advisory to the editors in New York, in capital letters:

> TAPE CUTS HERE. DEPARDIEU'S THOUGHT CHANGES AND HE SAYS A LAST FEW WORDS TO CONCLUDE WITH THE SUBJECT. AN HOUR LATER WE TRANSCRIBE FROM MEMORY HIS TWO FINAL REMARKS:
>
> GD: *Tout ca me fait rire. C'est des elements d'enfance.* (All that [talk] makes me laugh. That was just part of my childhood.)

So on January 11, 1991, more than two weeks before the story was published, the *Time* stringer who actually interviewed Depardieu sent a memo to *Time* headquarters in New York characterizing the rape issue as "ticklish." Her memo included a transcript of the relevant quotes in both their original French and her translation into English, and Foote-Greenwell said twice in her memo that all the relevant quotes were not on tape. Furthermore, before setting down Depardieu's final remarks, she states that "Depardieu's thought changes. . . ." She then sets down two more sentences from Depardieu, recorded an hour later from memory. It was the last of these two sentences, of course, that became the final, clinching part of the damaging published quote which portrayed Gérard Depardieu to the world as an avowed, unrepentant rapist.

For further clarifications, on November 1, 1993, I talked with Robert P. Marshall, Jr., associate general counsel of Time Inc. We discussed many of the issues involved in the Depardieu controversy and *Time*'s handling of the story. I did not tape-record the telephone conversation, but at the end of our talk I went back through the remarks I thought I might want to quote, and he confirmed their accuracy. All of the following quotes from Marshall were among those he confirmed.

Marshall told me that *Time* lawyers read every story in the magazine before publication. He also said that after Depardieu claimed he had been misquoted, Marshall went back through the relevant files, and he examined Foote-Greenwell's transcript and the tape of the interview. Marshall said that while he does read French, he also reviewed the transcript and tape with Joelle Attinger, a *Time* editor who he said is a native French speaker. At the end of this comprehensive review, Marshall said, he concluded that the account published in *Time* was an accurate description of Depardieu's remarks on the subject of rape. "It seemed to me an accurate description of his statement," Marshall said.

In order to go through the relevant quotes with me, Marshall took from his file a transcript that he said had been sent to *Time* by Foote-Greenwell in a memo dated January 11, 1991. He said her memo included three question-and-answer exchanges, plus a final remark from Depardieu. Her memo gave both the original French and her translations into English, Marshall said. He also read to me an introductory note to the editors in New York. In that note, he said, Foote-Greenwell said the issue of rape was "ticklish." He read to me the exchanges and then a final note beginning "Tape cuts here" and including the passage "Depardieu's thought changes. . . ." Everything Marshall read me exactly matched the copy of the memo that I had obtained in the first days of the controversy. (After our conversation, Marshall sent me a copy of the Foote-Greenwell memo, and it exactly matched the one I already had.)

Marshall and I went through the issues of *assister,* the shifts in verb tense, the adding of the words "in those circumstances," and the fact that all the quotes published in the story were not on Foote-Greenwell's tape, despite *Time*'s public statements to the contrary. In response, Marshall raised several points. He said that during the course of the interview, Depardieu had "plenty of opportunity" to say that the earlier published story was wrong and to say that he was not a rapist. He said that Foote-Greenwell's statement that "Depardieu's thought changes" was ambiguous and did not mean that he was no longer speaking specifically about rape. He said that the fact that the last sentence of the quotes published in *Time* was not on tape was only a minor point. "That's not the incriminating part of the statement," he said. The incriminating part, he said, was Depardieu's one-word response of *"oui"* to the question turning on the verb *assister*.

After we went through these points, I asked Marshall if there were any important aspects of this matter that we had not covered. He said no. In conclusion, I asked Marshall if he was comfortable with the way the story had been handled. He said: "I'm comfortable that Mr. Depardieu's comments were not taken out of context, certainly by the writer in New York, in light of the previously published story and the files he received from the stringer. I'm relying on her to properly interpret the meaning of Mr. Depardieu's comments, but that's her job."

Many newspapers, magazines, and news organizations in America have specific guidelines on how quotes should be handled by writers and editors. I asked Marshall if *Time* had any such guidelines, and in response he read to me from what he said were *Time*'s official editorial guidelines. I took down what he read, and afterward went back through it all with him to confirm accuracy. Here is what *Time*'s associate general counsel quoted from those guidelines:

"Quotes must be accurate. If edited or cut, there must be no alteration of the meaning or context. If a quote is paraphrased, it must not be in quotation marks. Grammar and spelling may be corrected, but it is unacceptable to add or delete a word or phrase that alters the meaning."

My discussion with Marshall completed the interviews that I conducted at *Time*. To my mind, many of the basic elements of the controversy were now clarified. The entire international uproar had not been triggered by anyone coming forth and accusing Depardieu of rape. It had been triggered by what *Time* claimed was Depardieu's own avowal of rape, as affirmed in his own words in an interview with *Time*. But as *Time*'s own tape and official transcript show, the quotes portraying Gérard Depardieu to the world as a rapist were not accurate. His responses to *Time*'s questions about rape were not just edited, cut, and taken out of their larger context. Words he did not say were added. Some of his verb tenses were changed. Two sentences drawn from two different parts of his remarks were cut, edited, and drawn together inside the same quotation marks.

In my interviews, Corliss, the writer of the story, acknowledged that Depardieu's words had been changed. He also stated that he had not verified the quotes against the French transcript, either before he wrote the story or after Depardieu claimed he had been misquoted. Foote-

Greenwell, the reporter who interviewed Depardieu, acknowledged that she had asked Depardieu about the rape issue only in vague terms. She also acknowledged that although she knew the verb *assister* could be interpreted and translated in very different ways, she did not make clear her usage of that verb when questioning Depardieu.

Furthermore, Foote-Greenwell's memo of January 11, 1991, makes clear that at least two weeks before Corliss's article was published, the reporter who conducted the interview informed the Showbiz section that she thought "the issue about the rapes is ticklish." She also advised that not all the quotes going into the magazine were on tape. Marshall, the *Time* attorney who reviewed the story and the supporting *Time* files after Depardieu claimed he had been misquoted, confirmed the contents of Foote-Greenwell's memo, including her advisory that not all Depardieu's remarks were on tape and that his concluding thought had been transcribed from memory an hour later. Marshall, who said that he and a native French speaker had reviewed the tape, also admitted that a portion of the quotes published in *Time* was not on tape. This, of course, was contrary to what *Time* had declared in its public statements and in its later article about the ensuing controversy.

This long, detailed account, then, is an inside look at how *Time* magazine came to portray Gérard Depardieu to the world as an avowed rapist. It is an account based on *Time*'s own tape and official transcript of Depardieu's remarks, and it is an account told, in large measure, by four people at *Time* who were directly involved in writing the original article or in responding to the ensuing controversy. Their explanations shed light on how *Time* handled this very serious allegation and on the origin of those explosive and damaging quotes. Their explanations also shed light on how *Time* responded to Depardieu's formal denials and his allegation that he had been misquoted, misinterpreted, and smeared in the pages of one of the world's most prominent publications.

Perhaps the last word on this sad affair should go to Robert Pondiscio. In explaining to me why *Time* had chosen to put out such a strongly worded statement at the start of the furor, after Depardieu claimed he had been misquoted and was demanding a retraction, Pondiscio said that Depardieu had leveled a very serious charge. He was challenging the credibility of *Time,* and such an attack had to be firmly rebutted and refuted. As Pondiscio put it:

"You're only as good as your reputation."

On the set of *1492* with director Ridley Scott, 1992

18

Columbus

In the spring of 1991, when Gérard was still off in Mauritius, how the *Time* affair would unfold was far from clear. At this stage, Gérard was still under siege from the media, he still felt hurt and embittered by the accusation that he was a rapist, and some of his closest advisers in France and America were still fearful that the entire affair could do irreparable damage to his career. And far away on the island of Mauritius, where he was wrapping up the shooting of *Mon Père, Ce Heros,* Gérard was still on his binge of food and drink. Indeed, by now, according to many people close to him, he had completely lost his mental and emotional equilibrium. The shoot in Mauritius ended satisfactorily, and *Mon Père, Ce Heros* became a small, charming film. But Gérard's depression then spilled onto a new movie set, with nearly disastrous consequences.

This was *Tous les Matins du Monde,* a French homage to baroque music and the creative spirit. Gérard had a small but key role, and he wanted to be on hand to give guidance and moral support to his son, Guillaume, who was making his screen debut alongside Anne Brochet, who had played Roxane in *Cyrano.* Livi was producing, and the director, Alain Corneau, was a close friend, and the shoot promised to be a congenial family affair. But from day one, Gérard was in horrible shape, putting Corneau into a very difficult bind. He and Gérard had done *Choice of Arms* and *Fort Saganne* together, and the two men shared another bond: Corneau had grown up in the 1950s in a French provincial town with a NATO base alongside. But as close as they were, Corneau now found his friend moving at a breakneck speed, hurtling toward catastrophe.

"Gérard is always like an intercontinental missile, but now he was even more so," Corneau says. "He knew he was only going to be shooting with us for fifteen days, so he moved to a higher speed."

When Gérard's spiral of drinking and depression threatened to disrupt the shoot, Corneau threatened to throw him off the film. Chastened, sobered, Gérard snapped into line. Indeed, from then on he started to calm down. The film was being shot in central France, in the Creuse, near Le Berry, and Gérard wandered around the area of his childhood. He went fishing and kept a nervous but distant eye on Guillaume, who was doing brilliantly. With Brochet and the film's main star, Jean-Pierre Marielle, giving fine performances, *Tous les Matins* became a huge critical and commercial success in France, and Guillaume was acclaimed as one of the most promising young stars in France. The film won nine Césars, and Livi was hailed as France's producer of the year.

Now, though, Gérard's self-destructive spiral began taking a new toll on his family, and especially on Elisabeth. He became involved with a Franco-American model, and in January 1992, she gave birth to a child. Gérard formally recognized the child and agreed to provide the mother and child with financial support. But the affair was reported in the press, causing the family further embarrassment and suffering. On the eve of his departure for America to make *Green Card,* Depardieu had prophesied to me that he was beginning what would "be either a great adventure or a tragic mistake." By the summer of 1991, about all Depardieu could see were tragic mistakes. His great American dream and his family life—up until then the anchor of his existence—now seemed to have crashed down around him and shattered into pieces.

As usual, Gérard's response to crisis was to throw himself even deeper into his work and into a new fictional character. This was a golden role for Gérard, a huge international role carrying bigger risks than he had ever faced before. But risks or no, in the summer of 1991 he felt certain that playing this character was part of his own unique odyssey as an actor. For a restless, wandering youth who had grown up dreaming of one day sailing to America, of conquering America, of establishing a following in America, what greater role could there be than that of playing Christopher Columbus?

The Hotel Melia sits on a quiet square overlooking the medieval town of Cáceres, Spain, a half-day's journey southwest of Madrid. The Melia, like Cáceres itself, combines what travel books often refer to as Old World charm and modern conveniences. In size and feel, it is more of an inn than a hotel, and even after a thorough refurbishing the Melia has managed to remain tasteful, discreet, and thoroughly European. The hotel caters to traveling businessmen and sophisticated tourists exploring the backroads of Spain, and for years its notion of big crowds and high excitement was a Rotary Club gala or an off-season convention of some obscure society of dentists or radiologists.

That notion, however, was forever transformed on the night of December 1, 1991. For on that rainy winter night, the little town of Cáceres and the Hotel Melia abruptly became a major crossroads of international cinema. By plane, by train, and by limousine they streamed into town, coming from Madrid, Paris, London, and even from Hollywood: cameramen, soundmen, lighting crews, carpenters, electricians, makeup artists, wardrobe specialists, stuntmen, and all the other support staff needed to make a big-budget Hollywood-style movie. Attracted by the irresistible perfume of movie stars, glamour, and big money, there also came a steady stream of celebrity sniffers: photographers, reporters, groupies, gawkers, autograph hunters, and scores of movie fans looking for work as extras and filled with dreams of meeting the stars. Throughout the entire day of December 1 and long past midnight, the tiny square in front of the Melia was filled with a throng of onlookers, a stark reminder for any skeptics tempted to doubt the incredible magnetism of the movies and their impact on our popular culture and imagination.

The scene inside the Melia was far more frenetic. Long past midnight, faxes and phone calls were still pouring in and out of the hotel, at a rate surely never seen in Cáceres before or since. In one suite, director Ridley Scott was going over final plans with his assistant directors and closest advisers. In other rooms of the hotel, film producers were on the phone to agents and moneymen in Hollywood, technicians were going over the equipment, and deep into the night at least one American actor was busy fretting over his lines for the following day's shoot. Room service was kept busy long after it usually shuts down, and long past midnight the bar just off the lobby was still jammed with serious drinkers, most of them Englishmen consuming vast quantities of beer.

But in the midst of all this frenzy, one small suite of the hotel went dark and quiet just after midnight: the suite belonging to Depardieu. Let everyone else go into a last-minute fury; Gérard wanted a good night's sleep. He had been through a terribly upsetting year, his personal life was still in an uproar, and on many nights throughout the year Gérard had been unable to sleep at all. Tonight, though, after dinner and a bit of reading, he fell into a deep, relaxed sleep, and he passed the night as contentedly, as he described it the next morning, "as a beet in the field." The next morning, long before dawn, Gérard was up smoking Gitanes and getting ready to go. Alone in his suite, he had coffee, took a shower, and as he awaited the hour specified on his call sheet, he busied himself arranging some of the clothes, books, and newspapers strewn about his makeshift home away from home.

On a morning as climactic as this one, many actors carrying a role like his might have come down with a rebellious stomach or an attack of nerves; not Gérard. His life was chaos, but now his work made him surprisingly calm. Like those athletes who perform extraordinarily well in big games, or those reporters who are at their best when covering a big breaking story, Gérard has a rare quality that might be referred to as "crisis cool." Unusual tension and chaos sharpen his focus and increase his concentration; the more demanding the role, the more calm he usually becomes. This morning, in other rooms of the Melia, several actors and actresses were putting themselves through a final primp in front of the mirror; Gérard did not even bother to shave the stubble from his chin. Right now, some of his fellow actors were undoubtedly doing a final run of their lines for the day; Gérard's script lay closed on the nightstand and he had no intention of opening it now. For months he had been studying that script, and now every scene and every line were engraved in his mind. For months he had slaved to improve his English. For months he had been reading histories, biographies, and diaries. For the past several weeks he had been crammed full of seamanship, horsemanship, and swordsmanship. Now Gérard could not bear one more second of preparation. This morning he was like a pregnant woman with her water burst: all he craved was physical release.

Finally, it was time to go. Gérard stepped into his faded Levi's and pulled on a black hooded sweatshirt, discreetly adorned with the logo of his winery, Château de Tigné. The sweatshirt was thick and warm, perfect for what promised to be a long, cold day on the set. Then he climbed into his favorite pair of cowboy boots, the black ones with the heels worn down and the hide begging for a lick of polish. Using his fingers for a comb, Gérard then drew back his long, damp mane and with an elastic band fixed it into a ponytail. Now he grabbed his script and two fresh packs of Gitanes and hurried down the old stone staircase to the lobby. Several members of the crew were standing in the doorway of the hotel waiting for their van; Gérard greeted them with a burst of high spirits:

"Hola!" The Spanish greeting came naturally to his lips.

"Hola, Gérard. *Hola."*

"Good shape?" he asked.

"Good shape, Gérard. And you?"

"Perfect!"

Gérard's Mercedes and driver were waiting out front. On this cold winter morning, with the sun not yet up, the medieval town of Cáceres was dark and gloomy, and as the big Mercedes wound through the narrow streets, its yellow beams swept across ancient ramparts and cobblestones, across the façades of tiny shops and shuttered cafés. They drove down along the Avenida de España and past the central esplanade, its great circular fountain now silent, its palm-shaded promenades now completely deserted. Heading north out of town, they passed through a zone of small factories and depots, and then the road led them past the railroad station, across the main highway to Madrid, and out past a village of abandoned adobe huts. The road then climbed a hill, and when Gérard and his driver came up over the top, spread before them was the vast plain of southwestern Spain, undulating in dimly lit swaths of russet and green. Down on the plain, the driver turned in at a sign scrawled "Columbus" and pulled the Mercedes into the site of this first day of the shoot. A raw, penetrating wind was blowing in off the plain, and when Gérard stepped from the car it was whipping the trucks and the trailers and the wings of the lunch tent, and blowing straight up the hill toward La Rábida.

Everyone on the set this morning was extremely tense; Gérard felt it as soon as he greeted the crew. After twenty-five years as an actor, there was nothing new to him about the frenzied kick of day one of a shoot, but this time was different: *1492* was going to be a mammoth production, a $45 million extravaganza, and for many of the people involved, this entire project was a colossal gamble. The film aimed to match Hollywood in terms of quality and scale, but *1492* was being written, financed, produced, and directed by Europeans, men and women coming from three different countries and from three very different film traditions and cultures.

Gérard and the originators of the project considered it a noble venture, but they had no illusions about the enormity of the risks. If it succeeded, *1492* would be a major triumph for European cinema, at a time when Europe's national film industries were feeling severely menaced by America's growing dominance of world cinema. If it succeeded, *1492* could lead to many more pan-European projects and it could even prove to be a symbolic triumph for the "New Europe," the unified trading and political bloc that was to come into being in 1992, exactly five hundred years after the Italian-born Columbus, sailing under a Spanish flag, landed his ships at an island in the "New World." But what if *1492* failed? Then it would be seen in Europe and America as a resounding defeat, yet more proof that the Europeans, with their boutique approach to filmmaking and their insistence on prizing art over commerce, just cannot make blockbusters of industrial scale and global box-office appeal. And if *1492* failed, Gérard knew it could prove to be a terrible setback to his hopes of making more movies in English and of extending his reputation and following in America and the rest of the English-speaking world.

With so much at stake, Gérard naturally harbored a whole range of worries and doubts, but this morning he was not about to parade them before the cast and crew. Like most of the old pros on board he knew that the chemistry generated this first day on the set might well set the mood for the long months to come, first here in Spain and later on in Costa Rica. So once he sensed all the tension around him, Gérard naturally started to clown, wrestling with the stuntmen, joking with the makeup crew, and teasing Gil Noir, his personal wardrobe aide for the past ten years. "Gérard is trying to make everyone relax," Gil confided. "That's *sympa,* no?"

While *1492* was thoroughly international in scope, cast, and crew, its roots were purely French. The movie was the brainchild of Roselyne Bosch, a French journalist working for the newsweekly *Le Point.* In 1987, she went to Seville to do a piece on how Spain was planning to commemorate the five hundredth anniversary of Columbus's expedition. Seville has archives containing some forty million documents relating to Columbus, and in them Bosch found fascinating glimpses of the man, including books from his personal library and letters handwritten by the explorer himself. In some of his books, she found in the margins tiny notes and drawings, such as a hand pointing to a particular passage. The more time Bosch spent in the archives, the more she became enthralled, and the more this hazy, almost mythological figure of Columbus became real to her—a man of flesh and blood. "I was deeply moved by seeing his handwriting and signature," Bosch says. "Suddenly, instead of being like Santa Claus, Columbus was a human being. . . . It was very powerful, and I thought, This ought to be a movie."

Bosch felt the idea was a natural, especially given the attention that Spain, Italy, and America were planning to lavish on their Columbus celebrations. Moreover, no one so far had brought Columbus convincingly to the screen. In 1949, the British had done a voyage-to-America movie with Fredric March playing the lead, but the general assessment was that the movie was mediocre and not what Columbus deserved. Bosch, excited by her many discoveries in Spain, called a friend of hers in Paris, Alain Goldman, a young French film distributor. He flew to Seville for a firsthand look at the Columbus material and a visit to the Seville cathedral, where Columbus is said to be buried. (Some historians are not convinced.) Goldman, too, was very impressed and he urged Bosch to stay on and pursue her research.

Soon they became partners in a fledgling film venture, Goldman as producer and Bosch as reporter-turned-screenwriter. Initially, they envisioned the film as a French project, but they found little support among French producers. The budget was too big for France, the producers said; try Hollywood. Rank amateurs though they were, Bosch and Goldman went knocking on doors in Los Angeles. But they found no encouragement and understandably so: they had no director, no star, and no track record in screenwriting or production.

Bosch became very discouraged, but finally she knocked on the right door: that of Britain's Ridley Scott. In style, he was a European director, and thanks to *Alien, Blade Runner,* and *Black Rain* he had excellent credentials and connections in Hollywood. And he had just made *Thelma & Louise,* a film that would bring him an Oscar nomination for best director. By odd coincidence, or destiny, Scott had already been toying with the idea of making a film about Columbus, and when Bosch set before him her idea and a rough synopsis of a script, Scott had just one response: "Yes—if we can get Depardieu to play Columbus."

This took Bosch by complete surprise; Depardieu had not even occurred to her. She and Goldman, aiming at the English-speaking market, had been focusing on American stars such as Kevin Costner and Michael Douglas, big names they figured would be the only way they could secure the financial backing they needed. But as soon as Scott said it, Bosch knew Depardieu would be perfect for the role: "I knew right away there would be no problem with energy; Gérard would burst upon the screen. And from that moment on, thinking of him in the role gave me a big push. Instead of having an abstract idea of Columbus, I knew it was Gérard. It was a liberation."

But would Depardieu agree? Bosch sent him a draft script and then set up a meeting with him in Paris, at the Hôtel Raphaël, a favorite rendezvous for the French film community. She and Scott arrived in the bar at the appointed hour of 7 p.m., but there was no sign of Gérard. After a half hour's wait, and torn between nerves and pique, Bosch finally telephoned Depardieu at a pied-à-terre he kept in Paris. Gérard answered with a very soft, very shy voice. Had he forgotten? Was there some sort of problem? Over the phone, Bosch got no clue. But soon Gérard was storming into the Raphaël and sallying into one of his torrential streams of consciousness. For nearly an hour, he burst forth, about Columbus, about himself, about how perfectly they were paired. Gérard's performance left Scott and Bosch dazzled and a little bit dazed.

"To my astonishment," she says, "I realized that in only one or two readings he had understood all the subtleties behind the lines. In Hollywood when I tried to explain Columbus's relationship with Queen Isabella, I had great difficulty, because their rapport was ambiguous, it was an unresolved sexual attraction. In sum, it was not Hollywood. Gérard got it right away, like a laser. . . . Ridley and I came away very excited. Gérard is larger than life. And Ridley films larger than life. It seemed a perfect match."

With Depardieu aboard, Goldman and Scott went to see Gaumont, the French production house controlled by the Schlumberger family. They met with Nicolas Seydoux, the head of Gaumont and a friend of Gérard's. Scott was expecting a Hollywood-type negotiation, with offer, counteroffer, and niggling over details. But when they named a price of 43 million francs—some $8 million, one of the largest sums ever paid for distribution rights in France—Seydoux just smiled and said yes. "We shook hands," Scott recalls, "and a moment later a waiter came in carrying a silver tray with a bottle of champagne, from the family winery, of course."

With their startup costs now covered, and with Gérard on board, what the young team needed next was some American backing. And Gérard knew just where to turn. When he was making *Green Card,* he had met Peter Weir's agent, John Ptak, a tall, refined, erudite man not at all in the mold of the stereotyped Hollywood agent. Ptak had several European clients, including the director Costa-Gavras, and he signed Gérard on as his client with Creative Artists Agency, the most influential agency in Hollywood. Through Gérard, Ptak now became instrumental in bringing Paramount into the *1492* project for $10 million, in exchange for distribution rights in North America. According to Ptak, Paramount was fully aware of the *Time* scandal but raised no objections to Gérard being in the movie. Just the opposite—they felt he was one of the few actors in the world who could carry off this ambitious historical epic.

As Goldman, Scott, and Bosch began putting together the mammoth enterprise, Gérard went into a cocoon and began the long creative process by which he would emerge as Columbus. The process is always a bit mysterious, but this time it was even more so. Columbus the man was so wrapped in myth and legend and revisionist politics that Gérard had no clear avenue into his being and spirit. Early drafts of the *1492* script also failed to provide him with a satisfactory feel for the man, so Gérard turned to outside reading. He first read histories and biographies of the explorer, and then he pored through Columbus's own letters. But what was the most helpful in finding the man inside the myth was reading the diary that had been written by Columbus's youngest son, Fernando. The diary, with its wealth of human and family detail, made Columbus come alive for Gérard and it stimulated his imagination; he even came to feel a strong sense of identification with the explorer.

By August 1991, Gérard was fully immersing himself in the role of Columbus. He spent several weeks at his picturesque summer cottage on the Normandy coast, in the hills above Trouville. Here he was far away from the lingering strains of the *Time* affair and he was surrounded by supportive family: Hélène, Patrick, Gérard's daughter, Julie, and at times by Elisabeth. In the embrace of his family, Gérard nursed his multiple wounds, his spirits improved, and he spent several hours a day concentrating on Columbus. One Sunday morning in mid-August, Gérard went into Trouville to buy tools for the house and to lay in provisions for a big Sunday lunch he was cooking with Patrick. Before lunch, he sat in his garden and discussed his preparation for what he knew would be one of the most challenging roles of his career. He was busy working on his English regularly now, and he was learning his lines from a draft script he had received from Bosch. From the script and his outside reading, Gérard had come to feel that he and Columbus shared a whole range of common attitudes, appetites, and desires, and he said that he was developing a strong personal bond with Columbus. So strong that Gérard said he could now feel Columbus inside him, emerging from the shadows and starting to grow and take form.

"Columbus and I are basically the same," he explained. "I am starting to feel how our two characters mesh. He and I are very similar. We are both voyagers, and we both travel light."

As he deepened his intellectual understanding of Columbus and explored their emotional affinities, Gérard also began physically transforming himself into Columbus. He let his hair grow long, as long as Columbus's appeared in drawings and paintings. To lead his men across the sea and to the New World, Columbus had to be strong and fit, so now Gérard began dieting and exercising. Very quickly he lost weight and his posture and bearing improved. The more he came to look like Columbus, the more Gérard felt like Columbus, and by the fall of 1991, with shooting just two months off, Columbus had taken clear form inside his being. Now in his visual and sensory imagination Gérard could see Columbus walking into the court of Queen Isabella and he could smell her perfume. He could see himself riding his mule through a herd of goats, and he could see his little son Fernando running up alongside. Gérard could feel himself in the arms of his common-law wife, Beatrix, and on her breast he could smell the scents of their hearth, and he could feel the softness of her hair brushing his cheek. By the time the shoot was a few days away, Gérard was strong and fit, his hair was so long it flowed down across his shoulders, and he had lost forty pounds and was carrying himself with purpose and authority. He and Columbus were now one in flesh and blood, and their fusion had reached beyond the physical into the spiritual.

"We are both artists and mediums, able to absorb and transmit forces larger than ourselves," Gérard told me. And at the annual French Film Festival in Sarasota, Florida, just before he left for the shoot in Spain, he told a group of American reporters, only half joking: "Now I *am* Columbus; I see all of you as Indians."

Gérard had completed his preparations with a few working sessions in Madrid with Ridley Scott and key members of the cast, and now here in Cáceres everything was set to begin. Replicas of the *Niña,* the *Pinta,* and the *Santa María* were manned and training at sea, and here on the set Ridley Scott and his crew were preparing their very first shots. With the magic of the movies, Scott's team had turned the sumptuous villa of a sixteenth-century nobleman into La Rábida, the humble Franciscan monastery where Columbus had waited a frustrating seven years for royal approval to lead his expedition westward. The first shot was to be inside what had been the villa's stable, and as Gérard went to his trailer for wardrobe and makeup, Scott moved into a final whirl. Sharpening camera angles. Adjusting lights. Placing his monks at their drafting tables, with their plumes in hand, their eyes fixed to their maps of the world, each map elegantly drafted on parchment, and each map embodying the unshakable conviction that the Earth was flat.

Scott comes from the very north of England, and by temperament he is cool, detached, and sure of his command. Appropriately, his English crew calls him "Guv'nor," with a great deal of respect. As a young man, Scott trained as a painter and graphics designer at the Royal College of Art in London, often in drawing classes beside David Hockney. Through such early films as *Alien* and *Blade Runner,* Scott won acclaim for his lush and startling visual effects; Pauline Kael has called him a "visual hypnotist," though with a tendency to be too slick. Scott envisioned *1492* as a sweeping epic, and he wanted to give it an especially rich texture and visual vocabulary, starting with the composition of this very first scene inside La Rábida. In keeping with his sketches and storyboards, the embers glowing in the fireplace and the candles flickering above the drafting tables now bathed the monastery in glimmering hues of yellow and orange, making the scene look as though it had been painted by Caravaggio or Georges de La Tour.

As Scott fussed with final details, swirling around him was what a euphemist might call "creative tension." The floor looked like a plate of spaghetti; wild confusions of cables and electrical wires spilled in every direction. Some two hundred members of the cast and crew were crammed into the small enclosure; orders were being barked out in a bizarre mix of English, Spanish, and French. After weeks of working ten, twelve, and even fifteen hours a day, many of Scott's technicians and field lieutenants were tired and snappish, and as the cold wind whipped and whistled through the set, you could read all the gathering tumult right on the face of the chief sound engineer, Pierre Gamet. The Frenchman had his headphones pulled down tight over his ears, his face was ashen, and his usually calm, methodical fingers were now flailing at the dials of all the gear stacked on his trolley.

"This is chaos," Gamet whispered. "There are just too many people in here." For Gamet, this set was a nightmare. Goats and horses had once used this stable for shelter, and it may have been fine for them. But now the heavy stone walls and the low, vaulted ceiling turned the cramped enclosure into a cavern of echoes; every sole scraping across the cobblestone floor scraped even louder into Gamet's headset and onto his tapes. This was supposed to be an intimate, hushed scene, but what was reverberating through Gamet's ears was the wind rattling through the sheets of cellophane that the crew had taped to the windows, to soften the light. The echoes and the rattling might not have annoyed an American soundman; in Hollywood, disturbing audio intrusions are routinely snuffed out in the lab. But Gamet is a purist, an artisan of Old World values: he wanted the sound he recorded to be exactly what would ultimately accompany the images on screen. This was his truth, his guiding ethic. So Gamet worked in a frenzy, muffling echoes, taping down the offending cellophane, fussing with noisy smoke machines, and signaling across the room to his partner and "boom," Bernard Chaumeil, using a verbal and gesticular code known only to them.

Gamet and Chaumeil were regarded as one of the finest sound teams in the movie business; in France, their craftsmanship had already been crowned with two Césars and they would soon win a third, for *Tous les Matins du Monde.* They had worked before in English, in New

York, when Gérard had made *Green Card* with Peter Weir, and they had also worked on *Cyrano de Bergerac,* a $20 million production Gamet had considered colossal in size. But they had never before worked on a project as ambitious as *1492.* And Gamet had never before worked with a director quite like Ridley Scott. Though the cameras were about to roll, Gamet had not had a single substantive conversation with Scott about the style and quality of sound the director wanted to achieve. Gamet was used to working on small, intimate sets and in close harmony with a director; now he felt like only a tiny cog in a giant, impersonal machine grinding away in a language and manner he could barely fathom.

Gamet was on this project for reasons extending far beyond his expertise as a sound engineer. Over the years, Gérard has forged symbiotic relationships with Bertrand Blier and a number of other directors who write roles expressly for him. But his rapport with Gamet was sometimes even closer: on more than a dozen films, Gamet had served as Gérard's ears. When they work together, every breath, every pause, every flub Gérard makes goes straight into Gamet's ears and onto his tapes. During a shoot, it is to Gamet that Gérard frequently turns to see how clearly his voice and his character are coming across. In making *Cyrano,* for instance, when Gérard was called upon to simultaneously duel and recite intricate alexandrine couplets, Gamet was his anchor; with a glance to Pierre he could gauge his performance. At the end of a take, if Gamet was pleased, Gérard knew his Cyrano was striking just the right chords.

On the set of *1492*, Gamet was also helping anchor Gérard's surrogate French family. Gamet, Chaumeil, and Gil Noir had worked with Gérard for more than a decade, often in distant corners of the globe, and the three of them had become close friends and dinner companions. When need be, they also served as a vital support group for the temperamental and sometimes volatile Depardieu. All three were highly respected professionals, and they did take on projects without Gérard. But the main reason they were on the *1492* set was because Gérard wanted them there and needed them there.

Completing the French contingent was Louise Vincent, a perfectly bilingual writer, actress, and dialogue coach who had worked with Laurence Olivier and Sophia Loren before coming to the rescue of Gérard's English. In the months leading up to the shoot, Louise had spent countless hours trying to prune his English of its heavy Gallic tones and accent. She had even taken the waters with Gérard at Brides-les-Bains, a spa in the French Alps; for two weeks they spent every day dieting and exercising and drilling his lines. In her doting, maternal way, Louise would even quiz Gérard between laps in the communal pool. Here on the set, Louise would be helping Gérard drill his lines, and she would be on hand to straighten out any problems with pronunciation. Now for the first shot, she was strategically positioned right behind Ridley Scott, her script open across her lap.

At last, with everything in place, Scott and his team moved into position. Adrian Biddle, the cinematographer, stepped aside to give Scott a final look through the lens of the big Panavision camera, mounted on rails and ready to track. Scott put his eye to the cup, and Fernando Rey moved out into position. Rey, the dean of Spanish actors and a man of great calm and dignity, was portraying Marchena, Columbus's political and spiritual guide. Angela Molina, a beautiful, dark-eyed Spanish star, was playing Columbus's wife. Billy Sullivan, an all-American kid from Long Island, New York, was playing Columbus's youngest son, Fernando. Armand Assante, a Latin-looking and very accomplished American actor, was playing Sanchez, treasurer to the Spanish crown and an arrogant Spanish aristocrat who would duel Columbus, mentally and literally. And part of the tension this morning stemmed from the fact that no one knew who was going to play the key role of Queen Isabella. Anjelica Huston was the first choice, but Scott was furious with her Hollywood agent and all her escalating superstar demands.

"Screw them all," Scott would huff a few days later, when he still had no queen. "I'll take me mum."

Now, though, Scott had his eye to the big Panavision camera, aiming it to the far end of the stable and zooming it in tight on an ancient wooden door rising majestically to the ceiling. Fernando Rey turned toward that door, and the monks, bent down over their maps, also gave it surreptitious glances. Now Gamet, Chaumeil, Gil Noir, Louise Vincent, and everyone else on the set turned toward that door, eager for a first sense of how this bold pan-European gamble was going to unfold.

"Silencio por favor!" bellowed Terry Needham, one of Scott's assistant directors. "Quiet, please. All right, boys. Shhh, shhh, shhh . . . Okay, a little more atmosphere. Bring up the smoke. . . ."

At the call of "Action!" that massive door, creaking on its hinges, slowly opened and in came Depardieu. He strode forward into the light, and as he did a collective gasp rippled through the cast and crew. Gérard appeared totally transformed. He was wearing a medieval robe the color of burnt orange, his dark-blond mane flowed down over his collar, and his blue-gray eyes were burning with determination; one look and you knew that here was a man launched on a mission, a man ready to pursue his vision no matter where it might lead. The impact was stunning: Depardieu *was* Columbus, come to life. And in one magical instant, this legendary and somewhat mysterious historical figure was once again just a man, flesh and blood, soul and will.

Columbus walked forward and Marchena held up his hand. "I have something for you," he said, drawing a parchment from the folds of his robe. "You are to be heard at the University of Salamanca."

At this stage in his life, and in the script, Columbus was an experienced navigator and explorer, but he had been unable to test his absolute conviction that the Earth was round and that the gold and other riches of the East could be reached by sailing west. In the halls of power in Spain, Columbus and his theories had become objects of scorn and ridicule, and despite seven years of trying in nearly every royal court in Europe, this brash commoner from Genoa had been unable to secure the necessary royal approval and financial backing. Now Columbus read this invitation to present his case in Salamanca, and his face lit up in hope and wonder:

"Blawd, that izzzz eeeen a weeeek!"

Another gasp rippled through La Rábida. Louise Vincent, after all those months of working on Depardieu's English, cringed in barely concealed shock, and Lord only knows what went sailing through the mind of Ridley Scott. But whatever it was, it wasn't pretty, and it came wrapped with a price tag reading $45 million. Scott hesitated a moment, then made up his mind. This had been only a dry run, with no cameras rolling, but he went over to Rey and Depardieu and in a friendly banter offered them a few directorial suggestions, and a bit of warmth and encouragement. Everyone else stood in silence, holding their collective breath.

Depardieu's face gave nothing away, but those who knew him best could easily imagine the worst. Gamet did not even have to imagine; he had already lived the worst with Gérard. Gamet had made three films with Gérard over the past year, and he had been with him throughout the *Time* affair, first in Mauritius and then on the set of *Tous les Matins du Monde.* No one close to him believed for an instant that Gérard had been a rapist, at nine or any other age. But Gamet had seen firsthand the terrible toll the scandal had taken on Gérard and his family. And though he would not admit it too loudly, Gamet was not at all sure Gérard could now cope with all the strains of working in English and of carrying so much responsibility for the success of this venture.

Indeed, with their intimate knowledge of Depardieu's physical and psychological state, Gamet, Chaumeil, and Gil Noir shared a host of worries, and others on the set had their doubts as well. Faced with the biggest opportunity, and the biggest risk, of his career, how was Depardieu's equilibrium now? Would he be able to keep his weight down? How was his drinking? How comfortable was he going to be working in English? To Ridley Scott, and to Bosch, Goldman, and their various financial backers, these were serious professional questions; to Gamet, Chaumeil, and Noir they were personal worries about the head of their film family. Louise Vincent had even graver worries. If Gérard's English proved a flop, she faced eighty very painful days on the set, and her reputation as a language and dialogue coach could be severely damaged.

Gérard, of course, had his own doubts. On the eve of making *Green Card,* his first major test in English, he had been on the verge of panic about working in another language. But pulling off *Green Card* had not been so difficult. Peter Weir had written his comedy expressly for Gérard, and he had wisely encouraged him not to fret about his heavy French accent; it would just be part of the character's charm. But as Gérard knew full well, *Green Card* had been a cakewalk next to carrying on his shoulders a historical epic like *1492*. Columbus was a role of grandeur and lyricism, and a heavy French accent on Columbus's lips would not be charming or endearing; it would be downright catastrophic. With that in mind, he had been working with Louise toward a single goal: "I wanted to get Gérard to not talk like a discernibly French actor speaking English," she says. "I want people who don't know him to say, 'I wonder where he's from?' "

So now here was the first day of shooting, and the question on everyone's mind was not where was Depardieu from; the question was, can he bring forth a whole sentence in clear, intelligible English, no matter what the accent? Should his English fail, there was still the option of looping, having Depardieu reread and resynch his lines in postproduction. But loop an entire film? The costs would be killing, and so would the delays. So after all the morning chaos and tension, what floated inside La Rábida right now was a faint whiff of panic, and to Louise Vincent it was not a whiff, it was a blast. And when two more dry runs proved only marginally better, she might have been forgiven for using the ten-minute break to mentally pack her bags and storm off in disgrace. For long days on the set, Louise travels with a tiny portable chair, and as Scott and his team prepared their first take with cameras rolling, she hunched down into her chair, head bowed, her body rocking gently, as though she were silently praying for some form of divine relief.

Gérard appeared unfazed by the episode. During the break, he stood out in the wind and cold, joking with the makeup crew, and stoking himself up with several Gitanes. If he was feeling any panic, any rush of doubt, no one around him could detect it. With his usual high spirits, he endured a touch of powder to his nose and forehead, and a fast, deft brush through his hair. Gil Noir fussed over his robe and his black felt hat, and when Terry Needham called "Places!" Gérard was ready to go. Inside, the monks were back at their drafting tables, the Panavision camera was loaded and aimed, the candles over the tables were relit, fresh kindling was on the fire, and once more every single eye on the set settled nervously upon that massive door at the far end of the monastery.

"Silencio por favor! Quiet everybody! Okay, boys, enough atmosphere. Cut those generators! Good. Rolling. . . . Columbus, Scene One, Take One. . . . Action!"

The door, again creaking on its ancient hinges, inched open and once again Columbus strode in and greeted Marchena. Then he carefully examined the parchment Marchena handed him, running a finger over the royal seal and studying the invitation to state his case in Salamanca. Now his face again lit up with hope and wonder:

"God, that's in a week!"

Spot on. It might not have been Laurence Olivier, but the words came forth in clear, understandable English, and by the third take, Gérard was on his way. He started to let go and feel at ease in English, and when the words started flowing, the rest settled into place. Gérard's initial physical awkwardness molded into grace, his face relaxed until his cheeks looked gaunt and hollowed, proof of the fact that he had shed more than forty pounds to become Columbus. Even his head started easing back, elevating his eyes and conveying just the impression Gérard was working for: that here was a man launched on a mission into the pure unknown, spirited by God himself. By the third take, Ridley Scott was satisfied.

"Cut! Print! Very good," Scott called. "We'll do one more, just to get a little more smoke and atmosphere."

Louise, Gil, Pierre, and Bernard all breathed sighs of relief, and so did everyone else in the room. And soon Scott was exchanging his cigarettes for a huge Cohiba cigar. As for Gérard, he soaked up the general sense of relief and luxuriated in it, then he added his own inimitable touch, bellowing across the monastery: "Loooouise! Come! I neeeeeeed you!"

Hearing that bellow, and the way it reverberated through his headphones, Pierre Gamet broke into a huge grin, for the first time this morning: "That's it, he's starting to cut loose. That's a good sign. A very good sign."

As the predominantly British and Spanish crew soon discovered, Gérard works like almost no other actor in the world. At the close of this first morning session, most of the actors up at La Rábida waited for a van to ferry them down to the lunch tent; Gérard raced down on foot, his long robe flapping in the wind. That afternoon, after a scene where Columbus rode his mule through a nearby pasture and a flock of sheep, again the vans stood at the ready, but Gérard preferred to trek back up the hill. "What's this?" a friend called. "A star without his Cadillac?"

"Ah, stars," Gérard waved. "Leave them where they are! In Heaven. And in Hollywood."

As the crew soon discovered, what Depardieu seeks on a movie set is not glamour or status, it is warmth and camaraderie; he doesn't want to be treated like a star, he wants to be treated like one of the guys, one of the family. But as his French family knew, working on the set was something else for Gérard: therapy. He was plunging into the role, entering the skin and spirit of Columbus, and in so doing he was distancing himself from all the trauma of the *Time* affair. Being far away in Spain, dressed in medieval robes, was not work; it was pure relief. Depardieu also hoped the movie would be a way for him to earn back some approval in America. Money was not his motivation. By the Hollywood standards of 1992, his package of fees and points on Columbus was surprisingly modest: some $3 million up front, plus a share of worldwide profits and a hefty cut of French receipts. In this same period, Michael Douglas demanded and got $15 million for making *Basic Instinct.* Depardieu could not have cared less.

Even though the budget of *1492* was ten times the cost of a typical French film, on the set in Cáceres Depardieu moved quickly to establish the kind of familial informality and intimacy in which he likes to live and work. Between scenes, he did not retreat to a corner or his trailer to rework his lines or "stay in character." Instead, he stayed with the cast and crew to joke around. During one complex sequence outside La Rábida, a riding scene where Ridley Scott used a 360-degree camera whirl to capture Assante's Sanchez strutting his stallion, Gérard had no role in the shot. And he might well have profited from a breather in his trailer. But throughout the sequence, there was Gérard, stomach to the ground, nose in the dirt, right beside Gamet as he tried to record the actual sound of the horse and rider from a position protected from the camera's view.

In order to remain at the top of his form, Gérard needs to stay loose and relaxed, and so on the set he frequently played the Prankster. One day later in the shoot, when he was cavorting around Costa Rica exploring the New World, Columbus was to lead his men across a river deep inside a tropical rain forest. The river looked sinister, and many of the actors feared there might be snakes. At the cry of "Action!" everyone waded in, and sure enough, soon one of Columbus's fellow commanders felt something cold slithering up his leg. Right behind him came Gérard, his eyes gazing innocently toward the camera, his hand hidden under the water and wielding a stick with devilish delight. "Gérard is very relaxed and works with great humor," says Fernando Rey. "He does all sorts of things to make us laugh. That's the *only* way to work. The other way leads to catastrophe."

The importance of Depardieu's form of comic relief became clear during a tense moment one afternoon later in the first week, in the middle of a tender scene between Columbus and his common-law wife, Beatrix, played by Angela Molina. Earlier that afternoon, the shot had been delayed for well over an hour because of problems with Molina's hair, and on a shoot where operating costs had been calculated at $200 a working minute, nerves were becoming a bit frayed. The scene was being shot in the couple's tiny kitchen, at very close quarters, and during the first several takes the chemistry was just not working. On the next take, the couple were deep in conversation with Queen Isabella, and Molina completely forgot a segment of her lines. Without missing a beat, Gérard took over her part and delivered her lines in a voice so soft and sweet and feminine it sent everyone into hysterics.

"Cut! That's a print!" Scott roared, to Molina's enormous relief. All her tension gone, the next take was perfect.

On the very first afternoon of the shoot, the cast and crew had a revealing look into the way Gérard works. Once again the action was to take place in the monastery, but now Columbus was to explode in frustration and rage. It was a very physical scene, and Depardieu had been rehearsing it for days with stuntman Gregg Powell. After a word or two from Ridley Scott and a brief rehearsal with the monks, everything was set. Fernando Rey's Marchena stood at the ready, the monks huddled down over their parchments, Pierre Gamet signaled to Bernard to draw the mike forward, and the cameras zoomed in close.

"Silencio por favor! Settle down, boys," Terry Needham called. "Shhhh, shhhhh . . . Rolling . . . Action!"

At this point in the story, Columbus was so pent-up from waiting that he was right on the verge of cracking. He had waited seven long years to launch his voyage; he felt the time had come to act. Act! To calm the tempestuous Columbus, Marchena counseled more patience, but that only sent Columbus exploding into rage: "Wait! Wait! I've waited seven years already! How much more do you want me to wait?" Losing all composure, Columbus started in on the monks: "You never leave the protection of your gardens! Your books are full of phony assumptions. Lies! Lies! Damn God! Damn God!" Suddenly Columbus started heaving books in all directions and fending off any monk who dared to intervene. It was a display of raw power and rage, but as soon as Gérard was beyond camera range, he burst out laughing. He was not torturing his soul, he was having the time of his life.

To gauge how well he was communicating, Depardieu kept an eye on Gamet, on Scott, and on Gil and Louise. They were his audience, his chorus. Depardieu now has so much technical expertise that he pays little attention to the camera; he instinctively knows where it is. He also pays little attention to the way he looks; the staff will do that for him. And if, as on day one of the shoot, he does not feel like shaving in the morning, so what? He *is* Columbus, so Columbus just did not feel like shaving that morning either. By discarding such concerns, by freeing himself of mental work, Depardieu can keep himself on course, following the map of his interior emotions and bringing them to the surface.

But the script of *1492* did not really tap into his emotional richness. Indeed, the script had been a problem from the beginning. Bosch had done the first drafts, and she and Scott had done several more rewrites. In the summer of 1991, Paramount executives were not happy with the results. They wanted a radical rewrite and proposed bringing in professional script doctors from Hollywood. But according to several insiders, the script then became a lightning rod for a potentially devastating cross-cultural clash.

The Americans, in line with their taste for plot-driven movies, wanted more action and suspense woven into the script. Bosch, in line with traditional European taste for character-driven movies, insisted the script remain an ambiguous and subtle portrait of the enigmatic Columbus. The clash over the script brought into conflict two very different systems and ideologies about filmmaking: Hollywood and its collective, industrial approach to cinema versus Europe and its *auteur* tradition; Hollywood's conception of the screenwriter as a small cog in a giant wheel versus Europe's conception in which the writer, the *auteur,* is king and sovereign—a king who has guaranteed artistic freedom and who need brook no interference from moneymen. The way Bosch and some of the Europeans saw it, the conflict came down to this: Heathens and Dollar Grosses versus Artists and High Culture.

By the end of the first day, however, everyone was starting to feel a bit less tense. The crew was also very impressed with Depardieu, and this was not an easy lot to impress. No crew is. They see actors naked, without makeup and costumes, before their lines are polished. Michael Stevenson, one of the assistant directors, had worked on *Lawrence of Arabia* with David Lean and Peter O'Toole, and several of the other members of the crew had worked with some of the best actors in the business. "The first day is a terrible thing for an actor," says Terry Walsh, who was Depardieu's fencing instructor. "He has to think, 'How am I going to look and behave at this particular place in the script, but also before this and after?' And he has to get it right. If the actor is too tired, or he gets pissed off, the film goes to hell. Gérard got it right."

Still, several people on the set guarded private worries about how this project was going to unfold. With actors of so many different nationalities, Louise Vincent worried that a hodgepodge of accents would show up on the screen. With the production being controlled by tight-fisted Englishmen, the French were worried that the routine would be like a production line, with barely a break for lunch. And in several quarters there were continuing concerns about the script. It may have been historically accurate, but many people on the set felt it was too academic, with little conflict or emotional subtext. Depardieu's character was clear enough, but several of the supporting roles seemed to be little more than props and walk-ons, making this too much of a one-man show. And right from day one, some of the actors were frustrated with Ridley Scott; there had been little time for rehearsals, and he seemed more concerned with perfecting his painterly visuals than he was with giving the actors the guidance and vision they wanted.

"Depardieu is a thoroughbred, and just a nudge or two is enough to guide him," one insider confided. "But some of the other actors need more direction. And they're not getting it."

No one had to tell Depardieu the weight of responsibility he was carrying in this $45 million extravaganza, and even when he left the set he was unable to cut loose. Playing the off-camera role of Gérard Depardieu, actor and artiste extraordinaire, is never easy, and in Cáceres he was under constant siege by mobs of fans, reporters, and paparazzi. At times he was accosted right at his hotel-room door. Leaving the hotel to go for a walk or out to dinner became too much of a hassle, so Gérard would hole up in his room, with his books, his phone, and room service.

"I am literally a prisoner in my hotel room," he lamented. "But it is all right. I adapt. Like a blind man, it is improving my sense of smell."

To the relief of his French film family, Depardieu was sticking to his diet, skipping the chocolate binges and keeping his drinking to a glass or two of wine with dinner. In Cáceres, where twelve-hour days were the rule and fifteen-hour days were not uncommon, Depardieu did go on a few benders, but most of his depressurizing antics were confined to the set, and to the kitchens of his hotel and restaurants in town. As always, he barged into kitchens, inspected the fare, and even nibbled off a plate here or there. This routine at first shocked but then delighted local waiters and chefs.

Being a Frenchman, Depardieu holds Sunday lunch sacrosanct, and on one Sunday outing with Pierre, Bernard, and me, Gérard as usual marched into the kitchen for a look at the *plats du jour.* He spied a tray of suckling pigs and that made up his mind. Depardieu is not a gifted linguist, but he speaks good menu English, Spanish, and Italian—priorities, priorities—and now he certainly could have ordered in passable Spanish. But when the waiter came to take our orders, Depardieu screwed up his face and brought forth a roaring "Oink!" By the following morning, the story was legend in Cáceres, and word of his antics was spreading to the national press in Madrid.

One night, imprisoned in his hotel room, Depardieu was immersed in a letter when I paid him a call. The letter was from Jean-Luc Godard. He and Gérard had never worked together, and Godard was not Depardieu's favorite *auteur.* But Godard was dangling a role Gérard could not refuse: God. Godard's letter was rambling and poetic—the seed of the film—and I could see that Depardieu was being swept into another high-risk adventure. In a burst of excitement, he read me aloud fourteen pages of Godard's wit and fancy, and I couldn't help but remark, "It seems, Gérard, that for you Columbus is already over."

"Absolutely," he said. "The hardest part took place before I stepped on the set. . . . In many ways, I have the impression I have accomplished my task. The quest is over. The rest is denouement."

During a phase of the shooting in Seville, Elisabeth arrived for a brief visit. The Columbus crew saw that around her Depardieu was a changed man. He was gentle and subdued, caring and attentive; his rough edges and bawdy humor magically vanished. As one member of the crew put it, "Elisabeth really tames the beast. Suddenly there were no more cunnilingus jokes."

Gil Noir, having worked with Depardieu for so long, has come to see Elisabeth as his rock of stability, especially in moments of crisis. "She weighs all of forty-seven kilos, no bigger than your finger, but what strength. What intelligence. This is a woman! Without her, Gérard would be lost. And he knows it."

Exactly eight-one days after shooting had begun, Columbus and his weary crew were on the *Santa María,* off the coast of Costa Rica. The sun was murder. Bow and aft there was a breath of wind, but under the canvas tarp shading the central deck, it was too hot to breathe. The crew and most of the extras were stripped to their shorts, and many of the ship's hands were stretched out on burlap sacks and on the raw wood of the deck. From that first day of shooting, *1492* had been racing against time, climaxed by a grueling sprint here on the steaming coast of Costa Rica, and now had come the day that Ridley Scott hoped to wrap up the shoot.

The shoot had been exhausting. Depardieu's usual routine had been to rise at 4 a.m., and for the past several weeks everyone had been on the boats by 6 a.m. Shooting almost always went straight on until the light was too far gone for Scott to squeeze out another take. Returning to his hotel, Gérard would then polish some of his lines, with Gamet recording, and then he would study his script for the next day's scenes. Demon for work and precision that Scott was, Gérard felt sure the director would have the film looped, edited, polished, and out on October 16, 1992—five hundred years to the day after Columbus's discovery of America. *Ça sent bon,* Gérard had said early on in Spain—it smells good—and his feeling had not altered. But his enthusiasm for Hollywood-scale moviemaking had now dimmed. He admired how well the Anglo-Saxon managerial team had guided the mammoth production through with nary a hitch, but by the end, Gérard missed the warmth and intimacy of making films French-style, family-style.

As with most artists, what worried him now was not how hard he had worked but the quality of the final creation. And here he had some doubts. He had felt good as Columbus, and Scott was a visual master, but the film was heavy on pageant, and he felt that his own emotional resources had barely been tapped by the script. Still, Gérard felt in fine form. The long days, the sun, being at sea—all these had made him tanned and fit. His weight was down, and a lot of the pain and bile from the *Time* affair had been cleansed from his system. The heat was running now at well over 100 degrees Fahrenheit, but Gérard did not care. This was his life, moving from adventure to adventure, from discovery to discovery, and he felt a strong kingship with old Columbus. He also felt a strong kinship with the English and Spanish crews. Whatever happened with *1492*, he felt that the future of film was going to be international. Through film he had encountered creators as different as Truffaut, Satyajit Ray, Peter Weir, and lately Kenneth Branagh. To his mind, movie people really all belonged to one culture, and despite differences of accent, they all spoke the same language—the universal language of tears and laughter.

1492 traced twenty years in the life of Columbus. It showed him in frustration, as he waited for royal approval to sail, and it showed him in triumph, discovering the New World and its riches, and proving to himself that his initial intuition had been right. The movie also showed Columbus in defeat and humiliation, the victim of jealous rivals out to achieve glory at his expense. He had soared too high; he had to be cut down to size. All through the making of the movie, Gérard had felt emotionally and spiritually connected to Columbus. And this afternoon, for his final shot in this epic journey, Gérard was to embody Columbus as an old man—sadder, wiser, but still unbroken. Now, in the shade of the tarp, Gérard's makeup man made his hair look gray and thin and he touched the lids of Gérard's eyes with red, to convey the effects of wind and age.

The makeup worked its wonders, and finally Gérard was ready as old Columbus. To prepare for this somber and melancholy final scene, Gérard moved off into a corner to collect his thoughts and feelings. There he was joined by Kevin Dunn, an American actor who was playing one of Columbus's fellow commanders. Dunn, an intuitive actor himself, immediately understood Gérard's mood, and at the very same time they began singing: "Hey, you, get offa my cloud. . . ."

"People tell me I look just like Mick Jaggar," Dunn jived.

"Yeah," Gérard said. "Mussa be da lips, mussa be da lips."

Dunn is a native of Chicago. He worked in the theater there but then he moved to Los Angeles to work in movies. His time with Gérard had been an education. "Years ago, I vowed to work with him, because, watching his movies, I couldn't keep my eyes off him. There was so much going on," Dunn says. "In this day and age, there aren't many actors who just look like regular men. He does.The way he acts is completely natural, too. One day here in Costa Rica, we were all going up a path through the jungle. Most of us tried to make it look easy, out of the ego of not wanting to look clumsy. Not Gérard. He just let whatever was going to happen, happen, and when at one moment he staggered and nearly fell, I'm sure it looked great on camera and wholly believable."

At 5:25 p.m., with the heat of the day finally subsiding, and the bow of the *Santa María* framed by the orange sun lowering on the horizon, old Columbus stood with his shoulders hunched and his face to the wind. Now Ridley Scott, his cinematographer, and the rest of the camera crew zoomed in for closeups. This was to be their last shot of Columbus, and a hush settled over the ship, while everyone in the cast and crew and extras looked on. Their long, punishing voyage was drawing to a close; their multilingual, multicultural family was about to split up, and now everyone was to go his separate way and return to his real family. This was the end of the journey and it was a solemn moment—until Gérard pinched a cameraman on the arm and let out a cackle, as if to say, Hey, gang, lighten up! It's only movies! It's only make-believe!

Still, when the camera halted and Scott said, for the last time with Gérard, "Cut! Print! Great job, Gérard," the cast and crew stood on the decks of the *Santa María* and gave him a standing ovation.

For Gérard, and for almost everyone else on the ship that day, *1492* would wind up a deep disappointment. Many critics mocked it, and while small pockets of the viewing public adored the movie with a passion, the film failed to click with big-number audiences. In America it was a total flop, earning only about $7 million in its commercial run. In the view of Vincent Canby and many other critics, the film lacked emotional interest and resonance. "*1492* is not a terrible film," Canby wrote. "Yet because it is without any guiding point of view, it is a lot less interesting than the elaborate physical production that has been given it. Only a very great writer could do justice to all the themes the Columbus story suggests. Ms. Bosch may be a very good researcher, but she's not a very great writer. With the great hulking figure of Mr. Depardieu at its center, the movie at least has the presence of an actor who can suggest passions that the screenplay never pursues with any consistency."

In many ways, the *Time* scandal and the disappointment of *1492* brought to a close one of the guiding themes of Gérard's life: his American Dream. The rape charge would leave him with a sense of hurt and betrayal that would be difficult to cleanse from his system. Playing Columbus had been a great adventure, with wonderful warmth and camaraderie, but *1492* had punctured any illusions he may have had about Hollywood-style extravaganzas; now he knew they could not bring him the kind of artistic nourishment and fulfillment he craved. Out of an overwhelming urge to make it in America, Gérard had moved away from his own artistic credo, and he had paid a price for it. Now he wanted to go back to his roots, back to smaller, more personal films, back to authenticity and purity of emotion. And first and foremost he wanted to go back to his vineyards, back to his private corner in the valley of the Loire.

Working at Château de Tigné in Anjou

Epilogue

The road of excess leads to the palace of wisdom.

—WILLIAM BLAKE

Travel into the region of Anjou and you can easily see why it so well suits Depardieu. This part of the valley of the Loire has rugged terrain, thick forests, rich soil, and no pretense. Anjou is known for wines that are light and full of flavor, and their character, like Gérard's, is often described as expansive and earthy. These are not wines generally served at state dinners at the Elysée Palace; they are wines everyone can appreciate and almost everyone can afford. At Château de Tigné, Depardieu makes several different wines, and if there is one word to best describe them all, the word is "festive."

Many chateaus in the Loire valley are surrounded by manicured lawns and gardens; Depardieu's is surrounded by sixty-two acres of very hard-working vineyard, set in a landscape rich in the colors and scents of La France Profonde. The chateau itself is a twelfth-century fortress, guarded by two medieval turrets of massive stone. Once upon a time, the tops of the turrets were lined with lookout posts and cannon emplacements; now thick growths of ivy curl up the turrets and across the face of the castle. Next to the brawn of its turrets, the castle itself has a look of lightness and delicacy. Tall, elegant French windows give the façade a cheerful look, and on clear days, sunlight dances across their panes.

Depardieu bought the chateau in 1989, and the story of the sale has some of the peasant flavor of Marcel Pagnol's *Jean de Florette.* In the beginning, the local villagers and grape growers did not want the chateau and its vineyards to go to Gérard; they felt he was just a Parisian celebrity looking for a short-term investment, and they presumed he had no serious interest in wine or any knowledge about the way it was made.

But when they actually met Gérard, talked wine with him, and saw him plunge that celebrated nose of his down into a snifter of Anjou wine, they changed their minds. To their amazement, by his nose alone Gérard could identify regions, he could measure alcohol content, divine the process of vinification, and he could often tell for how long the juice had been soaked in the *rafle,* the skins and pulp that give the wine its richness and character.

In fact, by the time Depardieu sought to buy his own chateau he was already a passionate connoisseur, winemaker, and collector. He had started making wines in the mid-1980s, with a Rhône valley grower named Alain Paret, and the craft rapidly became to him a second calling. When he first found the Château de Tigné, it was in a state of miserable decline and decay; the owners had even given up pruning the vines. Long before he began negotiating to buy it, Gérard insisted on paying the cost of pruning; he knew the vines would die if not properly tended. Since then, he has pumped a small fortune into rebuilding the chateau and reinvigorating its life blood: the making of wine.

Those who know Gérard best—Elisabeth, Carmet, and Patrick Bordier, for instance—say that something quite dramatic comes over him when he sets foot in his *terroir,* the word the French use to define a vineyard's location, climate, and soil. When Gérard is in his vineyards pruning, or down in his cellars arranging bottles, or in the vegetable garden tending his carrots, leeks, potatoes, and scallions, just the way he used to do with his Grandma Denise, Gérard becomes a different man. He leaves the world of cinema far behind and becomes a peasant. Tigné is his home, his land, his roots. Here he is close to Le Berry, and in many ways the region has the same feel as where he grew up, though the soil in Anjou is better for the kind of wines Gérard likes to make and drink and share with friends. He and his family have lived in Bougival for twenty years, and in July and August he likes to spend time at his summer house above Trouville. But Tigné has a special hold on Gérard. It is like an ancestral property inherited from some distant cousin Gérard never had, but imagines he did.

Gérard has a manager running the chateau, but he comes in often, sometimes by small plane, sometimes by helicopter, and on these trips he often meets with international wine merchants and potential clients. Since 1991, he has been selling his wines throughout much of Europe and in the United States. But Gérard's real joy comes in working his vines, his grapes, and his wine. He loves doing hard physical work in the sun and digging his fingers into the soil. This to him is good, honest work, and it gives him a lift, clarifies his thoughts, and animates his spirit. Absorbed in making his wine, Gérard can forget the world of cinema, and all the falseness that so often goes with it.

At the close of 1992, after the disappointment of *1492,* Gérard needed this safe haven and its tonic effects. His life, in many ways, was in crisis. His marriage was in turmoil, his weight had ballooned again, and he was drinking too much. Then, just before Christmas 1992, his son, Guillaume, ran into trouble. At a time when he was being hailed by audiences and critics around the world for his acting debut in *Tous les Matins du Monde,* the young man was arrested on a charge of selling drugs. The incident was a terrible blow to the entire Depardieu family, and of course it was even worse for Guillaume, who was then twenty-one. Once again, reporters and photographers set up camp in Bougival, and once again Gérard and Elisabeth felt they were under siege. But the crisis drew them together, and they did what they could to help Guillaume. Gérard was deeply upset by it all, especially when he saw his son convicted and sent to jail for several months. Gérard knows full well how hard it is to be the son or daughter of Gérard Depardieu, and he knew how hard it had been for his entire family to struggle through the *Time* affair. But Gérard was also deeply impressed by the way his son responded to the multiple shocks. According to Gérard and Elisabeth, Guillaume pulled himself together and entered a period of reflection and positive personal growth. "He sees more clearly now," Gérard said a few months later. "In fact, he has responded magnificently."

Through this maelstrom, as through so many others, Elisabeth, all ninety-seven pounds of her, devoted herself to anchoring her family and returning them to calm. By the summer of 1993, the family had regained some stability. Guillaume was coming through the crisis, and he was allowed to spend his days out of detention, though he returned to jail at night. By now, Julie had matured into a graceful, sensitive young woman, and she was doing studies at the Sorbonne in philosophy and psychology. Elisabeth was working on several projects, including a screenplay, but almost all of her energy and concentration was focused on Guillaume.

By now, though, Elisabeth was frequently feeling angry and bitter. Genius always has its price, and Elisabeth felt that she and Gérard had paid their share. Genius always has its jealous critics, and she and Gérard had suffered more than their share of those as well. Her husband had become a national monument and a perpetual news story, and their private lives and the lives of their children were now under constant public scrutiny; Elisabeth resented their loss of privacy and the incessant media intrusions. She was also feeling angry at the milieu of cinema, and at some directors in particular. For too many years, she felt, too many *auteurs* had been putting Gérard in psychological jeopardy, using him as their foil, using his gifts and his force as their tickets to glory. In her view, too many directors just let their wildest fantasies spin, in the name of art, and then they would enlist Gérard to act them out, as their knight valiant. Then off Gérard would go on another quest, ever ready to be bloodied in battle.

"Gérard will always go where they themselves are afraid to go," Elisabeth says. "They live through his courage."

By 1993, Gérard, too, was tiring of suiting up for battle, and he was sick of all the public and media fanfare that went with being a movie star and national icon. In some of his quieter moments, he even started to talk about retiring from acting and settling down in Anjou. At the same time, of course, he was busy penciling three or four more movies into his frenzied schedule. In many ways, Depardieu cannot stop working now; powerful patriarch that he is, the Atlas who often seems to carry the whole of French cinema across the beam of his shoulders, if he stepped back from making movies, his film family would suffer, and the health of French cinema would surely suffer as well. Gérard never wants to let anybody down.

But there was another reason Gérard could not slow down: he still had enormous creative appetites to sate. By 1993, the year he turned forty-five, his taste in roles was once again evolving and maturing. His interest in playing thugs was long gone; now he wanted to focus on roles and stories which were life-affirming. In making *Mon Père, Ce Héros,* he was happy to play a father getting back in touch with his teenage daughter, and he was eager to do the remake in English with Disney studios, which had brought out *Green Card.* Gérard had developed a friendship with Jeffrey Katzenberg, Disney's organizational and creative whiz, and he was eager to work with him again. The feeling was mutual.

"Making *Green Card* was a great opportunity to become a real pal of Gérard, not just a fan," Katzenberg says. After the shooting of *My Father, The Hero,* which was to be released in early 1994, Katzenberg was ecstatic. "I think the movie's got the potential to be a smash," he said. "Gérard's such a genius as an actor that he completely understands what he's doing in every scene. This movie is exploring a universal theme—a father and his daughter—and it works from every point of view. This movie could make Gérard into a major American star."

At the end of 1993, however, becoming a major American star was no longer one of Gérard's ambitions; he was still very leery of the

Hollywood whirlwind in general and of the American media in particular. Most important to him now was his private creative quest, which was taking another turn into history and classical literature. During the first twenty years of his career, he had made *Danton* and *The Return of Martin Guerre,* he had played Rodin and Cyrano, and he had produced and starred in a film version of Molière's *Tartuffe.* After *1492* came Berri's *Germinal* and *Une Pure Formalité,* by Italy's Giuseppe Tornatore, who did the Academy Award–winning *Cinema Paradiso.* At the end of 1993, Gérard completed work on Balzac's *Colonel Chabert,* the ironic story of a soldier who miraculously survives a bloody massacre on the battlefield only to succumb in a legal battle with his wife. Gérard also had plans to tackle another classic role he had long seemed destined to play: Jean Valjean in Victor Hugo's *Les Misérables.*

Gérard's taste was also turning to Shakespeare. When Kenneth Branagh did *Henry V,* Gérard lent his voice to the French version, and he hoped to do more Shakespeare with Branagh and the brilliant Emma Thompson, Branagh's wife. Ever the *entremetteur,* Gérard also had plans to sponsor Shakespeare festivals in French universities, just as he had established a foundation to preserve and promote the work of his friend Satyajit Ray, the late Bengali director. The way Gérard sees it, the language and power of cinema are universal; movies can bring people together by transcending all barriers of language and culture. And Gérard wanted to be part of it all, to work with Disney in America, with Branagh in Britain, with Tornatore in Italy, all the while staying true to his own roots in La France Profonde, right in the soil of his own chateau in the heart of Anjou.

"My life demands a power of perpetual adaptation," Gérard says. "That's why I feel myself to be a citizen of the world, someone who belongs to every country and who accepts all cultures, even in their contradictions."

But how long could Depardieu keep up this punishing pace? What more did Gérard need to do to sate his creative demons? Watching him push himself, and exhaust himself, Elisabeth frequently found herself torn between anger at Gérard and compassion for his endless quest for applause and approval. Still, it had been like this throughout their marriage, and as exasperated as she often became, Elisabeth understood full well why Gérard drove himself to such punishing extremes. "Gérard needs to be loved all the time, and loved totally," she told me. "He always has inside him the root of a lack of love, which makes him work and work and work. Again and again, he makes terrible demands on himself, even if, at the same time, he is being showered with love."

Though they see each other only rarely now, Michel Pilorgé also worries about his old friend's excesses. Like Elisabeth, though, Michel sees those excesses as inexorably tied to Gérard's raging creative genius. In Michel's view, what often appears in Gérard to be a self-destructive streak is actually part of Gérard's unique creative process; it is part of the way he sheds one fictional identity, in order to take on another. "I believe that Gérard's self-destructive tendencies are often part of a process of development and growth," Michel says. "He usually manages, somehow, to construct the most positive things out of elements which are incredibly insidious."

I have frequently witnessed the extremes of Gérard; I have seen his bright, radiant side, and I have seen his dark, tormented side. Gérard does not talk easily about the interiors of his creative process, but during our many hours of conversation, Gérard said that he feels that his quest as an artist demands that he explore both sides of his being, the bright and the dark, and he also believes that he has an artistic obligation to push himself deep into those interior realms that he has not yet discovered or explored. This quest is his passion, his need, his fix, and yet he also knows full well that he pursues his artistic quest at a great price, both to himself and to his family.

"There are always zones of shadow within me," Gérard told me. "Which is why I always go to the bottom of things, to the extremes. Now, with age, that becomes more and more dangerous, and more upsetting to those who love me. I'm a protector, but at the same time, I'm the one who goes out and lives experiences for everyone else, so they will not have to go live them themselves."

In Gérard's mind, true artistic creation always involves a deep interior search, a plunge into the unknown, a painstaking exploration of his own psyche and its hidden "zones of shadow." Of course, this exploration carries risk and danger and psychological jeopardy, but that is a price he is willing to pay. For he believes that it is deep inside the psyche of the artist that the real creative gold is mined. "Schizophrenia is interior spaces burst open," Gérard told me. "Artists share a similar fate. Inner research, bursting open those interior spaces, is the work and the suffering of any serious creator."

"Cinema is war with blanks," Gérard once told me, long before I understood what he meant, and when I think of him at his twelfth-century castle in Anjou, I see Gérard not as a modern movie star but as a medieval knight-errant who has somehow stumbled into the latter half of the twentieth century. Some knights show their courage by going off to war to kill; Depardieu shows his courage by going onto the public stage to bare his weaknesses and to bare his soul. That is how he feels he can draw people together and fulfill his destiny, not just as an actor but as an *entremetteur.*

Like some knight-errant of old, looking for some private grail, Depardieu is constantly losing his way, and in his quest he is often blindest to the ones he loves. But his castle in Anjou is an ideal place for Gérard to bring himself back on course, and it is an ideal place for him to bring his values back into focus. Just by running his hand over the gnarled trunks of his vines, or by walking through the ancient hollows of his wine cellar, or by inspecting the massive beams of his chateau, Gérard can clarify his vision and see what truly endures. By tasting grapes, blending their juices, selecting wood for his barrels, or just by cooking a meal in his big country kitchen, Gérard can return to the basic ethics and virtues that he believes govern and inspire the sister arts of acting, winemaking, cooking, and living: Authenticity. Purity of flavor. And generosity of spirit.

Start with a fresh, plump farm chicken, one that has been raised naturally and allowed to run free, and with a bit of flair an artful cook can create a celebration and a joyous communion for his family and friends. Start with passion, a bit of expertise, and a discriminating nose, and an artful winemaker, like a medieval alchemist, can turn a humble Anjou grape into a majestic Cuvée Mozart. And if he starts with a big heart and a burning need to communicate everything that's in it, an artful actor can reach out and touch millions of people around the world, through the universal medium of cinema and through the universal music of his own emotions.

"In World War I, it was the women who made the wine," Gérard once said to me over a glass of his wine, "and for generations afterward, you could drink that wine and say, 'Ahhhh, yes. That's the wine of my grandmother.' Or your father might die, but later you would drink his wine and you would say, 'Mmmmm, that's my father's wine.' Through their wine, they live on."

Appendix

The Works of Gérard Depardieu

FILM

Le Cri du Cormoran le Soir au-dessus des Jonques

French release: February 18, 1971; 85 min; C
Production company: Gaumont
Director: Michael Audiard
Actors: Michel Serrault, Bernard Blier, Paul Meurisse, Jean Carmet, Marion Game, Maurice Biraud
Depardieu: Henri, Kruger's right-hand man
Filming dates: September 10–November 5, 1970

Un Peu de Soleil dans l'Eau Froide

French release: October 29, 1971; 110 min; C
Production company: SNC
Director: Jacques Deray
Actors: Claudine Auger, Marc Porel, Bernard Fresson, Judith Magre, André Falcon
Depardieu: Pierre, Nathalie's brother
Filming dates: June 8–August 3, 1971

Le Viager

French release: January 19, 1972; 90 min; C
Production company: Les Artistes Associés/Dargaud Films
Director: Pierre Tchernia
Actors: Michel Serrault, Michel Galabru, Jean Richard, Odette Laure, Claude Brasseur, Jean-Pierre Darras, Rosy Varte
Depardieu: A young hoodlum
Filming dates: June 14–August 9, 1971

Le Tueur

French release: March 1, 1972; 110 min; C
Production company: Cofci/Gabfer/Europa/Mondial Tefi (Rome)/Rialto Film (Berlin)
Director: Denys de La Patellière
Actors: Jean Gabin, Bernard Blier, Fabio Testi, Félix Marten, Ginette Garcin

Depardieu: Fredo
Filming dates: November 8, 1971–January 3, 1972

La Scoumoune

French release: December 13, 1972; 105 min; C
Production company: Lira Film (Paris)/ Président (Rome); France-Italy
Director: José Giovanni
Actors: Claudia Cardinale, Michel Constantin, Jean-Paul Belmondo, Michel Pereylon, Alain Mottet
Depardieu: A young delinquent
Filming dates: May 2–July 4, 1972

Au Rendez-Vous de la Mort Joyeuse

French release: January 25, 1973; 90 min; C
Production company: Les Artistes Associés; France-Italy
Director: Juan-Luis Buñuel
Actors: Françoise Fabian, Jean-Marc Bory, Yasmine Dahn, Jean-Pierre Darras, Michel Creton
Depardieu: Beretti
Filming dates: May 15–July 12, 1972

Nathalie Granger

French release: September 27, 1973; 85 min; B/W
Production company: Moullet et Cie
Director: Marguerite Duras
Actors: Jeanne Moreau, Lucia Bose, Luce Garcia-Ville, Valérie Mascolo, Dionys Mascolo, Nathalie Bourgeois
Depardieu: A washing-machine salesman
Filming dates: May 1972

L'Affaire Dominici

French release: March 7, 1973; 100 min; C
Production company: Claude Giroux/Eric Rochat; France-Italy
Director: Claude Bernard-Aubert
Actors: Jean Gabin, Paul Crauchet, Gérard Darrieu, Geneviève Fontanel, Daniel Ivernel, Victor Lanoux, Danile Boulanger, Louis-Emile Galey, Jeanne Allard
Depardieu: Zézé, a young peasant
Filming dates: October 2–mid-December 1972

Rude Journée pour la Reine

French release: December 6, 1973; 90 min; C
Production company: Polsim Productions (Paris)/Citel Films S.A. (Geneva)/ O.R.T.F.; France-Switzerland
Director: René Allio
Actors: Simone Signoret, Jacques Debary, Orane Demazis, Michel Pereylon, Olivier Perrier
Depardieu: Fabien
Filming dates: May 7–June 22, 1973

Deux Hommes dans la Ville

French release: October 25, 1973; 100 min; C
Production company: ADEL Production (Paris)/Medusa (Rome); France-Italy
Director: José Giovanni
Actors: Jean Gabin, Alain Delon, Victor Lanoux, Mimsy Farmer, Michel Bouquet, Christine Fabrega, Jacques Monod
Depardieu: A young delinquent
Filming dates: May 21–July 30, 1973

Les Gaspards

French release: February 6, 1974; 94 min; C
Production company: Albina Production/Films de la Seine/ O.R.T.F.; France-Belgium
Director: Pierre Tchernia
Actors: Michel Serrault, Philippe Noiret, Michel Galabru, Charles Denner, Jean Carmet, Annie Cordy, Chantal Goya
Depardieu: The mailman
Filming dates: July–August 1973

Les Valseuses (U.S. title: *Going Places*)

French release: March 20, 1974; 115 min; C
Production company: C.A.P.A.C. Uranus
Director: Bertrand Blier
Actors: Miou-Miou, Patrick Dewaere, Jeanne Moreau, Brigitte Fossey, Isabelle Huppert, Michel Pereylon, Eva Damien, Jacques Chailleux, Marco Perrin
Depardieu: Jean-Claude
Filming dates: August 16–October 8, 1973
Available on video

La Femme du Gange

French release: April 12, 1974; 100 min; C
Production company: Sunchild Production
Director: Marguerite Duras
Actors: Catherine Sellers, Nicole Hiss, Christian Baltaun
Depardieu: A crazy beach bum

Stavisky

French release: May 15, 1974; 120 min; C
Production company: Cerito Films/ Ariane Films/Euro International
Director: Alain Resnais
Actors: Jean-Paul Belmondo, François Périer, Charles Boyer, Anny Duperey, Michael Lonsdale, Claude Rich
Depardieu: A young inventor
Filming dates: October 4, 1973–January 25, 1974

Vincent, François, Paul et les Autres (U.S. title: *Vincent, François, Paul and the Others*)

French release: October 2, 1974; 120 min; C
Production company: Lira Films (Paris)/Président (Rome); France-Italy
Director: Claude Sautet
Actors: Yves Montand, Michel Piccoli, Serge Reggiani, Stéphane Audran, Antonella Lualdi, Marie Dubois, Catherine Allégret
Depardieu: Jean, a young foreman and amateur boxer
Filming dates: February 14–May 15, 1974
Available on video

Pas Si Méchant Que Ça

French release: February 19, 1975; 110 min; C
Production company: Citel Films/ Artco Films (Geneva)/M. J. Productions (Paris); France-Switzerland
Director: Claude Goretta
Actors: Marlène Jobert, Dominique Labourier, Philippe Léotard, Michel Robin, Jacques Debary, Paul Crauchet
Depardieu: Pierre
Filming dates: June 17–August 1974

1900/Novecento (U.S. title: *1900*)

French release: September 1, 1976 (1st part), November 17, 1976 (2nd part); 325 min; C
Production company: P.E.A. (Rome); Italy
Director: Bernardo Bertolucci
Actors: Robert De Niro, Dominique Sanda, Burt Lancaster, Laura Betti, Stefania Sandrelli, Donald Sutherland, Sterling Hayden, Alida Valli, Mario Monti
Depardieu: Olmo Dalco, a sharecropper's son
Filming dates: July 1974–January 1975
A 234-minute version is available on video

Maîtresse (U.S. title: *Maitresse*)

French release: February 11, 1976; 112 min; C
Production company: Gaumont/Films du Losange
Director: Barbet Schroeder
Actors: Bulle Ogier, André Rouyer, Holger Lowenadler, Nathalie Keryan, Royland Bertin, Jeanne Herviale
Depardieu: Olivier, a young provincial
Filming dates: May 26–July 18, 1975
Available on video

Sept Morts sur Ordonnance

French release: December 3, 1975; 105 min; C
Production company: Jet Films/Belstar/Paris 66/T.I.T. Films; France–Spain–West Germany
Director: Jacques Rouffio
Actors: Jane Birkin, Charles Vanel, Michel Piccoli, Marina Vlady, Michel Auclair, Coline Serreau
Depardieu: Dr. Berg
Filming dates: June 30–August 16, 1975

La Dernière Femme/L'Ultima Donna (U.S. title: *The Last Woman*)

French release: April 21, 1976; 112 min; C
Production company: Faminia (Rome)/Jacques Roitfeld (Paris); France-Italy
Director: Marco Ferreri
Actors: Ornella Muti, Michel Piccoli, Renato Salvatori, Zouzou
Depardieu: Gérard, an unemployed engineer
Filming dates: September 1–November 1975
Available on video

Je T'Aime, Moi Non Plus

French release: March 10, 1976; 90 min; C
Production company: Président Films and Renn Production
Director: Serge Gainsbourg
Actors: Jane Birkin, Joe Dalessandro, Hughes Quester, René Koldehoff, Jimmy Loverman Davis
Depardieu: A peasant
Filming dates: September 11–October 27, 1975

Barocco

French release: December 8, 1976; 110 min; C
Production company: La Boëtie
Director: André Téchiné
Actors: Isabelle Adjani, Marie-France Pisier, Claude Brasseur,

Jean-Claude Brialy, Juline Guiomar, Hélène Surgère, Jean-François Stévenin
Depardieu: Samson, an assassin
Filming dates: March 1–May 14, 1976

Baxter, Vera Baxter

French release: June 8, 1977; 90 min; C
Production company: Sunchild Production/I.N.A.
Director: Marguerite Duras
Actors: Claudine Gabay, Delphine Seyrig, Noëlle Châtelet, Claude Aufort, Nathalie Nell
Depardieu: Michel Cayre, a journalist
Filming dates: April 5–April 30, 1976

René La Canne

French release: February 16, 1977; 100 min; C
Production company: Président Films/Rizzoli Films (Rome); France-Italy
Director: Francis Girod
Actors: Michel Piccoli, Sylvia Kristel, Valérie Mairesse, Jean Rigant
Depardieu: René La Canne
Filming dates: August 2–mid-November 1976

Le Camion (U.S. title: *The Truck*)

French release: May 25, 1977; 80 min; C
Production company: Cinéma 9/ Auditel
Director: Marguerite Duras
Actor: Marguerite Duras (as herself)
Depardieu: Himself
Filming dates: January 10–14, 1977

La Nuit, Tous les Chats Sont Gris

French release: November 23, 1977; 105 min; C
Production company: Sam Films and FR3
Director: Gérard Zingg
Actors: Robert Stephens, Laura Betti, Anne Zacharias, Charlotte Crow, Albert Simono, Dominique Laffin, Virginie Thévenet
Depardieu: Philibert Larcher
Filming dates: January 24–March 25, 1977

Dites-Lui que Je L'Aime

French release: September 28, 1977; 107 min; C
Production company: Prospectacle Filmoblic/FR3
Director: Claude Miller
Actors: Miou-Miou, Dominique Laffin, Claude Piéplu, Jacques Denis, Christian Clavier, Josiane Balasko, Véronique Silver, Jacqueline Jeanne, Michel Such
Depardieu: David Martinaud
Filming dates: March 28–June 3, 1977

Violanta

French release: March 22, 1978; 95 min; C
Production company: Condor Films (Zurich)/Artcofilm (Geneva); Switzerland
Director: Daniel Schmid
Actors: Lucia Bose, François Simon, Lou Castle, Maria Schneider, Ingrid Caven, Raúl Gimenez
Depardieu: Fortunat, Violanta's brother

Préparez Vos Mouchoirs (U.S. title: *Get Out Your Handkerchiefs*)

French release: January 11, 1978; 118 min; C
Production company: Films Ariane/C.A.P.A.C. (Paris)/S.O.D.E.P. and Belga Films (Brussels); France-Belgium
Director: Bertrand Blier
Actors: Patrick Dewaere, Carole Laure, Michel Serrault, Tiron Liebman, Sylvie Joly, Eléone Hirt, Jean Rougerie
Depardieu: Raoul, the husband
Filming dates: June 20–September 2, 1977
Available on video

La Femme Gauchère/Die Linkshändige Frau

French release: October 18, 1978; 110 min; C
Production company: Road Movies/Film Produktion/M.B.H. (Berlin)/Wim Wenders Productions (Munich); West Germany
Director: Peter Handke
Actors: Edith Clever, Bruno Ganz, Michael Lonsdale, Jany Holt, Markus Muhleisen, Angela Winkler, Rudiger Vogler
Depardieu: Man in a T-shirt

Rêve de Singe/Ciao Maschio (U.S. title: *Bye Bye Monkey*)

French release: May 26, 1978; 114 min; C
Production company: December 18 (Rome)/Prospectacle/Action Film (Paris); Italy-France
Director: Marco Ferreri
Actors: James Coco, Marcello Mastroianni, Gail Lawrence, Geraldine Fitzgerald, Mimsy Farmer
Depardieu: Gérard Lafayette, a museum employee
Filming dates: September 12–December 2, 1977
Available on video

Le Sucre

French release: November 15, 1978; 100 min; C
Production company: Cinéproductions/S.E.P./Gaumont
Director: Jacques Ruffio
Actors: Jean Carmet, Michel Piccoli, Roger Hanin, Claude Piéplu, Georges Descrières, Marthe Villalonga, Nelly Borgeaud
Depardieu: Raoul, the count Renaud d'Homecourt de La Vibraye
Filming dates: April 3–June 9, 1978

Le Grand Embouteillage/L'Engorgo

French release: November 21, 1979; 115 min; C
Production company: Clesi Cinematografica (Rome)/Greenwich Production/Filmédis, Gaumont (Paris)/José Frade PC (Madrid)/Albatros Produktion (Munich); Italy–France–Spain–West Germany
Director: Luigi Comencini
Actors: Miou-Miou, Ugo Tognazzi, Patrick Dewaere, Fernando Rey, Angela Molina, Alberto Sordi, Annie Girardot, Marcello Mastroianni
Depardieu: Franco, Angela's husband

Filming dates: June 26–late August 1978

Les Chiens

French release: March 7, 1979; 100 min; C
Production company: AJ Films/AMS Productions (Paris)/Les Films de La Drouette/Pacific Films (Tahiti)
Director: Alain Jessua
Actors: Victor Lanoux, Nicole Calfan, Pierre Vernier, Gérard Séty, Stéphane Bouy, Fanny Ardant
Depardieu: Morel, the kennel owner
Filming dates: July 31–September 30, 1978

Loulou (U.S. title: *Loulou*)

French release: September 3, 1980; 110 min; C
Production company: Gaumont
Director: Maurice Pialat
Actors: Isabelle Huppert, Guy Marchand, Humbert Balsan, Bernard Tronczyk, Xavier Saint-Macary, Christian Bouchet
Depardieu: Loulou
Filming dates: February 5–March 30, 1979
Available on video

Rosy la Bourrasque/Temporale Rosy

French release: August 20, 1980; 118 min; C
Production company: Les Artistes Associés; Italy-France
Director: Mario Monicelli
Actors: Faith Minton, Roland Bock, Gianrico Tedeschi, Helga Anders
Depardieu: Raoul Lamarre, a dethroned boxer
Filming dates: Spring 1979

Buffet Froid (U.S. title: *Buffet Froid*)

French release: December 19, 1979; 95 min; C
Production company: A2/Sara Films
Director: Bertrand Blier
Actors: Bernard Blier, Jean Carmet, Genviève Pagé, Michel Serrault, Carole Bouquet, Jean Benguigui, Jean Rougerie
Depardieu: Alphonse Tram
Filming dates: August 20–October 5, 1979
Available on video

Mon Oncle d'Amérique (U.S. title: *Mon Oncle d'Amérique*)

French release: May 21, 1980; 125 min; C
Production company: Philippe Dussart, in co-production with Andrea Films and TF1
Director: Alain Resnais
Actors: Nicole Garcia, Roger Pierre, Marie Dubois, Nelly Borgeaud, Pierre Arditi, Jacques Rispal
Depardieu: René Ragueneau, the farmer's son
Filming dates: September 28–late December 1979
Available on video

Le Dernier Métro (U.S. title: *The Last Metro*)

French release: September 17, 1980; 132 min; C
Production company: Les Films du Carrosse/TF1/SFP/SEDIF

Director: François Truffaut
Actors: Catherine Deneuve, Jean Poiret, Andréa Ferréol, Heinz Bennent, Paulette Dubost, Sabine Haudepin
Depardieu: Bernard Granger, actor and member of the Resistance
Filming dates: January 28–April 18, 1980
Available on video

Je Vous Aime (U.S. title: *Je Vous Aime*)

French release: December 17, 1980; 100 min; C
Production company: Renn Production/FR3
Director: Claude Berri
Actors: Catherine Deneuve, Jean-Louis Trintignant, Serge Gainsbourg, Alain Souchon
Depardieu: Patrick, singer and saxophone player
Filming dates: April 23–August 29, 1980
Available on video

Inspecteur La Bavure

French release: December 5, 1980; 100 min; C
Production company: Renn Production/FR3
Director: Claude Zidi
Actors: Coluche, Dominique Lavanant, Julien Guiomar, Dany Saval, Marthe Villalonga, Martin Lamotte, Alain Mottet-Dumeze, Hubert Deschamps
Depardieu: Roger Morzini, Public Enemy No. 1
Filming dates: July 7–September 5, 1980

Le Choix des Armes (U.S. title: *Choice of Arms*)

French release: August 19, 1981; 135 min; C
Production company: Sara Films/A2/Parafrance/RMC
Director: Alain Corneau
Actors: Yves Montand, Catherine Deneuve, Gérard Lanvin, Michel Galabru, Marc Chapiteau, Jean-Claude Dauphin, Richard Anconina
Depardieu: Mickey, a young delinquent escaped from prison
Filming dates: January 5–March 29, 1981
Available on video

La Femme d'à Côte (U.S. title: *The Woman Next Door*)

French release: September 30, 1981; 106 min; C
Production company: Les Films du Carrosse/TF1 Films Productions
Director: François Truffaut
Actors: Fanny Ardant, Henri Garcin, Michel Baumgartner, Roger Van Hool, Véronique Silver
Depardieu: Bernard Coudray
Filming dates: April 1–May 15, 1981
Available on video

La Chèvre (U.S. title: *La Chèvre*)

French release: December 9, 1981; 90 min; C
Production company: Gaumont International/Fideline Films (Paris)/Conacine (Mexico)
Director: Francis Veber
Actors: Pierre Richard, Michel Robin, André Valardy, Corynne Charbit

Depardieu: Campana, a private detective
Filming dates: June 8–September 9, 1981
Available on video

Le Retour de Martin Guerre (U.S. title: *The Return of Martin Guerre*)

French release: May 14, 1982; 111 min; C
Production company: SFPC/SPFMD/FR3
Director: Daniel Vigne
Actors: Nathalie Baye, Roger Planchon, Tchéky Karyo, Dominique Pinon, Bernard-Pierre Donnadieu
Depardieu: The "false" Martin Guerre
Filming dates: September 9–November 6, 1981
Available on video

Le Grand Frère

French release: September 1982; 115 min; C
Production company: Partners and Odessa Films Production/SFPC/TF1 Films Productions
Director: Francis Girod
Actors: Jean Rochefort, Roger Planchon, Jacques Villeret, Souad Amidou, Hakim Ghanem, Christine Fersen
Depardieu: The older brother
Filming dates: December 7, 1981–February 5, 1982

Danton (U.S. title: *Danton*)

French release: January 7, 1983; 136 min; C
Production company: Les Films du Losange, with Groupe X of Warsaw
Coproduction: Gaumont/TF1 Films Productions/S.F.P.C./T.M., with the French Ministry of Culture and Film Polski; France-Poland
Director: Andrzej Wajda
Actors: Wojciech Pszoniak, Roland Blanche, Patrice Chéreau, Stéphane Jobert, Roger Planchon, Jacques Villeret, Angela Winkler
Depardieu: Danton
Filming dates: April 21–July 17, 1982
Available on video

La Lune dans le Caniveau (U.S. title: *The Moon in the Gutter*)

French release: May 18, 1983; 137 min; C
Production company: Gaumont/TF1 Films Productions/S.F.P.C. (Paris)/Opéra Film Produzione (Rome); France-Italy
Director: Jean-Jacques Beineix
Actors: Nastassia Kinski, Vittorio Mezzogiorno, Victoria Abril, Dominique Pinon
Depardieu: Gérard Delmas, a docker
Filming dates: July 12–late December 1982
Available on video

Les Compères (U.S. title: *Les Compères*)

French release: November 23, 1983; 92 min; C
Production company: Fideline Films/E.F.V.E. Films/D.D. Productions
Director: Francis Veber

Actors: Pierre Richard, Anny Duperey, Stéphane Bierry, Michel Aumont, Philippe Khorsand, Roland Blanche, Jean-Jacques Scheffer
Depardieu: Jean Lucas, a reporter
Filming dates: April 26–July 20, 1983

Fort Saganne

French release: May 11, 1984; 180 min; C
Production company: Albina Productions/Films A2 SFPC
Director: Alain Corneau
Actors: Philippe Noiret, Catherine Deneuve, Sophie Marceau, Michel Duchaussoy, Salah Teskouk, Robin Rebucci, Florent Pagny, Hippolyte Girardot
Depardieu: Charles Saganne
Filming dates: August 8–November 30, 1983

Tartuffe (U.S. title: *Le Tartuffe*)

French release: September 5, 1984; 140 min; C
Production company: Gaumont/Les Films du Losange/TF1/D.D. Productions
Director: Gérard Depardieu
Actors: François Périer, Elisabeth Depardieu
Depardieu: Tartuffe
Filming dates: January 9–28 and March 13–17, 1984
Available on video

Rive Droite, Rive Gauche

French release: October 31, 1984; 104 min; C
Production company: T. Films/ Films A2
Director: Philippe Labro
Actors: Nathalie Baye, Carole Bouquet, Jacques Weber, Bernard Fresson
Depardieu: Paul Sénanques, a Paris lawyer
Filming dates: June 18–August 24, 1984

Police (U.S. title: *Police*)

French release: September 4, 1985; 113 min; C
Production company: TF1 Films Productions/Gaumont
Director: Maurice Pialat
Actors: Sophie Marceau, Richard Anconina, Sandrine Bonnaire, Pascale Rocard, Jonathan Leïna, Franck Karoui
Depardieu: Inspector Louis Mangin
Filming dates: October 29, 1984–January 18, 1985
Available on video

Une Femme ou Deux (U.S. title: *One Woman or Two*)

French release: November 6, 1985; 97 min; C
Production company: Hachette Première/Philippe Dussart S.A.R.L./ FR3 Films/D.D. Productions
Director: Daniel Vigne
Actors: Sigourney Weaver, Michel Aumont, Zabou, Jean-Paul Muel
Depardieu: Julien Chayssac, a French scientist
Filming dates: March 4–May 21, 1985
Available on video

Jean de Florette (U.S. title: *Jean de Florette*)

French release: August 26, 1986; 120 min; C
Production company: Renn Productions/A2/RAI2/D.D. Productions
Director: Claude Berri
Actors: Yves Montand, Daniel Auteuil, Elisabeth Depardieu, Armand Meffre, Ernestine Mazurowna, Marcel Champel
Depardieu: Jean de Florette
Filming dates: May 20–December 7, 1985
Available on video

Tenue de Soirée (U.S. title: *Ménage*)

French release: April 23, 1986; 84 min; C
Production company: Hachette Première/D.D Productions/Ciné Valse, Philippe Dussart
Director: Bertrand Blier
Actors: Michel Blanc, Miou-Miou, Bruno Cremer, Jean-Pierre Marielle, Jean-François Stévenin, Mylène Demongeot, Michel Creton
Depardieu: Bob, a burglar
Filming dates: December 1985
Available on video

Les Fugitifs

French release: December 17, 1986; 89 min; C
Production company: Fideline Films/EFVE Films/D.D. Productions
Director: Francis Veber
Actors: Pierre Richard, Anaïs Bret, Maurice Barbier, Jean Carmet
Depardieu: A gangster, released from prison, taken hostage in a holdup
Filming dates: Summer 1986

Sous le Soleil de Satan (U.S. title: *Under Satan's Sun*)

French release: September 2, 1987; 103 min; C
Production company: Erato Films/A2/Flach Films/Action Film/C.N.C.
Director: Maurice Pialat
Actors: Sandrine Bonnaire, Maurice Pialat, Alain Arthur, Yahn Dedet, Brigette Legendre, Jean-Claude Bourlat, Jean-Christopher Bouvet
Depardieu: Father Donissan, a priest
Filming dates: October 20–late December 1986
Available on video

Camille Claudel (U.S. title: *Camille Claudel*)

French release: October 5, 1988; 149 min; C
Production company: Films Christian Fechner/Litih Films/Films A2
Director: Bruno Nuytten
Actors: Isabelle Adjani, Laurent Greville, Alain Cuny, Madeleine Robinson
Depardieu: Auguste Rodin
Filming dates: September 14, 1987–February 15, 1988
Available on video

Drôle d'Endroit pour une Rencontre (U.S. title: *A Strange Place to Meet*)

French release: October 5, 1988; 93 min; C

Production company: René Cleitman; Hachette Première et Cie
Director: François Dupeyron
Actors: Catherine Deneuve, André Wilms, Nathalie Cardonne, Jean-Pierre Sentier, Alain Rimoux, Vincent Martin
Depardieu: Charles
Filming dates: February 15, 1988–April 15, 1988

Deux

French release: February 15, 1989; 113 min; C
Production company: Films 7/D.D. Productions/Orly Film
Director: Claude Zidi
Actors: Maruschka Detmers, Michèle Goddet, Philippe Leroy-Beaulieu, Béata Tyszkiewics, Wojcieh Pszoniak
Depardieu: Marc Lambert
Filming dates: May 30–August 15, 1988

Trop Belle pour Toi (U.S. title: *Too Beautiful for You*)

French release: May 12, 1989; 91 min; C
Production company: Ciné Valse
Director: Bertrand Blier
Actors: Carole Bouquet, Josiane Balasko
Depardieu: The husband
Filming dates: October 31, 1988–January 1989
Available on video

I Want to Go Home

French release: September 27, 1989; 105 min; C
Production company: MK2
Director: Alain Resnais
Actors: Adolph Green, Linda Lavin, Micheline Presle, Laura Benson, John Ashton
Depardieu: Gauthier
Filming dates: August 29–October 28, 1988

Cyrano de Bergerac (U.S. title: *Cyrano de Bergerac*)

French release: March 28, 1990; 135 min; C
Production company: Hachette Première et Cie
Director: Jean-Paul Rappeneau
Actors: Anne Brochet, Vincent Perez, Jacques Weber
Depardieu: Cyrano de Bergerac
Filming dates: May 8–September 30, 1989
Available on video

Green Card

American release: December 24, 1990; French release: February 1991; 107 min; C
Production company: Disney
Director: Peter Weir
Actors: Andie MacDowell, Bebe Neuwirth, Gregg Edelman
Depardieu: A French composer in New York
Filming dates: March 26–June 12, 1990
Available on video

Uranus (U.S. title: *Uranus*)

French release: December 12, 1990; 100 min; C
Production company: Renn Production
Director: Claude Berri
Actors: Philippe Noiret, Michel Blanc, Fabrice Luchini
Depardieu: A bartender/poet

Filming dates: June 1990–August 1990
Available on video

Merci la Vie

French release: March 13, 1991; 117 min; C
Production company: Ciné Valse
Director: Bertrand Blier
Actors: Charlotte Gainsbourg, Anouk Grinberg
Depardieu: A maniacal doctor
Filming dates: July 30–August 22, 1990

Mon Père, Ce Héros

French release: October 23, 1991; 103 min; C
Production company: Film Par Film
Director: Gerard Lauzier
Actors: Marie Gillain, Patrick Mille, Catherine Jacob
Depardieu: The father
Filming dates: March 25–May 1991

Tous les Matins du Monde (U.S. title: *Tous les Matins du Monde*)

French release: December 18, 1991; 114 min; C
Production company: Film Par Film
Director: Alain Corneau
Actors: Anne Brochet, Jean-Pierre Marielle
Depardieu: The elder Marin Marais
Filming dates: June 3–late August 1991

1492

American release: October 9, 1992; French release October 12, 1992; 150 min; C
Production company: Paramount-Gaumont
Director: Ridley Scott
Actors: Armand Assante, Sigourney Weaver, Fernando Rey
Depardieu: Christopher Colombus
Filming dates: December 2, 1991–March 25, 1992

Germinal

French release: September 29, 1993
Production company: RENN Production
Director: Claude Berri
Actors: Renaud, Miou-Miou
Depardieu: Maheu
Filming dates: September 1, 1992–February 15, 1993

Une Pure Formalité

French release: Spring 1994
Production company: Film Par Film
Director: Giuseppe Tornatore
Actor: Roman Polanski
Depardieu: The writer
Filming dates: March 1, 1993–May 1993

My Father, The Hero

American release: February 1994
Production company: DD/FPF/Disney
Director: Steve Miner
Actor: Katherine Heigl
Depardieu: The father
Filming dates: June 2–August 15, 1993

Hélas pour Moi

French release: September 8, 1993
Production company: Les Films Alain Barde
Director: Jean-Luc Godard
Actor: Laurence Maslish

Depardieu: Simon Donnadieu
Filming dates: July 15, 1992–September 1992

Colonel Chabert

French release: Fall 1994
Production company: Film Par Film
Director: Yves Angelo
Actor: Fanny Ardant
Depardieu: Colonel Chabert
Filming dates: August 23, 1993–December 1993

THEATER

Boudu Sauvé des Eaux, by René Fauchoix, directed by Jean-Laurent Cochet, 1968

Les Garçons de la Bande, by Mart Crowley, directed by Jean-Laurent Cochet, 1968

Une Fille dans Ma Soupe, by Terence Frisday, directed by Pierre Mondy, 1970

Galapagos, by Jean Chatenet, directed by Chatenet, with Nathalie Baye and Bernard Blier, 1971

Saved, by Edward Bond, directed by Claude Régy, with Hugues Quester, 1972

Home, by David Storey, adapted by Marguerite Duras, directed by Claude Régy, with Michel Lonsdale and Dominique Blanchar, 1973

Isme, by Nathalie Sarraute, directed by Claude Régy, with Michel Lonsdale and Dominique Blanchar, 1973

Isaac, by Manuel Puig, directed by Claude Régy, 1973

La Chevauchée sur le Lac de Constance, by Peter Handke, directed by Claude Régy, with Jeanne Moreau, Delphine Seyrig, Michel Lonsdale, and Sami Frey, 1974

Les Gens Déraisonnables Sont en Voie de Disparition, by Peter Handke, directed by Claude Régy, with Patrice Kerbrat, Andréa Ferréol, and Jean-Luc Bideau, 1978

Tartuffe, by Molière, directed by Jacques Lassall, with Elisabeth Depardieu, 1983

TELEVISION

Rendez-Vous à Baden-Berg, by Jean-Michel Meurisse, 1966

Le Cyborg, by Jacques Pierre, 1967

Tango, by Jean Kerchbron, 1967

Menaces, by Jean Denesle, 1969

L'Inconnu, by Youri, 1969

Un Monsieur Bien Range, by Agnès Delarive, 1972

FILM AWARDS

Academy Awards

Best Actor nomination:
Cyrano de Bergerac, 1991

Best Foreign Film:
Préparez vos Mouchoirs, directed by Bernard Blier, 1979

Best Foreign Film nominations:
Le Dernier Métro, directed by François Truffaut, 1981
Camille Claudel, directed by Bruno Nuytten, 1990
Cyrano de Bergerac, directed by Jean-Paul Rappeneau, 1991

Césars

Actor of the Decade: 1991

Best Actor:
Le Dernier Métro, 1981
Cyrano de Bergerac, 1991

Best Actor nominations:
Sept Morts sur Ordonnance, 1976
La Dernière Femme, 1977
Dites-Lui que Je L'Aime, 1978
Le Sucre, 1979
Danton, 1983
Le Compères, 1984
Fort Saganne, 1985
Police, 1986
Sous le Soleil de Satan, 1988
Camille Claudel, 1989
Trop Belle pour Toi, 1990

Best Film:
Le Dernier Métro, directed by François Truffaut, 1981
Camille Claudel, directed by Bruno Nuytten, 1989
Trop Belle pour Toi, directed by Bertrand Blier, 1990
Cyrano de Bergerac, directed by Jean-Paul Rappeneau, 1991

Best Film nominations:
Sept Morts sur Ordonnance, directed by Jacques Rouffio, 1976
Barocco, directed by André Techiné, 1977
Loulou, directed by Maurice Pialat, 1981
Mon Oncle d'Amérique, directed by Alain Resnais, 1981
Danton, directed by Andzej Wajda, 1983
Jean de Florette, directed by Claude Berri, 1983
Tenue de Soirée, directed by Bertrand Blier, 1983
Sous le Soleil de Satan, directed by Maurice Pialat, 1988

Cannes Film Festival

Palme d'Or:
Sous le Soleil de Satan, 1990

Jury's Special Grand Prize:
Rêve de Singe, 1978
Mon Oncle d'Amérique, 1980
Trop Belle pour Toi, 1989

Other Prizes

1973 Grand Prize Gérard Philipe of the City of Paris

1983 Association of Executives of the Cinemagraphic Industry Prize for outstanding work
Montréal Festival, best actor for *Danton*

1984 Association of American Critics best actor of the year for *Danton* and *The Return of Martin Guerre*

1985 Venice Film Festival, best actor for *Police*

1989 British Film Institute prize for lifetime accomplishment

1991 Golden Globe, best actor in a comedy for *Green Card*

Acknowledgments

This book is based on more than two years of research and on hundreds of hours of interviews I conducted with Gérard Depardieu and scores of people close to his life and work. As the preceding text makes clear, I received extraordinary cooperation from his family, his teachers and mentors, his fellow actors and directors, and from countless people in Paris, Châteauroux, and throughout the worlds of French and international cinema.

I cannot possibly salute individually everyone who made this book possible, but I do want to give special thanks to several people who were indispensable to my work. First, and foremost, I want to thank Gérard Depardieu. With extraordinary patience and candor, Gérard led me through his turbulent life and into the mysteries of his creative process. Thanks to his openness and cooperation, writing this book was for me both an adventure and an enlightenment. I hope that readers can find in his story their own sources of stimulus and inspiration.

I also want to thank Elisabeth Depardieu. As an actress, a psychologist, and the anchor of Gérard's family life, Elisabeth patiently guided me to invaluable insights about Gérard's life and turmoils. I also want to give special thanks to Hélène Bordier, Gérard's sister and aide-de-camp, and the guardian of family lore and memorabilia. For nearly three years, Hélène put up with all my pestering and shared with me a wealth of invaluable information and most of the family photographs which enliven the preceding pages.

For their generous cooperation, I also want to give special thanks to Catherine Deneuve, Nathalie Baye, Jean-Louis Livi, Michel Pilorgé, Patrick Bordier, Jean Carmet, Alfred Tomatis, Bertrand Blier, Jean-Paul Rappeneau, Peter Weir, Ridley Scott, Alain Corneau, Alain Depardieu, Fanny Ardant, Agnès Varda, Jean-Laurent Cochet, Claude Régy, Pierre Gamet, Bernard Chaumeil, Michael Barker, Tom Bernard, Marcie Bloom, John Ptak, Daniel

Toscan du Plantier, Roselyne Bosch, Alain Goldman, Bertrand de Labbey, Alain Vannier, Louise Vincent, Gil Noir, Dominique Cavé, Maurice Croze, Dominique Meunier Arroyo, Michel Arroyo, Monique Dagaud Marcon, Joe, Janine, and Annette Gagné, and Roger Lucas. For their research in three different countries, I want to thank Donna Evleth, Jill Ibrahim, Catherine Verret, Claire Blondell, and Fannie Sambor. For their help with double-checking all my French translations, I want to thank Elisabeth de Kerret and Micheline Manoncourt. For their help in guiding me through this process, I want to thank my literary agents, Maureen and Eric Lasher.

On a more personal note, I want to thank Jonathan Segal, my editor at Knopf, whose patience and wisdom guided me all the way through this complicated project. I also want to thank his colleague Ida Giragossian for all her help with logistics and organizing photographs. I also want to give a special public hug to my wife, Eda, who with great spirit and tolerance shouldered so many family burdens while I was doing research and writing. Eda was also essential to the detail work of proofreading and handling photographs. I also want to give special thanks to my parents, Ruth and Rupert Chutkow, for giving me a lifetime of support and encouragement. For years of unstinting friendship and support, I also want to thank Peter Cohen, David Wirtz, David Schneiderman, Peggy Rosenthal, Gordon Mott, Bill Borders, Mike Leahy, Larry Van Gelder, Marilyn Bender, Joe and Gussy Stanislaw, Philippe Guilbert, Marie-Christine Halpern, and Jean-Claude Zylberstein.

I dedicate this book to my two sons, Justin and Ethan. Through them, I also want to dedicate it to Guillaume and Julie Depardieu, and to all the young artists and creators of tomorrow.

P.C.

Index

Academy Awards, 4, 28, 62, 206, 209, 221, 238, 253, 256–7, 295, 319
  and *Time* affair, 256–62
Academy of Motion Picture Arts and Science, 260
Adjani, Isabelle, 11, 198, 229, 260
  in *Barocco*, 198, 199, 202
Affaire Dominici, L' (film), 215
Afrika Korps, 56
agents, 195–8
Alice's Restaurant (film), 188
Alien (film), 295, 298
Allen, Woody, 201, 279
Almendros, Nestor, 220–1
American cinema, 83, 109, 188–9, 220–1, 224, 307–8
  Depardieu's roles in English, 243–51, 292–313, 318
  and *Time* affair, 256–62
  see also specific directors and films
American distribution of Depardieu's films, 4–6, 221, 231–2, 256
American Graffiti (film), 104
American press, 8, 188, 189, 200, 201, 204–6, 218, 220–1, 229–30, 232, 237–8, 251, 254–87, 319
  Time affair, 254–87, 289, 296, 305, 312, 317
  see also specific publications
American Red Cross, 90
American television, 63
American theater, 188
And God Created Woman (film), 112
Apocalypse Now (film), 221
Ardant, Fanny, 16, 222
Arletty, 59
Armeé des Ombres, L' (film), 62
Arnaut, Lucien, 123
Around the World in 80 Days (film), 83
Arroyo, Michel, 126, 127–8, 129, 130, 150
Artmédia, 32, 33, 197, 212, 233
Assante, Armand, 301, 305
Attali, Jacques, 259
Attinger, Joelle, 285
Australia, 56, 241–2, 250
Austria, 51, 62
Auteuil, Daniel, 231
Awakenings (film), 247, 260

Badinter, Elisabeth, 206, 259
Baie des Anges, La (film), 174
Balance, La (film), 195
Balashova, Tanya, 163, 166
Ballon Rouge, Le (film), 83
Balzac, Honoré de, 61, 69, 162
  Colonel Chabert, 33, 319
Barbie, Klaus, 63
Bardot, Brigitte, 112
Barker, Michael, 220–1, 231, 232, 256–7, 260
Barocco (film), 198–9, 202
Baroncelli, Jean de, 188
Barrault, Jean-Louis, 129
Basic Instinct (film), 305
Baxter (film), 177
Baye, Nathalie, 180–3
  and Depardieu, 180–3, 195
Bay of Millionaires, 112–14
BBC, 53
Beatles, 27, 104
Beauvoir, Simone de, 157, 178, 206
Belgium, 21–3

Bellier, Pierre, *La Vie à Châteauroux, Juillet 1940–Août 1944*, 53
Belmondo, Jean-Paul, 109, 111, 122, 196, 233
Bennett, Tony, 95
Benson, Sheila, 251
Berlin Film Festival, 7
Berlin Wall, 7
Bernard, Tom, 221, 232, 256–7
Berri, Claude, 23, 28, 29, 31, 178, 185, 215, 319
  and Depardieu, 34–42, 178
  directing techniques of, 38, 40–1
  and *Germinal*, 23, 31–2, 34–42
  and *Jean de Florette*, 7, 8, 28, 41, 231–2
Berry, Le, France, 48–54, 70, 78, 101, 210, 316
Bertolucci, Bernardo, 32, 188, 194, 200–1, 211
  and *1900*, 194, 200–1
Besset, Valérie, 78
Biddle, Adrian, 301
Birth of a Nation (film), 220
Black Rain (film), 295
Blade Runner (film), 295, 298
Blake, William, 315
Blier, Bernard, 180–2, 183, 194–5, 196
Blier, Bertrand, 3–7, 8, 12, 180, 182–90, 197, 203–5, 221, 229, 245, 251, 264, 300
  and Depardieu, 3–7, 12–13, 15–16, 182–90, 197–8, 231–2
  and *Get Out Your Handkerchiefs*, 203–6
  and *Too Beautiful for You*, 231–2
  and *Les Valseuses*, 3–4, 27, 132, 160, 183–90, 197–8, 204
Bond, Edward, *Saved*, 175
Bonheur, Le (film), 173
Bordier, Hélène, 9, 31, 34, 58, 59, 60, 61, 65, 66, 67, 69, 70, 73, 86, 92, 98, 154, 156, 171, 194, 209, 210, 297
Bordier, Patrick, 34, 42, 194, 297, 316
Born on the Fourth of July (film), 39
Bosch, Roselyne, 294–6, 297, 303, 307–8, 312
Boudu Sauvé des Eaux (play), 157
Bougival, France, 8–9, 29, 193–4, 227, 258, 316–17
Bouquet, Carole, 231–2
boxing, 104–6
Boyer, Charles, 27, 196, 232
Boys in the Band, The (play), 175, 202
Branagh, Kenneth, 311, 319
Brando, Marlon, 83, 105, 109, 200
Brassens, Georges, 116
Brasseur, Pierre, 161, 234
Breathless (film), 109, 111, 188
Brel, Jacques, 116, 189
Bresson, Robert, 83
Bride Wore Black, The (film), 180, 212
Bridges, Jeff, 201
British press, 238, 256, 262
Brittany, 56
Broca, Philippe de, 233
Brochet, Anne, 235, 237, 289–90
Bruce, Lenny, 184
Bruce, Tammy, 260
Buffet, Bernard, 161
Burgess, Anthony, 188
Byron, Lord, 162

Camille Claudel (film), 7, 22, 28, 229, 260
Camion, Le (film), 177
Camus, Albert, 54, 61, 168, 178
Canada, 56
Canby, Vincent, 201, 218, 229–30, 238, 312
Cannes, France, 112, 128, 180
Cannes Film Festival, 34, 62, 112, 157, 195, 238
Cardin, Pierre, 176
Carmet, Jean, 14, 29, 36, 37, 38, 42, 70, 181, 182, 316
Carrière, Jean-Claude, 234
Cartier-Bresson, Henri, 47
Caruso, Enrico, 141
Cassavetes, John, 185, 197
Cavé, Dominique, 142–3, 144, 147
Centre Tomatis, Paris, 135–51
César et Rosalie (film), 196, 199
Césars, 9, 28, 195, 218, 238, 290, 299
Chabrol, Claude, 178
CHAD News, The, 103, 115
Chaplin, Charlie, 83
Château de Tigné, 315–17, 320–1
Châteauroux, France, 9–10, 36, 47–63, 65–75, 77–87, 89–99, 101–18, 150, 153–7, 189–90, 210–11, 254, 259, 264
Chaumeil, Bernard, 299–300, 302–3
Checker, Chubby, 93, 94
Chekhov, Anton, 168
Chevalier, Maurice, 27, 196
Chèvre, La (film), 33, 223–4

Chiens, Les (film), 202
Choice of Arms (film), 222, 289
Chopin, Frédéric, 162
Churchill, Winston, 114
Ciby 2000, 32, 194
cinema, *see* American cinema; French cinema; *specific films*
Cinema Paradiso (film), 319
Cinémathèque Nationale, 178
cinéma vérité, 185
CinéMonde, 59, 112
Cleitmann, René, 234–5
Clément, René, 62
Cleo from 5 to 7 (film), 173
Clockwork Orange, A (film), 188
Clouzot, Henri-Georges, 13
Cochet, Jean-Laurent, 127–8, 129–34, 148, 149–51, 156, 157, 163, 164, 165, 166, 168–70, 175, 179, 212
Cocteau, Jean, 83
cold war, 154
Colonel Chabert (film), 33, 319
Coluche, 184, 189, 222
Columbus, Christopher, 28, 42, 290–312
Combat (newspaper), 54
Comédie-Française, 128, 235, 236, 237
Comencini, Luigi, 211
Communist Party, 61
Compagnons du Tour de France, Les, 37, 49
Compères, Les (film), 33, 224, 243
Conformist, The (film), 200
Coppola, Francis, 40, 221
Corliss, Richard, 254, 264
  and *Time* profile of Depardieu, 254–87
Corneau, Alain, 222
  and *Tous les Matins du Monde*, 289–90
Corneille, Pierre, 168
Costa-Gavras, 296
Costa Rica, 310–12
Costner, Kevin, 260, 295
Cours Dullin, Paris, 122–7
Creative Artists Agency, 32, 296
Croze, Josette, 82
Croze, Maurice, 55, 81, 91, 117, 155
Cruise, Tom, 11, 39, 201, 229
Cyrano de Bergerac (film), 7, 28, 38, 221, 232–8, 244, 247–8, 250, 253, 256–7, 259, 270, 300
  critical acclaim for, 237–8
  and *Time* affair, 256–62
Czechoslovakia, 51
Dabadie, Jean-Loup, 196
Dagaud, Monique, 67, 69, 70, 90, 105
Dances With Wolves (film), 260
Danton (film), 229, 243, 319
Darrieux, Danielle, 59, 218
D-Day, 56, 78
D. D. Productions, 31
Dead Poets Society (film), 10, 241, 242, 244, 249
Dean, James, 83, 105, 109, 200
de Gaulle, Charles, 35, 53, 57, 62, 101, 102, 153–6, 158, 160, 188–9
Delacroix, Eugène, 162
Delon, Alain, 196
Demoule, Michel, 126
Demy, Jacques, 174, 175
Denby, David, 204–5
Deneuve, Catherine, 10, 16, 27, 33, 34, 174, 206, 212–21, 222, 228, 234
  and Depardieu, 214–21
  in *The Last Metro*, 214–21
De Niro, Robert, 11, 39, 200–1, 260
Depardieu, Alain, 58–61, 65, 67–9, 73, 82, 83, 86, 87, 90–1, 92, 94–5, 98, 103, 105, 107–8, 125, 126, 129, 150, 154, 194
Depardieu, Catherine, 83–4, 92, 98, 273
Depardieu, Dédé, 36–7, 50–63, 65–75, 79, 82–7, 90, 92–8, 102, 103, 108, 111, 116, 125, 146, 154, 170–1, 179, 190, 194, 210–11, 244, 247, 263
  death of, 227–9
Depardieu, Denise, 50–1, 61, 65–6, 111, 121, 126, 316
Depardieu, Eric, 92, 98
Depardieu, Franck, 92, 98
Depardieu, Gérard
  Academy Award nominations of, 28, 238, 253, 256–62
  acting style of, 11, 13, 26, 40, 176, 179–80, 216, 217, 236–7, 247–50, 301–7, 311–12, 320
  adolescent rebellion of, 89–99, 102–18, 254–5, 264–5
  American distribution of his films, 4–6, 221, 231–2, 256
  in American films, 243–51, 292–313, 318
  American influence on, 9–11, 83, 85, 87, 89–96, 101, 103–10, 189, 201–2, 232
  ancestry of, 36, 50–9
  appetite of, 21–9

Depardieu, Gérard (*cont.*)
apprenticeship in acting, 25–6
arrests of, 107–8, 158–9
bad-boy roles of, 27, 183–90, 199–206, 264
in *Barocco*, 198–9, 202
and Nathalie Baye, 180–3, 195
beginnings in acting, 122–90
and Claude Berri, 34–42, 178
birth of, 59
and Bertrand Blier, 3–7, 12–13, 15–16, 182–90, 197–8, 231–2
as a boxer, 104–6
in *The Boys in the Band*, 175, 202
in *Camille Claudel*, 7, 22, 28, 229
Césars won by, 28, 218, 238
in *La Chèvre*, 33, 223–4
in *Les Chiens*, 202
childhood of, 9–10, 16–17, 58–63, 65–102, 146, 148–9, 218–19, 228–9, 244, 254–5, 257–9, 263–4, 275, 276, 279
in *Choice of Arms*, 222, 289
and Jean-Laurent Cochet, 129–34, 148, 149–51, 156, 163, 168–70, 175, 179, 212
in *Colonel Chabert*, 33, 319
and Alain Corneau, 289–90
in *Cyrano de Bergerac*, 7, 28, 38, 221, 232–8, 247–8, 250, 253, 256–7, 300
in *Danton*, 229, 319
death of his parents, 227–9
and Catherine Deneuve, 214–21
and Marguerite Duras, 176–80, 194
early interest in movies, 83
early theater roles of, 157, 175, 180–3, 194–6, 202
education of, 16, 25–6, 85–7, 95–9, 102–3, 127
emotionalism of, 5–7, 10–14, 39, 67–8, 71, 110, 166, 182, 219, 320
extramarital affair of, 290
fame of, 7–8, 14, 34, 188–90, 211, 219–21, 228–32, 253–5, 308–9, 317–18
as a father, 191–4, 195, 209, 210, 211, 227, 253, 317
Film Comment article on, 264–80
first stage appearance of, 157
and food, 21–9, 33, 36, 309, 321
in *1492*, 28, 33, 38, 249, 290–313, 319
in *Galapagos*, 180–3, 194–5, 196
in *Germinal*, 23, 24, 26, 29, 31–2, 34–42, 319
in *Get Out Your Handkerchiefs*, 203–6
in *Green Card*, 7, 10, 25, 28, 243–51, 253, 278, 290, 296, 300, 303, 318
health of, 26–7
house of, 8–9, 193–4
influence on French cinema, 229–30
initiation into French cinema, 173–90
in *Inspecteur La Bavure*, 222
in *Jean de Florette*, 7, 8, 28, 41, 221, 227, 229, 231–2, 266
in *Je Vous Aime*, 222
in *The Last Metro*, 214–21, 266
in *The Last Woman*, 199, 202, 203
and Odette Laure, 131–3
and Jean-Louis Livi, 16, 32–3, 195–8, 233–5, 258
in *Loulou*, 200, 202, 230
and Andie MacDowell, 245–6
in *Maîtresse*, 199
marriage to Elisabeth Guignot, 163–71, 173, 191–4, 209–11, 219–20, 258, 262–3, 290, 297, 309–10, 317–20
memoirs of, 15, 71, 72, 165, 166, 228–9, 230, 244
in *Ménage*, 229, 238
in *Les Misérables*, 319
in *Mon Père, Ce Héros*, 28, 33, 253, 289, 318
and Jeanne Moreau, 180, 212–13
in *My Father, The Hero*, 318
in *Natalie Granger*, 176, 177
in *1900*, 194, 200–1
and 1968 student rebellion, 157–60, 189
in Paris as a young man, 121–70
physical appearance of, 13, 32, 103, 131, 164, 174, 196, 218, 251, 301
and Maurice Pialat, 230–1
and poetry, 161–3
in *Police*, 230
politics of, 157–60
as prankster, 65–8, 250
preparation for roles, 39, 248–50
press on, 7–8, 15, 187–8, 199–201, 204–6, 218, 229–30, 237–8, 250–1, 254–87, 312, 317–18, 319
and prostitutes, 107–9
and psychology, 29, 202, 248–50
public mask of, 8, 199–200
in *Une Pure Formalité*, 319
rape controversy involving, 255–87, 289, 296, 305, 312
and Jean-Paul Rappeneau, 233–7
and Claude Regy, 175–6, 177, 179

in *René La Canne*, 202
in *The Return of Martin Guerre*, 7, 28, 182, 195, 229, 266, 319
roles in English, 243–51, 292–313, 318
and Ridley Scott, 295–312
and scripts, 39–40
sexual initiation of, 106–7
sexuality on screen, 202–4, 217–18, 222, 245–6
speech disorders and hearing problems of, 5, 9, 11, 16, 17, 60–1, 63, 72, 74–5, 103, 128, 133–4, 135–51, 164, 174
"Super César" of, 28, 238
in *Tartuffe*, 319
and *Time* affair, 254–87, 289, 296, 305, 312, 317
and Alfred Tomatis, 137–51, 156, 245, 249, 250
in *Too Beautiful for You*, 4–6, 12, 205, 221, 231–2, 238
in *Tous les Matins du Monde*, 28, 32, 179, 289–90
training in acting, 122–7, 129–34, 148–51, 156, 161–70, 175–6
travels of, 111–15
and François Truffaut, 211–21, 222–3, 230
in *Under Satan's Sun*, 229, 230
in *Les Valseuses*, 3–4, 27, 132, 160, 183–90, 197–200, 202–3, 254
and Agnès Varda, 173–4
and violence, 110–11, 258, 278
and Peter Weir, 243–51, 296
and wine, 5, 10, 11, 24, 26, 33, 34, 36, 42, 180, 193–4, 258, 279, 315–17, 321
in *The Woman Next Door*, 222–3
and women, 106–9, 113, 114, 117, 128, 163–71, 173, 187, 190, 199, 202, 217–18, 245–6, 255–87, 290
Depardieu, Guillaume, 8, 26, 28, 179, 191, 194, 209, 210, 227, 258, 317
birth of, 191
in *Tous les Matins du Monde*, 290, 317
Depardieu, Julie, 8, 26, 193–4, 209, 210, 227, 253, 258, 297, 317
birth of, 193
Depardieu, Lilette, 36, 37, 52–63, 65–75, 83–7, 90, 92–8, 102, 103, 108, 111, 116, 125, 146, 154, 170–1, 179, 190, 194, 210–11, 244, 263
death of, 227–9
Depardieu, Marcel, 50–1
Descartes, René, 148
Dewaere, Patrick, 184, 186, 187, 203, 204, 222
death of, 223
Disney Studios, 7, 10, 33, 34, 224, 244, 318, 319
Don Juan (play), 125
Dostoyevsky, Fyodor, 279
Douglas, Michael, 295, 305
Dubreucq, Serge, 95–6
Dullin, Charles, 122
Dunn, Kevin, 311
Durand, Father, 95, 96, 97, 102, 103, 111, 159
Duras, Anthelm, 178
Duras, Marguerite, 173, 176–80, 206, 230–1
and Depardieu, 176–80, 194
Dylan, Bob, 189

Easy Rider (film), 188
Einstein, Albert, 148
Eisenhower, Dwight D., 56, 78, 114
Emmanuelle (film), 202
Espace Cardin, Paris, 176
Esquire magazine, 269
European Common Market, 101
Everly Brothers, 104

Femme du Gange, La (film), 177
Femme Nikita, La (film), 188
Fernandel, 59
Ferrer, Jose, 233
Ferreri, Marco, 199, 211
Field, The (film), 260
Fields, Bert, 261–2
Fifth Republic, 101–2, 153–60
Figaro, Le (newspaper), 187, 259
Film Comment article on Depardieu (1978), 264–80
Film Par Film, 32
food, 21–9, 33, 36, 309, 321
Foote-Greenwell, Victoria, 267, 268, 270, 272, 277–87
Ford, Harrison, 242, 247
Fort Saganne (film), 289
Fossey, Brigitte, 62, 186
Foster, Jodie, 229
400 Blows, The (film), 91–2, 212
1492 (film), 28, 33, 38, 249, 290–313, 319
Fourth Republic, 67, 101
France
Fifth Republic, 101–2, 153–60

France (*cont.*)
Fourth Republic, 67, 101
NATO bases in, 77–82, 101, 102, 114, 153–5
1968 student rebellion, 157–60, 189
postwar, 61–3, 67, 77–9, 101, 153–4
in World War II, 50–7, 58, 61–3, 212, 213–14
French Army, 51–2, 53, 81, 155, 211
French cinema, 7–8, 12, 32–4, 55, 59, 62–3, 178–9, 211–12, 224, 259
Depardieu's influence on, 229–30
Depardieu's initiation into, 173–90
mid-1950s, 83
New Wave, 178, 211, 213
and *Time* affair, 258–62
World War II themes in, 62–3
see also specific directors and films
French press, 7–8, 15, 145, 187, 188, 200, 205, 237, 238, 250, 257, 258–9, 265, 270, 272, 282; *see also specific publications*
French radio, 184
French Riviera, 111–15, 128–9
French television, 62
French theater, 26
Depardieu's early roles in, 157, 175, 180–3, 194–6, 202
Freudian analysis, 146
Frey, Sami, 176, 197, 215
Fugitifs, Les (film), 33, 224

Gabin, Jean, 7, 59, 122, 180, 181, 182, 190, 196
Gagné, Janine, 79–81
Gagné, Joe, 79–81, 105, 153, 155
Gainsbourg, Serge, 221
Galapagos (play), 180–3, 194–5, 196
Gallipoli (film), 242
Gamet, Pierre, 299–300, 302–7, 310
Gaumont, 233, 234, 296
Gere, Richard, 229
Germany, 7, 62, 63, 154
in World War II, 51–7
Germinal (film), 23, 24, 26, 29, 31–2, 34–42, 319
Gestapo, 51–5
Get Out Your Handkerchiefs (film), 4, 203–6, 223, 264
Gibson, Mel, 242
Girod, Francis, 202
Godard, Jean-Luc, 28, 109, 157, 178, 188, 200, 309
Going Places (film), see *Les Valseuses*
Golden Globe awards, 253, 263
Goldman, Alain, 33, 295, 296, 303
Goodfellas (film), 39
Grant, Cary, 27
Grappelli, Stéphane, 186
Great Britain, 74
press, 238, 256, 262
in World War II, 55, 56
Green Card (film), 7, 10, 25, 28, 243–51, 253, 270, 278, 290, 296, 300, 303, 318
Guignot, Elisabeth, 8, 10, 12, 17, 26, 42, 163–71, 173, 218, 316
emotionalism of, 165–6
in *Jean de Florette*, 227, 231
marriage to Depardieu, 163–71, 173, 191–4, 209–11, 219–20, 258, 262–3, 290, 297, 309–10, 317–20
as a mother, 191–4, 195, 209, 210, 211, 227, 317
and *Toute Différente et la Langouste*, 227
and Agnès Varda, 173–4
Guitry, Sacha, *Moi, sous l'Occupation*, 213

Hair (play), 188
Haldeman, E. Barry, 261–2
Haley, Bill, and the Comets, 93
Halliday, Johnny, 109
Handke, Peter, 176
La Chevauchée sur le Lac de Constance, 215
Harris, Richard, 260
Haskell, Molly, 266, 269
Heigl, Katherine, 335
Hemingway, Ernest, 33, 114
Hicks, Joseph, 77, 78, 81
Hiroshima, Mon Amour (film), 178
Hitchcock, Alfred, 212, 279
Hitler, Adolf, 51–2, 54, 213
Hitler Connais Pas (film), 183
Ho Chi Minh, 102
Hockney, David, 298
Hoffman, Dustin, 11, 39, 201
Holland, 51
Holly, Buddy, 104
Hollywood, 12, 32, 34, 180, 188–9, 195, 238, 244, 256–62, 291, 295, 307–8; *see also* American cinema
Hollywood Foreign Press Association, 253
Holocaust, 62–3
Holocaust (TV series), 63

Hotel Terminus (film), 63
Hugo, Victor, 61
Les Misérables, 180, 319
Humanite, l', 61, 87
Hungary, 62
Hunt, Linda, 247
Huppert, Isabelle, 186, 200, 202
Huston, Anjelica, 301

improvisation, 123, 124, 127, 185
India, 14–15
Indochina, 102
Inspecteur La Bavure (film), 222
International Herald Tribune, 259
Irons, Jeremy, 259, 260, 261
Italian cinema, 62, 211–12, 319

Jean de Florette (film), 7, 8, 28, 41, 221, 227, 229, 231–2, 266, 315
Jeux Interdits (film), 62
Je Vous Aime (film), 221
Jews, 53–4, 62
Jourdan, Louis, 27, 196
Journey of Hope (film), 261
Jouvet, Louis, 59
Jules and Jim (film), 180, 212, 221
Jung, Carl, 16, 248–52
Memories, Dreams, Reflections, 248–9
"The Spirit in Man, Art, and Literature," 250, 251
Jura, 52

Kael, Pauline, 205, 298
Karyo, Tchéky, 188
Katzenberg, Jeffrey, 34, 318
Keaton, Buster, 83
Keats, John, 162, 169
"Ode to a Nightingale," 169
Korean War, 78
Kristel, Sylvia, 202
Kubrick, Stanley, 188

Labbey, Bertrand de, 33
Lacan, Jacques, 202
Lacombe, Lucien (film), 63
Laforgue, Jules, 150
Lancaster, Burt, 201
Lang, Jack, 156, 258
Lanzmann, Claude, 63
Last Emperor, The (film), 200
Last Metro, The (film), 7, 9, 28, 213–21, 266
American premiere of, 220–1
Last Tango in Paris (film), 188, 200
Last Wave, The (film), 244
Last Woman, The (film), 199, 202, 203
Laure, Carole, 204
Laure, Odette, 131–3
Lauzier, Gérard, 16, 253
Laval, Pierre, 55
Lawrence, D. H., *Lady Chatterley's Lover*, 187
Lawrence of Arabia (film), 308
Lean, David, 308
Lebovici, Gérard, 212, 221
Lennon, John, 189
Lettres Volées (Depardieu), 15, 71, 72, 165, 166, 228–9, 230, 244
Libération (newspaper), 187
liberation of France, 56–7
Liszt, Franz, 162
Livi, Jean-Louis, 16, 32–3, 195–8, 211, 212, 221, 233–5, 253, 258, 289, 290
Loire valley, 47, 70, 315
London *Daily Mail*, 256
London *Observer*, 261
Lonsdale, Michel (Michael), 176, 215
Loren, Sophia, 300
Los Angeles *Times*, 238, 251
Loulou, 113–15
Loulou (film), 200, 202, 230
Lucas, George, 104
Lucas, Roger, 86–7, 97–8, 102, 103, 259
Lune Est Bleue, La (play), 165
Lynch, David, 32

MacDowell, Andie, 245–6
Maîtresse (film), 199
Malle, Louis, 63, 233
Malraux, André, 156
Mann, Judy, 256, 277, 280
Manon des Sources (film), 41
Maquis, 54, 56, 62
March, Fredric, 294
Marielle, Jean-Pierre, 290
Marillier, Colette, 52, 53, 94
Marillier, Suzanne, 52, 73, 87
Marillier, Xavier, 52, 53
Marivaux, Pierre, 168
Marseillaise, La (newspaper), 79
Marshall, Penny, 247
Marshall, Robert P., Jr., 285–7
Marshall Plan, 67
Martin, Dean, 95

Martinerie, La (military base), 77–82, 153–5
Maslin, Janet, 200, 204, 251
Mastroianni, Marcello, 215, 224–5, 232
Mauriac, François, 69
memorization, 150
Ménage (film), 229, 234, 238
Merci la Vie (film), 12, 14
Merveille, Jacky, 98, 103, 108, 155–6, 265
Method, the, 175–6, 247
Milice, 54, 55, 62
Miller, Henry, 127
  Tropic of Cancer, 187, 205
Miou-Miou, 184, 222, 223, 229
  in *Les Valseuses*, 184–7, 203
Misérables, Les (film), 180
Mitchell, Eddie, 109
Mitterrand, François, 178, 222, 259
Molière, 61, 125, 127, 130, 149
  Tartuffe, 319
Molina, Angela, 301, 306
Monaco, 112
Monde, Le, 10, 188
Monestier, Robert, 56–7
Monicelli, Mario, 211–12
Mon Père, Ce Héros (film), 28, 33, 253, 289, 318
Montand, Yves, 27, 32, 196, 222, 231, 234
Moreau, Jeanne, 173, 174, 176, 177, 186, 206, 215
  and Depardieu, 180, 212–13
Morgan, Michèle, 59
Mosquito Coast, The (film), 242
Mouilleron, Michel, 126, 129
Mozart, Wolfgang Amadeus, 138, 142, 143, 144, 146, 147, 149, 223
Museum of Modern Art, New York, 220
Musset, Alfred de, 133, 161–3, 171, 279
  Confession d'un Enfant du Siècle, 162
  On ne badine pas avec l'amour, 131
Muti, Ornella, 199, 202
My Father, The Hero (film), 318
Mystère Picasso (documentary), 13

Natalie Granger (film), 176, 177
National Organization for Women, 255–6, 260
National Society of Film Critics, 205
Nazism, 16, 51–6, 58, 62–3, 79, 139, 189, 211, 212, 213–14, 216
Needham, Terry, 301, 304, 306
Newsweek magazine, 7, 188, 266
New Wave, 178, 211, 213
New York, 25, 188–9, 220, 257
New York *Daily News*, 188
New Yorker, 205
New York Film Festival, 220–1, 231, 268
New York magazine, 204–5
New York *Observer*, 238
New York *Post*, 255, 257, 277, 278
New York Times, The, 5, 6, 7, 200, 201, 204, 206, 218, 238, 245, 251, 259
New York Times Magazine, The, 266
1900 (film), 194, 200–1
Noir, Gil, 35, 300, 302–3, 309–10
Noiret, Philippe, 234
Nolte, Nick, 33, 201, 224
Normandy, 56
North Africa, 53, 56
North Atlantic Treaty Organization (NATO), 77–82, 101, 102, 114, 153–5, 289
Nouvelle République du Centre-Ouest, La, 77, 81, 190
Nuremberg trials, 57
Nuytten, Bruno, 185

Occupation, 51–6, 58, 61–3, 212, 213–14
Olivier, Laurence, 300, 304
On the Waterfront (film), 83
Ophuls, Marcel, 62–3, 83
Oradour-sur-Glane, France, 57
Orion Classics, 221, 256
Osborne, John, 175
O'Toole, Peter, 308

Pacino, Al, 11
Pagnol, Marcel, 28, 58, 231, 315
Paramount, 197, 296, 307
Paret, Alain, 316
Paris, 6, 15, 31–2, 48, 49, 50, 52, 80, 102, 118, 121–2, 161, 195
  Depardieu as a young man in, 121–70
  1968 student rebellion, 157–60, 189
  World War II, 52, 56, 57, 139–40
Paris Conservatory, 128, 181, 235
Paris-Match, 7, 257
Paris Opéra, 133
Perez, Vincent, 235
Perier, Jean-François, 188
Pétain, Marshal, 54, 55
Piaf, Edith, 122
Pialat, Maurice, 200, 229
  and Depardieu, 230–1

Picasso, Pablo, 13, 26
Pilorgé, Michel, 116–18, 121–7, 128, 129, 150, 151, 157, 160, 162–3, 167–8, 170–1, 195, 211, 320
Pinter, Harold, 175
Point, Le (newspaper), 294
Poland, 51, 62
Police (film), 230
Pompidou, Georges, 188–9
Pondiscio, Robert, 262, 267–8, 272, 278, 284, 287
Porterfield, Christopher, 283–4
Powell, Gregg, 306
Presley, Elvis, 27, 93, 94, 101, 104, 189
press
  American, 8, 188–9, 200, 201, 204–6, 218, 220–1, 229–30, 232, 237–8, 251, 254–87, 319
  British, 238, 256, 262
  on Depardieu, 7–8, 15, 187–8, 199–201, 204–6, 218, 229–30, 237–8, 250–1, 254–87, 312, 317–18, 319
  French, 7–8, 15, 145, 187–8, 200, 205, 237, 238, 250, 257, 258–9, 265, 270, 272, 282
  Time affair, 254–87, 289, 296, 305, 312, 317
  see also specific publications
prostitution, 107–9
Ptak, John, 296
Pure Formalité, Une (film), 319

Racine, Jean Baptiste, 127, 130
racism, 107
Radio Moscow, 87
Raging Bull (film), 201
Raimu, 59, 190
Rain Man (film), 39
Rappeneau, Jean-Paul, 28, 38, 233–7, 246, 251
  and *Cyrano de Bergerac*, 233–7
Ray, Nicholas, 109
Ray, Satyajit, 11, 311, 319
Rebel Without a Cause (film), 109
recitation, 130–1
refugee camps, 52–3
Regy, Claude, 175–6, 177, 179, 180, 202
Renaud, 38
René La Canne (film), 202
Renoir, Jean, 157
Resistance, French, 53–7, 62, 212
Return of Martin Guerre, The (film), 7, 28, 182, 195, 229, 266, 319
Reversal of Fortune (film), 259
Rey, Fernando, 301, 302, 306
Richard, Pierre, 223, 224
Rive Droite, Rive Gauche (film), 182
rock and roll, 93–4, 189
Rodin, Auguste, 22
Rohmer, Eric, 178
Roissy Films, 221
Rolling Stones, 104
Rommel, Erwin, 56
Ross, Steve, 263
Rossellini, Roberto, 211
Rostand, Edmond, *Cyrano de Bergerac*, 127, 232–8
Rugoff, Donald, 189
Russia, 53, 77

Sacks, Oliver, 247
  The Man Who Mistook His Wife for a Hat, 247
Sahl, Mort, 184
St. Claude, France, 52
St. Tropez, 112
Sand, George, 70, 162, 279
Sarasota, Fla., French film festival in, 278, 298
Sarraute, Natalie, 176
Sarris, Andrew, 238
Sartre, Jean-Paul, 61, 157, 178
Sautet, Claude, 196, 197, 199
Sauvage, Le (film), 234
Saved (play), 175, 176
Schneider, Romy, 196
Schroeder, Barbet, 199
Scorsese, Martin, 279
Scott, Ridley, 38, 291
  and *1492*, 291, 295–312
Seberg, Jean, 109
Serreau, Colline, 24
7300th Material Control Group, 78
Seydoux, Nicolas, 296
Seyrig, Delphine, 176, 215
Shakespeare, William, 319
  Henry V, 319
Shelley, Percy Bysshe, 162
Shoah (documentary), 63
Short, Martin, 224
Signoret, Simone, 62
Si J'Etais un Espion (film), 183
Simon, Michel, 59, 157, 190
Smith, Lois, 257
Smith, William Kennedy, 263

Société Nationale des Constructions Aéronautiques du Sud-Ouest (SNCASO), 78
Sommersby (film), 229
Sony Classics, 221
Sorbonne, Paris, 157–60, 317
Sorrow and the Pity, The (film), 62–3
Souchon, Alain, 221
Soviet Union, 53, 77
Spain, 290–310
SS, 54
Stallone, Sylvester, 11
Stanislavski, 175–6
Stanley & Iris (film), 201
Stein, Harry, 264–5, 266, 269–71
Stendhal, 61
Sternberg, Tom, 221
Stevenson, Michael, 308
Stolen Kisses (film), 212
Stolen Letters, see *Lettres Volées* (Depardieu)
Stone, Oliver, 32, 39, 40
Stoppard, Tom, 175
Storey, David, *Home*, 176
student rebellion (1968, Paris), 157–60, 189
Studio Canal Plus, 32
Sullivan, Billy, 301
Sutherland, Donald, 201–2
Swaim, Bob, 195
Switzerland, 52, 74

Tall Blond Man with One Black Shoe, The (film), 223
Tartuffe (film), 319
Tartuffe (play), 27
Tati, Jacques, 83
Taxi Driver (film), 201
Telluride Film Festival, 4–6, 231, 268
That Man from Rio (film), 233
theater, *see* American theater; French theater
Théâtre de la Madeleine, Paris, 181, 196
Théâtre Edouard VII, Paris, 129
Théâtre National Populaire, Paris, 122, 175
Thelma & Louise (film), 38, 295
Theroux, Paul, 242
Thomas, Kevin, 238
Thompson, Emma, 319
Thoreau, Henry David, 241
Three Fugitives (film), 33, 224
Three Men and a Baby (film), 224
Time magazine, 7
  controversy about Depardieu profile, 254–87, 289, 296, 305, 312, 317
Time Out (newspaper), 238
Time-Warner, 259, 263
Tomatis, Dr. Alfred A., 133–4, 135–51, 245, 249, 250
  The Conscious Ear, 139, 140, 143
  treatment of Depardieu's speech problems, 137–51, 156
Tomatis, Umberto, 140
Too Beautiful for You (film), 4–6, 12, 205, 221, 231–2, 238
Tornatore, Giuseppe, 319
Toscan du Plantier, Daniel, 8, 15, 16, 233, 234, 259–60
Tous les Matins du Monde (film), 28, 32, 179, 289–90, 299, 302, 317
Toute Différente et la Langouste (play), 227
Trintignant, Jean-Louis, 112, 221
Truffaut, François, 7, 10, 28, 40, 91, 157, 178, 206, 211–21, 222, 231, 279, 311
  and Depardieu, 211–21, 222–3, 230
  and *The 400 Blows*, 91–2, 212
  and *The Last Metro*, 214–21
  and *The Woman Next Door*, 222–3
TV Guide, 269
20,000 Leagues under the Sea (film), 83
Two of Us, The (film), 41

Umbrellas of Cherbourg, The (film), 174
Under Satan's Sun (film), 229, 230
United Artists, 220, 221, 256
U.S. Air Force, 79, 105
U.S. Army, 77–82
USA Today, 257

Vadim, Roger, 112
Valseuses, Les (film), 3–4, 27, 132, 160, 183–90, 193, 195, 197–200, 202–3, 204, 205, 206, 222, 223, 254, 264
Vannier, Alain, 6, 221
Varda, Agnès, 173–4
Variety, 238
Veber, Francis, 31, 33, 223–4
  and *La Chèvre*, 223–4
Venice film festival, 62
Ventura, Lino, 62
Vera Baxter (film), 177
Verne, Jules, 61
Vie du Château, La (film), 233–4
Vincent, François, Paul, and the Others (film), 199

Vincent, Louise, 300–1, 302, 303, 304, 308
Vogue, 12, 13
Voltaire, 61

Wajda, Andrzej, 243
Waldheim, Kurt, 62
Walsh, Terry, 308
Warner Brothers, 259
Washington *Post*, 256, 280
Weaver, Sigourney, 242
Weber, Jacques, 233, 234
Weil, Simone, 206
Weir, Peter, 10, 16, 31, 241–51, 311
  and Depardieu, 243–51, 296
  and *Green Card*, 243–51, 300, 303
Welles, Orson, 279
Wild One, The (film), 105, 109
Williams, Robin, 241, 242
wine, 5, 10, 11, 24, 26, 33, 34, 36, 42, 180, 193–4, 315–17, 321
witchcraft, 73, 247
Witness (film), 242
Woman Next Door, The (film), 222–3
World War I, 51, 52
World War II, 50, 51–7, 61–3, 77, 101, 139–40, 189, 212, 213–14

Year of Living Dangerously, The (film), 242, 247

Zimmerman, Paul D., 188
Zola, Emile, *Germinal*, 34–5, 39–40

Photographic Credits

Grateful acknowledgment is made to the following for providing photographs and permission for them to be reproduced:

Depardieu family, for photographs on pages 46, 64, 76, 88, 102, 120, 152, 162, 192; and on photographic insert pages 1, 2, 3, 4 (top), 6 (bottom), 8 (bottom), and 9 (bottom)

David Appleby for Percy Main Productions, 288; insert page 15 (top)
Paul Chutkow, insert page 6 (top)
Maurice Croze, insert page 8 (top)
Disney Studios, insert page 15 (bottom)
Film Par Film, insert page 6
French Film Office, Unifrance Film, U.S.A., 208; insert pages 11 and 12
Pierre Gamet, 240; insert page 14 (top)
Hollywood Foreign Press Association, 254
Interama, Inc., 172; insert pages 9 (top), and 10 (top)
Roger Lucas, insert page 4 (bottom)
Richard Melloul, Sygma Photos, 314; insert page 7 (bottom)
La Nouvelle République du Centre-Ouest, 20; insert pages 5 and 10 (bottom)
Orion Classics, 226; insert page 13
Michel Pilorgé, insert page 7 (top)
Renn Productions, 30
Paul Schumaker for Motion Picture Bookers Club, insert page 14 (bottom)
Dr. Alfred Tomatis, 136